The
Forever Initiative

The
Forever Initiative

A Feasible Public Policy Agenda to
Help Couples Form and Sustain
Healthy Marriages and Relationships

Alan J. Hawkins

ISBN: 978-1484850718
version 1.0
CreateSpace Independent Publishing Platform, North Charleston, South Carolina

Cover design by Bree Crookston
Book interior design by Marny K. Parkin

Printed in the United States of America

To the many dedicated educator–practitioners in the field who are working day-to-day to help individuals and couples form and sustain healthy relationships and enduring marriages, and to the policy makers and scholars who are getting their backs.

Contents

Chapter 1

Promoting Public Provisions
for Private Promises:
Rationale and Overview

A...couple entered the [Oklahoma City Family Expectations] program in a rapidly declining relationship. The couple mentioned to both their Family Support Coordinator (FSC) and their Marriage Educators that they were currently together because of their expected baby, and that FE [Family Expectations] was their last hope of finding a way to make their relationship work. The couple later attended a booster session 3 months after the beginning of their workshop. At the session they introduced their new child and announced that they were getting married. They reminded the class that they did not expect to stay together when they entered the program, but they credited FE for providing them with a solid foundation on which to build their strong relationship. At the start of the couple's participation in FE, the father was opposed to marriage and viewed it only as a "piece of paper." He attributed this belief largely to the failure of both his parents' marriage and the marriage of his partner's parents. After completing their workshop group and meeting with their FSC, he came to the realization that marriage is a commitment to the relationship and family, and is integral to establishing a healthy support system for children. The couple was married in April.[1]

Jorge saw the HARP [Hispanic Active Relationships Center, in Dallas, Texas] billboard as he was driving home one day. Since his relationship was about to end, the billboard caught his attention. He wrote down HARP's number and once he was home he told his wife about the billboard and that he wanted to call to get information. His wife, Emily, had given up on the relationship and was convinced that their marital problems did not have a solution. After Jorge called and received the workshop information he convinced Emily to at least go and try it out. He asked her to give their relationship one last chance before signing their divorce papers.

Emily was very angry, resentful, full of mixed emotions, and did not want to get hopes up too high. Both Emily and Jorge ended up staying for the whole 12-hour class. They are still together and are determined to make their marriage work. Thanks to the HARP workshops, they learned that it is okay to forgive each other and they discovered great tools to communicate better and resolve their issues. Emily and Jorge, standing in front of class with tears in their eyes, spoke about how their lives and relationship had changed for good and how they will be forever thankful to HARP for having such a huge impact on their lives.[2]

These are heart-warming, personal stories. But I share accounts of these families here not because they are inspiring anecdotes but because they are noteworthy public accomplishments. These couples were helped by free educational programs that are supported by significant government funding—our tax dollars. I don't know the ends of the stories, whether these distressed, lower income couples successfully achieved their dreams of a healthy, stable, long-term marriage in which to rear their children together. But the programs they participated in were designed to help interested couples form and sustain healthy marriages and relationships so that more children can grow up outside of poverty in a caring, stable family with both a mom and a dad.

This is not a book about how to strengthen your own marriage,[3] although I will write a lot about how marriage and relationship education services are helping many couples form and sustain healthy marriages and relationships. Similarly, this is not a book that goes into great depth to explain why forever is facing the challenges it is facing these days and how marriage and romantic relationships have changed dramatically over the past several decades. Other recent books by talented scholars provide trenchant analyses of the changing institution of marriage.[4] But what is missing from these books is an in-depth analysis of specific things we can do. These authors usually reserve just the last few pages for some brief thoughts about actions that we might take to deal with the problems they have analyzed. An action agenda was not the focus of their books; it is for this book. This book begins where other books leave off. It's about a specific set of actions that we can take as a society—specifically focusing on government-funded initiatives—to provide educational resources to help more couples form healthy relationships and enduring marriages. Thus, this is a book for policy makers who direct government funding, for scholars and professionals who seek to influence these policy makers, for practitioners who implement educational policies, and for involved citizens who are sincerely concerned and intellectually curious about what the government might be able to do to help couples form and sustain healthy relationships.

Facilitating couples' aspirations for forever is a worthy and feasible goal of U.S. public policy. But we need more than a vague hope. In this book I will propose a specific, strategic, integrated agenda of public policy actions that can strengthen contemporary marriage. I don't pretend that the public policy agenda that I propose here will solve the problems of family instability that we are experiencing. But I think that what I propose can improve the situation noticeably by assisting many more couples to form and sustain healthy marriages and relationships, which in turn will have significant benefits for their children and society, as well as reduce the costs to taxpayers of a weakening institution of marriage that places many people in poverty.

I don't think anyone will be surprised by my assertion that the problems associated with forming and sustaining healthy marriages these days are more than a private concern. Yes, decisions about forming and unforming families are highly personal. But as many eminent scholars have documented recently, marriage is both deeply and increasingly personal while at the same time it is fundamentally public.[5] Moreover, private decisions about family life have what economists call "externalities," that is, costs associated with private choices that are borne by society, in much the same way that private decisions about what to eat can have public costs when poor decisions create public health burdens. When marriages, or even just stable romantic unions, break down or fail to form, society bears real costs, from increased direct public assistance to poorer educational outcomes for children and more.[6] One economist tried to estimate what the public costs of family fragmentation were and conservatively calculated them to be $112 billion a year.[7] A pair of sociologists conservatively estimated the annual costs of fatherhood absence—a close kin to family fragmentation—at $100 billion annually.[8]

Can Anything Be Done?

Is there anything that can be done realistically through public policy directly to strengthen marriage and reduce the costs of marital breakdown? Or are the forces of cultural change so overpowering and relentless and our tools to intervene so constrained and limited as to make any policy efforts merely quixotic? There are certainly those who believe the answer to that first question is doubtful and to the second question, yes. The popular historian Stephanie Coontz has written about the historical forces reshaping marriage, foreshadowing, she believes, an inexorable future of deinstitutionalized marriage with an eventual flourishing of diverse but functional family forms.[9] These historical forces, she argues, are too powerful to be banked, channeled, or moved by the kinds of modest policy initiatives that I will propose here. Noted family sociologist James Q. Wilson believed that broad cultural change is needed to strengthen marriage, but he did not think that government action would be effective. Rather he believed the kind of cultural change that is needed must be done privately by individuals, families, churches, neighborhoods, and the media.[10] Talented sociologist Steve Nock argued that there needs to be deep cultural-level change to strengthen the institution of marriage, as well, although he did see a role for law and policy to help spark that cultural change.[11] But, alas, no one yet has invented a point-and-click control panel for cultural change. Likewise, Charles Murray, the public scholar at the American Enterprise Institute, in his recent book, *Coming Apart*, believes that cultural renewal is the only path to reinvigorating the institution of marriage.[12] But he is not optimistic about such prospects. Indeed, he lays much of the blame for the weakening of marriage on the modern welfare state, so he is not about to call upon policy makers to fix the problem with add-ons to welfare programs.[13]

Moreover, there are numerous scholars who see direct public policy efforts to strengthen marriage as ineffective and ill-advised. Melanie Heath's recent book, *One Marriage Under God*, illustrates this common scholarly skepticism.[14] Her thesis is that public "marriage promotion" efforts are, at their heart, "boundary work"—efforts to reinforce the outsider status of nonheterosexuals and assimilate heterosexual "others" (meaning unmarried individuals) into a normative conception of traditional marriage. "Activism to secure marriage's boundaries is akin to activism to defend the nation's borders as a way to safeguard America's future," she asserts.[15] For marriage advocates, "marriage is essentially about instilling American, middle-class, heterosexual values." She argues that these advocates' efforts promote a single, hegemonic family structure as ideal, excluding other family forms and not offering meaningful help to them. As a result, she calls for an end to public funding of such initiatives. She is troubled not only by the ideological problems of these initiatives but by how, she claims, they divert funds from the fight against structural poverty that makes the "marriage script" unrealistic for so many. She sees family instability as only a result of poverty rather than as a bidirectional cause and effect. She calls instead for more funds to be invested in addressing directly the structural causes of poverty, rejecting the notion that there are relational causes to family instability that can be addressed effectively by educational programs.

The conclusions about the impotence of public policy to strengthen marriage that scholars across the ideological spectrum draw from their analyses of the current problems are not unreasonable. On the other hand, "optimism is America's birthright," Maggie Gallagher insists.[16] And there is research emerging to challenge empirically the notion that policy is impotent in the face of change. I will review this research throughout the book. The emerging evidence, I believe, suggests more reason for modest optimism that government efforts can help stabilize families and strengthen marriage than many have surmised.

A few scholars over the past decade or two have provided some brief thoughts about actions that we could take, usually at the end of a long and careful analysis of the changes and problems facing marriage. As I mentioned earlier, an action agenda was not their central focus, so their action ideas are not thoroughly developed. For instance, Paul Amato is one of the most prominent scholars of marriage and divorce in the United States. Together with his Penn State colleagues, he outlines how marriage has changed over the past two decades in his book, *Alone Together*.[17] While these authors recognize the personal and societal challenges presented by these changes, they are generally optimistic that the institution of marriage will survive these changes and remain a fundamental institution in civil society supporting the well-being of children. They support the concept of reasonable government efforts to strengthen the institution of marriage, especially efforts to help lower income couples who struggle to form and sustain healthy marriages and relationships. But their book ends with only this general support; they do not outline a specific agenda as I will do here.

Andrew Cherlin, at John Hopkins University, is another prominent family sociologist who has written about the changes to marriage and the challenges it presents to society in a cleverly titled book, *The Marriage-Go-Round*.[18] He documents the troubling instability in American family life, the rapid formation and dissolution of cohabiting unions with children as well as marriages. He implies the need for better education for young adults, especially around the issue of cohabitation. "We don't want a cohabitation tax or a marriage police," he clarifies, but he does imply the need for educational efforts to send stronger messages to young adults to "slow down" and think carefully about rushing into relationships, especially when children's lives are at stake.[19] I agree. But his recommendations for how to deliver this message are vague.

Harvard sociologist Kathryn Edin and Maria Kefalas at Saint Joseph's University provide one of the most trenchant analyses of why poor women put motherhood before marriage in their book, *Promises I Can Keep*.[20] In short, the women they study find motherhood deeply meaningful but fear of a lack of marriageable men means they prioritize motherhood, which they can control, over marriage, which they can't, and involve themselves in a series of romantic and coresidential relationships that make for much family instability for their children. These scholars admit that some kind of relationship education is needed for these couples, but struggle to know what that would be like for the women they study who deal with issues of chronic infidelity, physical abuse, substance abuse, incarceration, and mental health challenges. These authors place greater emphasis on policies to help adolescent males and young men avoid destructive behaviors, delay fathering children until their later 20s, improve men's employment prospects, and reduce unwed pregnancies. I acknowledge the need for effective coterminous policy to improve the social ecology for healthy relationships and stable marriages for all. But I also will argue for the value of supportive educational services and provide some details as to what role relationship education could play in helping these disadvantaged young people.

Naomi Cahn and June Carbone, two respected legal scholars, intellectually tackle the culture wars around marriage and family formation in their stimulating book, *Red Families v. Blue Families*,[21] and conclude that public support for marriage and relationship education should be a part of the solution: "While those who prize autonomy may be wary of celebrating traditional marriage, most do not begrudge efforts to encourage commitment, educate young people in the qualities that effectively promote relationship stability, or establish voluntary marriage [education] promotion programs."[22]

I support their analysis. But the fuller agenda they embrace includes more controversial elements around fertility and abortion that I do not address here and that make their proposals politically problematic to implement. Nor have these legal scholars been as detailed as I will be about what effective relationship education for young people should look like.

University of Chicago sociologist Linda Waite and marriage policy activist Maggie Gallagher sparked significant public attention to strengthening the institution of marriage in their controversial book, *The Case for Marriage*.[23] They marshal the research highlighting the unique value of the institution of marriage. They worry about laws and policies that minimize the institution or diminish its special status, and call for reforms to tax, welfare, and other policies to strengthen marriage's status as a leading institution promoting child and adult well-being. They also call for reforms to no-fault divorce law for couples with dependent children, including longer waiting periods. I believe some of the reforms they advocate have significant merit. But I also believe that much of what they advocate is not politically feasible. In this book, I put an emphasis on feasible actions that we can take now to move forward.

Some public policy scholars at respected think tanks have addressed the question of what can be done to strengthen marriages. Ron Haskins, a conservative, and Isabel Sawhill, a progressive, both at the respected Brookings Institution in Washington D.C., have provided the most significant public policy agenda to date to help couples form and sustain healthy marriages for the sake of their children. Their first strategic proposal is to focus more effectively on reducing unwed births to both teens and twenty-somethings with an array of educational and policy efforts. Children growing up without the social capital of a stable, two-parent family is the driving trend behind public policy efforts to strengthen marriage; reducing the number of unwed births would go a long way in reducing the problems that policy makers are trying to address. I agree and support effective measures to accomplish this policy goal. In addition, Haskins and Sawhill come to a set of compromised agreements on ways to provide valuable marriage and relationship education services to individuals and couples. Also, they advocate for some tax policies that can help low-income married couples or make it easier for unmarried parents to marry. They also propose funding a major, long-term social marketing campaign to get out the message of the importance of two-parent, married families. They argue that without the kind of cultural change targeted by such a media campaign, other reforms will not gain enough traction to make a meaningful difference. My proposed agenda will incorporate much of their agenda but will add much greater detail.

Haskins and Sawhill do not pretend that these proposals alone will fix marriage. They understand that marriage exists in a social and economic ecology that helps or hinders the formation and maintenance of healthy marriages. In their book they give particular attention to employment policies to help men become more "marriageable." While my book will not focus on policy to improve the social and economic soil in which healthy relationships and marriages can germinate and grow, I acknowledge the need for this kind of policy progress. Good marriages clearly improve our collective social and economic well-being. But good marriages will be more plentiful in social and economic earth that is less toxic to healthy, stable relationships (and healthy marriages and relationships will facilitate social and economic progress). The ideal is to make progress on both fronts. I will return to this idea in Chapter 3.

Charles Donovan, at the conservative Heritage Foundation, briefly outlined his "Marshall Plan" for "rebuilding our shattered homes."[24] He commends a number of the educational strategies that I will recommend here (in more depth) but prioritizes some tax reforms that I think are politically infeasible and could have unpleasant side effects.

By the way, President Barack Obama, in his book, *The Audacity of Hope,*[25] endorsed a number of government policies to strengthen marriage, including providing marriage and relationship education services to needy individuals and couples, a policy initiative begun under the previous Bush administration and continued in the Obama administration:

> [P]reliminary research shows that marriage education workshops can make a real difference in helping married couples stay together and in encouraging unmarried couples who are living together to form a more lasting bond. Expanding access to such services to low-income couples, perhaps in concert with job training and placement, medical coverage, and other services already available, should be something everybody can agree on (p. 334).

A handful of scholars, then, have speculated in general terms what we might do to strengthen the institution of marriage. But their plans are not as specific or detailed as I will propose here, and perhaps some are not very feasible.

That most other scholars have been thin on the details of how public policy can seek to strengthen marriage should not be surprising. As Christian Smith and his sociologist colleagues said when they addressed the problems facing emerging adults in contemporary society, "It is not the business of sociologists to prescribe normative responses to the social realities they study. It is better, we generally think, to simply describe and explain the social world to and for others, and then to let various kinds of readers figure out what, if anything, they want to do about it."[26] Moreover, they warn: "Until we grasp and accept the challenges and difficulties involved [with social problems], proposed solutions and alternatives will likely be superficial and fruitless. The premature activism they would set in motion might make some people feel better about themselves and the world, but they will not likely effect actual substantial change."[27] This is a sober and serious challenge that deserves a careful but brief response. Is a book like this premature, a Polyanna-ish and fruitless exercise in "feel-goodism"? Is change realistic and can it be effected by government action? Smith and his colleagues warn: "Nobody is in a position to transform mass consumer capitalism, the globalizing economy, liberal individualism, and other macro-social factors that give form and content to [the problems of] emerging adulthood"[28] (which is the focus of their book). I want to address this challenge directly to defend the value of a book at this time that sets out an agenda to help reduce a social problem—the destructive increase in family instability.

First, Smith and his colleagues do not completely abandon the value of thinking about how to address a social problem. While they do not believe that policy can affect macrosocial change directly, they do believe there are "*middle-level* institutional reforms . . . that could ameliorate some of the problems" in emerging adulthood[29] and that policy can help move some of these reforms forward. I think the agenda I am proposing in this book fits comfortably into the kind of middle-level institutional reforms that these authors value and explore. Furthermore, within this framework of attempting to reform through middle-level institutions such as high schools and colleges, religious organizations, human service agencies, the Cooperative Extension System in land-grant universities, and others, I believe attempts to create change—to help more people form and sustain healthy marriages and relationships—will give us a more basic understanding about what the problems are. My master's degree is in organizational behavior, a discipline that focuses on the craft and science of organizational change. Scholars of organizational change emphasize that a full understanding of organizational problems actually is aided by efforts to change the system.[30] You try to change a system based on an analysis of the problem, and if the expected change doesn't occur, chances are you probably have some flaws in your diagnosis of the problem. Efforts to change the system and then observe what happens can lead to important clues about the problem that were unseen or poorly understood before. In other words, intervention isn't just about fixing a problem but it is also about understanding a problem.

I think there have been some excellent analyses of the problems facing the institution of marriage, as cited above. I think our understanding of the issues, although hardly complete, is certainly maturing. And some policy initiatives are beginning to get into the cultural conversation. Accordingly, I don't think it is premature or Polyanna-ish to start thinking in detail about how we could try to address the problems and help more couples form and sustain healthy marriages and relationships. In the process, I suspect that we will learn more about the nature of the problems we are trying to address.

The Problem in a Nutshell and the Contemporary Challenge

Let me see if I can put in a nutshell the fundamental challenge we are facing. A large and increasing number of children are experiencing family instability that puts at risk their well-being emotionally, socially, intellectually, spiritually, and financially.[31] In short, they are at greater risk for losing a better future due to their parents' relationship problems. I believe that family instability is one of the biggest social problems we now face as a society. Today, more than 40% of children are born to unmarried couples whose relationships are fragile and unlikely to last for more than a few years—or even a few months, for some—despite their hopes and dreams.[32] Among the least-educated, low-income Americans, as well as women under 30, more than half of children are born to unmarried parents.[33] And high school–educated, middle-class Americans are rapidly "catching up" to this figure (44% in 2008).[34]

Please understand something here. While people are choosing to bear and rear children outside the institution of marriage, their reasons for doing so are not inexplicable, even if they are not good for children. As Harvard University sociologist Kathy Edin has shown,[35] low-income youth and young adults often feel a sense of detachment from mainstream society and a sense that the American dream is beyond them. They doubt that they can achieve a stable social and economic life. In the face of this discouragement, many find the most meaningful thing they can do is give life and love to a child. And of course, that is the most meaningful thing that any individual can do. Some even feel that the child literally saves them from a street life that will eventually destroy them. The problem is that while parenthood for young people may be a path to a more meaningful life, the children raised in these circumstances too often suffer, despite the good intentions and efforts of their parents. They often repeat the cycle of poverty, poor outcomes, and unstable families and the private and public costs associated with those outcomes.[36] And rates of intimate partner violence are alarmingly high in low-income couples.[37] We don't know much yet about the motives for unwed childbearing among high school–educated, working-class individuals, but as researchers begin to examine this, I doubt they will uncover unintelligible reasons. People's motives are often rational, at least in a proximal sense, even if their behaviors are not particularly wise.

Children born to unstable and unmarried parents are not the only concern, of course. Demographers estimate that about 45%–50% of first marriages and about 60% of second marriages will end in divorce.[38] Lower income and less educated couples are less likely to marry, but if they do, they are much more likely to divorce.[39] This isn't too hard to understand when you realize that they are much more likely to start that marriage in more complex and challenging circumstances. For example, they are more likely to start the marriage with biological children already in tow and nonbiological children from previous relationships that make married life more complicated.[40] As a result, far too many children experience a series of family transitions that are hard to manage and a quality of family life that falls short of their birthright. Their parents live together with several partners, marry one, divorce, live with more partners, remarry another one, and redivorce. Along for the turbulent ride, children experience a constant churning of family life that makes the normative process of growing up tougher than it should be. U.S. children experience these adult union break-ups at three to four times the rate of children in other Western countries.[41] As Andrew Cherlin has written:

> There are more partners in the personal lives of Americans than in the lives of people of any other Western country. The most distinctive characteristic of American family life, then, the trait that most clearly differentiates it from family

life in other Western countries, is sheer movement: frequent transitions, shorter relationships. Americans step on and off the carousel of intimate partnerships … more often. … This merry-go-round property of American families is more than a statistical curiosity. We should be concerned about it, both as parents and as a nation, because it may increase children's behavioral and emotional problems. Simply put, some children seem to have difficulty adjusting to a series of parents and parents' partners moving in and out of their home.[42]

Forming and sustaining a stable and healthy marriage in which to rear children has gotten harder to do for less educated Americans. The knowledge and skills needed to achieve our family aspirations are higher now than they were a couple of generations ago. The primary reason for this is the rapid deinstitutionalization of marriage. Nine-syllable words in books should be avoided as much as possible, but in this case, I think *deinstitutionalization* is the best word to describe why we are struggling so much to form and sustain healthy marriages and why we need better knowledge and skills if we are going to alleviate the problem.

I think Cherlin may have been the first to use the term *deinstitutionalization,* and he does the best job of explaining what is meant by it.[43] I'll try to summarize his analysis briefly and as clearly as possible. Cherlin defines deinstitutionalization as "the weakening of the social norms that define people's behavior in a social institution such as marriage."[44] For centuries, there were powerful norms that guided people's actions with regards to sexuality, courtship, and marriage. Of course, norms have always been violated, but the norms were strong nonetheless. With strong norms about marriage, people know a lot about what is expected of them and there is a taken-for-granted notion about how to behave. So it easier to form and sustain a marriage; even the relationally challenged can get by if they know enough just to follow the rules and if their expectations are realistic. But these norms or social rules for marriage have eroded rapidly over the last 50 years due to a number of changes. Cherlin cites Americans' love affair with expressive individualism, unrestrained sexual freedoms, gender role changes, and affluence as some of the biggest contributors to the deinstitutionalization of marriage.[45] There is probably some good news along with the bad news in these changes. Some norms have probably made it harder to build a mutually satisfying emotional connection. And economic changes have made it harder to begin a family for the less educated. But the point is, as Cherlin notes, "individuals can no longer rely on shared understandings of how to act. Rather, they must negotiate new ways of acting."[46] Courtship and marriage used to have a pretty clear set of rules to live by. Now that is much less the case. Moreover, marriage used to be at the very core of how we organized society. Nowadays, not so much. Marriage is just one way that people choose to order their lives, and society is becoming more accommodating of the many different ways people "do" family today.

On the one hand, this deinstitutionalization provides us with unprecedented freedom to create deep, romantic relationships that satisfy our individual needs and circumstances rather than force-fit everyone into the same box. Not surprisingly, then, we have raised the bar on marriage. It now is supposed to be a kind of super-relationship that meets all of our needs and creates deep emotional satisfaction.[47] On the other hand, all this freedom presents more potential for disagreement, misunderstanding, tension, and conflict among romantic partners, not to mention unrealistic expectations that lead to conflict, dissatisfaction, and disappointment. Greater potential relationship conflict and disappointment combined with a fierce American cultural value of expressive individualism creates a perfect storm for the relationship churning we see today. The contemporary reality is that we have extremely high expectations for marriage and romantic relationships and those expectations are hard to meet. Moreover, the courtship system has broken down in ways that make getting to marriage, or getting there without a lot of baggage, much harder. Chief among these is having children before establishing a committed, enduring romantic union. This relationship churning doesn't seem to be very good for most adults, but from a public policy perspective, the bigger concern is that it isn't good for children. As resilient as children are, family instability puts children at much higher risk for poverty[48] and debilitating problems that diminish their future potentials. This is true in the United States and around the globe in middle- and high-income countries.[49]

Accordingly, as a society we need to do a better job of educating people for the changed reality of contemporary relationships and marriage. We need to get smarter about marriage and relationships.[50] We need better relationship knowledge and skills. The "till-death-do-us-part" commitment that sustains relationships now comes more from the inside than the outside, more from our personal dedication than from societal structures, constraints, and norms.

About a decade ago, the U.S. government and a few states began actively experimenting with public policies supporting various educational initiatives to help couples learn better the knowledge and skills needed to form and sustain healthy marriages and relationships. I will describe these policy experiments in Chapter 2 and illustrate a number of specific initiatives and programs throughout the book to give the reader a clearer idea of what these government-supported efforts look like. I will also summarize the research that has been trying to evaluate how effective these initiatives have been.

The Bottom Line and a Preview of the Policy Agenda

The message of this book is that there are things we can do to improve the quality of romantic relationships, strengthen the institution of marriage, and provide greater family stability for children. There are some feasible, inexpensive policy actions we can take with government support that will make a positive, cost-effective difference in the number of couples in the United States who can form and sustain a healthy and stable relationship in which to rear their children. The policy actions I propose promote preventative educational services targeted primarily to needy, less educated families, at no cost, to help them form and sustain healthy relationships and stable marriages. But we need to implement a strategic, integrated *package* of educational efforts and we need to start early. To preview, my agenda consists of the following package of six proposals.

1. Increase and improve relationship literacy education for youth and emerging adults to help them gain the knowledge, attitudes, and skills needed to form healthy romantic relationships, avoid unhealthy relationships, and understand better the institution of marriage. (Chapter 4 will focus on this proposal.)

2. Provide marriage preparation education for engaged couples to prevent unwise marital choices and help them gain the knowledge and skills needed to form a healthy marriage. In addition, help cohabiting parents who aspire to marriage to assess their relationship and build their confidence for marriage with relationship development education. (Chapter 5 will focus on this proposal.)

3. Provide more support for marriage maintenance education to help couples deal with the inevitable challenges and transitions that can rattle

couples in the early years of marriage (and beyond). (Chapter 6 will focus on this proposal.)

4. Require divorce orientation education before filing for divorce to help individuals at the crossroads of divorce think clearly about their decision and prevent some preventable divorces. (Chapter 8 will focus on this proposal.)

5. Support this strategic public policy agenda with a 1% set-aside of TANF block grant funds to the state and a modest set-aside or surcharge on marriage licenses. Provide state TANF-office leadership to state-directed initiatives and guide efforts with a volunteer, active, expert advisory board. (Chapter 9 will focus on this proposal.)

6. Provide federal support to state-directed initiatives by funding rigorous evaluation research and disseminating the knowledge gained. Also, employ federal funds for media campaigns to increase awareness of the value of marriage and relationship education and participation in these services. (Chapter 9 also will explore this proposal.)

For readers who would like to view these proposals graphically with a little more detail and context—that is, see the beginning from the end—you may want to browse the first part of the final chapter. It will give you a clearer idea of where I am headed in the next eight chapters.

I want to admit up front that the specific proposals in this strategic agenda certainly are not new; we are already doing each of them here and there with support from government funds. But I think the agenda is innovative in the packaging of several proposals into an integrated strategy of what to do when and how to coordinate and fund them. Each proposal by itself has some but probably limited value; no single dosage of marriage and relationship education is a vaccine that can inoculate individuals against relationship problems. The full package will have greater impact. While we have been experimenting over the last decade with supporting a wide variety of educational programs to help individuals and couples, we have not developed an overarching strategy that may provide cumulative help at the right times across the early life course to make a real difference. I'll provide more details about this point in Chapters 9 and 10. Explaining and advocating for this strategic agenda and its potential is the purpose of this book.

In addition, I want to say something about priorities. My first and second points in the agenda—supporting educational opportunities for youth, young adults, and premarital couples—happen to be chronologically ordered, but they are also my highest priorities in this agenda. We've got to do a better job of helping young Americans stay on better paths that will make forming and sustaining healthy marriages a more realistic endpoint. Similarly, we need to help them avoid some of the mistakes that make this destination hard to find. Just to name the most obvious issue, we need to help young Americans get to marriage—or a committed, healthy relationship—before they get to parenthood. Marriages that begin in such challenging circumstances are much less likely to succeed and thus marriage itself won't be a policy maker's panacea.[51] So in my proposed agenda I want to put the most emphasis on helping youth and young adults form healthy relationships and establish strong, stable marriages. There are some valuable things we can do to support people after they marry, but I think they will be effective mostly when we get marriages off to a solid start.

Clarifications

Let me make a few of clarifications before going further. First, my focus in this book will be on U.S. policy actions. For various reasons, over the last decade the United States is probably doing more to help couples—especially lower income couples—form and sustain healthy marriages and relationships. A handful of countries, such as Australia, the United Kingdom, and Singapore, have experimented with policies to support relationship education but not as much as the United States.[52] I suspect the agenda I propose here could be relevant elsewhere. But my focus here is on the United States and our current situation.

In addition, while my focus in this book is on state and federal government support of preventative, educational services for individuals and couples, I don't discount the contributions that other public institutions, such as religion, healthcare, and business, can make to strengthen the institution of marriage. Indeed, I will propose that government support mostly be channeled through these institutions, stretching those efforts to help. And there are important policy changes that these institutions of civil society can make to strengthen marriages independent of government support. I will mention a few ideas throughout the book. Nevertheless, my focus will be on policy efforts supported by federal and state government initiatives, even though most of the programs will be integrated into nongovernmental or quasigovernmental organizations that already do educational work and have a stake in strong families.

Moreover, I will stay focused on support of educational initiatives. I do not include in my agenda such things as marriage-friendly tax policies, primarily because my focus will be on feasible things that we can do now. Changes to tax policy in our current economic and political environment do not fit my idea of feasible action items. Other good scholars have explored potential ways to use tax policy to strengthen marriages and some changes in tax policy already have occurred.[53]

Let me make one more important clarification. The reader likely has noticed that I have said nothing so far about same-sex marriage. I won't be addressing that topic in this book other than through my brief clarification here. Same-sex marriage is an important issue and debate. In fact, it dominates academic discussions and media coverage of marriage and public policy, sometimes to the point that people are not even aware of the kinds of efforts to strengthen marriage that I discuss in this book. Much more light needs to be shed on these efforts, so that is where my focus will be. There are many good books and articles that people can read to get a perspective on whether same-sex marriage would strengthen or weaken the institution of marriage. The scope of this book is already so large that including a substantial treatment of same-sex marriage is unwise. For some who support same-sex marriage and some who oppose it, the issue is a funnel through which every other discussion about the institution of marriage must first pass. I resist this funnel, and not because same-sex marriage affects only a fraction of a fraction of American adults who have a homosexual identity.[54] I resist this because marriage among the 95%-plus of adults who have a stable heterosexual orientation and who often make babies with their sex is deserving of attention without having to pass a prior litmus test. Those individuals for whom same-sex marriage is a prerequisite issue will be disappointed in this book because I will not take a stand here. Certainly I have personal and professional views on how the legalization of same-sex marriage may affect the meaning of marriage and whether it will ultimately strengthen or weaken the institution. But I believe the agenda I put forth here stands independent of my views and others' views on this important issue. The agenda I propose can go forward regardless of the outcome of the legal debate.

Certainly same-sex couples, married or unmarried, also may benefit from marriage and relationship education because, like too many children in heterosexual families, children in homosexual families also experience a great deal of family instability from the churning relationships of their parents.[55]

Finally, I use the phrase "help couples form and sustain healthy marriages" a lot in this book. That phrase is shorthand for some important issues that I should clarify. First, helping couples is important, but I believe we also need to go upstream and help single individuals stay on positive trajectories to healthy marriages. So even though I will often just refer to helping couples, I also intend to include within that phrase the importance of helping single individuals. Furthermore, my ultimate interest is to strengthen the institution of marriage, so my focus is on marriage. But when using that term, I acknowledge the need to help couples form healthy relationships regardless of when or whether they choose to marry. Pragmatically, healthy relationships are much more likely to lead to stable and healthy marriages. So I am concerned about all romantic relationships and hope to help all of them even though sometimes I just employ the term, *marriage* rather than the more generic *relationships*.

Underlying Principles of the Policy Agenda

There are some important principles underlying the strategic agenda I am proposing that I should clarify.

Feasibility. I will stress feasible proposals, not pie-in-the-sky ideas. By *feasible,* I mean actions that, for the most part: (a) can be supported mostly with a rechanneling of existing funds; (b) can be integrated into existing educational infrastructures to supplement existing efforts; (c) are likely to be appreciated by the general public and have widespread support; (d) avoid strong political opposition; (e) minimize the need for passing new legislation; and (f) create mostly voluntary educational opportunities rather than mandated participation. To be serious about a policy agenda to strengthen marriage is to see what can be done realistically now with current resources.

Timing. We need to deliver quality marriage and relationship education at multiple key time points. Starting early to reach youth is crucial. Then, we need continuing education in emerging adulthood, the engagement (or premarital cohabitation) period, and the early years of marriage. Education for remarrying couples is important, given that many marriages now include at least one partner who was previously married. Education and help for individuals thinking about getting a divorce is needed, too. Effective education benefits from repeated doses at key times.[56] One marriage and relationship education experience is not a lifelong inoculation. It's more like a booster shot for the various communicable diseases that need periodic doses to keep up the immunity.

Target. Everyone can use some help. But the research shows that well-educated folks are actually doing pretty well with marriage. Overall, well-educated individuals are marrying in high numbers and have relatively low levels of divorce. Nevertheless, lower income individuals are struggling to form and sustain healthy and stable romantic relationships and marriages in which to rear their children. Moreover, the moderately educated working class is now in nearly the same situation. Individuals with only a high school education, regardless of race or ethnicity, have seen divorce rates continue to go up while for the well-educated the rates have gone down substantially.[57] Similarly, reports of marital happiness have gone down for high school–educated Americans while they have held steady for well-educated Americans. And since the early 1980s, the percentage of nonmarital births has risen by more than 30 percentage points overall (to more than 40%) while it increased by only three percentage points (to about 6%) for well-educated Americans. Nearly 60% of Americans fall into the high school–educated category. And while they are not necessarily poor, their ability to form and sustain healthy marriages has decreased significantly. Add this group to roughly 10% of even less educated and poor Americans in the same leaky boat and that means 70% of Americans are struggling to get downriver to their destination of a healthy, stable marriage. So I am not talking about another program to help just a small fraction of the most disadvantaged members of our society, as valuable as that would be. I'm talking about a significant majority of citizens who are at greater risk for unhealthy and unstable relationships and the problems that can cause for them and their children. The marriage and relationship educational opportunities I am proposing here could benefit a majority, not a minority, of Americans. At the same time, I admit that a series of marriage and relationship education programs to help the most disadvantaged individuals in our society, those who struggle with dire poverty and severe personal problems, may not be enough to help.[58] But among the less advantaged are many who could benefit from the kinds of programs that I will be discussing here.

Scale. I am not proposing educational programs that look like large government bureaucracies. These programs will need to look to the participants like small, personal services, services probably provided by well-known and trusted community organizations and institutions. Small and local is not only beautiful but functional. I'm not proposing massive programs.

Implementation. It is not enough to provide funding for well-intentioned programs. You have to pay attention to the details, learn, evaluate, and improve. Success is in the details. Plenty of research documents how important effective implementation is for a well-intentioned program in order to achieve what it is supposed to achieve. Support for the kinds of programs I am proposing here must be accompanied by real attention to implementation details. I include some of those details in the chapters that follow.

My Credentials

I've been observing policy efforts to help couples form and sustain healthy marriages and relationships for more than a decade. I've been professionally involved consulting with federal and state efforts. For instance, I was a visiting scholar with the Administration for Children and Families, consulting with this federal agency that administers welfare policy in the United States and has experimented with new policies to help support healthy relationships and responsible fatherhood. I have consulted with major federal research projects to rigorously evaluate educational programs to help lower income married and unmarried couples form and sustain healthy marriages and relationships. I have been a member and chair of the Utah Commission on Marriage, which advises a state agency on ways to strengthen marriage in the state where I live. I serve on the Research Advisory Group to the Oklahoma Marriage Initiative, the premier state-level effort to provide free educational services to help individuals and couples form and sustain healthy marriages and relationships. Similarly, I serve on the Research Advisory Group that advises "Twogether in Texas," the Texas Healthy Marriage Initiative. And I have consulted on research matters with the California Healthy Marriage Coalition, now known as "Healthy Relationships California," which is funded by a federal grant. I have also consulted briefly with policy makers in Louisiana and Kansas on past and present policy efforts there.

I have attended numerous conferences and participated in formal conversations with other scholars, policy makers, legislators, and practitioners discussing government efforts to strengthen marriage, including some sessions in which strong conservatives and liberals were finding much common ground. I have ongoing relationships with the major think tanks that have strong interests in this area, such as the National Marriage Project, the Center for Marriage and Families at the Institute for American Values, and the Brookings Institute. I was an associate editor for a scholarly journal with an ongoing focus on couple and relationship education. Moreover, I've written more than 20 scholarly articles and chapters over the past decade relevant to policy efforts to strengthen the institution of marriage, including a study documenting the impact of government-supported healthy marriage activity in all 50 states and the District of Columbia.[59] I also was a co-editor of an edited volume on strengthening the institution of marriage.[60] And I regularly read the work of other scholars on this topic.

But I haven't been looking at these efforts just from an ivory-tower perspective. I've visited a number of organizations in a handful of states that are providing marriage and relationship education services to their communities, helped by government funding. While writing this book, I sat in on a wide variety of classes and I interviewed in-the-trenches instructors and program administrators. I think I have a feel for the challenges they face in delivering classes to diverse and often disadvantaged individuals and couples.

As a result of all this, I think I know about as much as anyone does these days about the kinds of government-supported efforts being employed to strengthen the institution of marriage and whether these efforts may be making a difference. Still, my graduate school training was in human development and family studies (Penn State, 1990), not social policy. I became interested in the policy dimensions of strengthening marriages and families in 2000 as a result of some experiences as a visiting scholar at the National Fatherhood Initiative. I have bootstrapped my learning in social policy since then without formal academic training. Reading books and articles, attending conferences with a strong policy focus, and burying my head in related issues, I've tried to teach myself how to think like a public policy scholar.

What is Marriage and Relationship Education?

I've used the term *marriage and relationship education* quite a few times already (often abbreviated hereafter as MRE). I have argued that the challenge of our time is to combat family instability by helping people become more relationally literate and skilled. This is the task of MRE. Maybe now would be a good time to define generally what I mean by it. I have learned that this term is not clear to many people. It is not the same as marriage counseling or therapy.[61] Certainly therapists provide education to their clients about healthy relationships. And therapists will sometimes recommend that their clients attend an MRE workshop to learn some better communication skills, in addition to personal counseling sessions. But counseling or therapy involves a trained counselor or therapist meeting with an individual—or better yet, a couple—to deal with specific, often deep-seated relationship and personal problems, the origins of those problems, and potential specific resolutions. And therapists often work on more than just relationship issues; they will take on such things as mental health issues (e.g., depression) or problematic behaviors (e.g., alcohol abuse) that are contributing to relationship problems. Therapists are trained to deal with the strong negative emotions with regards to the relationship that may emerge in therapy with couples. MRE educators, on the other hand, usually state explicitly that their programs are not the public place to work out serious private problems, nor are they an effective place to air strong, negative emotions or even highly personal experiences.

MRE is usually thought of as a way to prevent serious problems rather than a way to resolve them. My colleague, Kim Halford, at the University of Queensland (Australia), refers to MRE as "an attempt to steer couples away from the cliff of relationship distress, whereas couple therapy is the ambulance at the bottom of the cliff available to treat those couples who have fallen."[62] The field of prevention science talks about three different levels of prevention programs: universal prevention (targeted to everyone regardless of risk); selected prevention (targeted to individuals at particular risk for developing serious problems); and indicated prevention (targeted to individuals generally in the early stages of serious problems). MRE programs exist at all three of these levels. Some programs target couples in healthy relationships who want to make them even stronger. Other programs focus on identifying individuals and couples at risk, such as lower income and less-educated couples, but who are not yet experiencing serious distress. Most of the programs that I will highlight in this book target at-risk individuals and couples. Individuals and couples with serious relationship distress also sometimes seek out educational programs in addition to or in place of therapy, but the program does not focus on their specific problems; they receive only generalized rather than personalized help. For lower income couples, an MRE program may be their only option because no-cost therapy is very difficult to get. So, sometimes distressed couples participate along with others in learning from a set curriculum designed to help them improve their relationship skills and knowledge. These MRE programs can't take on helping specific couples with severe problems, such as infidelity or drug abuse, but good programs will refer couples with these problems for additional help.

Generally, those who participate in MRE are trying to work on strengthening their relationships or getting help to prevent little problems from becoming bigger ones or big problems from becoming terminal ones.[63] In other words, MRE participants are working on their relationship, with some doing more heavy lifting than others. We say it a lot—relationships need work. MRE is about working on a relationship or learning skills and knowledge for a future relationship.

Some MRE practitioners are trained as therapists, but many are not. Some scholars argue that MRE educators should also be clinically trained so that they can better recognize clinical problems and refer couples for more intimate and in-depth therapy. Some individuals who participate in MRE do have serious problems or mental health issues, so there could be some advantages to having a trained clinician as an instructor. But many MRE practitioners are not trained as therapists. And I have one colleague who argues that therapists make lousy educators because they tend to struggle to get outside of their therapeutic, diagnostic mindset that sees deep dysfunction in every little problem. Many educators are just people with a passion for helping individuals build healthy relationships.

MRE traditionally is provided in a workshop format to small groups of individuals or married couples, often in groups of 10 to 30 individuals. It takes place in varied settings—community centers, churches, community colleges—but involves face-to-face interaction with instructors and other individuals and couples in the group. (In Chapter 7 I discuss the need for more nontraditional means of delivering MRE.) Some MRE programs have a fee, anywhere from $20 for the cost of materials to several hundred dollars. But the ones that I will focus on in this book are free because of the support they receive from government funding, so they are more accessible to lower income couples. Participation in MRE programs that receive public support is voluntary. But in a few cases, *voluntary* means that participants have chosen an MRE class from a set of options, but they have to take one of the options. This is usually the case when parents are involved with state child and family services or have some kind of court order to take positive steps to address a problem that impacts their children.

The length of MRE programs varies widely. The average appears to be about 12 hours.[64] Government-supported programs generally are at least 8 hours in length and a few are much longer than that. In later chapters I will describe some programs with 30 to 40 hours of planned instructional time. A common approach is to divide the curriculum into 2-hour sessions offered once a week for several weeks to afford time to absorb program content and practice skills learned. But sometimes multiple sessions can make it more difficult for couples to attend regularly, especially lower income couples who may have transportation challenges, child care struggles, and whose lives and schedules are often less predictable. So many MRE providers now emphasize all-day weekend workshops to steer clear of some of these potholes.

Curriculum is usually pretty set in terms of what and how it is presented. Curriculum is usually programmatic; that is, it covers a variety of important topics, often in a sequence that builds on previous ideas and skills. Some curricula do not require any special certification, but most programs being offered to lower income couples these days are using set curricula that require instructors to attend a 2- to 3-day (or longer) training workshop before they can be certified to teach. A few MRE programs are less structured, emphasizing group discussion of issues that concern participants without much didactic presentation from instructors. Of course, MRE can take other forms. A fairly common form is a 1- to 3-hour presentation by an educator to a large auditorium of individuals and couples. This is more of a lecture than a workshop, but many people enjoy and benefit from this less interactive format. But this isn't what is usually meant by MRE and my focus in this book is on the more traditional group workshop.

In the traditional workshop, time typically is divided between some brief presentations by instructors or group facilitators, group discussion of principles, questions to instructors, role playing, viewing video enactments of principles and skills, and couples practicing a new skill just taught. Often the group instructors are a male–female team, sometimes married to each other. As a couple, they try to model the skills that they are teaching the participants. Many programs take care to match the instructor couple characteristics with the dominant demographic characteristics of the target participants, although there is no strong evidence yet that this produces better learning. (It may yield better recruiting of participants.) Some programs will have trained assistants as well as instructors who listen in and give feedback to couples while they practice a new skill. Programs targeted to lower income couples have learned to put an emphasis on more active learning processes rather than didactic presentation of material to match the preferred learning style of their participants. Sometimes these programs also include family support coordinators who work to help couples attend sessions and solve other problems that can make their participation in the program less effective.

Also, many lower income married couples feel isolated as a married couple—they don't know a lot of other married couples like them—so the group interchange and discussion that is common in MRE can take on the feel of a support group as well as an educational workshop. Sometimes married couples will form support groups or marriage enrichment groups and meet regularly to discuss issues, work on little issues, and draw support from other couples. This form of MRE does not have a set curriculum, although often there is a lead couple who have been trained as MRE educators.

The most common form of MRE involves a couple attending together. But increasingly practitioners are offering MRE to individuals or both individuals and couples attend classes together. MRE for youth and young adults is a rapidly growing form of MRE, and this doesn't assume that participants are in a romantic relationship. Usually the focus of MRE in these situations is on principles for building healthy romantic relationships and discerning warning signs of unhealthy relationships. I'll describe this kind of MRE more in Chapter 4.

If MRE is a way to help people work on strengthening their relationships (a current one or preparing more effectively for a future one), this must mean we know something about how to do that. I want to emphasize the word *something*. I don't think we know everything. If fact, I think we have a long way to go yet to be as effective as we need to be. I provide specific thoughts (or guesses) about how to improve the practice of MRE throughout the book and devote Chapter 7 to some thoughts about improvement. Still, we know some things about what makes for a healthy relationship and successful marriage and we can provide people with this information and good ideas, curricula, and programs that can help them form and sustain healthy marriages and relationships. Good MRE is based on sound research, and a number of talented scholars have provided us with a solid start to guide our interventions. Over the next two decades, I think we are going to get much better as we learn more and more about mature love and what gets in the way of it.

In addition, my definition of good MRE programs includes the need that they be evaluated and empirically demonstrate that they can help people. I have reviewed hundreds of studies that evaluated many different kinds of MRE programs. There is solid evidence overall that MRE programs can help couples improve their communication and problem-solving skills as well as improve their relationship quality and satisfaction.[65] Most of this evaluation work has been done on more educated and mostly White couples. Recently there is evaluation work on programs targeted to less educated, lower income individuals, and, importantly, there is emerging evidence that MRE can help them, as well.[66]

Outline

To summarize, this purpose of this book is to explain and promote a feasible strategic policy agenda that will help more couples form and sustain healthy marriages and relationships for the benefit of their children. The next chapter will illustrate in broad strokes some of the policy initiatives that federal and state governments have implemented and begin looking at the research that is evaluating these initiatives. Chapter 3 will acknowledge and respond to legitimate concerns and critiques about these policy initiatives. Chapters 4 through 9 go into greater depth about each of the specific proposals that constitute the overall agenda I am proposing, illustrating along the way some specific programs, examining further the evidence for their effectiveness, and suggesting feasible means or delivery infrastructures for getting more educational opportunities to those who need them most. The final chapter provides a summary and some concluding thoughts.

My hope is that this book can inform and stimulate. I hope it can inform interested people about what may be possible right now to strengthen the institution of marriage and improve the quality of romantic relationships. But most of all, I hope it will stimulate legislators, policy makers, and professionals in key areas of influence to action that will provide more opportunities for individuals and couples to improve their knowledge and skills to form and sustain healthy marriages and relationships. Ultimately, my hope is that healthier relationships and stronger marriages will help facilitate more positive futures for our children.

Chapter 2

Federal and State Initiatives to Help Couples Form and Sustain Healthy Marriages and Relationships: A View of the Landscape

Before getting into the details of my specific proposals to strengthen marriage and reduce family instability, it would be valuable to understand the government-supported initiatives already operating. In this chapter, then, first I outline the federal government's healthy marriages and relationships initiative that began in 2001. In addition, beginning in the late 1990s, a few states have implemented their own significant initiatives. Thus, I will outline marriage initiatives in Utah, Oklahoma, and Texas. Some state legislatures have passed legislation over the past 20 years intended to strengthen marriage and reduce divorce; I review these efforts, as well. Finally, I begin to address the pressing, crucial question, "Are these initiatives working?"

The Federal Healthy Marriages and Relationships Initiative

Without question, the U.S. government has been the primary catalyst for public policy efforts to help couples form and sustain healthy marriages. The reason for this requires some explanation. After all, the U.S. Constitution has been interpreted as providing to the states, not the federal government, the right to regulate matters of marriage and divorce.[1] So how did the federal government take on this surprising role? The answer to this question rests with an understanding of federal welfare policy changes over the past 20 years.

In the early 1990s, a good deal of research began to document the structural changes that had been occurring to American families since the 1960s and the disconcerting outcomes associated with those changes. I think Barbara Dafoe Whitehead's controversial 1993 article in the influential *Atlantic Magazine*, "Why Dan Quayle Was Right,"[2] brought this scholarship into the public eye in a way and to a degree that had not occurred before. Referencing an accumulating body of scientific research, her thesis was that the unraveling of the two-parent, married family was substantially increasing harm to children and weakening the social fabric of society. Her title cleverly captured a media phenomenon of the time, when former Vice President Dan Quayle (who was a leading Republican party presidential candidate at the time) was widely ridiculed for criticizing a popular TV show character, Murphy Brown, for glamorizing single parenting by depicting on the show having a child out-of-wedlock. After the media circus died down, Whitehead marshaled the emerging scientific evidence on the importance of marriage to children's (and adults') well-being and published it in a leading progressive magazine. While this was hardly the beginning of the cultural war over family issues, this publication established a major front in that war. I mark Whitehead's article as the seminal moment for what some call the promarriage movement in the United States.

Also in the 1990s, another vice president was making a mark in a different way that tied into concerns about the American family. Vice President Al Gore began making headway in his efforts to make federal policy more responsive to the reality that fathers were important in children's lives and that policies and programs should take account of this reality. While his focus was on fatherhood rather than on marriage, these efforts likely tilled the soil for future concerns about family instability, couple relationships, and marriage.

Vice President Quayle's and Vice President Gore's concerns were based on emerging scholarship, not just personal opinions. Federal policy makers and some lawmakers also began paying attention to this scholarship and used it to raise questions about federal policies and welfare policy in particular. Congress and civil servants back in the 1960s constructed welfare policy when these dramatic changes in family life were barely beginning to be seen. One critique was that welfare policy was antifatherhood and antimarriage because it gave benefits to single mothers and took those benefits away if they married or if unmarried fathers were resident in the home with children (even if they remained poor). There were a few attempts to refine these policies over the years,[3] but I think it is safe to say that there wasn't a lot of real action, even though some policy makers and administrators were beginning to shift their thinking about serving not just mothers but families, and that included fathers as well as mothers and fathers together as couples.

But in the mid 1990s, with the Republican party gaining control of Congress after decades as the minority party, party leaders determined to make wholesale changes in America's welfare policies, including its alleged hostility (or indifference) to marriage. While there were a series of to-be-expected partisan political battles over how to change welfare policy, eventually Republicans pounded out a set compromises with the help of the Clinton administration in 1996 that scrapped the old welfare system for a new program called Temporary Assistance to Needy Families or TANF (pronounced "tan-if"). TANF provided block grants of federal funds to states that, in turn, would decide how to spend the funds to accomplish four broad goals, three of which dealt with family structure: reduce unwed births, encourage the formation of two-parent families, and reduce welfare dependency by encouraging marriage and work.

But the family structure goals in the new program received very modest attention from the states in the ensuing years. Most of the attention went to the controversial employment provisions of the new program that required work or efforts to increase employability by those who were receiving benefits, including single mothers. There was some attention to reducing unwed pregnancies (perhaps due to bonus funds that rewarded states that did the most to reduce unwed pregnancies), but there were only a few states that gave attention to marriage and two-parent families with their TANF funds. Perhaps this was because there were few ideas of how to do this and substantial skepticism that government programs could push back with any force against powerful tides of sociohistorical change that were altering family formation patterns in the United States and elsewhere. (I discuss this skepticism more in Chapter 3.)

A major shift occurred, however, during the (George W.) Bush administration. In 2001, President Bush appointed former Wisconsin Governor Tommy Thompson as Secretary of Health and Human Services. Under Thompson's state leadership, Wisconsin had been one of the few states that experimented with policies to reform welfare to make it friendlier to fathers and marriage. Furthermore, Secretary Thompson hired Wade Horn, a child psychologist by training, to be the head of the Administration for Children and Families (ACF), the agency that set, administered, and evaluated welfare policy in the country.

Horn was an experienced federal bureaucrat. He had served previously in ACF during President (George H. W.) Bush's administration as the director of the Children's Bureau. Horn was already a well-known player inside the D.C. beltway when he left his work as director of the nonprofit National Fatherhood Initiative for his post at ACF. Horn previously had done some work on fatherhood initiatives in Texas for then-Governor Bush.

While at NFI, Horn became increasingly convinced that public and private initiatives to promote responsible fatherhood in the United States needed to be wed with efforts to strengthen marriages. I was a visiting scholar at the National Fatherhood Initiative during the summer of 2000. My early scholarship had focused on increasing positive father involvement. I remember several long and stimulating conversations with Horn on the importance of strengthening the institution of marriage as a necessary step to rebuilding a culture of positive father involvement in children's lives.[4] Horn also was influenced by his association with Diane Sollee, the president of the Coalition for Marriage, Families, and Couples Education, in Washington D.C. Sollee, a charismatic progressive and a divorced grandmother, was the surprising but highly effective human hub of a burgeoning social movement to promote the value of marriage and relationship education as a way to strengthen families. Being in the same area and crossing paths on numerous occasions undoubtedly helped Horn to consider the possibility that policy makers could get behind the growing MRE movement to get these services to more disadvantaged individuals who potentially could benefit the most from them.

In 2002, President Bush set the stage for federal involvement when he announced that he would make strengthening marriage a central feature of his effort to improve welfare policy in the United States:

> Statistics tell us that children from two parent families are less likely to end up in poverty, drop out of school, become addicted to drugs, have a child out of wedlock, suffer abuse or become a violent criminal and end up in prison. Building and preserving families are not always possible, I recognize that. But they should always be our goal. So my administration will give unprecedented support to strengthening marriages. Many good programs help couples who want to get married and stay married.[5]

At ACF, Horn began to push federal agencies under his control[6] to take seriously the idea that welfare policy could and should help couples form and sustain healthy marriages. His first efforts were to use existing ACF programs, agencies, and funding streams to experiment with integrating healthy MRE programs into their existing efforts. This was intentional. For practical and political reasons, Horn did not want federal interest in healthy marriages to be dependent on a single funding stream; he was not after just another policy silo. He wanted existing efforts to help disadvantaged families broaden their perspective to explore ways to strengthen and stabilize couple relationships. These efforts eventually came to be referred to as the ACF Healthy Marriage Initiative (HMI).[7] Several terms are used to refer to this initiative, including Healthy Families Initiative and Healthy Marriages and Relationships Initiative (HMRI). I prefer HMRI because I think it is the most descriptive term, even though it is a little clunkier. So I will usually use that term in this book. The mission of the federal HMRI was to help individuals and couples gain greater access to voluntary MRE services in order to obtain the knowledge and skills needed to help them form and sustain healthy marriages and relationships.[8]

Horn massaged his message over the years to respond to various criticisms of the initiative and to clarify what the federal HMRI was and was not. It was not, for instance, a federal dating service, he would say countless times. More seriously, he clarified that the programs being implemented were not designed by the government, only drew support from it. Community organizations were responsible for choosing programs they thought were effective and implementing them in ways they thought would work best. Furthermore, early language about "promoting marriage" evolved into more refined language about supporting healthy marriages and relationships. (Many critics of the initiative still refer to the initiative by this early term, *promoting,* even though it is no longer particularly descriptive of what is actually happening.) This shift came in response to early concerns that the initiative was promoting marriage for marriage's sake and took no account of the reality that some marriages were abusive or destructive or necrotic. Horn increasingly emphasized that the initiative was not simply about getting people married; it was about helping couples form and sustain healthy marriages. Moreover, even if couples did not choose to marry, Horn argued that creating a healthy, more stable relationship was an important policy aim in itself. He did not back off, however, using the "M word." He joked that he was a one-man desensitization machine in the federal government; he wanted to get policy makers comfortable with talking in serious ways about the institution of marriage and how it affected for good the lives of children and adults. Finally, he constantly reinforced the idea that the motive behind the federal HMRI was child-centered: to increase the chances of children growing up in a stable home with two invested parents in a healthy relationship. Over time, the message was refined in ways that made it tougher for critics struggling to dismiss the new policy initiative. This is not to say that Horn was merely polishing and spinning a message for public relations purposes. From my extensive observations, the federal HMRI accurately reflected the message that Horn was giving.

Horn did not want the federal HMRI to be perceived as having an ideological agenda to just serve up more fodder for the cultural wars. He wanted the initiative to be taken seriously by serious policy wonks and scholars. He felt that the question of whether the federal government had a role to play in promoting family stability for the sake of children was a serious issue and deserved some rigorous investigation and experimentation. This is one reason why in 2002 and 2003, ACF launched several long-term, large-scale, rigorous demonstration and evaluation studies of the effectiveness of programs to help low-income couples form and sustain healthy relationships. Two of these projects became known as the Building Strong Families study[9] and the Supporting Healthy Marriages study.[10] Initiating rigorous evaluations at the beginning of the HMRI would go a long way to getting people to take it seriously, Horn reasoned.

In the meantime, the TANF program had to be reauthorized by Congress in 2002. Seeing only a few, modest efforts by states to use TANF funds to help strengthen marriages, the Bush administration began promoting a more direct role for marriage-strengthening initiatives as a part of TANF reform. A series of continuing resolutions by Congress kept TANF going until 2005, when Congress finally agreed on some reforms and reauthorized TANF as a part of the Deficit Reduction Act of 2005.[11] The legislation allocated $100 million each year for 5 years for competitive grants to community organizations across the United States to fund programs to help individuals and couples form and sustain healthy marriages and relationships.[12] Some of these funds were set aside to support the serious, rigorous evaluation work that had already begun at ACF. Another $50 million was authorized for responsible fatherhood programs, some of which also included programs to strengthen relationships between coparents.

There were about 850 applications for these 5-year HMRI grants; only about 120 organizations were funded for demonstration projects to see what could be accomplished. (Similarly, there were more than 800 grant applications for responsible fatherhood programs, with only $50 million to allocate to them.) Only a few of these grants were to state entities and states did not coordinate any of the grant applications, as far as I know. The vast majority of grants went to private community organizations, including some faith-based organizations.[13] A couple of funded initiatives went to umbrella organizations to promote and coordinate a statewide HMRI working with MRE providers in communities across the state (e.g., Alabama, California; an early pilot project like this was funded in Kentucky). These grants were managed by the Office of Family Assistance (OFA) at ACF, an agency that was deeply involved in federal welfare policy. Funded programs generally targeted lower income participants, although some more advantaged couples and individuals have participated in the programs, as well. Funds could be used for eight allowable activities: public advertising campaigns on the value of marriage and skills needed to increase marital stability; education in high schools on the value of marriage, relationship skills, and budgeting; marriage and relationship programs for nonmarried, pregnant women and expectant fathers (which could include parenting skills, financial management, and job skills); premarital education and skills training; marriage enhancement and skills training; divorce reduction programs (with relationship skills); marriage mentoring programs; and programs to reduce economic disincentives to marry (in conjunction with any of the above activities).

In some work I did with my students at Brigham Young University, we found tremendous variation from state to state in the amount of federal funds used to support healthy marriage and relationship activity. Across the 50 states and District of Columbia, the estimated total funding allocated to these initiatives from 2000–2012 was nearly $800 million, with an average of about nearly $15 million per state. California, Texas, Florida, and Oklahoma had the highest levels of activity based on raw funding allocations. Of note, three of these states (Oklahoma, Texas, and Florida) have (or had) a state office providing leadership to state efforts, and California has a federally funded statewide initiative that supports community organizations' MRE education efforts. Oklahoma and Texas also have contributed a measureable chunk of TANF block-grant funds allocated to their states to their healthy marriage initiatives, as I detail later in this chapter.

On the other end of the spectrum, a handful of states have very little federal government support for helping individuals and couples form and sustain healthy marriages and relationships. Rhode Island had no funding in this area that we could detect; Nevada ($127,000) had only a minimal amount. Table 2.1 lists the top and bottom 10 states in terms of raw funding activity for healthy marriage and relationship initiatives.

Table 2.1. *Top 10 and Bottom 10 States with Governmental Funds for HMRIs, 2000–2012*

Rank	State	Total Funding 2000–2012
1	Texas	$101,847,284
2	California	98,750,765
3	Oklahoma	41,605,582
4	Florida	40,113,437
5	Ohio	31,520,154
6	Pennsylvania	30,882,379
7	Colorado	29,179,888
8	Missouri	26,500,135
9	Michigan	24,742,043
10	Wisconsin	23,492,554
42	Hawaii	2,036,644
43	Nebraska	2,035,377
44	Vermont	1,973,916
45	Delaware	1,540,000
46	Montana	1,446,889
47	North Dakota	1,010,847
48	West Virginia	762,935
49	Idaho	544,000
50	Nevada	127,012
51	Rhode Island	0

But comparing raw numbers can be misleading because there are enormous population differences between states. Accordingly, a fairer comparison would be to divide these total funding figures by the average population to produce per capita funding figures, or in other words, the average amount spent per resident over the period 2000–2012. These figures, given in Table 2.2, provide a somewhat different picture of governmental support for healthy marriage and relationships initiatives.

Table 2.2. *Top 10 and Bottom 10 States with Governmental Funds Per Capita for HMRIs, 2000–2012 (total spending ÷ average population)*

Rank	State	Per Capita Funding 2000–2012
1	District of Columbia	$27.76
2	Oklahoma	11.57
3	Alaska	8.37
4	Wyoming	7.79
5	New Mexico	7.63
6	South Dakota	6.66
7	Colorado	6.13
8	Missouri	4.54
9	Texas	4.35
10	Wisconsin	4.22
42	Iowa	1.09
43	North Carolina	1.04
44	Minnesota	0.99
45	South Carolina	0.77
46	New Jersey	0.72
47	Massachusetts	0.66
48	West Virginia	0.42
49	Idaho	0.37
50	Nevada	0.05
51	Rhode Island	0.00

Across the 50 states and the District of Columbia, the average total per capita funds allocated to these initiatives from 2000–2012 was about $3.22 per individual. Looking at the data this way, the District of Columbia ($27.76) by far comes out on top, allocating two and one half times as much per individual as the next highest state, Oklahoma ($11.57). The relatively small population in Washington, D.C., and the significant number of ACF-funded programs, including responsible fatherhood programs with a significant couple education component, made D.C. the per capita funding leader. Washington, D.C., has the highest rate of unwed childbearing and several of the grants serving D.C. were directed at serving unwed parent couples. (Later in the chapter I will mention a study that suggests that D.C. saw the most substantial positive changes in family stability during this period.) Oklahoma has the most significant state-directed, statewide initiative serving a moderate-sized population. (I will provide more details on Oklahoma's efforts later in this chapter.) Alaska benefited from a large number of grants targeted to help Native Americans from the federal Administration for Native Americans, and those grants covered a relatively small population. Wyoming ($7.79), New Mexico ($7.63), and South Dakota ($6.66) did not receive large amounts of dollars, but they have small populations. Wyoming has one of the highest divorce rates in the nation, so perhaps the high level of per capita funding there will be valued. Missouri ($4.54) and Texas ($4.35) are still in the top 10 states by this per capita measure, but Florida, California, Pennsylvania, and Ohio drop out of the top 10.

Rhode Island ($0.00), Nevada ($0.05), Idaho ($0.37), and West Virginia ($0.42) remain at the bottom in per capita spending on HMRIs, but per capita figures produce a different group in the next tier of lowest states: Massachusetts ($0.66), New Jersey ($0.72), South Carolina ($0.77), Minnesota ($0.99), North Carolina ($1.04), and Iowa ($1.09). Rhode Island and Massachusetts have some of the lowest divorce rates in the United States and about average nonmarital childbearing rates, so perhaps organizations in these states have not felt strong needs to try to provide MRE in their communities. Nevada, however, has the highest divorce rate; the lack of government funding for healthy marriage initiatives there is more noticeable. West Virginia also has a relatively high divorce rate.

Ideological differences in the states may explain some of the variation, but perhaps less than many might expect. Yes, some of the highest funding levels (per capita) are found in solid conservative states such as Oklahoma, Texas, South Dakota, and Wyoming, while some of the lowest funding levels are found in progressive states such as Rhode Island, New Jersey, Massachusetts, and Minnesota. Yet is it easy to find counterexamples. Some "red states," such as Idaho, are among the lowest-activity states, while liberal Washington D.C. is the highest-activity jurisdiction. Conservative and progressive states alike can ignore or embrace government-supported efforts to strengthen marriages and relationships.

While there is significant variation from state to state in the amount of government-supported efforts to strengthen marriage, still this variation does not overshadow a dramatic increase in the availability and usage of MRE services for more disadvantaged individuals and couples who struggle to form and sustain healthy marriages and relationships, and who in the past have had little access to such services.[14] This is an important development, one that would not have occurred without the policy push from ACF. For family life educators, this change is a welcome extension of their profession to an important and needy clientele. It also has thrust the work of marriage and relationship education into the world of public policy. For policy makers, this change adds a new stock to the portfolio of public assistance programs, one that directly addresses a known cause of poverty: family instability.

However, an uncertain cloud overshadows this important increase. The work that has been federally funded over the past decade was intended to show what is possible in making MRE programs available to more disadvantaged and needy families. What is unclear is whether these demonstration projects have taken root in organizations and agencies that serve lower income families. The availability of new funds attracted these organizations to add a new service or, in some organizations that were not typically serving lower income families, extend a service to more disadvantaged individuals. If these funds dry up, will these educational services wilt or will they find adequate resources elsewhere? That is, will these programs be dependent on a continued, specific, federal funding stream, a stream facing the serious possibility of prolonged drought given federal budget shortfalls, or can they be supported through other channels? Anecdotal evidence uncovered as my research assistants and I contacted several grantees whose federal funding had expired raises concerns. In many instances, MRE programs had been discontinued for lack of funding. In some instances, personnel contacted in these organizations did not even know that such a program ever existed, let alone could tell us anything about what has happened to the program since the grant ended.

What has happened to this initiative with a Democratic Obama administration? Sometimes administration transitions leave controversial policies from past administrations in the dust; a policy housecleaning occurs. But the HMRI policy initiative has continued in the Obama administration, evolving somewhat to put a little more emphasis on healthy relationships between parents and on responsible fatherhood; the "M word," marriage, is used more judiciously now. Such terms as the Healthy Families Initiative are more common. Another linguistic adjustment occurred in the name of the National Center for Marriage Research. In 2007 the federal government funded a new research center called the National Center for Marriage Research that resides at Bowling Green State University (in Ohio). When the Obama administration started putting its stamp on things, the name of this center was changed to the National Center for Family and Marriage Research.[15] While some language has changed in the Obama administration, most of the same purposes and goals of HMRI remain—to promote healthier and more stable families in which to rear children.

The first round of major funding for healthy marriage demonstration programs ended in 2011 during the Obama administration. The federal initiative could have died in the transition, and there were proposals floated to subsume any couple relationship education efforts under an umbrella of responsible fatherhood programs to be run through state governments. But this did not occur. Instead, a second major round of grants for organizations to support healthy relationship education efforts were competitively awarded for 2011–2014. The original $100 million for HMRIs was reduced to $75 million (and the original $50 million for Responsible Fatherhood demonstration grants was increased to $75 million). The new round of grants emphasizes integrating MRE services with other social services for lower income individuals and families, such as employment programs, substance abuse programs, childcare, and so forth. A handful of programs that have integrated MRE services with other human services, such as employment services, are being formally evaluated by ACF.[16] The continued support for MRE and evidence of its effectiveness appear to be more than just governmental inertia. As I mentioned in Chapter 1, President Obama has publicly acknowledged:

"Expanding access to such [marriage and relationship education] services to low-income couples, perhaps in concert with . . . other services already available, should be something everybody can agree on."[17] And this seems to be more than political rhetoric. At a recent conference that I attended, a White House aide who works with these kinds of programs told the group that President Obama regularly asks him about how these initiatives are going.

So current policy efforts are still exploring the potential utility of a wide range of programs to strengthen marriages and healthy romantic relationships. Nevertheless, a question about program sustainability remains, despite the noteworthy advances making MRE services available to lower income couples and individuals over the past decade. Wade Horn left ACF in 2007, shortly after major funding became available to support HMRIs. According to Horn, one reason he left was that he did not want the federal HMRI to become dependent on his presence for its intellectual and administrative support; he wanted the initiative to stand on its own logic and merits. He was a champion for the initiative while at ACF and was an involved leader, regularly peppering department heads under him about progress on these initiatives. But he did not want the initiative to be a personality cult. Although the HMRI was not his only policy emphasis during his administration, it may be his most significant mark on the agency, or at least the most prominent because it was new and visible and controversial. When Horn left, the initiative did seem to lose some of its steam. For example, in 2011, I contacted ACF to get information about the number of individuals who had participated in the programs supported by the federal HMRI. What I discovered is that no one had gathered that basic information. It exists buried in reports from the grantees over the years, but no one had taken the time and effort to aggregate it and make it public.

Despite some reduced focus on the institution of marriage, it appears that much of the formal policy initiative to help couples form and sustain healthy relationships will continue on with a somewhat different rhetoric that emphasizes stable and healthy families for children regardless of the legal bonds between parents. Regardless, I think there is a more effective way to continue these policy efforts that would downsize direct federal leadership. I have appreciated this leadership, but I worry that it could disappear in a political haze or budgetary purge. In Chapter 9, I propose a potentially more sustainable way, other than federal ACF grants to community organizations, to support these kinds of programs. As mentioned earlier, I think it is time for states to take on the leadership role, and a mechanism for doing so already exists. States just need to step up.

A more important critique of current federal HMRI efforts may be that they have had a scattershot approach without much strategy. The funding has supported demonstration grants to see what programs might be effective in helping couples form and sustain healthy relationships and marriages. But there was not a carefully constructed, overarching strategy or logical model to make a difference in the long run. Chapters 4–8 in this book present my proposal for this needed strategic plan, which I summarized briefly in Chapter 1.

I don't want to sound overly critical of the federal HMRI. Unquestionably, the energy, intellectual investments, and funding that came from the initiative changed the landscape and produced what I believe are some valuable lessons. I admire what Wade Horn was able to do. The kind of change he created in federal policy is difficult. But I think we know a lot more now about what is possible and what is needed, and from this we can refine our strategy to be more effective at helping couples form and sustain healthy marriages and relationships. Part of that strategy is to get states to provide the leadership. So in the next section of this chapter, I will review the few state-directed HMRIs that currently exist.

State-Directed Healthy Marriages and Relationships Initiatives

If I am calling on states to step up and lead HMRIs rather than to depend on federal grants to community organizations, then it would be helpful to learn what has been happening in a few states that are trying to do this. Two states have established healthy marriage initiatives that have endured for a significant period of time: Utah and Oklahoma. In fact, the Utah and Oklahoma initiatives preceded the federal HMRI by a couple of years. To be clear, these state-directed efforts were using almost exclusively federal, not state dollars—TANF block grant funds given to states by the federal government to support needy families. While there are various requirements and guidelines, states have some leeway in how they use these funds to achieve the goals of the TANF program. In the late 1990s, a few states embraced the purposes of TANF to help strengthen two-parent families and marriages and began exploring what could be done from a public policy perspective. This section of the chapter outlines state initiatives in Utah and Oklahoma that began in the late 1990s and continue to be active today. Virginia just launched a state initiative with the help of the same organization that runs the Oklahoma Marriage Initiative, which bodes well. But it is too soon to know what will develop there. Louisiana has a formal Commission on Marriage and Families that was established by executive orders in 2004 (by Governor Blanco) and again in 2008 (by Governor Jindal). But from reading their annual reports to the governor and talking to a few commission members, this effort appears still to be in the fact-finding and research-and-recommendation phase. I don't see evidence that funding is being allocated and directed by this group to implement recommendations. A few other states experimented with a state-level initiative (e.g., Florida, Kansas, Texas) but they didn't stick for various reasons. I include a brief discussion in this chapter of the Texas initiative that began in 2007 with much fanfare and funding but was cut back severely in 2011 and is now only a shadow of the original initiative. The level of detail I provide in these sections may be more than what many readers want. So those readers may want to skip to the summary paragraphs at the end of each section.

The Utah Healthy Marriages Initiative

Utah was the first state to quietly launch a government-supported initiative to strengthen marriage. Utah is where I reside and I watched the beginnings of this initiative closely. Then, in 2004, I became a formal member of the initiative's volunteer advisory board, serving as the chair from 2009–2011. My association with this state initiative has influenced my thinking considerably about how government can be an active agent in helping couples form and sustain healthy marriages.

The Utah Healthy Marriages Initiative (UT HMI) had its genesis in 1998. Then–first lady of Utah, Jackie Leavitt, was involved in a commission called the Governor's Initiative on Families Today (G.I.F.T.) that was formed in 1993 and sponsored out of the governor's office. G.I.F.T. organized an annual conference on strengthening families. While the conference gave some attention to marital relationships, Mrs. Leavitt felt that there needed to be a stronger emphasis on marriage.

Around this time, Mrs. Leavitt had a conversation with a colleague of mine at Brigham Young University, Dr. Brent Barlow, who had a particular interest in strengthening marriages. Barlow endorsed the value of a government effort to strengthen marriages. Mrs. Leavitt approached her husband, Governor Mike Leavitt, for support to begin a separate initiative on strengthening marriages with a separate advisory board. The governor approved this change and the Utah Governor's Commission on Marriage was born.

The governor formed a voluntary commission of marriage scholars, practitioners, and activists. Abbie Vianes, a staff member of G.I.F.T., was tapped to provide initial staff coordination for the commission. Brent Barlow was appointed to be the first chair of the commission, serving on a voluntary basis. Mrs. Leavitt was a key member of that commission early on. In 2000, Vianes left to work with another commission sponsored by the governor's office. She was replaced by Melanie Reese, who had been working in the Utah Department of Health. Reese had been involved in the successful and award-winning public health campaign, "Baby Your Baby." She brought this public health background to her work as coordinator of the Utah commission. She has been the full-time staff coordinator since 2000, providing the initiative with tremendous continuity.

In the first 3 years, the commission received no specific government funding other than the coordinator staff position. To fund its activities, it had to seek out private sponsorship. This changed in the early 2000s when the Administration for Children and Families began to encourage support of programs specifically designed to help couples form and sustain healthy marriages and relationships. In 2001, Reese wrote a successful proposal to Utah's Department of Workforce Services for $600,000 in TANF funds to support the commission's efforts to strengthen marriage. These funds supported a major project to produce a video called, *Marriage News You Can Use,* for newlywed couples (in English and Spanish). These videos were distributed for free through 29 county clerk offices to marriage license applicants in 2002 and 2003. The videos also were distributed to all Utah State University Cooperative Extension offices, 11 Family Support Centers, 7 PTA Family Resource Centers, and to many high school Family and Consumer Education teachers. It was a very modest beginning, but it was a start.

A set of piecemeal initiatives characterized the early years of the Utah Healthy Marriages Initiative. In 2001, the commission launched its own website, utahmarriage.org. The website included content on forming and sustaining a healthy marriage and relationship. It also listed available MRE services across the state. In 2003, the commission funded the training of 76 community marriage education instructors in the PREP (*Prevention and Relationship Enhancement*)[18] program in return for offering the program for free for at least 32 participants. This was done with the hope of increasing the number of trained MRE providers in the state. While it did increase the number of providers, many of these providers are no longer active in offering PREP classes in the state. Also in 2003, the commission funded a project to add materials on building successful marriages to home-visitor packets for fragile families. These were distributed through Head Start and Baby Watch Early Intervention nurse home visitor programs. But these materials are no longer distributed. Sustaining worthy initiatives proved to be difficult in the early years. Also in 2003, the commission began offering a low-cost continuing education seminar for therapists (and educators) in the state featuring high-profile experts in the field. These seminars have continued every year and have grown in popularity. The rationale behind offering these continuing education seminars was that marriage therapists were a key human infrastructure for helping couples strengthen their marriages and prevent divorce. The commission wanted to do what it could to enhance therapists' efforts.

In 2004, a change took place in the Governor's Commission on Marriage that proved to be important in the long term. The commission was moved from the Governor's Office to the Office of Work and Family Life in the Department of Workforce Services (DWS).[19] DWS administered TANF funding and programs in Utah. Since the commission had been operating primarily on TANF funds and because state TANF agencies were now reporting to ACF on state efforts to help couples form and sustain healthy marriages and relationships, DWS administrators welcomed the opportunity to oversee the commission. At this time, the name of the commission was changed to the Utah Commission on Marriage, and a program name was added—the Utah Healthy Marriages Initiative (UT HMI).

With this bureaucratic relocation, in 2005, DWS and the UT HMI worked to create a clearer strategic plan for their activities that helped focus their efforts. That strategic plan emphasized four areas of activity. The core of the strategic plan was to strengthen existing infrastructures in the state that were delivering MRE services: (a) capacity building of the state's infrastructure to deliver MRE services, including the Cooperative Extension Service; (b) strengthening the Adult Roles curriculum delivered in public high schools in its ability to help youth develop greater relationship literacy; (c) developing capacity by supporting a continuing education workshop for marriage therapists and educators; and (d) outreach through the UT HMI website and a media campaign to promote use of services to help couples form and sustain healthy marriages and relationships.

In accord with this strategic plan, in 2005 the commission supported a number of activities. For instance, they provided some financial support for a revision and updating of the Adult Roles curriculum that was taught by Family and Consumer Science educators in high schools across the state. The class provided relationship literacy education to students. Funds also helped to advertise the elective class. The next year, the commission worked with state educators to create an option for high school students that combined the mandated financial literacy curriculum with the elective Adult Roles curriculum into a year-long course. This option increased the usage of the Adult Roles course in many schools.

Also in 2005, the UT HMI began piloting a project to support some local Community Healthy Marriages Initiatives (CHMIs) in three counties, with funding funneled through local Cooperative Extension Services. Early efforts in these communities included a National Marriage Week USA conference and developing some ongoing MRE services. These pilot projects were a fertile learning ground for a major initiative that would bloom in 2009.

Efforts to make MRE available to more Utahns, especially lower income Utahns, received a boost in 2006 and 2007. In 2006, Brian Higginbotham, Family Life Specialist with the Utah State University Cooperative Extension Service, received a large, 5-year federal Healthy Marriages and Relationships Initiative grant from the ACF Office of Family Assistance to demonstrate the value of remarriage and stepfamily education using the *Smart Steps* program. Nearly a third of Utah marriages are remarriages for one or both spouses. This program was delivered in communities by local Cooperative Extension Service family life specialists and other educators. It was re-funded in 2011 for 3 more years. Also in 2007, Higginbotham added to the state's potential to help remarried couples and stepfamilies with a demonstration grant from the ACF Office of Head Start to support making Smart Steps available to parents of children attending Head Start programs. The Smart Steps program is one of the premier MRE services available widely across Utah and serves a more at-risk population of participants. It has reached about

800 individuals a year in Utah. Similarly, the Ogden–Weber Community Action Partnership Head Start program also received a grant to offer the 16-hour, PREP-based Within My Reach/Within Our Reach program to parents of Head Start children in Head Start facilities. This smaller effort in its first few years of operation reached about 150 people a year. These federally funded program efforts have not been directed by the UT HMI, but the program administrators participate on the UT HMI Commission. And the UT HMI's website advertises these services. The UT HMI benefited by harnessing valuable infrastructures in the state—the Cooperative Extension Service and Head Start—to deliver MRE services to more state residents.

In 2006, the UT HMI funded the production and distribution of a *Building a Successful Marriage* booklet to all marriage license applicants in the state. The next year, the commission decided to adopt and revise slightly a handbook for newlywed couples developed by the Cooperative Extension Service. Thus, in 2007 the commission began offering the *Utah Marriage Handbook* to marriage license applicants in county clerk offices. Many Family and Consumer Sciences educators across the state also started using this handbook in their classes with high school students. Handbooks were made available for free to students in these classes in 2009 and 2010. Higginbotham's renewed Smart Steps grant in 2011 included funds to keep making these handbooks available for free to couples getting their marriage licenses.

Perhaps the most significant development in the brief history of the Utah Healthy Marriages Initiative came in 2007. Funding the UT HMI's activities had been a chronic worry. The UT HMI had applied for federal funds in 2006 that would have provided a federal grant to support the activities from 2006–2011. The grant proposal was not successful, but that may have been a blessing in disguise. In 2007, Melanie Reese, the coordinator of the UT HMI, sent a proposal to the leadership of the Department of Workforce Services to set aside 1% of TANF funds that came to Utah to support preventative efforts to help couples form and sustain healthy marriages and relationships. This so-called "1% solution" proposal was endorsed by DWS, which has provided steady, modest funding of about $700,000 a year for the UT HMI from 2007 through 2012. Utah was the second state to implement this "1% solution" for funding healthy marriage activities. (Ohio was the first, although Ohio was unable to sustain this policy for more than a few years, as far as I can tell.) This source of funding for the UT HMI has influenced my thinking about how other states can support their own healthy marriage initiatives and is part of my proposed agenda.

To help make Utahns more aware of the MRE services available to them, the UT HMI decided in 2008 to launch a major media campaign that would pique interest in services and drive people to the UT HMI website where more information was available. The Commission contracted for five years with a leading social marketing firm, Richter7, to execute this campaign. It focused primarily on 18–29-year-old emerging adults. After some market research, they developed creative ad strategies using television, print, Internet, and other venues, including social media and booths at bridal fairs. The media campaign has resulted in substantially increased traffic to the website and more participants at MRE programs. In the first 3 years of the campaign, ads were seen more than 33 million times in the targeted demographic of young adults. In addition, the campaign placed nearly 10 million online paid search banner ads, producing more than 17,000 clicks on the ads with an average visit to the website of 3 minutes. The UT HMI has a presence on Facebook and Twitter, with a following of nearly 1,000 individuals. An internal study in 2011 documented that awareness of the Utah HMI had doubled since 2008, with television ads having the most impact. More important, the number of recently married couples participating in marriage preparation education in Utah increased from 36% in 2008 to 50% in 2011, an increase that seems too large too fast to have happened without some help. My observations of our media campaign here in Utah have influenced my thinking about the value of funds to increase awareness of MRE services, a key element in my proposed agenda.

Also in 2008, the commission supported the development of a pilot program offering for free the *Couple C.A.R.E.* program and *RELATE* inventory to Utah residents who accessed the programs through its website. *Couple C.A.R.E.* is a research-based, self-directed, at-home program developed and evaluated by Kim Halford at the University of Queensland (Australia). It emphasizes relationship self-regulation and effective communication skills.[20] The *RELATE* inventory is a relationship evaluation questionnaire developed by a team of researchers at Brigham Young University. The researchers recruited participants to be involved in an evaluation study of the effectiveness of the *Couple C.A.R.E. + RELATE* program. The free services continued through 2012.

Another important development in building an infrastructure to deliver MRE services began in 2009 with a decision to partner with Utah State University Cooperative Extension to help establish local Community Healthy Marriages and Relationships Initiatives (CHMRIs) in counties and communities across the state. Until this time, most efforts were administered at the state level. However, a few years earlier the UT HMI had begun to support some local CHMRIs. Limited funding was given to local family life Cooperative Extension Service agencies in these communities to support their educational efforts to help couples form and sustain healthy marriages and relationships. Through these pilot projects, the UT HMI leadership saw the potential of establishing successful initiatives all across the state. The decision to decentralize commission efforts was made and the UT HMI contracted with Utah State University Cooperative Extension Service to develop these local initiatives through their team of trained family life educators throughout the state. Competitive grant proposals were reviewed and contracts were allocated to about half (14 of 29) of the county extension offices in 2010, including both urban and rural counties. Funding levels varied from less than $5,000 to as much as $25,000 for CHMRIs that were further along in their development. The task of these CHMRIs was to build up and provide effective MRE services in their communities, with a special emphasis on reaching more disadvantaged couples in the state. In 2011, funding was provided to five additional counties to establish CHMRIs in their communities.

The UT HMI monitors these efforts with visits from Utah State University Family Life Specialists and annual reports, and has been pleased with the progress being made. Nevertheless, these agents could only spend a small portion of their time on HMI activity, so progress has been slow at making regular MRE classes available. As a result, a further evolution of this strategy to work though the Cooperative Extension System came in 2012 when the commission authorized using funds to hire part-time educators in a handful of county offices in high-population counties. These educators' sole focus is on marketing MRE services and teaching classes at convenient times. This has increased the number and regularity of MRE opportunities in the state and in turn the number of participants.

Also in 2009, the commission supported training of the CHMRI leaders in domestic violence protocol. My colleague and former graduate student Kay Bradford at Utah State University, an expert in this area, conducted the training. The commission also funded a study of the effectiveness of the training that revealed that these leaders were trying to implement the protocol in their initiatives, but also found several areas for improvement.[21]

The UT HMI is an example of what can be done with limited funding but steady leadership and sustained efforts. The UT HMI received only about $9.5 million in government support from 2002–2012 (about $700,000 a year). Much of this came from a 1% set-aside of TANF block grant funds that come to the state to help needy families. This was done as an executive policy decision rather than a legislative act. Even without the legislation, the funding was steady through 2012 due to ongoing support of administrators in the Department of Workforce Services that oversees TANF efforts.

Unfortunately, shortly before this manuscript was finalized, this support changed. A new set of administrators, facing cutbacks in TANF funds, decided to terminate the Utah Commission on Marriage and reallocate the small amount of funding to other programs. The commission's efforts, it turns out, had been funded with supplemental streams of federal TANF funds and those supplemental funds have now dried up. The commission's work was not seen as core, so the funds will be reallocated. Commission supporters fortunately gained the support of a few key legislators who were successful in placing the commission in a bill in the 2013 general legislative session (and scraped up a small appropriation to keep some momentum until an innovative funding solution can be found). The reborn commission will be housed in the Department of Human Services rather than the Department of Workforce Services. The commission plans to pursue legislation to fund the UT HMI by directing $20 of the marriage license fee to support its efforts.[22] If this legislation succeeds, it would provide a steady funding source (about $500,000 a year). Of course, it was disappointing that the administrative unit that directs TANF funding in the state abandoned its commitment to enhancing MRE services as part of its effort to reduce family instability. Obviously, even well-established, well-respected, and well-functioning HMIs are vulnerable. In the long run, however, the demise of the commission in the Department of Workforce services may prove to be another blessing in disguise if it eventually results in a more solid funding situation.

Summary. The UT HMI has helped more than 250,000 individuals in Utah receive some kind of MRE at a cost of about $3.72 per person (2000–2012). It has supported and coordinated efforts to increase relationship literacy education for youth in the public schools and emerging adults in various community settings, premarital education to engaged couples, and marriage maintenance education for married couples.[23] It has promoted awareness and usage of these services with an ongoing media campaign. The various programs reach out—some more effectively than others—to lower income couples who have the greatest need. Day-to-day leadership for the UT HMI has come from a dedicated and experienced full-time staff person guided by a volunteer advisory board of scholars, practitioners, and activists in the state. Accordingly, the UT HMI is a working model in many respects of the policy agenda I am promoting in this book, even if it is on the ropes now due to a change in administrative leadership. Assuming the initiative survives, it still has a way to go to hit its stride to find the most effective and efficient ways to serve the state. But I think it is a good and feasible model of what other states could begin to implement with only a modest investment of available funds (TANF block grants). Of course, feasible does not mean easy to implement and sustain. But I discuss these challenges more in Chapter 9.

The Oklahoma Marriage Initiative

Although Utah was the first (by a year) to launch a state-directed healthy marriage initiative, Oklahoma has gone the farthest. It now has the most comprehensive and strategic approach to helping couples form and sustain healthy marriages and relationships. Since 2009, I have served on the Research Advisory Group for the Oklahoma Marriage Initiative (OMI). Like the Utah Healthy Marriages Initiative, the OMI has influenced my thinking a great deal about an integrated set of public policy efforts to strengthen marriages. In the late 1990s, Oklahoma Governor Frank Keating became concerned about the state's rising poverty rate. A commission analyzing the reasons for rising poverty identified high divorce and nonmarital childbirth rates as leading causes of poverty in the state. This is hardly newsworthy. I doubt Governor Keating was the only state chief executive to learn that family structure change was adding to the need for public assistance. What is newsworthy was Governor Keating's response. He asked, "What can we do about it?" This response has been rare. The thought that the state could do some things directly to reduce the need for divorce, increase the number of children born into stable, two-parent families, and generally strengthen the institution of marriage was novel. With the encouragement of Jerry Regier, Oklahoma Secretary for Human Services at the time, Keating decided to take action to strengthen Oklahoma's families. Leaders across the state were brought together to discuss issues and pledge support to the cause. With goals to substantially reduce the divorce rate and increase the number of children in two-parent families in Oklahoma over the next decade, Oklahoma became the first state to provide substantial public funding to develop a statewide initiative directed by the state. Since the early beginnings of the OMI, a new governor and new director of OK DHS, Howard Hendrick, have embraced it. Director Hendrick gave strong leadership to the initiative until his retirement in 2012; he was not an absentee landlord. At our annual OMI Research Advisory Group meetings,[24] Secretary Hendrick has been there for nearly the entire time and constantly asking questions and exploring "what ifs."

A rather unexpected decision early in the OMI has proven to be very effective. Rather than administer the initiative from their own offices with civil servants, OK DHS contracted with Public Strategies, Inc. (PSI), a private, for-profit public relations firm in Oklahoma City, to give direction to and run the day-to-day operations of the OMI. PSI reports regularly to DHS on the initiative. Mary Myrick is the president of PSI. This entrepreneur with a strong Midwestern twang brings a savvy public relations mindset to the initiative and an innovative energy to its efforts to strengthen marriages in Oklahoma.

OMI's priorities were to build capacity to deliver marriage and relationship education services, build demand for those services, and evaluate their effectiveness. OMI selected PREP as its educational curriculum because it had the most research support and the organizational capacity to adapt the curriculum to different populations in the state.[25] Their goal was to make 12-hour PREP-based classes available to all within the state at no cost. Private and public organizations including education, corrections, health, social services, military, schools, and churches were recruited into the OMI effort. PREP-based workshops were adapted to specific populations in need or at-risk. For example, the PREP curriculum was tailored to TANF recipients and became the Within Our Reach (for couples)/Within My Reach (for individuals) curricula. Similarly, Connections is a modification of PREP for youth in high school classes. A PREP curriculum specially modified to be culturally relevant to African American couples is called Heart & Soul. Walking the Line is a PREP-based curriculum for incarcerated inmates.

After learning that training volunteer educators did not necessarily translate into year-round sustained capacity, the OMI put special efforts into building up, supporting, and sustaining the ongoing delivery of workshops in specific geographical areas and among certain groups, such as Latinos and Native Americans. PSI staff provided the labor to help solidify this initiative as a long-term service. They helped communities and organizations to schedule and coordinate classes year-round, identify referral sources, locate facilities for workshops, and provide program supports such as childcare for the participants. OMI had trained more than 3,500 PREP instructors to deliver services.

To help support service delivery and create demand in the public for educational services, many public events were created. Community-level events provided a condensed version of PREP that could be taken in a single, day-long sitting to stimulate further interest. This, coupled with frequent in-person presentations at community and public agencies, also helped generate publicity for the OMI and its educational services.

A marquee component of the OMI is the Family Expectations (FE) program for lower income, unmarried, expectant parents as well as lower income married parents in the Oklahoma City area. FE is based on Pam Jordan's (University of Washington) PREP-based Becoming Parents curriculum.[26] It is a 30-hour curriculum that includes a wide variety of topics related to forming and sustaining healthy marriages and relationships, as well as infant care and parenting modules. The Oklahoma City site for *FE* became a part of two federally funded, large-scale, long-term, rigorous demonstration and evaluation studies. (Details of these studies will be provided in Chapters 5 and 6.) To preview, *FE* has scientifically demonstrated that it can help some lower income couples form and sustain healthy marriages and relationships.

The OMI has received sustained TANF block grant funding through OK DHS of about $2.5 million per year since 2000. In addition, from 2006–2011, OMI received $1 million a year from an ACF grant from the federal Office of Family Assistance. Overall, from 2000–2012, Oklahoma has received a little more than $40 million in support of its efforts to help couples form and sustain healthy marriages. On a per capita basis, Oklahoma is the number-one state in terms of direct coordination for these kinds of efforts. (The District of Columbia has the highest per capita investment, but there is no coordination of its efforts; all those funds come from separate federal grants.)

From that investment of funds more than 315,000 individuals, including 125,000 youth, have completed PREP-based marriage and relationship education. That number represents 8% of the state population. The estimated cost of the initiative per participant is about $12.50.

Summary. The OMI from the beginning has had strong political support and firm leadership from the Governor's Office and the Department of Human Services. Day-to-day management comes from Public Strategies, Inc. Like Utah, but more extensively, it delivers research-based curricula to youth, emerging adults, cohabiting parents, engaged couples, and married couples. It is beginning to build cutting-edge services to help ambivalent couples on the brink of divorce think carefully about how they might be able to repair their relationship. It has learned how to reach out and involve diverse lower income participants in MRE services. It is an effective partner with domestic violence prevention organizations across the state. An ongoing media campaign, public relations efforts, and community activities build awareness and use of services. Rigorous research efforts have documented the ability of some of its programs to help couples. The OMI is the best example of the policy agenda I am proposing in this book. It takes political leadership and talented day-to-day management over many years to make this kind of initiative work. But there is nothing about the OMI that is inherently difficult to replicate. And the OMI leaders regularly share what they know with interested others.

The Texas Healthy Marriages Initiative

Texas has an extensive and complex history of supporting activities to help individuals and couples form and sustain healthy marriages and relationships. Overall, Texas has received more than $100 million in federal and state government support since 2004 for efforts in this regard, more than any other state. Between 2006 and 2011, state TANF block-grant funds for the Texas Healthy Marriages and Relationships Initiative totaled just over $50 million. Other funds came directly from federal grants for MRE. In 2011, dramatic budget cutbacks were made to the state initiative in Texas, and it is now essentially dormant as a public policy initiative. So some readers may not be interested in the details of the initiative that I outline in this section. The genesis of the Texas Healthy Marriages Initiative (TX HMI) occurred in 2003, when the Texas legislature passed H.B. 2292, directing the Texas Health and Human Services Commission (HHSC) to establish the "Healthy Marriage Development Program." The goal of this program was to promote marriage and relationship education and support services for recipients of public assistance in Texas. In 2007, the Texas legislature passed H.B. 2683 and 2685. H.B. 2683 directed HHSC to set aside a minimum of 1% of TANF block-grant funds each year to administer a grant program to provide MRE services and support the development of healthy marriages and strengthening of families by providing free services to participants, developing programs, enlarging program capacity, and paying for program expenses, including provider training and technical assistance. H.B. 2685 directed HHSC to develop and maintain a website (twogetherintexas.com) on which individuals and organizations could electronically register and provide information about available MRE services. It also amended the Texas Family Code, increasing the marriage license fee to $60, while providing a waiver of that fee for couples that complete at least 8 hours of premarital education from an approved-provider program. This fee incentive has increased the number of lower income couples participating in marriage preparation education.

To provide direction, leadership, and coordination to these legislatively mandated efforts, HHSC set up the Healthy Marriage Program (HMP), also referred to as the Texas Healthy Marriages Initiative. The goal of TX HMI is to increase the well-being of Texas children by providing marriage and relationship education services. Nearly a quarter of Texas children live below the federal poverty level and Texas ranks near the top in terms of its teen pregnancy rate.[27] TX HMI administers a partnership of public, private, community, and faith-based organizations and leaders who work together to build awareness of MRE services, provide relationship training and support, and participate in research to improve existing programs and policies, targeted especially to low-income families.

Oversight of the TX HMI comes from Jeff Johnson in the HHSC Office of Family and Community Services. In addition to the set-aside 1% TANF block-grant funds, TX HMI also provided some coordination and technical assistance to state efforts that were funded with more than 20 federal ACF grants for various healthy marriage demonstration programs between 2004 and 2011.

There are numerous components to TX HMI. The largest and probably best-known component is collectively referred to as "Twogether in Texas."

This is a program to provide free premarital education to Texas couples throughout the state. Local leadership and coordination of Twogether in Texas came from 12 Regional Intermediaries (or RIs), local TX HMI staff with responsibility to build up a service delivery infrastructure in their region. Working with local MRE service providers, including both voluntary and contracted providers (with TX HMI grants), they worked to build awareness of premarital education services, encourage couples to invest in approved premarital education programs, and facilitate the process of these couples receiving the legislated discount on their marriage license. From Fall 2008 through 2010, these RI efforts resulted in coordination of more than 8,600 marriage and relationship workshops, with nearly 90,000 participants in 2009–2010. An HHSC report estimates that Twogether in Texas reached about 11% of its potential audience (couples who married during that time). Severe budget cuts to TX HMI in 2011 required that Twogether in Texas rely more heavily on volunteer providers rather than providers with TX HMI grants. Volunteer providers were much more likely to be faith-based organizations.

Another component of TX HMI is coordination of a set of Community Healthy Marriages Initiatives (CHMIs) in Texas that receive either TANF block-grant funding from the state or federal ACF-grant funding (or both). Specifically, TX HMI supports CHMRIs in the Austin area (through Child Inc.), Houston (through Family Services of Greater Houston), Nueces County (through Nueces County Community Action Agency), and Tarrant County (through The Parenting Center of Tarrant County).

Another component of TX HMI was the AVANCE program with AVANCE Houston. This was a program designed to provide low-income Hispanic married couples with services to strengthen their marital relationships and improve the well-being of their children. The state TANF block-grant funding for this program ended in 2010 due to severe state budget cutbacks.

Another component of TX HMI partnered with Lutheran Social Services of the South, Inc., to run educational retreats for postadoptive couples to help them strengthen their marriage relationships against the stress of family transitions associated with adoption.

Another component of TX HMI was the Research Advisory Group, on which I serve. This group of national and state scholars provided direction to efforts to evaluate TX HMI effectiveness. Steven Harris provided leadership for this group. (He did so from Texas Tech University, and has continued to do this despite joining the University of Minnesota faculty in 2009.) The Research Advisory Group conducted a baseline survey of attitudes about marriage and related matters among Texans. The survey also explored attitudes about and experiences with MRE.[28] The Research Advisory Group has been involved in other ongoing evaluation efforts, as well. Recently, due to budget cuts, this advisory group has been mostly inactive.

Another component of TX HMI was the Supporting Healthy Marriage (SHM) program. SHM is a marriage education program designed to help low-income married couples. It was evaluated in a rigorous 8-year study (2004–2012) funded by the federal Office of Planning, Research, and Evaluation. Texas participated in this study with two sites: Family Services Association of San Antonio and El Paso Center for Children. Program participants received more than 30 hours of marriage education along with various family support services. About 400 couples (almost all Hispanic) were enrolled in this study in the two sites between 2007 and 2009. Results of this evaluation study are highlighted in Chapter 6.

A final significant component of TX HMI is called the Healthy Marriage Development Project (HMDP). It was funded in 2006 by a 5-year grant of $900,000 a year from the federal Office of Family Assistance to Texas HHSC. The HMDP managed a public advertising campaign and provided MRE to married couples and unmarried couples considering marriage, as well as to unwed expectant couples in Fort Worth, Fort Bend County, Laredo, and Corpus Christi. It also provided booster classes that include budgeting, nutrition, and parenting education. Also, HMDP worked to reduce the financial disincentive to marriage among welfare program recipients.

Another significant program in Texas was passed in 2007. It is under the direction of the Texas Office of Attorney General, while the other programs I have described are under the direction of or at least receive coordination and support from HHSC. H.B. 2176 directed the Texas Board of Education to work with the Office of Attorney General to develop and implement the parenting and paternity awareness (p.a.p.a.) program for mandatory use in high school health curricula beginning in the 2008–2009 school year. The curriculum has 14 units that include information about healthy relationships, the benefits of a healthy marriage, the importance of a two-parent family to children's well-being, the "success sequence" (i.e., Education ➜ Marriage ➜

Children), and intimate partner violence prevention. Nearly six thousand educators in Texas were trained on the p.a.p.a. curriculum and it has been delivered to about 500,000 high school youth through 2010. (I'll outline a preliminary evaluation study of this program, which has found some promising results, in Chapter 4.[29]) The program is funded through child support funds, with two thirds of the funding federal and one third state.

Despite its achievements so far, the future of the TX HMI is unclear. Large budget shortfalls in 2010 resulted in big budget cuts to the initiative that handicapped efforts. Remaining funds were transferred to the general budget (rather than taken from TANF funds). And in 2012 the legislature cut the program down to the bare bones, leaving Twogether in Texas barely on life support with one full-time coordinator for the whole state serving more than 2,500 volunteer educators (mostly faith-based). Perhaps it is worth noting, too, that the TX HMI is a more diffuse and complex initiative than the UT and OK HMIs. It has a wide range of activities, but HHSC funds and directs only some of these initiatives, coordinates with others, and is relatively uninvolved with others. Perhaps this more diffuse control of the initiative makes it harder to sustain over time.

Summary. Texas launched its initiative with specific legislation and funded it with a 1% set-aside of TANF block-grant funds and a handful of direct ACF grants. It built an infrastructure of community organizations to deliver primarily marriage preparation classes, incentivized with a significant deduction on the marriage license fee for those who took the classes. But funding was withdrawn in 2011 with severe budget cutbacks. Thus, the Texas case, like the Utah case, reminds us that these kinds of initiatives can be difficult to sustain, even when launched with legislative direction, substantial funding, and good leadership. So I'm not naïve about the budgetary and political challenges facing government support for HMRIs. In Chapter 9 I will deal with these realities and propose a feasible way to sustain these efforts, but I know it will be hard.

State Legislation to Strengthen Marriages and Reduce Unnecessary Divorce

Most of the activities from the state healthy marriages initiatives described above have been a result of policy decisions rather than enacted legislation. The TX HMI was launched with legislative support, but the implementation of the initiative has been done at the policy level. And Oklahoma and Texas passed bills providing incentives for engaged couples to invest in formal premarital education. Otherwise, policy makers have pushed these initiatives forward by administrative policy rather than legislation.

Given historically high divorce rates over the past 40 years (although they have come down somewhat since their 1980s peak), as well as dramatically increased rates of nonmarital childbearing and family instability (that continue to rise), one might expect states to be more active on the legislative front to counter these trends that impact civil society and the well-being of children and adults. But my research on this indicates that half of the states (25) have enacted no substantive legislation since 1990 intended to strengthen marriage or reduce divorce. Arizona, Arkansas, Florida, and Minnesota have been most active enacting this kind of legislation. A second tier of modest-activity states includes Georgia, Indiana, Louisiana, Maine, South Carolina, Tennessee, and Texas. After that, activity levels are uniformly low or nonexistent.

I have been personally involved over the last decade in efforts to enact legislation in Utah designed to encourage involvement in educational programs to help couples form and sustain healthy marriages. But even in conservative, profamily Utah, these efforts have failed to pass.[30] It's not just me. I have influential colleagues in other states who have been trying to promote legislation without much success either. When legislation does pass, it is usually because of dogged efforts at the right time by a skilled legislator who strongly believes in the value of law to support a stronger institution of marriage. But legislative success is uncommon.

For states with some level of legislative activity, the most common action has been to raise the age of legal marriage (18 states). Marriage in the teenage years is a strong predictor of marital dissolution, so widespread efforts to raise the age of legal marriage seem rational. But marriage rates for teens have dropped dramatically over the past 40 years, and no state has raised the legal age to 20 when the risk curve that maps the relationship between age at marriage and divorce quickly flattens out.[31] So it is hard to know how effective these laws have been. They have probably helped to reduce the divorce rate slightly.

There have been a handful of other legislative initiatives intended to strengthen marriages and reduce divorce, including financial incentives for engaged couples to participate in marriage preparation education, covenant marriage with voluntary stricter grounds for divorce, and "time-out" laws that can temporarily halt no-fault divorce proceedings to allow for counseling efforts to save the marriage. But I describe these legislative actions in more depth in later chapters, so I will not dwell on them here. Unfortunately, little research has attempted to evaluate the effects of these laws.

Do These Policy and Legal Initiatives Work?

As the reader of this chapter can see, there is a good deal of government-supported effort intended to help couples form and sustain healthy relationships and enduring marriages, probably much more than the average person—even the well-educated and informed person—knows. Of course, compared to other kinds of policy initiatives, such as efforts to increase the employability of young adults or reduce the number of unintended pregnancies, the amount of healthy marriages initiative effort is quite modest. Still, there is enough that we should take notice of it. And these efforts have accelerated since the mid-2000s.

But what do we know about how effective these efforts have been? Obviously, that is a crucial question. So to conclude this chapter, I turn to a review of the research on this question. My focus in this chapter will be on the research that evaluates broad policy initiatives as opposed to specific programs, even when these programs are supported with government funding. Specific program evaluation studies also are important to look at, but I will do so in later chapters when they are associated with a particular agenda point. For instance, when an evaluation study is focused on a program to help at-risk married couples strengthen their marriage, I will review that in the chapter dealing with the proposal to increase marriage maintenance education to married couples (Chapter 6).

Before proceeding, however, I offer two caveats. First, in order for healthy marriage programs to be effective, they have to be implemented effectively and reach the targeted population in sufficient numbers. There have been a number of formal implementation studies, and overall, these studies have provided reason for some optimism.[32] Diverse, low-income couples (married and unmarried), as well as high school students, young single mothers, Head Start parents, refugee families, military couples, stepfamilies, and others are participating in nontrivial numbers in government-supported MRE programs in many communities throughout the United States. Similar to other voluntary programs, recruitment and retention is challenging, but practitioners are learning more effective ways to do this. Those who engage in the programs self-report that they are learning new behaviors and relationship skills (e.g., communication, conflict resolution, cooperation), about the nature of commitment, what a healthy, nonabusive relationship is, how to manage their finances cooperatively, how to nurture and sustain the positives in their relationships, positive parenting and responsible fatherhood skills, and more. Participants generally highly value and enjoy the educational experience and report that it helps them be better partners and parents.

Second, efforts to evaluate government-supported HMRIs are still young. Good evaluation of major policy initiatives often takes decades. Take for instance evaluation of the popular national Head Start program launched in the 1960s and designed to help low-income preschool children improve their readiness for school and their physical health and overall well-being. It received billions of dollars of funding for many years without strong evaluation support. Only recently has strong evaluation of the effectiveness of this program emerged with somewhat mixed results.[33] Efforts to evaluate government-supported HMRIs are emerging now but are hardly definitive. At least policy makers and scholars have been pushing evaluation from the beginning of these initiatives, which itself is unusual and noteworthy.

In the last section of this chapter, I describe a handful of studies that shed light on whether these kinds of initiatives are working.

50-State Comparative Study of Healthy Marriages and Relationships Initiative Impacts on Family Demographic Outcomes

As the previous sections makes clear, there has been a considerable amount of government-supported effort intended to strengthen marriages and relationships and reduce divorce, especially since 2006. The amount of effort across states has not been uniform, however. From a research perspective, this variation is fortuitous. It enables researchers to ask a straightforward question: Are states that have more HMRI activity supported by government funds improving their situations compared to states that have less activity? In other words, can we see differences in things like marriage and divorce rates, poverty, and family stability between states with greater and lesser investments in these kinds of efforts?

A few years ago, Paul Amato, a prominent family sociologist at Penn State, and I set out to try to answer this question. Amato had become curious about this question and did his own, informal, back-of-the-envelope test based on early and limited data. He was surprised to find some results suggesting that HMRIs might be having a small but statistically noticeable impact on important population outcomes. But he knew that a much more extensive and sophisticated study would be needed to fairly test his initial findings. I sensed the value of this study when he discussed it informally with a small group of scholars at a meeting I attended. I volunteered to help get the data needed. While seemingly straightforward, it was in reality a complex and labor-intensive process. For instance, there is no central repository of information on federal and state efforts to strengthen marriage. ACF did not have a central, comprehensive record of their funds and what they had accomplished. While various sources and documents exist, most information about these projects has not been aggregated and culled systematically.

So to answer our research question, we first had to launch a large project to collect information about these government-supported initiatives. With a team of spunky research assistants at Brigham Young University[34] and a small grant from the National Healthy Marriage Resource Center, I managed a project to find, sort, and organize all the data we could get about these government efforts. (This work resulted in the state-by-state comparison data presented earlier in this chapter.) We combed through various documents published by ACF and other organizations documenting these efforts (especially funding information). We directly contacted many organizations that had received government grants to implement healthy marriages and relationships programs. We talked to state leaders about initiatives in their states. We did research on various laws passed over the past 20 years intended to strengthen marriage and reduce divorce. We invested hundreds of student-hours in efforts to collect this information. We were thorough and dogged. Still, I'm sure we weren't able to document everything. Nevertheless, through our research, we documented about $800 million of government funds invested in healthy marriages initiatives between 2000 and 2012. Getting good information on the numbers of participants served by organizations with these funds was much harder. As I mentioned earlier, we have been unsuccessful so far in discovering how many participants have been served by these programs and initiatives. We were able to make direct contact with a fraction of these organizations and have documented more than one million participants. But this number vastly understates the actual number reached. So unfortunately, the study I am describing here uses only funding information. I suspect that there is only a modest correlation between funding and number of participants served, but using funding data is the best we can do at this point. We organized the funding data by state and year to see if differences between states and changes from year to year could predict some positive changes at the demographic level. We divided these numbers by state populations to yield per capita funding figures so we could better compare the figures across states with vastly different populations.

Meanwhile, Amato took on the challenging task of creating a data set with state-by-state and year-by-year population-level outcomes, such as marriage and divorce rates, the proportion of two-parent families, and the percent of births to married parents. You might think that these data would be straightforward to get from such sources as the U.S. Census Bureau, but you would be wrong. For instance, a handful of states do not collect and report marriage and divorce rates, and many other states have missed reporting in various years. So Amato had to be creative and diligent in finding other sources to find missing data. He culled most of these data from the American Community Survey conducted by the government each year since 2000, which is currently the best source of information about the kinds of child and family variables we were interested in. We combined the state-by-state, year-by-year record of government-supported HMRI funding with these state-by-state, year-by-year population-level outcomes to create a data set that could finally answer our research question.

To be honest, we were a little skeptical about finding strong, positive results. First, our data were not perfect and complete, so there would be what researchers call measurement error in our data that would make it harder to find a statistical relationship between HMRI funding and population-level outcomes. Even more sobering, while we had documented what seemed like a lot of government-supported activity, in reality these efforts were reaching a small proportion of the population, so it would be difficult to push the outcome numbers by much. Moreover, the amount of time for these initiatives to push the outcomes has been small—a decade of activity but only about 5 to 6 years of significant activity that has produced variation between states. In addition, we were pinning our hopes on first-generation programs and initiatives that were still very much exploratory and experimental. And the programs were trying to impact personal and relationship behaviors and decisions that are hard to change. Finally, we were aware that many economic and social policy efforts, as logical and well-intended as they seem, often have limited impact when evaluated, especially in early evaluation studies. So the odds were stacked against us. Nevertheless, the research question was valid and needed to be addressed: Does variation in state efforts to help couples form and sustain healthy marriages and relationships predict differences in important population-level outcomes that logically would be connected to the goals of these efforts?

Here, in a nutshell, is what we found.[35] Cumulative per capita funding for HMRIs between 2000 and 2010 was positively associated with small changes in a few of the outcomes. But when we looked just at 2005–2010— the years with the most funding and activity—we found that cumulative per capita funding for HMRIs was positively and significantly associated with several outcomes, including the percentage of married adults in the population and children living with two parents, and it was negatively associated with the percentage of children living with one parent, nonmarital births, and children living in poverty. Although the changes were small, they were noticeable and statistically reliable.

Although our study found statistically significant associations between per capita funding and several demographic outcomes, it's fair to ask whether these associations were large enough to matter to policy makers. So we took Oklahoma, a high-activity state, and applied our numbers to see what happened there. In Oklahoma, between 2000 and 2010, government funding for MRE totaled a little more than $30 million. This amount represents approximately $8 (cumulatively) for every state resident in 2010, about three times the national average level of spending. Our findings suggested that this level of funding in Oklahoma corresponds to a 3-point increase in the percentage of children living with two parents, a 2-point decrease in the percentage of children living with one parent, a 2.7-point decrease in the percentage of children born to single mothers, and a 1.4-point decline in the percentage of children in poverty. These estimated changes are not as large as the general increase since 2000 in single-parent homes, nonmarital births, and child poverty, so these trends still moved in negative directions during that decade, just not as far as they would have otherwise. Nevertheless, these numbers suggest that states that invested in MRE services in significant ways during the last decade may at least have slowed the movement of family trends in directions that many people find troubling.

Researchers often test and retest their analyses to see how they hold up under different analytical circumstances. We did this and our findings were pretty robust. However, we found one important change in our findings when we removed from our analyses an influential outlier—Washington, D.C. Washington, D.C., had the highest level of HMRI funding (per capita) by far of any state and some of the largest changes in the demographic outcomes we were measuring, as well. We worried that D.C. might be unduly impacting the results of our study, so we took it out and re-ran our analyses. When we did this, the results were no longer statistically significant. Interpreting this finding takes some careful thinking. On the one hand, the exclusion of D.C. suggests that the encouraging results we got earlier are an artifact of an outlier case—D.C.—that received by far the largest allocation of government funding (per capita) for HMRI efforts. Without this case the small effects observed with the 50 states are no longer statistically reliable (though in the hypothesized direction). Thus, one interpretation of the data is that HMRI-support policies have yet to prove their ability to impact population-level family stability and economic well-being outcomes; an outlier case is giving a false impression that these positive effects are going on in the other states when, statistically speaking, this isn't reliable. But when the D.C. outlier is reduced (by dividing it in half) rather than deleted from the analyses the small effects for the 50 states remain significant. Hence, the interpretation of the findings depends on how one thinks it is best to handle a significant outlier case. This is a lengthy and technical discussion for another time and place.

On the other hand, the effect observed for Washington, D.C., is interesting in its own right. In a small geographic region with high percentages of lower income couples that has seen the largest concentration of HMRI funds, we found several demographic outcomes moving in hypothesized, positive directions. A significant need combined with significant opportunities may be the ingredients needed for these policies to have their intended effect. Moreover, note that D.C. has the largest concentration of African Americans of any state. Previous research has raised the intriguing possibility that HMRI programs may be more effective for African Americans. In one of the most rigorous evaluation studies of large-scale HMRI programs targeted to lower income couples, researchers found a significant, positive effect for African American cohabiting parents but not for other couples.[36] Perhaps the observed effect for D.C. also is a result of target population demographics favorable to these kinds of programs.

It is not crystal clear whether our findings support the utility of HMRIs. There is some evidence that they can make a small difference, but Washington, D.C., may be driving that association. But the D.C. case is a positive sign in itself. And remember that we weren't able to test our hypotheses with data on the actual number of individuals who participated in these government-supported HMRI efforts. In theory, the number who participated would have more impact on our outcomes than just funding levels. So overall, I think our study provides some encouraging results. Again, given the relatively low level of HMRI activity in the states, the limited amount of time to produce effects, the exploratory nature of these programs, and the limitations of our study, it was surprising that we found any encouraging results. Also, I want to be clear that our study did not assess the effectiveness of implementing the full agenda of policies that I am proposing in this book. The study essentially evaluated the impact of a hodgepodge of various programs designed to demonstrate their potential to help couples form and sustain healthy marriages and relationships. I think a more strategic, full rollout of these efforts would likely produce stronger impacts.

We can't assert from our research that the HMRIs directly caused slightly better outcomes—correlation does not equal causation—but our findings do lend some support to a hypothesis that government-supported educational programs and initiatives to strengthen marriages and romantic relationships and reduce family instability improve important population-level outcomes that indicate stronger families. And stronger marriages and families mean less poverty and reduced needs for public assistance to needy families and better outcomes for kids.

Along these lines, Bob Lerman, a hard-nosed economist at American University in Washington, D.C., and a fellow with the progressive Urban Institute, tried to estimate what the cost savings would be over a period of 10 years if these HMRI programs were creating healthier, more stable families. These kinds of studies are challenging and rely on all sorts of assumptions. But he made a host of very conservative assumptions (and left out a large set of costs that could not be estimated) and still came out with an estimate of a little more than \$100,000 in government costs that would be saved for each relationship "saved" by these programs.[37] Lerman did not conclude from his study that these initiatives were working and producing large savings, but he did conclude that HMRIs have the potential for substantial return on investment. So even small improvements in the kinds of trends we looked at in the study just described could result in big savings to the government.

Community Approach to Supporting Marriages and Relationships Education

Another interesting and relevant study of the impact of HMRIs comes from a rigorous evaluation study funded by the federal government of Community Healthy Marriages and Relationships Initiatives or CHMRIs. CHMRIs are not a single program. Instead, CHMRIs are a collection of community-based efforts to provide a wide range of MRE services to fit the needs of a local community. Hundreds of CHMRIs are scattered all over the United States. The logic behind community-based efforts to strengthen marriage goes like this: First, CHMRIs recognize that marriage is a public institution that undergirds societal well-being; it is not just a private and personal relationship. We are all stakeholders in each other's marriages and families. Healthy marriages support healthy communities (and vice versa). In addition, grassroots efforts are closer to home, and thus tend to be more responsive to community needs and more sustainable. Finally, marriages are more likely to thrive in communities where individuals feel their marriages are not isolated but rather supported by services in their communities and acknowledged as important by their neighbors.

The vast majority of CHMRIs are not government-supported. They exist on small grants, corporate sponsorship, and volunteer labor from passionate proponents. Some of these CHMRIs self-report that they have reduced divorce rates in their communities. For instance, probably the premier CHMRI, "First Things First" in Chattanooga, Tennessee, reports on its website that it has reduced the number of divorces in the community by 22%.[38] It is hard to rely on this straightforward figure; more sophisticated studies are needed to control for other factors and discern just how much the CHMRI efforts effected this change. One study a few years ago of privately supported CHMRIs employed a research design that at least can give a sense of how much CHMRIs may be impacting divorce rates, although this study has its shortcomings.[39] It evaluated the impact of Community Marriage Policies (CMPs). CMPs are, in essence, a religious cartel of faith-based organizations in a community that pledge to require couples to receive premarital education before marrying and provide ongoing marriage mentoring to newly married couples, among other things.[40] This study examined divorce rates in more than 120 CMP communities around the United States. (Note that some CMPs were operating successfully but some were operating ineffectively or even defunct.) The study found that CMP communities had experienced a divorce rate decline that was 2% greater than comparable communities without CMPs, perhaps preventing about 30,000 divorces nationwide.

A few CHMRIs have received significant government funding from ACF and made significant outreach to more disadvantaged members in their communities. The federal government funded a sophisticated study of three of these CHMRIs in Dallas, Milwaukee, and St. Louis, and compared them to outcomes in Fort Worth, Kansas City (Missouri), and Cleveland. (MRE services were targeted to areas that had higher concentrations of lower income individuals, and researchers surveyed comparable areas of the comparison cities.) The study surveyed behaviors and attitudes about marriage and relationships, as well as direct participation in MRE activities, from a representative sample of about 3,000 adults who responded to interviews in 2007 (when the CHMRIs were just beginning) and 2009. The results suggest that these CHMRI efforts did not produce significantly better outcomes in their communities compared to matched, similar communities. The lack of differences includes no greater proportion of adults participating in some kind of MRE service or even being more aware of opportunities. Of note, however, the researchers did document that the matched communities had significant private (and some public) efforts going on to help couples form and sustain healthy marriages, although there was more going on in the three focus communities (Dallas, St. Louis, Milwaukee). In addition, the study only examined a 2-year window during the implementation of these community efforts; it may take a longer period of time to see effects emerge. There were also some methodological complications that emerged over the course of the study, which is not uncommon for these kinds of studies. For instance, it became apparent over time that there was a substantial amount of relationship education for youth initiated in high schools in these focus communities, but the researchers did not include youth in their surveys. (Including minors in research is complicated.) So this study wasn't able to make as strong a test of the effectiveness of CHMRIs as I would like to see. On the other hand, I was encouraged to see that nearly 10% of adults in these communities received some kind of MRE service during the course of this study.

A second aspect of the evaluation study was another survey of individuals in the focus communities who had participated in some kind of MRE service during the 2-year timeframe of the study. Most of the classes were 6–8 hours long. More than 80% of respondents to the survey said that the classes improved their relationships, often a great deal, and that what they learned also helped them in their parenting and with relationships at work. The most common area of improvement identified by survey respondents was in communication skills. So although effects were not evident at the community level, those who received services said they benefited from them.

OFA Grantee Programs Meta-Analysis

I'll share one more study that evaluates, albeit less rigorously, the effectiveness of federally supported HMRIs. In 2011, I tried to contact all organizations that received a federal grant from the Office of Family Assistance to provide MRE services. I asked if they had collected basic data on the outcome of their programs. By basic, I meant did they collect data on participants as they entered the program and then again at the end, and did they follow-up later on? More specifically, I asked if they collected data on such things as relationship quality, commitment, communication skills, and father involvement. While not required to do so by their federal grant, many of these organizations had collected these kinds of data for their own evaluation purposes. I asked if they would be willing to share these data with me so that I could combine them with data from other HMRIs to get a sense of whether these programs were having their intended impact. I asked specifically for programs that were serving primarily low-income individuals and couples. About 30 organizations responded with their data; some of these organizations were running multiple programs. So I was able to collect basic evaluation data on program outcomes on about 50 programs supported by federal OFA grants.[41] I got data on programs serving youth, unmarried young adults, unmarried parents (mostly cohabiting), engaged couples in premarital education programs, and married couples in enrichment programs. Overall, there were about 50,000 participants assessed in these 50 programs.

Before reviewing those results, a caution. These kinds of evaluation data are not as rigorous as the data collected in some of the large-scale studies I will review later on in the book. These organizations collected data from participants before and after the programs. But they did not collect data from nonparticipants, or from a nontreatment control group. The most rigorous studies don't just compare a treatment group before and after an intervention to see what happened. Rather, they randomly assign study participants to either a treatment group, who go through the program, or to a nontreatment comparison or control group to see if the treatment group ends up different from the nontreatment control group. Research done in this way controls for a host of potential problems that can reduce the confidence in the findings of the experiment. Also, the most rigorous studies generally follow participants over a significant period of time to see if any changes persist or fade away (or get stronger), and if any differences between the treatment group participants and the control-group participants remain or diminish (or strengthen). The data I collected from these organizations was short on long-term follow-up assessments. (It's expensive to follow up and these organizations were not funded to do rigorous evaluation.) Also, the most rigorous studies employ multiple kinds of measurement strategies rather than just asking individuals to report on themselves. All my data were self-report surveys. So the results from my study using these less rigorous data have to be interpreted cautiously. Still, asking people about their relationships after they complete a program and comparing their answers to what they reported just before they began the program does give a picture of how people feel they have changed. So it is one way to get a quick assessment of whether the program is successful, at least in the eyes of the participants themselves.

Now that I have been appropriately cautious about how strong this study is, what did we find? We conducted a meta-analysis that essentially combined data from 50 different programs reporting on the participants' change as a result of attending a MRE program of some kind.[42] Combining data from all these programs gives a better picture of what may be happening overall than any single program. In technical terms, we found that the overall pre-to-post change effect size for these programs was $d = .40$, a statistically significant effect (that is, it is unlikely that this result occurred by chance). A significant effect size was found for each target population served (e.g., youth, unwed parents, premarital couples, married couples). Similarly, a statistically significant effect was found for all outcomes assessed including relationship quality, communication skills, relationship confidence, relationship aggression (small but still statistically significant), unhealthy relationship knowledge (youth), and coparenting/fathering. There were no significant differences in effects for men and women. Not surprisingly, moderate-dosage programs (9–20 hours) tended to have somewhat higher effects than lower dosage programs (8 hours). Programs with larger proportions of participants who did not have a high school education appeared to benefit a little more than those with greater education. It might be worthwhile to point out that the strength of the effects I found in this study are in the same ballpark as effects found for other intervention programs aimed at improving family-related behaviors, such as parenting, coparenting for divorcing parents, and teen pregnancy prevention.

While this study has important limitations, as I acknowledged earlier, the results provide some early, encouraging evidence that OFA MRE programs may be successful in helping many individuals and couples improve the quality of their relationships. As a result, policymakers who have followed with interest these demonstration programs may have a little more reason to support them in the future and to call for more rigorous efforts to assess their effectiveness.

So, What Does It All Mean?

I certainly haven't reviewed all the relevant research on the effectiveness of HMRIs yet. As I mentioned earlier, some of the research is about programs directed to specific kinds of couples and measures the effects of a program on the participants rather than the effects of a large policy initiative. I'll give plenty of attention to the former studies in subsequent, relevant chapters. In this chapter I've tried to focus on the latter studies. It's hard to take the research I've reviewed in this chapter, stuff it into an intellectual box, and wrap it up with a pretty conceptual bow. But I'll do my best. Here's what's I think the bottom line is: I think the early evidence from studies of policy initiatives to help couples form and sustain healthy marriages and relationships is that the kinds of programs being supported by government funds look like they are producing small but significant positive effects in important relationship outcomes and that these positive effects are beginning to register at the population level as small improvements in child and family outcomes. Although these changes are small, the sizable return on investment of these small effects means they may be saving taxpayers money.

In this chapter, I have tried to give the reader a better idea of what state and federal governments are doing to promote educational opportunities to help individuals and couples form and sustain healthy relationships and enduring marriages, as well as some brief histories of how these policy initiatives got started, unfolded, and struggled to maintain themselves. In addition, I reviewed the early research evidence on whether or not these kinds of policy initiatives are helping. I concluded that the early evidence suggests that they may be making a small but valuable difference. But I think we can do better. The work in this area is still young and we are learning more about how to do it better. With steady improvement and implementation of the full, strategic agenda I am proposing in this book, I think there is a good chance that future research will find that these initiatives can have more substantial effects.

Admittedly, we still have a long way to go to get better at helping couples form healthy relationships and enduring marriages. But I'm optimistic that we are going to get a lot better at this over the next two decades. I think we will see important advances in our understanding of mature love and what makes love work and last. With better basic understanding, we will find better ways—and I suspect more efficient ways—to help people achieve their relationship aspirations. So in one sense, I think the work we have been doing over the past decade to make more marriage and relationship education available, especially to those who may need it most, is more akin to laying down the tracks to strengthen and improve romantic relationships rather than building the trains that will run on them. Or maybe a more ambitious but timely analogy is the Internet. We built the infrastructure for what has become the Internet in the 1970s and 1980s and 1990s. But the early hardware that was connected by the Internet and the original software that powered the hardware were limited and slow at first. Over the past 20 years, we have seen dramatic improvements in hardware and software (and continued advancement of infrastructure) that are now making incredible use of that infrastructure. There was a needed, substantial public policy commitment at local, state, federal, and international levels to building that infrastructure.

The general public's early experience with the Internet was clunky, but it still created new, functional possibilities in our work and personal lives and the future potential was readily apparent and exciting. Twenty years later we are reaping tremendous benefits with dramatic improvements in hardware and software. Similarly, the educational hardware and software being used with the MRE infrastructure that we are laying down now are probably a bit clunky and slow. But if we continue to invest more resources and energy, we will see significant improvements over time. I don't think we will somehow make mature love and healthy marriages as easy as sending an e-mail or text message. But we can do a lot better, and the efforts that I have described in this chapter are the early efforts to lay down an infrastructure and experiment with what can be done with it to help couples form and sustain healthy marriages and romantic relationships. Important questions, then, are whether we will continue to invest those resources, and more specifically for this book, is public policy needed to help build this infrastructure and will public policy makers support this?

I'm convinced that public policy will play a crucial role. But I don't know whether that support will continue. I do know that there are a lot of questions and reasonable skepticism about the value and potential of state and federal healthy marriages and relationships initiatives. So before going on any further, I want to acknowledge and address the questions and skepticism directly. That is the task of the next chapter.

Chapter 3

Responding to Critiques about Government-Supported Efforts to Strengthen Marriage: Anticipating the Barricades on the Road

Most mornings while I munch my breakfast I read *Time* magazine rather than the morning paper. On the very morning that I began writing this chapter, I came across an essay from a prominent journalist, Rana Foroohar, who took shots at government-supported efforts intended to strengthen the institution of marriage.[1] The context for the essay was the 2012 Republican Presidential Primary and the emphasis candidates were placing on conservative social issues. Foroohar's basic point was worth noting, even though she said it in a journalistically typical snarky tone. She argued that if Republicans were serious about creating more stable families, then instead of throwing money at "Bush-era programs encouraging people to marry," we should do more to prevent unplanned pregnancies among young unmarried women and find better ways to help young men secure good jobs so that they would be more attractive candidates for marriage.

I think the journalist is right when she asserts that fewer unintended pregnancies and more good jobs for young people would help increase family stability, strengthen marriages, and improve children's well-being. But she got two things wrong. First, note the shallow understanding of what these policies actually are doing. Characterizing government-supported efforts to help couples form and sustain healthy marriages and relationships as simply pushing folks to "put a ring on it" paints a misleading portrait, as Chapter 2 should make clear. (In her defense, she was quoting from an interview with the distinguished Princeton scholar Sara McLanahan on this point. But McLanahan is well-informed about government marriage initiatives and the research around them, so I suspect that the journalist took her comment out of context.) Just as important, the journalist places these policy efforts in opposition to each other, as though efforts to prevent unintended pregnancies and increase good jobs for young people are somehow shortchanged by direct policy efforts to strengthen marriage.

In this chapter, I want to acknowledge and respond directly to a set of objections and critiques about government-supported Healthy Marriages and Relationships Initiatives (HMRIs). These concerns come from the ideological left, right, and center.

The *marital ecology* critique is perhaps the most common, so I address it first. The critique in the previous paragraph is a species of the genus of this concern. It emphasizes progressive policy that creates an economic and social ecology in which family stability and healthy marriages would flourish rather than direct efforts to strengthen marriages. A second common critique I label the *pragmatic skepticism* argument. It emphasizes the powerful historical, social, and economic forces behind the dramatic changes in the institution of marriage (which I reviewed briefly in Chapter 1) and the relative impotence of "soft," voluntary, educational efforts to counteract those forces and help couples form and sustain healthy marriages. In short, it is skeptical of the potential effectiveness of these efforts. A third critique that is sometimes added to the pragmatic skepticism critique I call the *family diversity* critique. It stresses a long history of adaptive change to the institution of marriage, of which recent changes are just another instance, and it predicts a future of many functional family forms. A fourth critique I call the *government intrusion* argument. It emphasizes a libertarian concern about the side-effects of government involvement in highly personal matters, including financial costs, but just as important, costs to personal liberty. Although I address these four critiques separately, operationally they are frequently intertwined.

Let me stress that I think these are generally fair concerns worthy of a serious response. Ultimately, however, I think they are just barricades in the road to public efforts to strengthen marriage that mark minor challenges that can be managed or repaired; they don't close the road or make it unnavigable. I believe the policy agenda that I propose in this book for strengthening the institution of marriage overcomes the concerns raised by these critiques.

The Marital Ecology Critique

The essence of the marital ecology critique is this: Providing voluntary educational services to help more people form and sustain healthy marriages and relationships may be a quaint idea, but it misses the point. It's the wrong approach. Marriages struggle when the socioeconomic ecology in which they exist is unsupportive or hostile to their thriving. The most significant reason that couples—especially lower income couples—struggle to form and sustain a healthy marriage, according to this critique, is not that they don't value marriage or that they don't have the skills for a stable, healthy marriage.[2] Rather, it is because the fertile social soil and healthy economic conditions needed to support a good marriage often are lacking.[3] Providing marriage and relationship education to couples who live in such stressful circumstances is, in the words of two noted psychologists, Ben Karney and Tom Bradbury, "akin to offering piano lessons to people with no access to a piano."[4] This critique emphasizes that it is hard for people to form or sustain a healthy relationship, even when they value their relationship and want a strong marriage. Instead, this critique argues that what we need to do to help marriages (and all romantic relationships) is to nurture policy that creates better social and economic conditions in which romance can take root and thrive and grow into healthy marriage.[5] This includes a society where young people can get a good education, a good job, and good healthcare, and benefit from public and corporate policies that allow couples to balance work and family. It also includes help with problems that take a toll on relationships, such as drug abuse, depression, and abuse, which are far too common, especially in impoverished communities.[6] And it is a society that helps young people plan their families rather than a society that accepts the inevitability of unintended pregnancies.[7] Laws that incarcerate an inordinate number of low-level offenders make it difficult to form stable, healthy families, as well.[8] Policy should be prioritized for funding that will support efforts to improve the conditions that support healthy relationships and marriages rather than divert funds to programs offering marriage and relationship education (MRE). This critique stresses that these kinds of social policies will create a greater hope for the future that is the DNA of forming healthy, stable marriages. In the absence of that kind of hope, argues Harvard professor Kathy Edin, young people will continue to shun marriage, not because they don't value it highly, but because they do, and they don't feel that they have what it takes to make it succeed.[9]

They do not, however, forgo children. They embrace the deep purposes associated with rearing children, which may have heightened meaning due to a lack of confidence about access to success in other domains. And unfortunately, the factors that diminish their ability to form and sustain a healthy marriage also work just as much against their ability to endow their children with a stable and hopeful life. Thus the lack of hope is passed on to the next generation. While I support the need for effective coterminous policies that create conditions of greater hope to nurture healthy relationships in ways that help marriages succeed, I don't think this marital ecology critique is an effective reason to reject the policy agenda I propose in this book. I propose an "and," not an "or" approach. It makes sense to me (and to other scholars[10]) to do both; we need to do both. There are already a lot of public policies trying to improve the social and economic conditions that indirectly support a healthy marriage or relationship. And I fear, as the *New York Times* columnist David Brooks says, that we expect too much of economic policy: "In short, modern societies have developed vast institutions oriented around the things that are easy to count, not around the things that matter most. They have an affinity for material concerns and a primordial fear of moral and social ones."[11] As a society, we need to pay as much attention to social processes as economic ones if we want happiness.[12] What I propose is a feasible and affordable additional policy tool that directly targets relationship skills and knowledge, not a replacement for these other policy initiatives.

The marital ecology critique does draw attention to the need for us as a society to continue to work to create conditions that give more young people hope, help relationships thrive, and make it easier for couples to form and sustain healthy marriages. When effective public policy helps create better conditions by improving our educational system, increasing the number of good jobs, promoting responsible fatherhood, reducing domestic violence and aggression, preventing and treating substance abuse and addiction, treating depression, and diminishing the number of unplanned pregnancies, then I have little doubt that we are also helping to strengthen the institution of marriage, and I feel that my tax dollars are well invested. Each of these policy areas has a clear connection to healthy relationships and marriages. None is a magic bullet, however, just as effective HMRI efforts alone are no panacea.

For instance, education is one of the best predictors of the ability to form and sustain a healthy marriage[13] and there is now a disconcerting educational divide among the marriage "haves" and "have-nots"[14] (as I briefly reviewed in Chapter 1). Thus, I think there is a straightforward connection between effective policy that promotes a stronger, more effective educational system and stable families and stronger marriages. I am a cheerleader for progress in this area. In fact, I put this at the top of my list of conterminous policy to support a stronger institution of marriage. We need an educational system that is capable of providing youth with hope for a good adult life. I don't pretend to be an expert in this area; I'm not sure what we need to do policy-wise to move this agenda forward.[15] I'll be an engaged listener and enthusiastic cheerleader for these kinds of efforts. But why does progress in this area prevent experimenting with the kinds of policies I'm promoting in this book to strengthen marriage? (I'll address the "limited funds" response to that question shortly.) Why target some known factors contributing to family instability and poverty but not others?

Similarly, I'm for effective employment policies to help create more and better jobs for young people. We know that young men who struggle to find and keep good jobs feel less prepared to take on the responsibilities of marriage, which is seen by many now as a capstone to a stable life in the young adult years, rather than a foundation for it (as I reviewed in Chapter 1). And understandably, underemployed men are not attractive marriage material to young women who value marriage but want the stability and security that is supposed to come with membership in that institution via their husbands' steady income and benefits.[16] There is some evidence that policies that increase low-income individuals' income increase marriage rates.[17] As a marriage scholar and advocate for a stronger institution of marriage, I'm a fan of effective employment policy, not to mention general economic policy that improves the overall economy. But a generation of policy experimentation with improving employment prospects for underemployed men (and women) has found mixed success.[18] And even when these policy efforts do improve job prospects, they do not appear to improve the overall life chances of disadvantaged youth and young adults.[19] Still, I appreciate even modest success in this area and I hope we can identify more effective policies. There has been a dramatic decline in support of these efforts[20] and I hope we can reverse this trend.

Also, social policy that effectively addresses the tragic problem of domestic violence is needed. I support policy that helps to prevent intimate partner violence and treats the psychological problems it creates in its victims. No doubt our justice system can also improve how it handles these crimes that undercut the moral meanings of love, romantic relationships, and marriage. And it's not just violence at the hands of an intimate partner that creates problems for forming and sustaining healthy marriages. Research also documents how the effects of abuse suffered as a child can poison adult romantic relationships.[21] Thus, we need more access to effective treatment for childhood abuse, especially among the poor, who are many times more likely to have been victims.

But again, this is not an "or" but an "and" situation. Early on in the federal government's efforts to help couples form and sustain marriages, critics raised the specter of preserving marriages that would only serve to trap abused wives or partners in destructive relationships.[22] In response, federal policy makers began consistently modifying the noun *marriage* with the adjective *healthy*. They acknowledged the reality of domestic violence and clarified that efforts were designed to support healthy marriages and relationships, not trap women in bad ones. By implication, this meant that a positive outcome of some individuals' participation in government-supported MRE programs could be for them to realize they were in an unhealthy relationship and seek help to end it. Moreover, in all federal- and state-supported HMRIs, programs are required to work with domestic violence prevention advocates and implement domestic violence protocol to protect participants from abuse and help any victims get help.[23] Some individuals who show up for MRE classes have experienced violence or are at significant risk for violence.[24] Furthermore, most MRE programs now directly address the issue of unhealthy relationships, teach couples to avoid violence and aggression, and help partners develop better communication and problem-solving skills.[25] Some early research suggests that MRE programs may be able to reduce or prevent relationship violence.[26] Accordingly, government-supported HMRIs are now a working partner with domestic violence prevention advocates to fight the plague of domestic violence in our society. Government-supported HMRIs are a supplement rather than a replacement for domestic violence prevention efforts; they work together rather than against each other.

One of the most important areas of policy progress that could help create a more supportive environment for couples to form and sustain healthy marriages is the prevention of unplanned pregnancies.[27] In fact, there are scholars who urge that this be the primary policy tool to strengthen the institution of marriage.[28] In the United States in 2009, 41% of births were to unwed parents,[29] a nearly 50% increase since 1990, and that trend continues to creep up. Moreover, 53% of births to women under the age of 30 were to unmarried women, a more than 50% increase since 1990.[30] While some of these births are planned, most are not. Unfortunately, these children are much more likely to experience high levels of family instability, poverty, abuse, poorer mental and physical health, and academic and behavioral problems, and to repeat the cycle of premature parenthood and poverty.

If more effective policies could substantially reduce the number of unplanned births to unmarried parents, then the need for HMRI policy would be reduced. The impetus for HMRI policy, after all, derives primarily from a concern for children's well-being. Unfortunately, our success in this area has not been enough to make a big dent in the problem. The limited success we've found has been with interventions to prevent unwanted pregnancies for teens, including providing free contraceptives.[31] We know much less about preventing nonmarital births to 20-somethings. Now a large majority of nonmarital pregnancies occur to 20-somethings,[32] not teens, and children's outcomes are not much different between the two parental age groups.[33] So we have a long way to go to reduce unplanned, nonmarital births.

Yet every little bit of progress will improve many lives and save taxpayer dollars. Moreover, it will strengthen marriages. It is more difficult to form a healthy marriage when children are born out-of-wedlock. This is so for a marriage between biological parents. It is more so for single parents seeking to marry a nonbiological-parent partner. Obligations to children outside a current romantic relationship and entanglements with previous partner coparents make it more difficult to tie the knot and create more stresses if the knot gets tied.[34] In addition, unplanned children make it more difficult for parents to complete their educational goals, which, as noted earlier, helps to sustain a healthy marriage. Hence, I want to see more success in policy efforts to help teens and young adults prevent unplanned pregnancies. For instance, it appears that expanding Medicaid eligibility to cover family planning services for more women reduces the number of unwed births and saves taxpayer dollars.[35]

But the HMRI policies I am proposing can supplement these efforts. Effective programs directed especially at youth and emerging adults that help them understand better the success sequence (1 = finish school; 2 = marry; 3 = have children), communicate what healthy relationships look like and how to avoid unhealthy relationships, and teaching good relationship skills may be a valuable supplement to efforts directly focused on preventing unplanned pregnancies. I review some of these programs in Chapter 4.

One element of this critique questions whether we can afford to support both HMRI policy and other social and economic policies like the ones I've described here. In an era when we are facing a long-term, difficult challenge to reduce crippling budget deficits but still fund essential services, this is a serious concern. As two prominent sociologists recently wrote: "Recent campaigns to promote marriage are based on the assumption that marriage will improve the well-being of individuals [which they challenged in their study], and in a context of scarce resources, they divert time and money away from other policy levers."[36] And as I was working on this chapter, I tuned into a session on National Public Radio that was discussing the problem of increasing numbers of children reared in single-parent households. In the broadcast a prominent sociologist at the University of Maryland, Philip Cohen, complained about HMRIs taking away from more legitimate welfare needs: "the Healthy Marriage Initiative took money from the welfare program, to the tune of several hundred million dollars, to promote marriage."[37]

My response to this fiscal concern is threefold. First, we have been and will continue to spend billions and billions of dollars every year for many policies that, when effective, help improve the social and economic environment for marriage (and all relationships), including policies dealing with education, employment, healthcare, domestic violence, abuse, and unplanned pregnancies. I don't have precise figures, but what we spend now and what we have spent in the past on these programs must dwarf the costs for the kinds of initiatives I am proposing in this book. In Chapter 2 I mentioned that I have identified about $800 million of government funding for HMRIs from 2000–2012, an average of about $60 million a year. If all the funds to support the initiatives that I will propose were instead invested in coterminous policy to improve the social and economic conditions that help marriages thrive, I suspect those additional funds would barely register as a rounding error. By contrast, in 2006 alone, and just looking at one modest policy effort—Medicaid spending on family planning services—the federal government spent $1.3 billion.[38] If $60 million more funding had been added to this figure for just one area of social policy intervention, it would have increased it less than 5%. So, I suspect the argument that we should divert the limited funds being allocated to these HMRIs may be a pretense for a distaste toward policy efforts to strengthen marriage. Second, I am proposing that states set aside 1% of TANF block-grant funds for preventative educational efforts to help couples form and sustain healthy marriages. TANF funds are already allocated to states, which have considerable discretion in how to use them to help needy families. So I'm not calling for new funds but for a small re-tasking of existing funds. And I think the research is showing these funds may actually save tax dollars in the long run. We can afford 1% for reasonable prevention efforts. And these funds do not detract from other effective policy efforts. Perhaps we need more funds for other worthy initiatives that indirectly strengthen marriages and families, but we need to be sticking our hands into deeper policy pockets than the HMRIs to find these funds. My third point is that the "affiliative economy" of family and human relationships—what the esteemed British policy expert David Halpern calls the "hidden wealth of nations"—is intricately intertwined with the money economy, has enormous impact on the money economy, and may be more strongly related to human well-being than the money economy.[39] A downturn in the affiliative economy has real effects, too. And it's why Halpern calls for greater public support for developing key human skills, including parenting and couple relationships.[40]

No question that publicly supported HMRI efforts, as well as all kinds of social welfare programs, will come under increasing pressure to prove their merit, given that the budget dollars to support them will almost certainly shrink as we wrestle with enormous budget deficits. A concern for effectiveness brings me to the next critique.

The Pragmatic Skepticism Critique

The pragmatic skepticism critique of government policy to help couples form and sustain healthy marriages and relationships is easily summed up: The policies won't work. This argument comes from critics all along the ideological and political spectrum, although different critics stress different reasons for the futility of these efforts.[41] The critique is an umbrella for a set of pragmatic concerns. First, some critics argue that MRE programs won't work because they are missing crucial things that create problems for relationships.[42] Some argue that it would be more effective to try to help people be better coparents than to be better partners or to help poor children directly with an array of programs and services. Other critics stress the reality that individuals are making bad marital partner choices that can't be overcome by merely teaching relationship skills.[43] Still others are concerned that the programs are not designed to be effective for lower income couples who need them the most, nor are practitioners reaching lower income couples with their programs.[44] Some raise concerns that these programs do not take account of the reality of poor women's risks for intimate partner violence and may subject women to greater risks.[45] Moreover, the critique continues, even if some programs were shown to be somewhat effective, it is extremely hard to bring promising programs to scale to be able to reach enough people to push the numbers in the right direction. And how could we afford to bring these programs to scale? Ultimately, even if programs appear promising, we could bring them to scale, and we could afford them, the critique goes, such success would be chimeric because the hard reality is we are up against social–historical forces that are just too powerful to change in the long term. For these and other reasons, policy efforts to strengthen marriage will be ineffective.

What is my response? Pragmatic skeptics have raised valid issues. For instance, noted psychologists Tom Bradbury and Ben Karney[46] argue that programs to help couples will struggle because they do not take account of individual, personal characteristics, such as personality, attitudes and values, educational achievement, and personal experiences, such as family-of-origin experiences and even ethnic or racial cultural experiences. According to this argument, these factors have large influences on the quality of couple relationships and they are often immune to interventions to change them. MRE programs that teach individuals healthy relationship skills have a hard time overcoming these individual characteristics.

For my response, I'll start with the argument that MRE programs don't target some of the most important factors that affect the success of romantic relationships, such as our personality characteristics.[47] And of course, they cannot change our family-of-origin experiences. But I respond with two counterarguments. First, the challenge facing MRE programs is no different or more daunting than that faced by other social policies that rely on educational interventions. Personality and personal characteristics certainly are involved in the effectiveness of, for instance, employment training and pregnancy-prevention education, and those characteristics constrain the potential success of publicly supported efforts to help in those areas, too. Efforts to help couples form and sustain healthy marriages and relationships share a similar burden with other policy efforts to help human beings who are not infinitely or easily malleable. That is the challenge that comes with the territory. MRE efforts should not be singled out because of this challenge. Second, early experiences cannot be erased by current MRE programs, but good programs can attempt to change how we understand and are affected by our early experiences in ways that reduce the potential harm they do to relationships. For instance, children who have experienced the divorce of their parents often struggle with commitment and trust issues in their adult romantic relationships and are at greater risk for divorce if they marry.[48] But educational programs can help these children understand their experiences and reframe how they view them (e.g., "I know I am greater risk, so I will worker harder at my marriage"). Isn't that the point of education? It doesn't change the past but it can help us understand the past and shift the course of the future. So while I acknowledge the barriers to change that MRE confronts, I'm not overwhelmed and discouraged by them. I believe strongly that knowledge is, if not power, at least strength. And let me make a brief point here that I touch on in later chapters, especially Chapter 7. While I believe in the potential of MRE programs to help individuals and couples form and sustain healthy marriages and relationships, I don't think we've arrived at any promised land; there need to be and there will be significant improvements in how MRE programs work that will lead to increases in their effectiveness.

Some critics believe—correctly—that the ultimate aim of these kinds of policies is to improve children's lives, not to improve couples' relationships. Thus, this argument goes, the educational focus would be better placed directly on improving coparenting skills of couples who have children together so that they are better at cooperating and supporting each other in their parenting responsibilities regardless of the status of their relationship. This would have a more direct effect on children's well-being than targeting the couple's romantic relationship. The implication here is that it is easier and more effective to target coparenting behaviors for educational intervention rather than romantic relationship behaviors. My response is, first, that both approaches have merit. We know that the quality of parents' romantic relationships impacts the quality of parenting, especially for mothers.[49] And in the absence of a good relationship between Mom and Dad, Dad is not likely to stick around and be involved day-to-day with his child.[50] So targeting improvements in couple relationships should lead to better parenting. Accordingly, marriage and relationship education makes sense to me. Limiting the scope of educational intervention just to coparenting issues unnecessarily limits what we can do to try to help. Targeting coparenting behaviors as well, such as supporting your partner's parenting efforts rather than undermining them and working together as a team, makes sense to me, too, and some MRE programs indeed include coparenting content in their programs and are finding positive changes in parenting practices and children's well-being.[51] Even studies of MRE programs that do not have a specific coparenting component but do address effective couple communication are beginning to find that changes in couple functioning spillover to produce positive changes in parenting behavior.[52]

As I was working on this chapter, I attended a conference at which a speaker argued that MRE doesn't work but that coparenting education does, so this should be the focus of policy to improve children's lives. Empirically, I challenge the assertion that the evidence so far does not support the potential effectiveness of MRE (and will review that evidence throughout the book). Moreover, the evidence for the effectiveness of coparenting education certainly is less advanced.[53] And logically, why do we think that helping disadvantaged couples learn ways to strengthen their romantic relationships would fall flat, while helping them learn how to support, respect, and cooperate with each other in their parenting behaviors would be highly effective? Rationally, it seems to me that we are in the same human relational zip code here with relationship education and coparenting education. Both are about knowledge and skills to improve how couples work together. One is more focused on the romantic relationship while the other is more focused on parenting together effectively. Both are a good idea. Parents who don't get along in their romantic relationship will likely struggle in their parenting relationship, and likewise, parents who undermine each other's parenting will see that play out negatively in their relationship. So I reject the argument that coparenting should replace relationship education in order to help children. Ideally, they go together for parents in a romantic relationship, and many MRE programs are doing both. If parents are not together, I support the interventions to help them cooperate effectively to rear their mutual offspring.

Another argument I've heard stresses the reality that individuals are making bad marital partner choices that can't be overcome by merely teaching relationship skills.[54] Without question good matchmaking is important to marital success.[55] And I don't doubt that people across the socioeconomic spectrum are making less-than-optimal choices about who to marry. Some let the stars in their eyes obscure a realistic assessment of the prospects for marital success, while others rush to a decision. By the way, cohabitation, which was supposed to help with this, seems to be falling down on the job. As recent scholarship has documented, people often rush into cohabitation without much forethought[56] and then end up sliding into marriage (rather than deciding and making a commitment).[57] As it turns out, there isn't much evidence that cohabitation offers an advantage for making a good judgment about the success of a marriage and some research suggests that it may actually contribute to the chances of divorce later on. I should note, however, that some research suggests that those who move in together after they get engaged don't seem to have this added risk[58] and the negative effects of cohabitation on marital stability may diminish somewhat as cohabitation becomes more common and marriages form with less commitment.[59]

If people make less-than-optimal choices, I agree with the critics that teaching them better communication and problem-solving skills may not be an easy way to overcome an unwise decision (although it might provide some help in some circumstances). But part of what I'm proposing here are educational efforts that would promote wiser choices and help prevent bad matches. Embedded in my recommendations for relationship literacy education for youth and young adults is an emphasis on what constitutes a healthy relationship, danger signs to avoid, how to form healthy relationships, and how to choose a marriage partner wisely. Moreover, my proposed agenda calls for support of premarital education programs to help engaged couples and relationship development education programs for cohabiting parents. Part of what these kinds of educational programs do is help couples to evaluate their strengths and weaknesses. Scott Stanley has found that a general outcome of these kinds of programs is that 10%–15% of couples decide not to marry as a result of what they learn.[60] So again, what I am proposing here should be able to make a difference with the problem of poor marital choices.

Another concern expressed under the rubric of pragmatic skepticism is that the kinds of programs I am proposing are not designed to be effective for lower income and at-risk couples who need them the most.[61] This was a common and accurate critique of the first generation of MRE[62] and of early government efforts to support MRE.[63] But a great deal of effort and money has gone into adapting programs in content and methods to be more effective for at-risk couples and people of color whose lives are often much different and more stressful than those of well-educated, White couples. Some critics argue that we don't know enough about relationship quality for the poor, so programs for them are unlikely to work.[64] No question we need to know a lot more about relationship and marital quality among the poor. But these are temporary limits, not complete restraints. We are learning more and more and this information is going into intervention programs to help more disadvantaged couples. Moreover, early evidence, including many studies that will be reviewed in upcoming chapters, suggests that these programs are even more effective, specifically for less educated couples,[65] lower income African American[66] and Hispanic couples,[67] and other at-risk groups.[68] So the research limitations haven't prevented some success in helping more disadvantaged couples. And these programs are reaching increasing numbers of disadvantaged individuals and couples as practitioners learn how to market their programs to this population and recruit and retain them in their programs.[69] Indeed, this growth is directly a result of the government support.

Another legitimate concern of pragmatic skeptics is whether any success generated in early efforts can be a basis for larger success. That is, can successful educational interventions be brought to scale throughout a community to push the numbers enough to make a dent in the outcomes that are negatively affected by family instability? A generation of hard-headed evaluation work in many areas of social policy has shown that we can produce an educational program that helps children and families, but taking that program to a larger scale is another matter. Perhaps the Head Start program, designed to help disadvantaged preschoolers be academically and socially ready to learn when they start school, is a prime example of the challenges of bringing a small program to a larger group. While the research shows that these kinds of early intervention programs can be successful and cost effective,[70] when we take the programs to scale we find that a lot of them don't work well and they don't produce the long-term effects we thought we would get.[71] So yes, taking programs to scale is a challenge. Again, this is not unique to MRE programs; it is shared by all policy efforts. Moreover, we are finding some success at taking family programs to scale. In the area of parenting education, for instance, the *Communities that Care* program developed by University of Washington scholar David Hawkins[72] has found ways to disseminate effective parenting education programs across a community. Similarly, research has documented the effectiveness of the effort to take the *Triple-P Positive Parenting Program* to scale in South Carolina.[73] And there is some emerging evidence that taking MRE programs out of the laboratory and into the community on a scale large enough to make an impact is at least possible.[74] The problem of scale is difficult, but it is not insurmountable, especially when there is a sustained policy effort that is guided by ongoing research.

Of course, taking effective programs to scale has costs. Can we afford such costs? The pragmatic skepticism critique approaches the cost issue a little differently than the marital ecology critique, which argues that HMRI funds should be diverted to support important economic and social policy efforts that improve the social and economic ecology. The pragmatic skepticism critique, in contrast, questions whether the investment in HMRI is likely to pay real dividends. In the case of efforts to support MRE, recent cost analyses point to real concerns. Two federally supported, large-scale, rigorous studies of MRE programs designed to help lower income couples strengthen their relationships produced eye-popping cost figures. The *Building Strong Families* (BSF) demonstration and evaluation program cost a little more than $11,000 per participant and the *Supporting Healthy Marriage* (SHM) program cost a little more than $9,000 per participant.[75] Figures like these would likely be unsustainable at scale. However, these figures need some context. First, these programs were firsts, so they had a lot of start-up, development, and research costs. The SHM program was a year or two behind the BSF program and learned a great deal from that project and that may have contributed to its lower (but still high) cost (a reduction of about 20% per participant). Given what we've learned from these major projects, costs will undoubtedly go down some more. Still, it is still pretty scary to consider such high costs. I have asked various program directors for estimate of their per-participant cost. Of course, costs differ depending on the target populations they are serving. For instance, it is relatively inexpensive to provide relationship education to youth in high schools. One administrator estimated her costs, from several years of data, at about $250 per student. For premarital couples, administrators estimated their costs between $1,000 and $2,000. But when programs are serving very disadvantaged individuals and couples, costs are much higher, perhaps $3,000 per participant. These figures bracket a much more reasonable cost figure.

Of course, costs also depend on the model for providing services. In my home state of Utah, we have developed an efficient way to deliver services with our small budget. With pretty good information on the number of individuals reached by Utah Healthy Marriages Initiative programs and accurate funding data, I estimate that the per-participant cost of the Utah HMI program is $14.35, which is obviously much less than the costs for the BSF and SHM programs. However, the Utah HMI programs are, for the most part, low-dosage programs, some only 1–2 hours of educational intervention, and probably do not reach as needy a population as served by other initiatives. And this figure includes getting MRE information to individuals and couples in the form of handbooks for newlyweds and other relatively minor interventions. So this is clearly a minimal estimate of the per-participant cost. If these calculations are limited to more substantive MRE opportunities, the per-participant figure increases to $38.98. But this is a figure that seems pretty affordable when funding is highly constrained. The Oklahoma Marriage Initiative estimates its per-participant cost at about $12.50.

I think hard-headed skeptics do us a service when they raise the affordability question. I have appreciated the Obama administration's greater emphasis on supporting policy initiatives that have strong evidence that they actually work and are cost effective.[76] Too much of what we do in the policy arena lacks evidence for effectiveness. As I outlined in Chapter 2 and will provide further evidence for in later chapters, there is emerging research suggesting that MRE programs can make a positive difference, and I think we are going to see substantial improvements in these programs over the next two decades. We don't have enough good information yet about cost effectiveness, that is, that MRE programs save us more than we spend by reducing the problems associated with family breakdown. But given the enormous public costs associated with family breakdown, cost effectiveness may not be that hard to achieve. As I mentioned in Chapter 1, the economist Ben Scafidi (2008) conservatively estimated that the U.S. cost of marital breakdown (i.e., divorce and unwed childbearing) was more than $112 billion a year.[77] Similarly, sociologists Steve Nock and Christopher Einolf estimate the annual cost of father absence at $100 billion.[78] Another set of researchers estimated the costs of divorce (not including unwed childbearing) in Texas at more than $3 billion a year.[79] If we are going to pay for ambulances at the bottom of the cliff, then it is prudent public policy that we build some fences at the top to see if they can prevent some unnecessary falls.

The point of this discussion is to show that there may be funding models and program methods that can efficiently support government efforts to help couples form and sustain healthy marriages and relationships. Certainly there are opportunity costs related to ways those funds might otherwise be used by states to help needy families. This is not a trivial concern, but as I argued earlier in this chapter, the amount set aside to support these HMRIs is microscopic compared to the funds going to support other efforts to help needy families. So I think the affordability concern voiced by pragmatic skeptics, though legitimate, can be answered effectively.

There is one further argument associated with the pragmatic skepticism critique to overcome. Ultimately, even if we had programs that worked for those that need them most and they could be taken to scale and we could afford to fund them, any short-term success we think we see will ultimately be chimeric, according to pragmatic skeptics, because we are up against forces of social change that are too powerful to fight with mere educational programs. Forces such as individualism, sexual freedoms, changing gender behavior, and economic affluence and materialism have been growing inexorably for decades, perhaps even centuries, the argument goes, and these forces have and will continue to change the way we organize society, including marriage and family life. We are naïve to think otherwise. Any short-term battles that we might appear to win as a result of our do-gooder social policies would ultimately be crushed by the powerful glacial forces of social change that have been altering the way we "do" marriage and family life.[80] We may think we are making progress, but we are only heading slowly north on a massive iceberg unmoored from the continent and drifting relentlessly south. Pragmatically, we would do better to roll with the tides of change and try to adapt more effectively. This is labeled the *family diversity critique.*

But first I need to respond to this important critique. I don't doubt that history packs potent forces. But I doubt that history is as linear as this critique would suggest. There are countless examples of how societies have confronted entrenched problems and effectively fought back, making a positive difference, even perhaps a cultural change. For example, I recently watched a documentary on the nineteenth-century Women's Christian Temperance Union. A small group of women eventually became a large group and then a nationwide cultural force that battled an entrenched, growing culture of alcohol abuse among men that left many wives and children neglected and abused. (The WCTU also helped to sow success for the women's suffrage movement.) With private and public tools, some more effective, some less, they changed the way society looked at and tolerated alcohol abuse. Furthermore, in my lifetime we have substantially changed attitudes and behaviors towards drunken driving that once seemed entrenched. A similar change has occurred with attitudes about smoking, especially smoking in public. These were changed with a long-term investment of public health education and some public policies (e.g., warning labels on cigarette packages, consumption taxes).[81] More recently we may be seeing another "inexorable" trend beginning to yield to counterforces of planned change. Public health practitioners for some time now have been warning us that obesity would soon become the nation's number one preventable health problem. Powerful historical forces have driven the dramatic increase in child and adult obesity. But we are hardly passive as a society, despite the enormous challenge it is to reverse this trend.

In each of these cases, the empirical evidence eventually made it clear that our tolerance of too much alcohol, tobacco, or unhealthy food was taking its toll on individual lives, which in turn produced deleterious effects for society and public costs. The weight of empirical evidence met with sustained do-gooderism to produce positive change. Of course, in a free society, people still make choices to do unhealthy things, but society nudges them in better directions, nudges that make a nontrivial collective difference.[82] Essentially, that is what I think can happen as we come to grips with the unhealthy patterns of couple and family formation that are creating serious problems for individuals and the communities in which they live. We can nudge them with messages and a series of educational opportunities that help them achieve their aspirations of real, sustained love and stable families.

Again, my point is that history is not linear. Societies all the time confront problems that seem intractable, beyond the efforts of do-gooders, progressives, or conservatives to control. Yet sometimes, somehow, we successfully stem the tides. Acknowledging the depth of the problem facing us in forming and sustaining healthy marriages and relationships and the powerful forces driving those problems should not be a call to step aside and watch; rather, it is a sober challenge to invest.

The Family Diversity Critique

Of course, it's possible that I am wrong about a very fundamental issue. Perhaps the family instability problems we are observing are not long-term problems at all. Perhaps they are, historically speaking, transitional problems that will eventually work themselves out. The marital ecology and pragmatic skepticism critiques are often proffered along side the family diversity critique that begins by accepting that we are going through a period of tremendous social change but reminds us that this is hardly new. We have gone through numerous eras of dramatic social change that have impacted families and changed the way we "do" family. Most recently, there was dramatic social upheaval during the transition from a rural, agrarian society to an urban, industrial society. Family life changed dramatically as a result and many at the time worried about those changes. But we survived. A new normal emerged. The sky didn't fall.[83]

According to the family diversity critique, we are certainly seeing a dramatic change in the institution of marriage. But this isn't bad; it's simply real life and misses the eventual fact that we adapt. Soon enough we will see a new normal and that new normal will likely consist of a flourishing of many different and fluid family forms that work not by virtue of their structure but by effective interpersonal processes and supportive contexts. Compatible with increasing trends of individualization, sexual freedoms, and prosperity, people will construct families in many different ways but they will find functional forms that will more fully meet the contemporary human needs of women, men, and children.[84] Change is inevitable but we are good at not only adapting to change but at riding it to a better place.

I had an interesting personal experience with this family diversity critique in 2005. I read an op-ed in the *Washington Post*[85] authored by perhaps the most public proponent of this critique, Professor Stephanie Coontz, at Evergreen State College (Washington). More eloquently than I did above, she articulated the family diversity critique, beginning with the powerful historical change argument delineated earlier:

> We may personally like or dislike these [historical] changes [that have transformed marriage]. We may wish to keep some and get rid of others. But there is a certain inevitability to almost all of them.
>
> Marriage is no longer the institution where people are initiated into sex. It no longer determines the work men and women do on the job or at home, regulates who has children and who doesn't, or coordinates care-giving for the ill or the aged. For better or worse, marriage has been displaced from its pivotal position in personal and social life, and will not regain it short of a Taliban-like counterrevolution.
>
> Forget the fantasy of solving the challenges of modern personal life by re-institutionalizing marriage. . . .

I admit that I took umbrage at being labeled an American Taliban counter-revolutionary for the work I was trying to do to strengthen the institution of marriage. I expressed that sentiment on an electronic listserv, unaware that Coontz apparently also was on that listserv. The next day I got a nice email from Coontz, whom I had never met. She had not intended to demean the work of folks in the promarriage movement by analogy to the Taliban. We had a pleasant and constructive exchange of messages over the next few days. I got to meet her in person a few years later and enjoyed getting acquainted with her. We weren't as far apart in our views as I would have thought.

But I suspect that we still disagree about whether the marriage glass is half full or half empty today. She argues that we are in a fundamental transformation of how we "do" love and sex and family and children, one that, like big historical changes in the past, will involve some temporary problems but ultimately will result in a flourishing of functional family forms for a new age. I can appreciate that change happens and that good can come of it. I like to think of myself as a progressive (although I suspect true liberals eat moderate progressives like me for breakfast). But I am not optimistic about a natural and sanguine end to the changes we are seeing that are leaving fewer children being raised in a stable family with two responsible, caring, and involved parents. If a better day is just over the horizon, that horizon is still a long, long way away.

In fact, and pardon the comparison, I think this argument is a bit like the global warming controversy. Even though we aren't 100% sure of all the causes of global warming, nor are we completely certain that it is a permanent rather than periodic change, we do know that the earth is warming right now. And if the causes are human—and the evidence is strong that they are—and we don't act quickly, we risk confronting a problem too big to solve later on. Hence, the prudent thing is to take reasonable action now to reduce the likely causes of warming. Those who deny global warming or choose a passive acceptance of it are doing so at an enormous risk.

Likewise, we are facing a kind of marital cooling now. And though we don't know for certain what the ultimate causes of family instability are, we have some pretty reasonable guesses. Nor do we know if these trends will continue unchecked or subside or reverse as we adapt to a new era. But we do know that families today are less stable now in ways that negatively affect children, women, men, and the communities in which they live. The negative trends, evident now for nearly two generations, do not seem to be abating yet. The prudent course, it seems to me, as we continue to increase our understanding of modern family life, is to assume that we need to act now to facilitate greater family stability and healthy relationships. And if we do this in a way that is voluntary, does not impose choices on people, and provides them with valuable knowledge and skills to help them achieve what they already want—a healthy, stable marriage and family—then we do so in a way that most will support. Perhaps we will find down the road that the family diversity critique had merit and things will arrive at a homeostatic positive place for families. It won't have cost us much if that is the case. Besides, such adaptation would require us to be better at relationship skills anyway, so the educational opportunities that I'm proposing would help usher in the new normal pointed to by the family diversity critique. Maybe we will discover some new social–technological fix to all our family concerns in the hazy future. But I don't think we should count on this. We should act based on our best understanding of the current situation and do the best we can to fix the problem before the problem potentially gets too big to fix.

The Government Intrusion Critique

The last critique is one I hear often from conservatives, although you don't have to be conservative or a Republican to voice it. The government intrusion critique comes from those who are deeply concerned about unnecessary (perhaps unconstitutional) government involvement in the private lives of its citizens. From this perspective, government has very little business sticking its nose into our private lives, and romantic relationships are outside the purview of legitimate government involvement. Good government is limited government. I have even heard influential conservatives argue that government has no legitimate regulatory interest in marriage, including granting marriage licenses. More often, however, I hear this critique expressed in this form: "The government will mess up anything it tries to do. The last thing we need is for the government to be running a dating service or telling us how to have a happy marriage!" Also, it's not unusual for the government intrusion critique to grab onto the affordability argument addressed earlier in the pragmatic skeptic critique: we just can't afford to be doing all this stuff.

My response? First, I'm sympathetic to the concern that individual liberties can be infringed when government gets involved in our lives, even by good-faith, well-meaning efforts. Marriage and our romantic relationships are, of course, deeply private. But the government involvement I'm proposing in this book is making educational services available on a voluntary basis—no coercion and minimal government intrusion. Most who choose to participate in these services would probably not even know that support for that service came from public coffers. Let me clarify that I am not proposing that government workers develop and implement these educational services. Instead, government invests in talented scholar–practitioners with expertise and experience in helping couples form and sustain healthy marriages and relationships. I think the federal government should help fund rigorous evaluations of these efforts, learn what works and what doesn't, and reallocate funding according to what we learn. But I don't think this support function is an intrusion into our personal liberties.

But there is a more fundamental issue. While marriage is deeply personal, it is more than a private relationship; it is also a public good, one that supports the general welfare of all citizens, including those most vulnerable—children. A problematic change over the past several decades is that we have lost track of how central the institution of marriage is to societal well-being.

We have emphasized the private nature of our personal romantic relationships at the expense of acknowledging their crucial public function. Treating marriage as only a private relationship obscures the public good that it is.[86] We are stakeholders in each other's marriages, not merely bystanders.[87] I believe that government has a legitimate role in supporting this public good that undergirds the optimal development of its citizens. Government should do so carefully, wisely, effectively, and as efficiently as possible. But I find short-sighted the argument that the institution of marriage is outside the scope of legitimate government interest.

Moreover, if you want government intrusion in your lives, just watch what happens when families break up. When couples divorce, they have more legal obligations to each other than when they are married. And the state will tell them when they can see their kids, how much money one needs to allocate to support children (which is never a realistic amount), and a host of other things. And forgoing the legal status of marriage doesn't do much to limit state intrusion. The government will still come after you and garnish your paycheck for child support and make other demands. Moreover, you are likely to fall into poverty when your relationship breaks up and so you will need some public assistance, at which point the state will have all sorts of rules that will intrude on your personal autonomy. The reality is that stable, healthy families keep government far from our private lives. If there are nonintrusive things we can do with government support that will keep more families intact and healthy, then this will translate into less government involvement in our private lives, not more. Thus, from a libertarian perspective, I think there is an important role for public policy to strengthen marriage so that there will be less need and demand for government involvement in our lives.

Conservatives and progressives alike appreciate the freedom we are given to choose our own life course and make our own decisions free of government coercion. But I believe a just and compassionate society needs to help its people to understand better the choices they make and the likely consequences of their choices, especially when those personal choices have significant public impact on their communities. It's not just or compassionate to leave people to make their own mistakes without any education. And if government is pulled in to pick up the pieces or deal with the consequences of these mistakes, then preventive efforts should make sense to libertarians and to all of us. I suppose that even in a worst-case scenario in which we found that nothing we do from a public policy perspective helps, educating people makes them more accountable—a conservative value—and is the fair thing to do—a progressive value.

Perhaps the worst-case scenario mentioned above does not appear so remote to libertarians. Government more likely than not, they might argue, will make things worse rather than better. Government do-goodism seldom helps and often just messes things up more. With some narrow exceptions, they argue, we should leave social problem solving to the market or to the church or other community organizations. Again, I appreciate the expectation that government funds be allocated wisely. But the effectiveness critique is best answered empirically rather than ideologically. Some early testing suggests positive potential for healthy marriage initiatives. Let's continue to test and evaluate. In fact, evaluation is specified in my proposed agenda.

Finally, for those who hold an extreme libertarian view that government should get out of the marriage status business, a view I have heard expressed by both conservatives and liberals, I would argue that this is at least impractical if not disastrous. Marriage is central to so many legal concepts; finding ways to take care of family issues and disputes without a legal status sounds to me like a full employment act for lawyers and an overwhelming challenge for individuals. Many people today are forming families without the legal status of marriage, but the law still has to get involved in many of these circumstances anyway. We can't just extricate the state from marriage and family concerns by returning the institution of marriage to the sole province of religion or private contracts. The state is involved with marriage because the institution is central to the lives of its citizens. And as long as children are being born and as long as couples link their lives economically and in other ways, the state will need some level of involvement in these personal parts of our lives.

In this chapter, I have tried to respond to the major objections, critiques, and concerns I have heard expressed about government-supported efforts to help individuals and couples form and sustain healthy marriages and relationships. No doubt my responses have been incomplete and imperfect but I hope they are not inadequate. That is, I hope that I have defended this kind of policy effort sufficiently to remove the intellectual and practical barricades that block progress and enable the reader to consider in concrete terms some realistic roads we could take to a better place. The next several chapters are a figurative map of those proposed roads.

Chapter 4

Relationship Literacy Education for Youth and Young Adults: Learning the Rules of the Road for Healthy Romantic Relationships

Proposal and Priority 1: Increase and improve relationship literacy education for youth and young adults to help them gain the knowledge, attitudes, and skills needed to form healthy romantic relationships, avoid unhealthy relationships, and understand the institution of marriage.

I'm a convert to the value of public support for marriage and relationship education (MRE) for youth and young adults. My past skepticism went like this: Given the typical age at first marriage (mid- to late 20s), teens are chronologically more than a decade away from marriage. Psychologically, perhaps, they are even farther away; for most young adults, that important (and desired) life event is still invisible over the marital horizon. And for some who have grown up with few examples of a healthy, stable marriage, the very idea of marriage exists more in fairytale land than in their day-to-day consciousness.[1] With something so temporally and psychologically distant, education on forming and sustaining healthy marriages seems like it would be (a) a hard sell and (b) unlikely to stick due to a short cognitive shelf life. Those who struggle developmentally to see past next Friday night, the next paycheck, or the next term paper are not prime candidates to absorb and use MRE that seems better suited for a time in the fuzzy future.

But my thinking about the value of MRE for youth and young adults has evolved. Long before young people are thinking seriously about marriage, they are making important romantic relationship decisions and transitions—lots of them—and many without forethought.[2] By age 18, two thirds of adolescents have been in a romantic relationship, many lasting more than a year.[3] Child development scholar Andrew Collins argues that youth romantic relationships are neither transitory nor trivial but instead have real effects, positive and negative, on adolescent development.[4] Nearly half of young adults 18–25 are cohabiting or seriously dating.[5] And more than 40% of young adult romantic relationships involve some kind of physical relationship violence.[6] Romantic relationships, sex, and even parenthood are not being delayed; only marriage is pushed back over the temporal horizon. Perhaps we once hoped that delaying the wedding until the late 20s would help young people form and sustain healthy marriages. After all, researchers have clearly documented that teenage marriage is one of the strongest predictors of divorce.[7] But romantic relationships and sex and, for many, bearing children and starting families, are filling the temporal gap between pubescent adolescence (which is arriving earlier and earlier) and marriage (which is occurring later and later). And each of these behaviors is not without important consequences for the ability to form and sustain a healthy marriage and family when the matrimonial moment finally comes. On a more positive note, research is beginning to illuminate the positive potential of healthy adolescent romantic relationships for current and future adult development,[8] so MRE may be able to help harness that potential.

The road that links adolescence to adulthood and a healthy marriage is not a paved interstate, with efficient on- and off-ramps, smooth driving, and numerous safety features on the road (and in the car) to prevent or cushion any wrong moves as young drivers traverse the distance to their eventual family destination. What may look to many young people these days as an exciting road trip is instead a daunting trek of winding and narrow roads, poorly marked and full of potholes; a route with unexpected detours that threaten not just when but if youth arrive at their intended destination and in what shape they (and others) are in when they get there. And once they get off track, finding an alternative route to the destination is difficult; there seems to be no relationship GPS device that smoothly recalculates their route for them. Moreover, they trek alone for the most part. In contrast to a few generations ago, society does not "interfere" much in regulating youth and young adult romantic relationships[9]; they are left "free" to chart their own courses, for the most part. Not surprisingly, then, as a society we almost guarantee that many young people will spin off the road in their romantic journeys and perhaps never arrive at their desired destinations.

Accordingly, we can't wait until youth and young adults eventually turn their attention to marriage. More than 75% of U.S. high school youth say that having a good marriage and family life is extremely important to them.[10] More than 80% of unmarried young adults say that it is important to them to be married someday; only 5% consider it unimportant.[11] But if they are going to get to their destination in good shape to form a healthy marriage, we need to educate them for the challenging road ahead. There is an analogy here to driver's education. Anticipating the challenges and dangers that young drivers face and the costs to individuals, families, communities, and society of driving mistakes, as well as the value of driving skills for adolescents' development of healthy autonomy and competence, our high schools make driver's education widely available to their students. We need a similar commitment from our schools to help our youth learn the relationship rules of the road and establish good relationship habits. As the esteemed psychologist Frank Fincham at Florida State University has put it, relationships need to become the "fourth R" in education: reading, 'riting, 'rithmetic, and relationships.[12]

So acknowledging the need to act early to try to prevent bigger problems later has changed my thinking about the potential value of MRE for youth and young adults. Galena Rhoades and Scott Stanley at the University of Denver have similarly argued:

> [I]ntervening earlier in relationship development, before individuals are committed or perhaps even partnered, has the potential to have an even greater impact on improving relationship quality [than for couples already committed to marriage], reducing divorce rates, and, perhaps most importantly, supporting stable unions for children to grow up in. . . . If we only intervene after a couple has formed and especially if we wait until a couple decided to marry before offering practical relationship education, we may miss many of the most important turning points in people's romantic lives. We also may miss opportunities to improve parents' relationship stability for the good of the children involved.[13]

Also, Ben Karney at UCLA, a sometime critic of federal policies to strengthen marriages, and his colleagues acknowledge the value of starting young: "Recognizing the importance of adolescent romantic relationships to healthy adult development suggests that targeting those relationships directly may lay the foundation for subsequent healthier marriages in adulthood." They interpret a wide range of research as "consistent with a model that views adolescent romantic relationships as a key period during which the foundations of healthy adult marriages may be strengthened."[14] Similarly, Ginger Knox, a noted social policy researcher, and her colleagues advocate for a policy goal that "every young person . . . leave high school with a basic understanding of the relationship skills that he or she will need to sustain employment, a satisfying long-term relationship with a partner, and effective parenting as an adult," including effective communication and emotion regulation.[15] Sociologist Wendy Manning at Bowling Green State University (Ohio) and her colleagues conclude that, "programs that start at earlier ages (in early adolescence) may be especially effective at promoting marriageability by preventing some of the early relationship experiences that shape negative future relationship trajectories."[16] Finally, adolescent development scholars Bonnie Barber and Jacquelynne Eccles argue that: "Well-designed curricula may help adolescents develop knowledge and interpersonal skills that improve their chances of experiencing positive relationships" and "extract themselves from risky romantic relationships," although they note that designing developmentally and contextually appropriate curricula will be challenging to do.[17]

Nevertheless, this conceptual logic supporting the value of MRE for young people would be insufficient if I still thought it would be fruitless. But I see some emerging evidence (that I will review throughout this chapter) that MRE targeted to youth and young adults can help young people chart a safer course to a healthy marriage and stable family. While the evidence so far is still limited, I think it is encouraging. The combination of a clear problem and a potential preventative tool has turned me from a reluctant skeptic to a cautious optimist and advocate for public resources to promote MRE to youth and young adults.

Other scholars have acknowledged the problem and pointed towards a response. The prominent University of Notre Dame sociologist Christian Smith, who may know more about the challenges of contemporary U.S. young adults than any other scholar today, recently wrote:

> We are failing to equip our youth with the ideas, tools, and practices to know how to negotiate their romantic and sexual lives in healthy, nondestructive ways that prepare them to achieve the happy, functional marriages and

families that most of them say they want in future years.... [T]he adult world is simply abdicating its responsibilities.[18]

Similarly, sociologists Mark Regnerus and Jeremy Uecker at the University of Texas–Austin, in their lengthy examination of premarital sex among young adults in the United States, noted "there is little effort from any institutional source aimed at helping emerging adults consider how their present social, romantic, and sexual experiences shape or war against their vision of marriage."[19] And Barbara Dafoe Whitehead, whose seminal essays gave birth to the marriage debate in our society 20 years ago, along with her colleague, Marline Pearson, an in-the-trenches, forward-thinking, community college educator teaching low-income young adults, wrote:

> [T]eens are afflicted with a knowledge deficit about relationships. Teens aspire to a life of successful work and future marriage but their attitudes are often at odds with the evidence on what it takes to actually achieve these goals. Consequently, they often behave in ways that undermine their ability to realize their aspirations. For all these reasons, it is time to . . . begin a hope-based strategy aimed at teaching teens [and young adults] about healthy relationships and marriage.[20]

Also, Anthony Chambers and Aliza Kravitz of The Family Institute at Northwestern University, in their analysis of low marriage rates among African Americans, called specifically for "educating [Black] teenagers about the benefit of children growing up in two-parent households as well as teaching them important relationship skills that foster relationship success."[21] They also called for more attention to marriage and relationship education at historically Black colleges and universities to reach young adults sooner.

This chapter, then, is my recommendation for how society can help to reclaim the responsibility of helping young people to "negotiate their romantic and sexual lives in healthy, nondestructive ways," as Christian Smith wrote,[22] and consider how their youthful romantic lives connect to their later goals for marriage. I give this recommendation my highest priority. Once couples commit to a permanent union and marriages form, there is still more we can do to support healthy, satisfying relationships and even prevent some unnecessary divorces. But there is only so much that realistically can be achieved if these marriages are formed on weak foundations that result from challenges brought into the marriage. Thus, this chapter outlines the public need for early action and the potential for positive results to help more young people safely navigate the lengthening road between early adolescence and a healthy marriage and intact family. Because we are dealing with such personal and private decisions and choices, a primary tool to accomplish this purpose is publicly supported, voluntary relationship literacy education made available to a large proportion of young people through preexisting educational infrastructure.

What Is Relationship Literacy Education?

For this younger age group, I call marriage and relationship education by another label: relationship literacy education (RLE). RLE is a subset of MRE. Relationship literacy education emphasizes general knowledge of the process of forming healthy romantic relationships, avoiding the pitfalls of unhealthy relationships, and understanding better the institution of marriage, rather than skills associated with making a healthy, long-term relationship with a specific romantic partner work. But it also includes some basic help with effective communication and problem-solving skills. RLE is the primer before the first coat of paint. Or, getting back to my traveling analogy, RLE is not the specific map of roads and highways you take to get to your destination; it's more like a general orientation to taking a safe and enjoyable road trip. The focus of RLE is on the relationship "rules of the road": how to form and sustain healthy romantic relationships (and what a healthy relationship looks like), the things that make that problematic, and an accurate understanding of the institution of marriage that most desire to join eventually.

More specifically, RLE blends a variety of topical ingredients together into a stew of helpful information and skills for youth.[23] (And many of these skills have broader application to other kinds of relationships, including and parent–child, employer–employee.[24]) Instruction is commonly provided in high school health or family and consumer sciences classes. In these formal educational settings, RLE may be just a component of a larger curriculum. Secondary education need not be the only setting for providing RLE, although it may provide the most efficient outreach; community youth programs, church youth groups, 4-H, and other settings can help.[25] Instructional dosage is usually between 8–15 hours.[26] RLE practitioners emphasize the need for RLE content to be relevant to the diverse lives and experiences of young people today.[27] The best curricula also should be sensitive to such things as teens' different family situations and upbringing and previous experiences (including abuse).[28]

Most RLE courses include a content module focused on self-awareness and self-efficacy, under the principle that a healthy relationship starts with two healthy individuals. Individuals struggling with a sense of self-worth or perceived inability to control the direction of their lives are more likely to struggle to form close relationships and experience disappointment and trouble when they do. Also, young people can benefit from understanding how their own personalities, family experiences, cultural norms, beliefs, and other factors may influence forming and sustaining a healthy relationship.

RLE also includes an understanding of healthy romantic relationship development. It discusses head-on how sex impacts youth relationships. RLE deals with sexuality, obviously, but it is not the same as nor does it take the place of sex education. Sex education is generally focused on body parts and biological functions, contraception, sexually transmitted diseases, and similar matters. While sex education tends to emphasize what to avoid (pregnancy and STDs), RLE tries to emphasize how to achieve the long-term relationship and family dreams that youth have. Barbara Dafoe Whitehead and Marline Pearson have argued: "teens are street-savvy about the attractions of sex and school-smart about its perils but increasingly uninformed or misinformed about the steps to building healthy relationships, now and in the future."[29] RLE emphasizes the relational aspects of sexuality, sexual decision-making, and how sex impacts relationship development. It raises the issue of sexual tempo—essentially slowing down—acknowledging the empirical relationship between rapid sexual involvement in a relationship, moving in together, and poorer relationship quality down the road.[30] RLE also addresses the issue of cohabitation from the standpoint of how it may affect healthy relationship formation, not so much as an issue of sexuality.

Some may be thinking that it makes sense to integrate sex education and relationship literacy education.[31] I think this is an interesting and important question, but I don't think we have a good answer to it yet. A recent policy push by the federal government may provide some needed evidence on this. With funding from the U.S. Congress (via the Affordable Care Act of 2010), the Administration for Children and Families has allocated significant funding to states to support programs that have been shown to be effective at delaying sexual initiation, reducing teen pregnancy, and increasing contraceptive use among sexually active teens. This initiative has been labeled the Personal Responsibility Education Program.[32] In addition to sexuality education (that must include both abstinence and contraception information), classes also must include curricula that address other important issues, such as healthy relationships, adolescent development, parent–child communication, healthy life skills, work/career success, and financial literacy. (Programs must include at least three of these adulthood preparation skill topics.) The legislated mandate to evaluate the success of this initiative may help us learn whether sex education and RLE work well in combination rather than apart. Along with other scholars,[33] I suspect that an integrated treatment may be effective. But it is also possible that the sexuality emphasis, which is primary, could drown out healthy relationships education.

RLE also includes learning effective communication and better problem-solving skills, which are central to healthy relationship development and maintenance. Poor skills in this area can set the stage for later, more serious problems in romantic relationships.[34] While some students may try to apply their learning in a current romantic relationship, there is nothing that precludes learning in a generic way such things as active listening skills and tools for de-escalating negative interactions (e.g., humor, self-soothing). And these skills can serve many different kinds of relationships, not just romantic ones, including parent–child and employee relationships. Also, a focus on effective problem solving in RLE includes frank discussions about the too-common reality of dating aggression and violence, and that these are signs of an immature and unhealthy relationship. A quarter of young adults say they have experienced relationship violence in their current relationship; a third of cohabiting couples have experienced relationship violence.[35] Physical and verbal violence are especially common among "churning" adolescent couples who breakup and reconcile, perhaps multiple times.[36] And being a victim of dating violence in adolescence significantly increases the odds that you will be both a victim and a perpetrator of intimate partner violence in young adulthood.[37] How to leave an unsafe relationship or just break up a low-quality relationship are also a part of good RLE curricula. Often RLE provides students with questionnaire tools for evaluating the quality of a specific relationship.

Most RLE programs also work to expose myths and misinformation about romantic relationships and marriage. I don't think it surprises anyone to learn that teens often hold unrealistic, romanticized, idealistic, and even wrong ideas about intimate relationships.[38] These distortions can set up unrealistic expectations and even unhealthy behavior patterns that undermine healthy relationships. Moreover, as a culture, and abetted by the popular media, we have hypersexualized young romantic relationships,[39] giving youth confusing and contradicting messages that sex is a natural part of early romance but that you should wait a while before becoming sexually active. Also, youth are exposed to confusing, inconsistent, and downright wrong messages about the institution of marriage.[40] On the one hand, they get messages that marriage is just a piece of paper; it's just another step. And many seem to be accepting these messages.[41] On the other hand, they also absorb messages that marriage is special and the best situation to rear children. RLE brings research-based information to this confusing situation to clarify, for instance, that early sexuality often has long-term negative consequences for youth, and, with appropriate sensitivity, that married adults are happier, healthier, safer, and richer than adults in other kinds of relationships.[42]

Relationship development is an important module in good RLE. The way relationships progress has an impact on later relationship and marital outcomes. Relationship development risk factors for later relationship success include cohabiting before commitment to a future for the relationship,[43] multiple sexual partners,[44] and initiating sexual involvement early in the relationship.[45] Many RLE programs deal explicitly with the risks of precommitment entanglements, noting that too many couples slide into romantic relationships and even marriage without a clear evaluation of the relationship or a strong commitment to each other and the institution of marriage. Commitment surfaces as a frequent topic in RLE; commitment is central to healthy, long-term relationships. Good RLE programs discuss how marriage generally is different from other relationships and that it has a set of rules and norms that place important boundaries on our behaviors. In a society that worships personal freedoms and unlimited choices, these boundaries can appear to youth and young adults as something that they may want to avoid. But these boundaries serve as a way to protect and preserve valued relationships, so they help us achieve a valued life goal. As my colleague Scott Stanley says, commitment is the choice to give up other choices in the service of a greater good.[46]

A close kin to commitment content is trust. Researchers are finding that many young women, especially lower income women, struggle with trust issues.[47] Much of the lack of trust comes from childhood or current experiences with childhood abuse (or witnessing abuse). Ironically, it appears that about half of these women do not gather any evidence about their romantic partners' potential trustworthiness before intertwining their lives with them. RLE programs should deal explicitly with trust and how to assess it, especially in the context of having experienced abuse and violence.

Mate selection is a valuable topic in RLE, as well. And although most won't marry until their mid- or late twenties, a nontrivial 25%–30% of young adults marry by the age of 25 (and many more desire to be married by age 25).[48] In RLE, young people can learn important characteristics of self, partner, and relationships that are associated with a positive or negative prognosis for a healthy, stable marriage. They can become familiar with warning signs for unhealthy relationships, such as relationship aggression and violence, jealousy, and controlling behaviors. One's parents' relationship history also impacts children's chances of marital success; children whose parents have divorced are at twice the risk of divorce themselves,[49] and children whose parents never married also face a much higher risk of relationship problems. While they can't change what has happened in the past, young people can recognize these risks and invest more in learning the skills needed to make romantic relationships and marriages work better than their parents' did.

A crucial message at the core of RLE is that adults and children and society do better in virtually all ways when youth follow what a number of scholars are calling the "success sequence": education à marriage à children.[50] Marriage is best built on a foundation of increased maturity, discipline, and opportunity that comes from education at least through (but best beyond) high school. Marriage—more so than other kinds of relationships, it appears—then provides a more stable platform to rear children with a mother and father in their daily lives who can provide the basic temporal and psychological necessities for them. Marriage also integrates adults—especially men—into societal institutions in productive ways for them and their children.[51]

But this success sequence is not a simplistic formula by any means. As the statistics show, it is problematic; many struggle to follow the formula for a variety of personal, familial, cultural, and societal reasons. This is especially so for poorer youth and young adults. Whitehead and Pearson acknowledge that the success sequence is a "high wire act":

It takes sustained effort, skill, practice, discipline, deferred gratification, parental dedication and social support to complete the success sequence. It is unrealistic—if not irresponsible—to expect teens to try to walk this high wire alone. They need information, guidance, skill and support to make it safely through a prolonged adolescence and into a flourishing adult life.[52]

The road to success is the long, uphill, and winding one; the easy road is downhill and easy, at least until you go around the first bend and find yourself in a ditch that's hard to get out of. Thus, there is a need for RLE to help young people, especially the more disadvantaged, understand the safer roads that are more likely to take them to their personal and family aspirations. Those who follow this success sequence and their children have significant advantages; they are unlikely to experience poverty and will be healthier and happier. Those who start at the end—bearing children before forming a commitment to a permanent relationship and increasing their employability with vocational or higher education—are at significant risk of poverty and a host of other personal problems with public costs.[53] The success of RLE efforts ultimately must be judged by how many youth it helps to sequence their lives in ways that promote optimal development for youth and young adults and optimal situations for the children that they will eventually rear. Again, this is no easy task, but it is the core challenge for RLE.

Kay Hymowitz, a scholar at the Manhattan Institute for Policy Research, approaches this success sequence idea in terms of a missing *life script* for young people. Marriage, she argues, can organize our lives during youth and adulthood in productive ways. It can serve to orient us to the future, foster economic independence, discipline our choices, and make us more child-centered. When that life script is lost, we may lose the productive ordering of the early life course. According to Hymowitz:

> Marriage is not a lifestyle choice, a bundle of [government] benefits, or a piece of paper. . . . As the core cultural institution, marriage orders life in ways we only dimly understand. It carries with it signals about how we should live. . . . When the poor lost the language of American marriage, they lost a great deal more than a spouse. . . . They lost a life script.[54]

In short, marriage is a core institution in our society that helps to order our lives in productive and meaningful ways. Of course, marriage is not the only path to a productive and meaningful life. But from a sociological perspective, marriage is the path most likely to lead to stronger families and personal happiness for the largest number of people. The fact that marriage seems so dim to so many young people today—especially disadvantaged ones—calls for a good and fair society to educate them to see more clearly the path to marriage. Without a strong conception of marriage as a realistic possibility for themselves, young people may not even think they can undertake the long journey. They need an identity that can imagine a healthy and stable marriage and effective behavioral strategies (and supportive environments) to provide a hope that they can realistically achieve their aspirations.[55] One youth educator I talked with in Alabama referred to the satisfaction she feels when she sees "the hope light come on." Contemporary young people need a North Star to guide their actions and decisions day to day towards their desired destination. As Whitehead and Pearson point out, our youth need something to aim at as well as knowing what to avoid.[56]

A comparison could be drawn between RLE and public efforts now in some places to teach young people about healthy personal financial management or healthy lifestyles. For instance, Utah high school students are required to take a financial literacy course (or pass an exam) to learn the basics of personal money management in the hopes of reducing the number of young adults making poor financial choices early on, such as acquiring excessive personal debt, which can create lasting problems and constrain future choices. Youth initiation into financial matters comes earlier than in the past, and in some ways, the financial services industry seems to be preying on young people these days before they figure out how to manage their financial lives. And apparently, parents and other youth leaders are not compensating with enough guidance in this area (perhaps because they, too, are struggling). Thus, youth need to become financially literate at earlier ages than in the past to avoid the problems that come from early, unwise financial decisions. And we can hardly pick up a paper or browse the news these days without hearing about the "epidemic" of childhood obesity. Youth obesity has exploded over the past generation. Noting that obesity is much easier to prevent than cure, and the earlier the better, schools are adopting more curricula dealing with healthy eating habits and exercise.

I think relationship literacy education fits comfortably into these categories of valuable preventative education for youth that tries to help them steer clear of long-term problems, thereby reducing societal costs of poor personal decisions. Effective RLE is needed to help young people make wiser relationship decisions before they make mistakes that constrain future family possibilities and bear significant societal costs. With greater knowledge comes greater hope for the future.

As I end my discussion on the content of youth RLE, let me add a little about parents and role models. I think a valuable element of RLE curricula would be involving parents in what their teens are learning. Some programs build this feature into their curricula. Students can practice their good communication and problem-solving skills with their parents. And indeed, one study of a youth RLE program showed that it improved communication with parents even several years down the road.[57] Maybe some of these skills the students are learning and practicing can rub off on the parents. This also gives parents a clearer sense of what their children are learning, which may build support for the class.

If my magic wand was functional, I would wish for every child growing up the gift of two married parents who modeled for their children what it means to be committed through good times and bad and treat each other with respect and kindness, and let them eavesdrop on how two people who are able to communicate effectively resolve their differences. Perhaps if this were each child's birthright, there might be less need for youth RLE. But this is not a birthright. Today more than 40% of children are born to unmarried parents who are unlikely to be together by the time that child starts school. On top of that, more children experience the divorce of their parents or experience a marriage based on less than respect. Accordingly, I think an important part of youth RLE should be to have each student try to identify a couple that models a good marriage and interview them several times about specific issues they are studying. Practically, it might be best if the curriculum were to suggest that a teen identify someone other than their parents to lessen the potential negative feelings for youth whose parents may not be the best role models. Certainly, if a teen wanted to work with her or his own parents, that would be fine. If there is a scarcity of such couples in the area, then I think teachers should work to identify a pool of volunteer role-model couples that students could get to know. Churches and other civic organizations could be tapped to help recruit them. Also, perhaps students who are blessed with two parents who model a healthy marriage or committed, enduring relationship in the home can volunteer them to help other students. Youth need to see a concrete model in order to see what is possible and internalize a hope for the future. This recommendation is not without some controversy, of course. Some single parents may be offended. But I think most would understand and support the benefits of this element of the curriculum.

Illustrating Relationship Literacy Education (RLE) for Youth

In the preceding section I tried to define in general terms what relationship literacy education is. A few concrete examples of RLE programs will help clarify this general portrait. First, I'll highlight the Alabama Healthy Marriages and Relationships Initiative's efforts to deliver a significant dose of RLE to a large number of high school youth, including a large proportion of disadvantaged or vulnerable youth. I didn't choose this example at random. Rather, I think this is one of the best programs and it has the most serious evaluation research agenda attached to it of all youth RLE efforts to date. Also, it has received considerable public support from the federal government's Healthy Marriages and Relationships Initiative (described in Chapter 2). In addition, I will briefly highlight the Texas *parenting and paternity awareness* program. It takes a different approach to youth RLE but shares similar aims, and it reaches an impressive number of youth. Some RLE programs target young adults rather than teens. To illustrate this type of program I will highlight a couple of curricula designed specifically to help young adults with their relationship decisions: *Within My Reach* and *How Not to Marry a Jerk(ette)*. *Within My Reach* and *"No Jerks"* have been employed by a large number of community organizations serving disadvantaged young adults that receive support from government funding. I will highlight just a few.

While presenting these illustrations, I will review the evaluation research that assesses whether these programs look to be successful. I wish the research in this first-priority area of my agenda was stronger. Some early research is encouraging but we need much more. For some reason, scholars haven't paid enough attention to these kinds of programs yet. The Administration for Children and Families funded one important, rigorous study of a youth-focused RLE program in Alabama that I will review here. But it did not fund a large-scale study of RLE as it has for programs targeted to married or cohabiting adult couples. I think this was a strategic error in their evaluation plan that has left us with fewer data on youth RLE than is warranted by its importance. So there is a larger element of faith in these programs than is good when you are promoting a policy agenda. Nevertheless, as I said, I think there is some encouraging early research, and I think we will get better at youth RLE as we do more and learn more.

The Alabama Healthy Marriages and Relationships Initiative Relationship Smarts Plus *Program for Youth*

The Alabama Healthy Marriages and Relationships Initiative (AL HMRI)[58] is a major effort funded by the federal Administration for Children and Families (ACF). Its mission is to strengthen families by addressing the quality of couple relationships in families and teaching relationship skills to youth. Francesca Adler-Baeder, with Auburn University's Cooperative Extension Service, directs the project, which involves a large number of partner organizations across Alabama. While the AL HMRI has many components, one of its most important pieces is outreach to youth with the *Love U2: Relationship Smarts Plus* (RS+) program. An original ACF grant funded a pilot program to test the effectiveness of the program and the RS+ curriculum.[59] Additional ACF demonstration grants in 2006 and 2011 supported a broad roll-out of this program, delivered primarily through high school classes to more than 1,000 students a year, including large numbers of youth from at-risk lower income families, single-parent families, and stepfamilies.[60]

The RS+ curriculum was developed originally by Marline Pearson, a talented practitioner whom I mentioned earlier in this chapter, and was revised somewhat for this project. (Two modules were added on adolescent identity development and relationship aggression, control, and abuse.) The content includes 13 lessons.[61] Together these lessons cover a wide set of the topics important to understanding and promoting healthy romantic relationship development for teens. Part 1, "Foundations for Understanding Romantic Relationships," includes four lessons: (1) Who am I and where am I going? (2) Maturity issues and what I value; (3) Attractions and infatuation; and (4) The meaning of love and intimacy. Part 2 of RS+ focuses on "Knowledge about Dating Relationship Processes" and includes four more lessons: (5) Principles of smart relationships; (6) The low-risk relationship strategy: Decide, don't slide! (7) Is it a healthy relationship? and (8) Breaking up and dating abuse. Part 3 focuses on "Communication Skills for Healthy Relationships and Marriages" with two more lessons: (9) A foundation for good communication; and (10) Communication challenges. The final part focuses on

"Marriage and Planning for the Future" with three more lessons: (11) Why parents' relationships really matter to children; (12) Increasing the odds of having a healthy marriage someday; and (13) Follow your North Star (review and setting personal success sequence plans).

The curriculum is delivered by family and consumer sciences or health educators in Alabama high schools who have received extensive training in the curriculum before teaching. More recently, many of these classes have used trained educators from community parenting/family resource centers to teach the classes rather than high school teachers. This strategy decreases the challenges and expenses of training high school teachers in a new curriculum. Also, they are experimenting with using younger graduate and undergraduate students from Auburn University and even experimenting with training volunteer high school students as peer educators. Health classes may be more effective to deliver the curriculum because they reach a more representative group of youth, including roughly equal numbers of girls and boys. I had the chance to observe a couple of these classes on a visit to Alabama and observed classes of about 25 ninth- and tenth-graders actively engaged in discussions about effective communication skills, as well as a module on relationship danger signs. I was impressed with how well the curricula were taught and how seriously the students took the class.

In student feedback about the program, the students are very positive. Here is a sampling of some of those comments collected by researchers at Auburn University:[62]

> "They should do the program more. I think it would help our society and help teens not lose sight of what's important."
>
> "I know for sure that I will take the lessons and apply them to the real life situations. I think that if I do that I would have more healthy relationships."
>
> "I gained respect for myself."
>
> "After attending these classes I know that I can have a successful relationship whether it be a marriage or a friendship. In the classes I gained knowledge of the areas I need improvement in. I had no idea how important it is to be a good listener. It can change a whole situation. I also learned how to handle disagreements with others."
>
> "I absolutely love this class. It made me realize how dumb I've been. I can figure out if someone is using me or really loving me. I won't get hurt now."

So students enjoy the program and say that they have learned important lessons that they will apply in their romantic relationships in the future. Of course, a set of positive comments from program participants is not the same as a formal outcome evaluation of the program's effectiveness. A rigorous evaluation study of this program was conducted by Jennifer Kerpelman and her colleagues at Auburn University.[63] They analyzed data collected from more than 1,400 high school students in 39 public schools across Alabama. Health classes were randomly assigned to either receive the RS+ curriculum (treatment group) or not (treatment-as-usual control group). A little more than half of the students in the study were female; 54% were European American and 35% were African American. A little more than half were eligible for free or reduced-cost lunches from the schools. About 40% of students were in intact families and 25% were in single-parent families; a third were in stepfamilies. The study focused on two important outcomes: faulty beliefs about romantic relationships, specifically, the belief that "love is enough" or "love conquers all," and conflict management skills (self-reported). Results at 1 year after the program showed that students in the RS+ health classes decreased more in their faulty belief "love is enough" and increased more in their conflict-management skills compared to students in the control-group classes. Moreover, improvements in faulty beliefs were found regardless of race/ethnicity, family income, and family structure. Improvements for conflict-management skills were found for students in less advantaged groups, but not the more advantaged groups. Students in stepfamilies seemed to benefit especially from the program. I find these results from a rigorous study of diverse youth taking a solid curriculum encouraging.

In another study using this same sample of youth, researchers found that students who took the RS+ program increased their disapproval of using aggression in dating relationships and, more importantly, that these attitudes were related to less use of physical aggression in their dating relationships 2 years later.[64] This corresponds with anecdotal comments from many students who say that the RS+ lessons on dating violence were the most important ones for them.

Of course, we still need to know how these initial lessons translate into relationship choices and behaviors for these students as they reach their 20s. Unfortunately, we don't have that research yet.

A later study of the RS+ program in Alabama with a larger number of students who all took the program (but with no control group to compare them to) reported significant, small-to-moderate, positive changes at the end of the program on all measures of individual well-being (e.g., self-worth, depression), erroneous attitudes and beliefs about romantic relationships (e.g., relationship violence is normal/acceptable, cohabitation is helpful to a successful marriage), and conflict management for both adolescent girls and boys. The effects for conflict management were concentrated in African American teens. Changes in beliefs about the value of cohabitation were concentrated in European American teens. Teen girls reported more improvement in self-esteem and less depression than teen boys. Teen girls reported a significant decrease in the belief that opposites attract and in acceptance of dating violence (but boys did not). While this study is not as rigorous (no control group and no follow-up a year after the program), it still gives a positive view of how students of the RS+ program are learning valuable relationship principles and skills that bodes well for the future.

The Texas p.a.p.a. Program for Youth

The *parenting and paternal awareness* or *p.a.p.a.* program in Texas illustrates a different approach to relationship literacy education that is interesting to explore.[65] The Texas legislature voted unanimously to require this 14-hour curriculum for high school students as a component of their mandated health class. In its first 2 years of operation (2008–2010), more than 500,000 students went through the curriculum. That kind of reach is unprecedented in RLE.

The Child Support Division of the Texas Office of the Attorney General, along with the federal Office of Child Support Enforcement, supported the development of this curriculum as an innovative step to try to reach youth before a pregnancy occurs rather than deal with the legal consequences afterward. Texas ranks almost dead last in the teen birth rate (and is dead last in repeat teen births).[66] While *p.a.p.a.* is a program designed to prevent premature parenting, the developers explicitly state that it is not a sex education program. Rather, its focus is on the rights, responsibilities, and realities of early parenting. What makes it an RLE program is that it sends a strong message to teens about the importance of the "success sequence": education à healthy marriage à children. And it educates youth about the realities and difficulties when that sequence gets out of order, including the responsibilities of parenthood, paternity establishment, and child support. The most prominent message is that becoming a parent prematurely is a big responsibility that is hard on adults and children. Key themes include both preventative issues and responsibility issues if a pregnancy and birth occur. Healthy relationship skills are stressed, including avoiding relationship violence. The legal and financial challenges of single parenting are presented, as well as the value of paternity establishment, meeting child support obligations, and the importance of father involvement and both a mother and father in the child's life if teens become parents.

A rigorous, long-term outcome evaluation study has not been conducted on the *p.a.p.a.* program yet, unfortunately. A short-term formative evaluation and assessment of how students' knowledge and attitudes changed was conducted by the University of Texas recently, led by the prominent sociologist Cynthia Osborne.[67] From a survey of more than 5,000 students before and after the program drawn from a representative sample of Texas high schools (but with no control group for comparison), researchers concluded that *p.a.p.a.* significantly improved students' knowledge and attitudes in targeted areas. For instance, there was a substantial increase in the percentage of students planning to delay childbearing until after marriage. Similarly, there was a significant increase in the percentage of students who agreed that it is important for children to have both a mother and father actively involved in their lives, even if the parents don't live together. There also was a substantial jump in the proportion of students who correctly specified the financial costs of raising a child and the percent of net income a noncustodial parent generally pays in child support. Also, the proportion of students who said they would establish legal paternity if they had a child outside of marriage increased significantly. Teachers and school principals were generally positive about the program and thought that it should be taught to their high school students. Still, despite the positive changes, there was still a lot of room for improvement on many indicators.

I chose to highlight this program for a couple of reasons, even though we can't be confident yet about its effectiveness. First, the reach of the program is impressive. I'm not aware of any similar program that reaches such a large number and proportion of youth with a healthy dose of RLE. But those numbers will decline because the state recently dropped the health requirement for high school graduation. Nevertheless, I spoke with a Texas official at a recent conference who said that despite the dropped mandate, a majority of students take the health class and thus get the *p.a.p.a.* curriculum.[68] And the fact that it is not required now may help eliminate the stigma that can accompany mandated classes. Second, the approach of the program is interesting. It is a premature parenting prevention program with a strong emphasis on the legal rights, responsibilities, and day-to-day realities of teen parenting. Yet it covers many of the same topics of more traditional RLE with many shared aims. The *p.a.p.a.* program in Texas shows that there is not a single way to approach relationship literacy education.

Other Evidence of the Potential for Youth RLE

Although there hasn't been a lot of research on the effectiveness of youth RLE, I want to bring attention to a few other studies worth noting. First, an important rigorous study on the potential value of youth RLE was conducted by Sarah Halpern-Meekin at Franklin & Marshall College (Pennsylvania).[69] She studied the effectiveness of youth RLE in six different high schools in Florida and Oklahoma. The Florida high schools had mandated the RLE class as a graduation requirement, while the Oklahoma schools simply offered and promoted the curricula. The Florida schools used various curricula while the Oklahoma schools used the *Connections: Relationships and Marriage* curriculum. Halpern-Meekin found that these curricula had the potential to improve students' interpersonal skills and social competence, although the specific results were more complicated. For instance, she found stronger effects for the mandated curricula, perhaps because the mandates brought in more at-risk students who stood to gain more from the curricula. The effects were measured 1 month after the class, so long-term effects are unknown.

The study of youth RLE with the longest follow-up evaluation (4 years) was conducted by Scott Gardner testing the *Connections* curriculum in a California high school with a diverse student body.[70] While these researchers found some initial positive results, they generally faded away when assessed 4 years down the road. Encouragingly, they did report at 4 years a decrease in relationship violence between students who took the RLE course and those who didn't—an intriguing and encouraging result—as well as an overall increase in self-esteem.

In addition, a meta-analytic study (a systematic study of studies) that I conducted recently lends further support to the potential of youth RLE. I described this research in more general terms back in Chapter 2. My research assistant, Kaylene Fellows, and I identified seven organizations that received support from ACF to offer RLE for youth and that also collected some data from youth before and after they took the programs.[71] There were more than

23,000 youth in these field studies. Combining the outcomes of these seven RLE programs, we found a statistically significant positive change on various attitudinal outcomes about relationship formation and marriage (the effect size was a moderate $d = .45$).

Another perspective on the potential for youth RLE comes from a recent report from ACF of a study of 15 youth RLE programs supported by ACF from 2006–2011.[72] In this study, researchers carefully examined 15 programs for clues about how effective these programs may have been. This was not an outcome study; it was an implementation study focusing on what these organizations were doing and how students were reacting. Among the study's major themes are three lessons relevant to the potential of youth RLE: (a) youth clearly desire better information about healthy relationships; (b) youth participants are able to develop a clearer vision about what a healthy relationship is and is not; and (c) RLE has the potential to be a powerful change agent within some youth relationships.

Of course, more rigorous research still is needed. But these early studies suggest that youth RLE programs could help youth gain valuable skills and knowledge that would help them stay on a better path to healthy and safe relationships in young adulthood and healthy, stable marriages later on.

Illustrating RLE for Young Adults

Effective RLE for teens is a necessary start to formal marriage and relationship education, but it is insufficient. As youth continue on the long road to adulthood, relationship decisions kick into high gear, often take on more weight, and are more readily connected to hopes for a healthy, stable marriage. Thus, my proposed agenda includes promoting a second dose of relationship literacy education in young adulthood to bridge that time between high school and marriage.

The Neighborhood Place (Louisville) Within My Reach Program for At-Risk Young Adults

In 2006, Becky Antle of the School of Social Work at the University of Louisville was awarded a 5-year grant from ACF to provide healthy relationship education to disadvantaged young adults in the Louisville, Kentucky, area. This educational opportunity is made available through a local agency, Neighborhood Place, a well-known social services delivery organization in the area. Like many others who received ACF grants to serve this target population, she decided to use the *Within My Reach* (WMR) curriculum. WMR targets individuals rather than couples in romantic relationships; typically MRE programs expect couples to participate together.[73] This program does not assume that the program is taken together by both individuals in a couple relationship, nor does it assume that the participant is even currently in a serious relationship. It is focused on relationship literacy rather than a specific couple relationship.

WMR was designed specifically with lower income individuals' circumstances and stresses in mind. It borrowed from Marline Pearson's RS+ curriculum (Pearson is a co-author of WMR). It also has roots in the Denver University PREP program.[74] PREP is the most evaluated, refined, re-evaluated, and re-refined MRE curriculum in the world. In addition, it has been adapted for many different audiences, including WMR for disadvantaged young adults. Over time, these research-based refinements and adaptations have made PREP-based programs some of the most valued and trusted programs in the field, and a leading choice for program providers who are accountable to funding organizations. Instructors are trained in an intensive 3-day training session by program developers, but there are no specific degree requirements for instructors.

The 15-hour WMR curriculum has three main sections. The first section covers the following topics: models of healthy relationships, mate selection principles and issues, expectations, personality issues (how they impact relationships), how relationships affect children, relationship tempo (going slow to make good decisions), and deciding about rather than sliding into relationship transitions. The second section focuses on romantic relationship safety, recognizing dangerous patterns, and ways to leave relationships safely. Also, participants learn effective communication skills to manage conflict and resolve problems. The last section deals with specific topics and problems in relationships, such as infidelity, commitment issues, and ways to manage coparenting with former romantic partners. The specific topics in this last section are less likely to be a part of RLE for youth.

This program has been formally evaluated a couple of times so far. (Others are in the pipeline.) Antle and her colleagues at the University of Louisville evaluated the short-term effects of WMR on 200 unmarried, disadvantaged individuals.[75] Comparisons of post-test scores to pre-test scores of those who went through the program indicated significant increases in healthy relationship knowledge, relationship quality, and self-reported communication skills. Another study by Antle and her colleagues followed a larger group of WMR program participants and found positive effects 6 months after the program. An encouraging finding in this study was that participants reported reductions in physical and emotional violence in their relationships and that improvements in relationship quality and communication skills contributed to the declines in violence.[76] In addition, there was very high satisfaction with the program as expressed by participants in surveys and also evident in the fact that more than 90% completed all sessions of the program.

A separate qualitative study evaluated the implementation of WMR in a small sample of low-income mothers who applied for TANF benefits in Oklahoma.[77] While the study did not assess the program effectiveness per se, the researcher conducted in-depth interviews with 11 mothers 2–3 months after the program to get a sense of their reaction to the program and what they felt they learned. The researcher found a good fit between the relationship lives of these disadvantaged mothers and the WMR curriculum. Most of the mothers reported learning and using some relationship-skill concepts from the program.

More rigorous research on WMR is needed, but I find these early results of RLE for young adults encouraging. This kind of curriculum fills a big need for quality relationship literacy education for at-risk young adults.

The No Jerks Program for Young Adults in Northern Utah

How Not to Marry a Jerk(ette) is the popular name of a well-used program. But it is known by several other names, including *How Not to Fall for a Jerk(ette)* and *P.I.C.K. a Partner*. (P.I.C.K. stands for "Premarital Interpersonal Choices & Knowledge.") I'll just call it *No Jerks* for short. This program was developed by John Van Epp based strongly on attachment theory.[78] The *No Jerks* program is intended for singles (and singles-again) and is designed to teach a way to build a healthy relationship that emphasizes engaging the head along with the heart to assess the future potential of the relationship, or as it cleverly says on its website (www.lovethinks.com), "how to follow your heart without losing your mind." It focuses on two major issues: pacing relationships and exploring key areas that predict the quality of a future marriage or relationship. In terms of pacing, the 6–10 hour curriculum explains a research-based model of how romantic attachment to a person grows, creating feelings of closeness and cohesion, and helps participants learn to pace a growing attachment by placing appropriate boundaries on the relationship. In addition, the curriculum describes the major things to look for in a potential mate that should be considered and observed during a dating relationship and identifies and corrects unrealistic expectations and potentially damaging interpersonal dynamics.

A number of government-supported programs are using variations of the *No Jerks* program, including some in my home state of Utah. In fact, while I was working on this chapter, a colleague forwarded to me a testimonial from a recent student who took this program. The former participant said:

> I wanted you to know how much I appreciated you teaching this class. I have learned so much and [gained] more confidence now [so] that when presented with another situation to date . . . I will have the criteria I need to judge whether it would be a good match or not. I am thinking about taking the course again. . . . [and] I thought it might be a good idea, when I am seriously considering marrying someone, to ask this person to read this manual and [take] some of the tests . . ..

No Jerks has been a popular staple program taught in several counties of northern Utah and receives state support from the Utah Healthy Marriages Initiative. In 2012, the program grew to include about 50 classes and 1,000 participants. Classes are regularly taught and often full. It is not difficult to recruit interested participants into this brief program, which is a common challenge in most family life education programs. The curriculum has been streamlined to 6 hours. Part-time family life educators staff the classes. A number of chaplains in the U.S. military have been trained in this program and offer it to military personnel. In addition, classes are being offered in domestic violence shelters, residential treatment facilities, Job Corps settings, and alternative high schools. One class targeted youth who were timing out of foster care.

But rigorous outcome evaluation studies of the *No Jerks* program are missing in action. None has been done on programs in Utah. Only one published study evaluated the program's immediate success at teaching the targeted concepts.[79] This study of soldiers on two Army bases who volunteered to take the program found that program participants put significantly more emphasis on getting to know the key predictors of marital success when dating a potential marriage partner compared to a similar (but not randomly assigned) comparison group of soldiers. Also, program participants were significantly more likely to say that they were more intentional in their dating strategies and less likely to adopt unrealistic or constraining beliefs (e.g., love conquers all, cohabitation increases chances for marital success, opposites attract and are good marriage partners, finding the right spouse is a matter of chance) in contrast to the comparison group. Program participants also reported that they improved knowledge and confidence in their abilities to use the relationship skills taught in the curriculum. But there are weaknesses in the design of this evaluation study, so a more hard-nosed assessment of the program's effectiveness must await a more rigorous study, especially one that targets disadvantaged youth who are at most risk for relationship formation problems.

There was one other qualitative evaluation study of the *No Jerks* program with a sample of low-income young adults (mostly women) by Wendy Manning at Bowling Green State University.[80] She and her research assistants conducted in-depth interviews with program participants 6 months after they went through the program. They reported that participants generally felt more confident and competent in setting appropriate boundaries for romantic relationships and that they had higher standards for relationships now. The participants said that they took more time to get to know potential partners before becoming physically intimate. And they also said they had better tools to break off unhealthy relationships. Finally, they said that they were still using skills learned in the program and some said that they were sharing their new relationship knowledge with others. While much more research is needed on this curriculum, I think it promises to meet a significant need to help young adults avoid the pitfalls and get smarter about healthy dating relationships that are more likely to blossom into healthy, stable marriages. The curriculum also is very appealing to young audiences; this helps to recruit and retain more participants.

Other Evidence of Effectiveness of RLE for Young Adults

Frank Fincham and his colleagues at Florida State University have been studying the effectiveness of the *Within My Reach* program integrated into a semester-long course. Funds to support this program came from an ACF grant. The 30-hour insert is referred to as *Relationship U,* and it has a bottom-line message of being intentional and smart about relationship decisions—deciding rather than sliding. In a quasi-experimental recent study, they found that, overall, students who took *Relationship U* became more mindful and intentional about decisions in their romantic relationships compared to students who did not get the curriculum.[81] While these students were not a particularly disadvantaged group, this is still an encouraging outcome.

Fincham and his colleagues also have been testing the potential effects of a one-hour, online PREP-based curriculum, called ePREP, with college students. In a set of three randomized controlled trial studies, these researchers found some intriguing and potentially important results from this brief, inexpensive intervention.[82] Those who took the ePREP curriculum showed modest improvements in various relationship outcomes, as well as reductions in physical and psychological aggression in their romantic relationships and substantial improvement in their problem-solving skills. Given the unacceptably high rates of relationship violence that have been documented in young adult romantic relationships, it is encouraging to see that a brief, online intervention may hold promise for reducing violence. In addition, there were also positive effects from ePREP on individual mental health. The researchers found effects when ePREP was taken by only one individual in the relationship and when both participated. One study found that those who were the most engaged in the curriculum—learned the material better, were more engaged in homework assignments, and mastered the communication skills taught—generally had even stronger outcomes.[83]

These studies evaluated programs that were a little more than relationship literacy education because they also tried to improve a specific relationship. But the target audience of programs like this is young adults, which is what I'm focusing on this chapter. Overall, I'm encouraged by early research that online technology can be harnessed to produce much greater outreach of relationship literacy education to techno-savvy young adults, and do so at much less cost. So I think we need to invest a lot of work in this area. And a lot of the good MRE programs out there are moving in this direction.

I hope these brief illustrations of government-supported youth and young adult RLE programs provide a better idea of what I am promoting in my policy agenda. I think the early research in this area is encouraging, but I wish we had more evidence, given how critical these first life course dosages of MRE are. Of course, even if we have great, highly effective programs, we need the means to get them to a substantial proportion of youth and young adults. Prevention scientists refer to this variously as the scaling, dissemination, or outreach problem (and I raised it briefly in Chapter 3 as a legitimate concern). I address this important topic in the next section.

How Do We Deliver RLE?

An effective educational infrastructure to deliver relationship literacy programs to youth is already in place, of course, in secondary education. Schools have enormous potential outreach and they are within the scope of governmental influence. This is the good news about RLE for youth: a good educational infrastructure to deliver it already exists. Teachers with backgrounds in the behavioral sciences, such as family and consumer sciences, psychology, sociology, or health, can deliver these curricula.

Should RLE be required in schools? Obviously, this would produce the greatest outreach. But for several reasons, I don't think this is a good idea. One reason is that a mandate is hard to get and it doesn't always stick. As I described earlier in the chapter, in Texas, administrators integrated the *p.a.p.a.* curriculum into the mandated health class in high school, but then a few years later the health class requirement was rescinded. Similarly, in 1998, the Florida legislature mandated a marriage and relationship curriculum in public high schools when they passed the Marriage Preparation and Preservation Act.[84] But it ran into implementation problems. The legislature did not allocate funding for such things as curriculum development and training, leaving educators on their own to figure out how to accomplish the unfunded mandate. Given the scope of the change—getting a new and potentially controversial curriculum out to millions of students—it's not surprising that there was resistance and foot-dragging and the mandate was never fully implemented and is no longer operational from all that I can tell. So mandates aren't a panacea. Moreover, mandated classes often gain a certain stigma among the students: "If it is required, it's probably lame." Also, if a curriculum like this is required, are there enough well-trained teachers who are enthusiastic about the course? Implementation research on RLE for youth stresses that the quality of the teacher is crucial to potential success.[85] These courses need teachers who can really connect and engage with the students and deal skillfully with a sensitive curriculum.

Rather than require RLE in schools, I'm in favor of a more back-door approach. With small amounts of public funds: build a good curriculum that students value, improve it over time, and disseminate it to other educators; provide solid professional training and continuing education opportunities in this content area for enthusiastic educators;[86] creatively market the content and importance of the program to youth and their parents. In short, take the long road to make RLE in schools a great class and build demand for it over time. Mandates may short-circuit the building of a quality program.

Moreover, mandates may not be needed to attract a large number of students to the curricula. Utah's relationship literacy curriculum is embedded in a nonrequired class that served nearly 13,000 students in 2012. RLE programs fit comfortably within the national health curriculum framework in most states. And recently the national sex education standards added healthy relationships and personal safety in dating relationships, both important topics in RLE. So the content of RLE is increasingly integrated into other standard curricula. RLE is inherently interesting and relevant to youth and can produce immediate benefits, such as better and safer dating relationships, not just more distant benefits such as a healthy, stable marriage. So I don't think mandates are needed. Having said this, I'm sensitive to the fact that the best research on the effectiveness of youth RLE suggests that it has stronger potential in schools where RLE is mandated compared to schools that just offer it, as mentioned earlier in this chapter.[87] This might be due to the fact that more at-risk students who need the curriculum are likely to be exposed to it than is the case with voluntary participation. I'm not opposed to a mandate, but if RLE is required, I think there needs to be a lot of attention to effective implementation.

Like Utah, Oklahoma has taken a more patient approach, not employing mandates. It has used federal TANF funds to train hundreds of public school educators in a scientifically based RLE program (*Connections: Relationships and Marriage* and *Connections: Dating and Emotions*) over the last decade. That effort seems to have paid off, significantly increasing the numbers of students taking the course. From 2004–2012, more than 125,000 high school students took it. Feedback from instructors and students is very positive.

One noteworthy barrier to promoting youth relationship literacy is the increased emphasis on traditional academic subjects spurred by federal legislation such as "No Child Left Behind" and "Race to the Top." This emphasis can limit the number of opportunities for students to take nontraditional subjects. I have a couple of ideas on how to deal with these barriers. One idea is to integrate RLE curricula into other mandated or widely taken courses. In Utah, a RLE course was merged with a state-mandated course on financial literacy to create a year-long course option that increased the number of students receiving RLE there. In Texas, as mentioned earlier in this chapter, state officials integrated the *p.a.p.a.* program with health classes. Another possibility, one I alluded to earlier in the chapter, is to combine RLE and sex education curricula in the schools, although I worry a little that sex will drown out relationships in such a combined curriculum. Regardless of how it is done, these kinds of initiatives can be supported within regular funding channels, for the most part, making their implementation more feasible.

Training high school educators to deliver RLE can be expensive. But some schools are holding down those costs by bringing in trained educators from community agencies that provide MRE services. I observed a talented male–female set of instructors in an Alabama high school class engage a diverse group ninth- and tenth-graders in lessons on effective communication and relationship warning signs. The female instructor was a recently retired high school health teacher with a passion for youth RLE. Using outside educators can hold down costs, reduce the burden on school teachers to learn a new curriculum, and provide them a welcomed break from being up front in the classroom.

Another barrier to promoting youth RLE in schools is that Family and Consumer Sciences, a discipline tailored to deliver it, has no leadership presence in the U.S. Department of Education, as most academic disciplines do. As a result, there is no advocate at the top of the national education bureaucracy to push an agenda and provide support for RLE. This is an action point that the federal government could address to help the states in their efforts to get RLE to more youth.

Finally, to overcome barriers to RLE in schools we can do more to help administrators see the connections between romantic relationship problems in youth and educational attainment. The research is clear that one of the biggest reasons why teens don't graduate from high school or struggle to pursue further education is that they have become adolescent parents.[88] This finding supports sex education efforts in secondary education; RLE efforts can add to this. In addition, I suspect that some of the other relationship issues common in adolescence in addition to pregnancy and parenting issues, such as dating violence and premature sexual involvement, also distract from academic performance. There is a substantial body of research on school-based efforts to enhance students' social and emotional learning that documents its effectiveness in improving students' academic performance as well as their social skills and emotional development.[89] Some might see youth RLE as a subset of social and emotional learning programs, and if it is, then we should not be surprised to see that RLE can improve students' academic performance and achievement.

While I have emphasized schools as the primary way to deliver RLE curricula to youth, that doesn't mean that other organizations can't help too. A wide spectrum of government organizations are tasked with helping youth involved in the child welfare and juvenile justice systems, and these could do a better job of integrating RLE into their services for disadvantaged youth. I recently attended a 1-day conference focused on this opportunity. Moreover, federal and state governments fund a number of positive youth development programs to strengthen those factors that help to prevent problems for youth. RLE programs would be natural companions to many of these programs. And private church youth groups, YMCAs, parenting/family resource centers, and other groups can play a valuable role.

Delivering a second dose of RLE to young adults, especially disadvantaged ones, will be more challenging. Educational infrastructure that can deliver RLE to 18- to 29-year-olds is more diffuse than it is for adolescents. Even with good curricula, finding good ways to deliver the curricula to young adults will take some creative effort. But there are a number of candidates. Social service and employment service agencies that work regularly with disadvantaged young adults potentially could be a good source for delivering RLE, although it will take some time and effort to help them see that this kind of service is appropriate to their organizations.[90] The Obama administration has spurred this kind of infrastructure development in its last round of grants to support MRE by giving preference to grantee organizations that work to integrate their services with employment and other human service agencies. Oklahoma has taken seriously the need to reach young adults with tailored programs delivered in traditional social service organizations that work regularly with at-risk youth and single parents.

I think another rich venue for reaching out to young adults is our system of community colleges, where many young adults get affordable post–high school vocational training and education. More than 6 million U.S. young adults are enrolled in more than 1,200 community colleges.[91] A small amount of public funds could be made available for modest grants to develop and test effective RLE programs in community college settings and to expand interest in such offerings.

Anecdotally, I have observed an increasing number of course offerings at U.S. colleges and universities, although they generally (but not exclusively) serve a more advantaged student population. These courses focus not just on the institutional aspects of marital and family formation but on the personal aspects of dating, cohabitation, marriage, sexual relationships, and relationship skills. Some formative evaluation research on these kinds of course offerings has been done with encouraging possibilities. For instance, as I mentioned earlier, Fincham and his graduate students have been testing the effectiveness of a PREP-based curriculum for college students that is integrated into a semester-long course. They have received some encouraging feedback from students on this curriculum.[92] Similarly, Linda Malone Colon, at Hampton University, regularly teaches a class on marriage and relationships in the African American community with an emphasis on valuable skills to help relationships succeed. The demand for the class far exceeds the number of seats available. To help more community college and university educators become familiar and comfortable with these kinds of programs, it would help to provide some minor training grants for this purpose.

No doubt creative web-based delivery of services will play a role in delivering relationship education to young adults given the omnipresence of web-based technologies in most of their lives.[93] Some early research on the potential of web-based relationship education reviewed earlier in this chapter is encouraging. Of course, at the rate that technological change is happening, the web may be too last-century to be of much help to the next generation. If our educational efforts aren't on smart phone or social networking platforms, they may struggle to reach enough of our youth and young adults. But I know that program developers are now developing interventions for these kinds of platforms. And traditional classes and new-age "relationship apps" could build on and complement each other.

While I am on the topic of technologically assisted relationship education, perhaps this is the right place to broach the topic of web-based dating services. I'm not going to get into my concerns about what they do and how they do it and whether there is a reliable science behind it. (Yes, I have some concerns and no, there is not a reliable science of relationship compatibility.) But there is no question that online dating sites are a big deal these days and I suspect they are here to stay. I just looked at the eHarmony web site and they claim that they are the starting point for 5% of all marriages in the United States these days. Millions of young adults now use dating service web sites to increase their dating success and find potential mates. So as long as so many young adults are using these sites, why not enlist them in providing research-based RLE to their users (maybe as a no-cost perk)? This would be a tremendous service. Rather than just "matching" couples, they could help dating individuals learn better the rules of the relationship development road so they have a safer and better journey and are more likely to end up where there really want to be. While this is not something I am suggesting that public policy should push, I do think these private providers could give a powerful assist by making their service more educational. They have the financial resources to do a great job.

Final Thoughts: Shortening the Road

I began this chapter by discussing the lengthy and difficult-to-navigate road from adolescence to a healthy, stable marriage. I'll conclude by questioning whether it is possible to shorten the road. Here I'm talking as much or more about cultural change efforts as I am about public policy initiatives. The road to marriage has been getting longer because youth are becoming relationally and sexually active earlier and because they are making a commitment to permanent unions later. In theory, we could shorten the road from both ends. At the earlier end, we could send stronger, more uniform messages as a culture that youth are not ready for sexual relationships and these should be postponed until a mature point in time later on. And without reservation, we could send stronger messages to youth that they should not become parents before they are more mature and in a committed, in-good-times-and-bad, two-parent relationship. This recommendation is not especially controversial, although some will say it is quixotic. Red-state conservatives, blue-state liberals, and the big mass of purple people in between can all agree that children and adults will be much better off in a society with lower rates of immature teen sex, pregnancy, and early parenting. I have argued in this chapter that we need more RLE (and better sex education) to help with this.

But it can't be all about educational policy. There needs to be a cultural-level shift activated by youth leaders, teachers, popular media, intellectual leaders, and parents to consistently reinforce this message.

What about the other end, though? Young adults are marrying later and later. The average age at first marriage now is nearly 29 for men and 27 for women. That means about a decade between high school graduation (we hope) and settling down (we hope). I think several things have fueled the longer waiting period. One has been a distorted interpretation of the research on age of marriage and divorce. As I mentioned earlier in this chapter, research consistently confirms that those who marry in their teens face a higher risk of divorce. But the risk curve flattens out quickly in the early 20s; there is not much difference in risk for those who marry at 23 compared to those who marry at 28.[94] While those who married in their later 20s have slightly lower risks of divorce than those who marry in their early 20s, those who married in their early or mid-20s report slightly higher levels of marital happiness than those who married in their late 20s.[95] Researchers aren't sure why this is the case, although it may be that it easier to weave two lives into one when marriage occurs earlier than it is when young adults have a longer history of independent living.

Regardless, young adults mature at different speeds; while many may not be ready for the commitment of marriage at 22, many are. One study finds that most young adults report that they want to be married by age 25, but that their parents think it should be a little later.[96] If young adults younger than 25 find a wonderful potential spouse and want to make the commitment, why should the collective voice of the culture gasp in horror? Probably the most representative voice of American culture is Oprah Winfrey. When popular teen singer Justin Bieber told her in an interview that he wanted to get married by age 25, she advised him to wait longer—"Rethink that, will you?"—in order to discover who he really was.[97]

Mature young adults choosing to marry in their early and mid-20s deserve our support, not our condemnation. Sociologist Mark Regnerus at the University of Texas has written about this with regards to young Christians,[98] but it deserves consideration on a larger scale. Twenty to thirty percent of young adults (ages 18–25) are married.[99] Should we shun them or help them? Young adults marrying in their early 20s can weave two pliable lives together from the foundations of adulthood rather than merge two independent lives together later on. Financial prosperity should not be a requirement for marriage the way most young adults and their parents now think it is. This notion sometimes is expressed as, "You shouldn't marry until you are economically prepared for divorce." But I think this undermines the very notion of commitment. A few years of living on a tight budget may actually be a good thing in the long run. Yes, economic stress takes a toll on marriage, but that research is talking mostly about established families with children, not newlyweds sans kids. And as Regnerus questions, why should parents and extended family members treat married young adults differently than unmarried young adults in terms of their willingness to offer some financial support? Parents reinforce the no-marriage-before-25 rule when they tell young adults that they won't pay for tuition and such if they get married in their early 20s. Abetted by many voices, young adults today have thoroughly internalized the cultural message that they should postpone marriage and enjoy their freedoms during their 20s.[100] Responsible use of that freedom is fine. But as the dreary statistics and stories show, many are not particularly responsible; looking back, freedom doesn't look so free and easy for many. If you question this last assertion, I suggest you read the book *Lost in Transition* by Christian Smith and his colleagues, who document with young adults' voices the painful and constricting harms associated with their sexual freedoms.[101] Let's reinvestigate the idea that maturity and commitment before your mid-20s is possible and even commendable.

Another thing fueling the later age of marriage has been an understandable but overhyped fear of divorce. Among richer and poorer, there is a sentiment that divorce is a big risk and the worse thing that could happen.[102] Better never to marry than ever to divorce. Admittedly, the risks are high. As I reviewed in Chapter 1, about 45% of first marriages and 60% of second marriages terminate in divorce. Obviously, you wouldn't get in a car if you faced those risks of getting in an accident. But there are two important points to make about these risks. (And I'll give more details about this in Chapter 8.) First, the risks are lower for some. Those who get a college education, make a decent income, practice a religious faith (especially practice together), and postpone children until after marriage actually have divorce rates that approach single digits.[103] Of course, the bad news is that those who don't have these factors in their favor face daunting risks well above 50% for divorce. That's one reason why government policies are experimenting with getting educational programs to these higher risk couples—to try to give them a fairer chance.

But the fixation on divorce is problematic for me. The word *divorce* isn't as meaningful as it used to be. It used to be a pretty good indicator of family instability; not so much now. Now much of family break-up occurs without the legal system involved because the unions are informal. But these are still union break-ups and many of them involve children, children who still suffer the consequences of family instability from these informal dissolutions. (Break-ups from informal unions are no picnic for adults either.[104]) Avoiding divorce doesn't shield children and adults from family break-ups because people are forming families without getting married these days, especially less educated couples. If fear of divorce meant trepidation of family instability and caution in forming unions with children in them, then that makes sense to me. But I think fear of divorce usually means just that: fear of legally marrying and then legally breaking up. Go ahead and live together, have kids together, break up, live with someone else, but for heaven's sake don't get married until you're sure it will all work out because divorce is the worst thing that can happen to you and your kids. This logic doesn't hold. A fear of divorce needs to be replaced with a fuller concern for union dissolution and family instability.

So the cultural fear of divorce is, to some extent, misplaced. What we need is a healthy desire to avoid family instability. The commitment associated with marriage provides a relationship with more power to hold itself together against contemporary relationship entropy. Of course, marriage is not omnipotent; marriages fail. But fear of divorce is not working as the answer. Hence, postponing a good match between reasonably mature individuals until their late 20s out of fear of divorce doesn't make sense to me. We can provide young adults the kind of information needed to minimize the chances of divorce and perhaps allow some to buck the cultural tide, choose to make a permanent commitment to a romantic partner, and shorten the road to their aspirations of a healthy marriage. And we can do this without setting them up for higher risk of marital failure.

These two issues—a concern for marrying too early and a fear of legal divorce—have fueled a cultural aversion to shortening the road and supporting healthy marriages for reasonably mature young adults in their early 20s. I think we should be more flexible about the right time to marry. The road doesn't have to be so long for everyone.

Conclusion

But I'm getting preachy now, so it must be time to close this chapter. Regardless of how long or short the road is between adolescence and a healthy marriage, youth and young adults still need the rules of the road that can get them safely to their destinations. I have argued in this chapter that government support for relationship literacy education for youth and young adults should be a first priority of a public policy agenda to promote healthy marriages and relationships for the sake of children. Although the quantity and quality of research evaluating the potential of these kinds of programs lags behind the need, still, I believe there are enough encouraging early results to invest further in this strategy. I have tried to show that this element of my policy agenda can be supported for the most part with existing infrastructure, personnel, and funding. Thus, it is not a pie-in-the-sky notion but a feasible path, if we will take it.

Earlier I compared RLE to driver's education in the high schools. Let me conclude by returning to that analogy. Shouldn't our commitment to creating safe and healthy relationships be as great as our efforts to create safe drivers? Yes, when young drivers don't learn and implement the skills for safe driving, the toll can be tragic in young lives. But the social carnage of poor relationship decisions by youth and young adults is no less heartbreaking and, from a policy perspective, no less damaging. It's time we make relationship literacy education for youth and young adults an educational priority.

Chapter 5

Marriage Preparation Education for Engaged Couples and Relationship Development Education for Cohabiting Parents: Improving the On-Ramps to a Healthy, Stable Marriage

Proposal 2: Provide marriage preparation education for engaged couples to prevent unwise marital choices and help them gain the knowledge and skills needed to form a healthy marriage. In addition, help cohabiting parents who aspire to marriage to assess their relationship and build their confidence for marriage with relationship development education.

If we are successful with efforts to reach a large proportion of youth and young adults with relationship literacy education (RLE), as described in Chapter 4, the next step in my proposed strategic policy agenda to help couples form and sustain healthy marriages will be easier. But even when we are successful, there are still challenges ahead that call for another dose of marriage and relationship education (MRE) when couples make a public commitment to a future together or are thinking about marriage. That is, even when young adults are "relationally literate," they will benefit from another round of MRE designed this time to assess carefully their personal readiness for marriage, the quality and prospects of a marriage to a particular partner, and to build a stronger knowledge and skills foundation for a successful marriage. They will benefit from formal marriage preparation education.

Let me continue the road trip metaphor from Chapter 4. If relationship literacy education, or RLE, for youth and young adults is learning the rules of the road, then marriage preparation education is the careful planning and preparation for a long, involved trip. Sure, it's exciting to think about the destination and even fun to think about the road trip to get there. But if people make a quick decision to go, hop in the car, and take off across country, they are at risk for trouble and breakdown that threatens their ability to get where they want to go. Or if they take off while knowing that the car's radiator is leaking and the tires are bald, their commitment to getting to their destination probably won't override the problems likely to cause a breakdown. The trip is more likely to be a smooth, safe, and enjoyable one if they do some route planning, get the car checked and tuned, and take other sensible actions before heading out. Similarly, when a couple makes a decision to join their lives together permanently, it's an exciting time but it is also a time when they need to make a careful assessment of the road they are choosing and the means they have to get to their destination. Engaging their heads as well as their hearts before they set out on the long and demanding journey that is contemporary marriage is the ticket to greater chances of success.

Of course, many couples are already forming families before making a strong commitment to the future for themselves and their children. Yet many of these couples aspire to marriage and a stable family. How do we help these couples to move forward for the benefit of their families? Cohabiting-parent couples who aspire to marriage but have not made the commitment need education to help assess their relationship and build skills that will give them the confidence to make a commitment to the future.

This chapter outlines my proposal to improve the on-ramps to marriage by promoting greater use of MRE to help couples strengthen the foundations of marriage for the benefit of the next generation (and themselves). First, I outline the problems and issues that create a need for more and better education. I divide the need into two approaches, one for engaged couples and another for cohabiting parents who aspire to marriage but have not committed to it. I call the former approach marriage preparation education, or MPE, and the latter approach relationship development education, or RDE. Then, similar to Chapter 4, I illustrate MPE and RDE with some noteworthy operational programs. As I do this, I review the research on the effectiveness of these kinds of educational interventions. Then, I address the challenge of how to deliver these educational programs to large numbers of premarital couples. I conclude the chapter with some thoughts about how to promote greater use of MPE and RDE with legislative and private efforts.

The Need for Marriage Preparation Education

More than 80% of young adults expect to have a marriage that will last a lifetime.[1] Yet demographers tells us that 40%–50% of first marriages and about 60% of second marriages will end in divorce, and the first 5 years of marriage carry the highest risk.[2] Good research finds that many marriages are preceded by doubts and begin with lower levels of satisfaction and significant problems, and that these are the marriages at most risk for decline and divorce.[3] But many of the reasons that people give for divorce are preventable issues, at least in theory, and could be addressed before marriage. A national survey in 2005 found that the number one reason for divorce given by divorced individuals was a lack of commitment (from one or both spouses).[4] Too much arguing was the number two reason given, with marrying too early, unrealistic expectations, and inequality in the relationship close behind. Good MPE addresses each of these issues. Another reason high on the list was simply ineffective preparation for marriage. Preparations for the most important journey we ever take in life could be better. The best time to prevent a divorce and save a marriage is before it starts.[5]

Of course, these days, many families form before couples commit to marriage. That's why I think the concept of premarital education applies to both formally engaged couples and cohabiting couples with children who have hopes for marriage. I'll say more about cohabiting parents later. Whether married or not, if the relationship dissolves, the lives of children already in that relationship or those likely to come soon are affected.

While the value of MPE applies to most, effective preparation may be especially important for groups of individuals who have high-risk profiles for divorce. For instance, those who have experienced the divorce of their parents have double the risk for experiencing their own divorce.[6] Second marriages are at more risk than first marriages.[7] Individuals with only a high school education or less have a higher risk.[8] Similarly, individuals who do not have a religious affiliation are more likely to divorce, and couples with differing religious affiliations or different levels of religious devotion also have higher risks. This is hardly an exhaustive list of risk factors for divorce. We know a lot about what factors put people at higher risk for divorce. Those with greater risks have a greater need to invest in effective preparation to ready themselves for greater challenges. Unfortunately, research also suggests that those with higher risk profiles are less likely, not more, to participate in MPE.[9] So we need to do a better job of getting MPE to those who need it most.

How many couples invest in formal MPE? The best estimates we have put the figure at only about 30% overall, although more recent marrying cohorts appear to be above 40% now.[10] Still, less than half are participating in MPE, and those who do may not be participating in high-quality programs. We have a lot of room for improvement when it comes to getting couples into strong MPE programs, especially those at greater risk for marital break-ups.

Why the low uptake? It's not because people generally don't think it's a good idea or are unwilling. In one nationally representative poll, more than 85% agreed that all couples considering marriage should participate in MPE before getting married and nearly half said participation should be required by law.[11] About 90% of Utah and Oklahoma adults think it is important for couples to participate in MPE.[12] A Texas survey showed that more than 75% of young adults were willing to participate.[13] Cost isn't likely an issue either. The large majority of weddings in the United States occur under religious auspices; religious institutions provide the large majority of MPE. Most of these are offered at no or low cost and any minor costs incurred probably wouldn't even register when stacked up against the bill for the wedding.

I'll discuss two important reasons that I think contribute to the low uptake of MPE. The first reason I just hinted at: giddy wedding preparations quickly overwhelm rational thoughts about marriage preparations. Rationally, preparing for a life-long marriage is more important than preparing for a one (or more)–day wedding event, but marriage preparation activities are helplessly sucked into the black hole of wedding planning in our culture. I talk to my students about this, but I worry about whether it really sinks in. Once a bride and groom and their families are caught in the gravitational pull of wedding planning, nothing escapes, including energy to invest in strengthening the foundations of the marriage. Weddings are valuable because they call for the public recognition of a couple's private commitment. But our hegemonic emphasis on the party aspects of weddings has become a big problem. *Father of the Bride* is one of my least favorite movies of all time.[14] (I'll talk a little more about the problem of wedding costs at the end of this chapter.)

What can we do to shrink this cultural tumor? I think many churches may have the right idea here. For instance, if you marry in the Catholic Church, you are required to go through their lengthy marriage preparation education program, which includes both religious education related to marriage and also principles for building strong, stable marriages that would be endorsed by most secular marriage researchers and practitioners.[15] Some other religious denominations have similar requirements, but certainly not all. I think religious organizations that offer quality MPE programs and require or strongly encourage participation before marrying in the church are doing a responsible thing. Churches should not be wedding factories, as one clerical colleague quipped to me once. They have a keen stake in the quality and longevity of the relationships they bless with formal church sanction, not just the number of wedding widgets they stamp out.

Should the state mandate MPE for marrying couples? No state has done this yet. I'll provide more of my thoughts about this later in the chapter. Here I emphasize that there is more that religious, community, educational, and social service organizations can do to encourage greater voluntary participation in MPE. Certainly inadequate supply should not be a factor that dampens demand.

But there is a second, big factor that I think dampens demand for formal MPE. In a word, it's cohabitation. While young people endorse the potential value of MPE, I suspect that in many young people's minds, formal MPE can be adequately replaced with living together before marriage. Some believe living together is an essential way to prepare effectively for a marriage. One survey found that two thirds of 18-year-olds agreed that living together before marriage was a good way to test the likely success of a marriage.[16] Cohabitation rates have increased dramatically over the last 50 years, with more than two thirds of couples now living together before first marriages.[17]

But the logic that premarital cohabitation will increase chances of a successful marriage by testing the relationship before firmly committing to marriage has struggled to find empirical support. In fact, most of the research to date suggests it has the opposite effect: if a couple cohabits before marriage, they generally run a higher risk of divorce.[18] Some of the difference in risk for divorce between those who live together before marriage and those who don't can be explained by what researchers call "selection effects," that is, by preexisting differences between those who choose to cohabit and those who don't (e.g., they are generally less religious, less educated) that also are associated with greater risk for divorce. But this seems to be only part of the story. Researchers at the University of Denver, Galena Rhoades, Scott Stanley, and Howard Markman, have found the greater risk of divorce associated with cohabitation comes mostly from couples who cohabit before getting engaged, before making a firm commitment to the long-term future of the relationship.[19] In the absence of this precohabitation commitment, they theorize that cohabitation inertia creates a situation in which some cohabiting couples slide into marriage without making a real commitment.[20] Cohabitation inertia comes from such things as sharing a residence, financial entanglements, and importantly, having a child together (usually unplanned). Thus, some cohabiting couples end up marrying who probably wouldn't if they had not been living together. Moreover, they seem to have less commitment to the marriage, having just ended up there rather than making a discrete and firm decision. (And remember that the number one reason given for a divorce is lack of commitment.) They are sliding rather than deciding. As a result, these researchers found that those who cohabit before marriage report greater likelihood of divorce, poorer marital quality, lower marital satisfaction, less commitment, and poorer communication than those who cohabited after getting engaged or those who married before moving in together.

So apparently, cohabitation isn't an effective way to prepare for marriage, although postengagement cohabitation doesn't appear to be a big risk factor and there is some evidence that if you only live together with one person whom you eventually marry, then cohabitation doesn't carry as great a risk.[21] Perhaps some couples are able to use the experience of living together to help them make better decisions about the future and to strengthen their relationship. Certainly, living together increases the possibility of gaining valuable information about your partner, yourself, and the relationship. But on average, those who are counting on living together as a way to test a relationship and prepare effectively for marriage likely will be disappointed. Perhaps marriage preparation education is not so old-fashioned after all. I think couples who are living together (the majority) as well as those who are not (the minority) can benefit from formal preparation for marriage.

What is Marriage Preparation Education?

When answering this question, I need to clarify the target of MPE and subdivide accordingly. As I mentioned earlier in this chapter, one target for MPE is formally engaged couples, usually without children, committed to a future together. Another target is cohabiting-parent couples aspiring to marriage. Some have been married before or been in other cohabiting relationships. These couples have children—his, hers, theirs, or some combination. As a group, statistically, they hope to marry but feel they are not ready for that step. There is overlap in good MPE for these different targets but there are important differences too. I'll start with formally engaged couples and then note differences for cohabiting-parent couples.[22]

MPE for Formally Engaged Couples

The overall purpose of MPE for formally engaged couples is to make sure engagement includes the brain as much as the heart and that relationship skills are up to the challenge of forever. It's not a problem if they have stars in their eyes as long as there are clear-minded thoughts in their heads, as well. Important tasks, then, include: (a) assessing one's own personal readiness and preparation for marriage; (b) evaluating the quality of the match and aligning expectations and plans; (c) improving relationship skills; and (d) understanding the institution of marriage.

Assessing personal readiness, preparation, and commitment. Assessing one's own readiness for marriage is the first step. A good marriage starts with two mature individuals who are ready for the challenges and commitment of a long journey together with all its thrills and chills. Ideally, this personal readiness assessment is done before making the commitment to marriage. But in reality, for most of us, I suspect this is a process, not just a single-point-in-time decision. Getting engaged is not the same as getting married. Engagement is a commitment to an individual to prepare for marriage, not an ironclad promise to marry. Making this commitment to prepare for marriage can be a big transition and we may learn a lot about ourselves in the process. Recent research among newlywed couples confirms that premarital doubts about getting married are common (nearly 50%) and that premarital doubts (at least for women) predict higher divorce rates (2.5 times higher) a few years down the road.[23] So Job One during the engagement period is serious introspection. Am I really ready for the commitment of marriage? What assets and liabilities do I bring? What skills and deficits do I have? What doubts do I have and what can I do about them?

Of course, the devil is in the details of such broad questions. That's why good MPE programs employ relationship questionnaires or inventories that ask literally hundreds of questions about each partner as well as the relationship. The questions are based on research such that responses to each item predict marital quality and stability down the road. The responses to these questions, then, can provide personal and couple food for thought. The relationship questionnaires don't produce some magical cut-off number above which you are guaranteed success. The science is nowhere near that level of certainty. Instead, the function of these relationship assessment questionnaires is to allow important issues to surface—issues that research shows are related to success later on—for introspection and discussion, to help individuals and couples anticipate potential challenges, gain greater confidence, and prepare more effectively for marriage. Questions deal with a wide range of things, from personal mental health (e.g., struggles with depression) to personality characteristics (e.g., introversion and extroversion) to family history (e.g., parental divorce) to personal beliefs and attitudes (e.g., religiosity, sexuality, acceptance of divorce) and more. While there are a handful of good relationship questionnaires out there used for MPE, such as PREPARE/ENRICH[24] and FOCCUS,[25] my favorite is RELATE.[26] It was developed more than 30 years ago by colleagues of mine at Brigham Young University. Since 1979, these dedicated scholar–practitioners have revised, updated, and tweaked the instrument, wrapping all their work in rigorous research on the effectiveness of RELATE as a tool to help individuals and couples learn about themselves and their relationships and to predict marital success. Some of this research documents that taking and receiving feedback from these instruments improves relationship satisfaction.[27] RELATE is the most thorough and most scientifically validated instrument available today.[28] Web-based relationship inventories now are being customized in real time to meet users' specific circumstances (e.g., relationship status, remarriages, religious affiliation), providing a more refined and relevant set of questions.

In addition, under this category of personal readiness and preparation, I think good MPE programs now need to urge individuals to assess the "sliding versus deciding" issue. I mentioned this briefly earlier in this chapter and in Chapter 4. Researchers have found that many cohabiting couples who marry slide into marriage from the inertia of living together without a firm decision point and commitment to marriage.[29] Instead of being the foot-loose-and-fancy-free relationship that many think it is, cohabitation over time often creates a kind of relationship inertia that pulls people into marriage who probably would not marry without that inertia. Couples who make the commitment to marriage (i.e., engagement) before living together do not have this same risk for divorce. I think good MPE programs need to build a "sliding versus deciding" check into their curriculum. They can't assume that engagement is a clear indication of a carefully considered decision and strong commitment to the future. If there has been a firm decision and commitment to marriage, then onward. But if an engaged couple is headed to the altar because it just seems to be the direction the current road is taking them, then they need to pull off the road and work through the decision to marry. Commitment is key to marital success. All the good relationship skills in the world may not be enough without a firm commitment to the richer-or-poorer, in-sickness-and-health, good-times-and-bad, till-death-do-us-part promise we need to make forever happen.[30] Cohabitation is not a reliable signal of commitment these days, especially for men. Individuals need to make sure they get the commitment thing worked out right before getting back on the road.

Evaluating the quality of the match and aligning expectations and plans. Relationship questionnaires are also helpful in the next major task of MPE: evaluating the quality of the match and aligning expectations and plans. It would be great if our responses to the questions would tell us clearly that we are a match made in heaven and there is nothing but celestial sailing ahead. Unfortunately, relationship questionnaires and MPE programs can only perform a more earthly function: they provide potential clues about problems that will likely emerge (or confidence that a couple has a lot going for them) and then invite couples to talk, make explicit what might remain implicit, plan, and negotiate. Some relationship assessment instruments require that you use their feedback in connection with a trained counselor to facilitate these discussions. Others, including the RELATE instrument, do not require a counselor, but provide computer-generated, detailed feedback and comparisons of partner responses with suggestions for topics to discuss.

Science has yet to solve the human mystery of why some matches are good and some are—well, not so good. The reality is that there is an infinite combination of factors that contribute to the quality of a match. But even more important than those matched characteristics are the relationship skills and values we employ to make our marriages succeed, sometimes even when it appears that two people are not well matched. There are some valuable hints, of course, about good matching. For instance, we know that even if opposites attract (which itself is a bit of a myth), similarities provide a stronger foundation for long-term love. For instance, sociologists and psychologists alike have shown that partners who share a similar set of beliefs, attitudes, and interests are more likely to have a happy marriage than those who try to integrate, live with, and work around such differences.[31] By the way, this is probably what web-based dating services are doing when they say they are creating "unique" compatibility matches for their clients. They capitalize on the simple empirical reality that people with similar beliefs, values, and interests are more likely to marry and succeed in marriage. These sites screen for problematic personality characteristics that make any relationship perilous (e.g., narcissism), toss those clients out of the pool, then match the remainder according to similarity profiles. It's not rocket science, although these sites may help by matching with larger pools of people and providing clearer information than is available in traditional dating.

So good MPE programs help couples explore and examine the quality of their match, anticipate some potential struggles, and do some preliminary work to minimize the problems. They also help couples assess whether their expectations for marriage and plans for life in general are aligned. Research confirms the commonsense notion that premarital disagreements about core values and misaligned expectations predict a greater likelihood for divorce.[32] Here again is the utility of relationship questionnaires posing questions about family plans (e.g., number of children), gender roles (e.g., egalitarian or traditional), parenting practices (e.g., authoritative or coercive or permissive), financial values (e.g., materialism), religious values (e.g., rearing children in a faith), and much more. Perhaps it is a bit obvious, but it is best that couples be clear with each other on these issues and work on aligning important differences before saying "I do." Scott Stanley at the University of Denver has one of the brightest minds in the profession about MPE. He argues that one of the reasons MPE is effective is that it stimulates formal deliberation on important issues.[33] Moreover, it provides a braking mechanism on a potential rush to the altar. Recall from Chapter 1 my summary of Andrew Cherlin's call for Americans to slow down their relationship-formation behavior. While he may have been referring more to cohabitation decisions than marriage decisions, still, MPE is one concrete way we get romantically involved couples to slow down.

And good MPE programs facilitate better disclosure. You might be surprised at what people choose not to disclose to their future spouse. I have taught a few formal MPE programs in my time and teach relevant principles in some of my university courses. I once learned after the fact that a bride-to-be who had taken my class had been too scared to tell her fiancé that she was $80,000 in debt. One day early in the marriage he was opening up the mail before she returned from work and discovered her debt, which was now his debt in their community property state. It helped that her debt was from expensive, uninsured medical procedures (rather than, say, excessive consumer spending); they survived this discovery after some difficult days. But you can easily imagine a different scenario when the connubial infrastructure of trust takes such an early hit. I've talked about this issue with students in my classes and they have volunteered their own nondisclosure anecdotes with friends and family members: a man who didn't disclose a previous marriage and children from that marriage; a woman who didn't disclose a medical problem that would make bearing children unlikely. In three states, Arizona, Arkansas, and Louisiana, couples can choose to marry under a "covenant marriage" statute that requires an oath before the county clerk (who issues the marriage license) that you have disclosed to your partner everything that could reasonably affect the decision to marry. I've heard enough nondisclosure horror stories that this sounds increasingly like a good idea to me. In some states such a nondisclosure would be considered fraud, and therefore grounds for annulment—but how much better to disclose the information before marriage and perhaps save the relationship from a fatal breach of trust.

A final thought on this topic comes from the fact that some people make a decision to marry but are not particularly confident that it is the right decision for them, and that individuals who are less confident of their decision have lower martial quality a few years down the road.[34] So MPE can provide a more formal assessment of that decision and a chance to back out or do more work to strengthen the relationship and provide more confidence for going forward.

Improving relationship skills. Good MPE programs don't just provide the means to assess personal and relationship issues. Importantly, they also try to provide the relationship skills that will facilitate the forever that couples want. MPE practitioners tell me that many engaged couples have poor communication skills. They don't know how to talk together calmly and solve problems effectively. They are committed to marriage despite the fights and the drama of their relationships. They realize that they need some better skills. Almost all MPE programs put a lot of emphasis on effective communication and problem-solving skills, including the use of positive communication techniques (e.g., careful listening, affirmation, appropriate humor, soft start-ups of complaints) and the avoidance of negative communication practices (e.g., criticism, contempt, defensiveness, stonewalling, escalation, physical and emotional aggression).[35] Relevant to the emphasis on teaching communication skills in MPE, I reviewed all the evaluation research on MPE programs in a formal meta-analytic study with a former doctoral student, Elizabeth Fawcett, and some other colleagues. We found, contrary to what the field thought, that MPE programs don't actually improve relationship satisfaction for premarital couples, probably because they already are bumping their heads on the ceiling of the scales used to measure satisfaction and don't have any room to grow. But we found that these programs lead to significant improvements in communication skills for premarital couples.[36] No ceiling effect here; even with stars in their eyes there appears to be plenty of room for improvement when it comes to communication skills.

Another set of relationship skills that are included in good MPE programs might seem more like values, but they can be learned and increased. For instance, asking for and giving forgiveness are two of the most valuable "skills" that spouses can improve to build a strong foundation for their marriage.[37] Fairness and equity are central to good marriages today; techniques for facilitating them can be learned. We often overlook simple things, such as expressions of appreciation, that go a long way to building and maintaining a healthy, stable marriage. Appreciation is a learned behavior, too.[38] Marriage is the most ethical thing we ever do and we can't assume that we come to it primed to be our most ethical selves. Good MPE gives its learners some practical ways to be their most ethical selves as they make the commitment to forever.

When MPE does these three things well—help individuals assess personal readiness and preparation, examine more clearly the quality of the match and the relationship and align expectations, and improve important relationship skills, then couples are more likely to find marital success. I'll review later in the chapter various studies suggesting that MPE does improve relationship skills and strengthen marriages in the early years of marriage.

By the way, a positive outcome of MPE is not always a stronger relationship—sometimes it provides enough information to some couples that they see their prospects for marital success are not very high. Whether it be personal readiness issues, worries about personality clashes, facing up to important dissimilarities, inadequate communication and problem-solving skills (including violence), or something else, some couples call off the wedding as a result of going through a formal MPE program. Some research suggests that perhaps 10%–15% of couples end the engagement as a result of participation in a MPE program (and this figure likely is higher for couples who take a course in plenty of time before the wedding).[39] Terminating the relationship before it creates a marriage that is probably headed for divorce should be viewed as a successful outcome of good MPE, especially if it leads to changes and better prospects for marriage down the road. And as the research finding just mentioned implies, MPE will work best when it isn't a rushed process shortly before the wedding. Ideally, MPE is taken early in the engagement period with adequate time to work on some issues or time to call off the wedding if marriage looks to be a perilous course.

Before moving on, a word about preparing for a second marriage is in order. In about one third of marriages in the United States today, one or both spouses were previously married.[40] Remarried couples are at greater risk for divorce—about 60% break up—and they break up faster than first marriages.[41] To me, this suggests an even greater need for marriage preparation, but there is no evidence that couples entering a remarriage seek out help at a greater rate. Research on this question is limited, but one study suggests that about one in three remarrying couples participate in formal marriage preparation and about one in six couples seek professional counseling (and there is probably overlap between these two groups).[42] This study found some evidence that participation in formal marriage preparation education was associated with higher relationship quality a few years down the road. Informal preparation, such as reading a book, was more common. Like never-married couples, many remarrying couples may see living together before marriage as the best way to prepare for remarriage.[43] It may help to provide programs designed specifically for couples in this circumstance. Remarriages face a set of additional issues that make building a strong marriage harder. So preparation for remarriage needs to supplement the regular curriculum with discussion of issues such as managing relationships with ex-spouses, financial responsibilities to previous children, stepparenting roles, and more.[44] I think the field needs to give a lot more attention to these kinds of programs.

Understanding the institution of marriage. Engaged couples need to assess their own personal preparation, evaluate the quality of the match, and work to improve their relationship skills. All of these are related to the fact that couples are intending to make a lifelong commitment to each other. But they make another commitment, as well, to the institution of marriage. Couples are not only marrying each other; they are joining a significant institution. And I think that many do not fully comprehend what this means. So I think MPE should include a discussion of the institutional aspects of marriage as well as the relational aspects.

The MRE field generally does not make much of a distinction between relationship education and marriage education. The field uses the conjunctive term "marriage *and* relationship education," usually to clarify that programs can target education for those already married as well as those in unmarried romantic relationships (who may or may not be thinking about marriage). The "R" part of MRE also encompasses educational programs targeted to youth and young adults who may not be in a serious romantic relationship but are interested in learning what it takes to have a healthy relationship and a good marriage.

But I think there is an additional meaning in this conjunctive term that is relevant to best practices for marriage preparation education. Often we use the terms *marriage* and *relationship* as if they were synonyms. The term *relationship* most precisely refers to the quality of the interactions between romantic partners and how they feel about their union. The term *marriage* encompasses a broader set of issues that come along when two people get married. Marriage is an institution. It comes with a set of external (and usually internal) expectations, norms, and rules, even if we are not fully aware of them. Also, marriage comes with baggage, for lack of a better word. For instance, children come along with most marriages and are a crucial part of the marital system. Spouses might have disagreements over child rearing that affect the quality of their relationship, but even when they can't resolve those relational disagreements they are still connected to their children and their children have a stake in the marriage. Similarly, money issues are more significant as married people comingle funds and make long-term financial plans. Again, fights over finances can sour relationships[45]—that's the relational part.

But regardless of how money affects the relationship, money still connects spouses to each other in nonrelational ways. Religious beliefs often are intricately intertwined with formal marriage; many spouses believe their relationship takes on a sacred quality and that God is a part of their marital system.[46] We know that shared religious beliefs and practices are associated with happier marriages,[47] the relational part. But there is an institutional aspect, as well. Religious people may believe that they should stay in the marriage, which is bigger than just their happiness in the relationship, because God wants them to overcome the problems or because divorce is a spiritual failure.

There are a lot of other things that come with a marriage; it's not simply about the relationship. We know this intuitively when we aren't very happy with our spouse about something but also sense that our problems don't define our marriage; they are just a part of it. So even when spouses are unhappy in their relationships, a marriage still exists, and people often stay together in unhappy relationships, usually hoping that eventually the relationship will improve. Marriage scholar Scott Stanley refers to this as *constraint commitment*.[48]

I draw this distinction between the terms *marriage* and *relationship* to make a point about the content of MPE programs. Yes, there is a lot of focus on evaluating the match and skills to improve the quality of our interactions, the way we communicate and solve problems, and the way we treat each other, each of which builds a stronger foundation for a happy relationship. But I think MPE also should include content that deals more directly with the institutional side of marriage. For instance, many programs talk a lot about the need for commitment to sustain a marriage, not just because commitment itself improves relationships, which it does, but because it is one of those rules of marriage.[49] We are committed and we can expect our spouse to be committed. We don't bail out easily. Infidelity is a big issue in marriages these days[50] and MPE programs would do well to talk about the rule of marital fidelity. As long as we are married we are sexually faithful to each other, no ifs, ands, or buts. It's a legitimate expectation that everyone must agree to. Even those outside of the marital relationship are supposed to support that rule and we look down on those who do not. There are norms or rules about time together and prioritizing our spouse over other interests. Spouses make sacrifices for each other. These and many other rules exist when we get our membership cards in the institution of marriage. Couples should be clear about this as they are preparing for marriage.

Illustrating MPE for engaged couples: The Parenting Center's Empowering Families Program (Fort Worth). The Parenting Center in Fort Worth, Texas, grew out of a vision in the 1970s to reduce child abuse and today provides wide-ranging parenting and family services to area residents. (Historically, Fort Worth has seen some of the highest rates of child abuse in Texas.) The Parenting Center recently added to its menu of services the *Empowering Families* program, which offers free 8-hour marriage and relationship workshops, case management services, and job/career advancement services. A bright and passionate family life educator, Jennifer Acker, oversees the program. The program expenses are supported by a federal grant. Without the grant, these new services would not be possible, according to Acker.

Potential participants are referred to the *Empowering Families* program by various social service agencies and through various creative marketing strategies. In addition, county clerks are a referral source. When couples getting a marriage license learn that they can get a significant discount ($60 state fee is waived, but $12 county fee is not) on their license by taking a free MPE workshop, many will call and attend a class quickly before they get married.[51] Lower income couples make up the bulk of the participants in the workshops. Program administrators work hard to eliminate potential barriers to participation by offering such things as gas cards, bus passes, and free childcare for the workshop. (Spanish-language classes for Hispanic families do not work without free childcare.) Classes are run regularly, including a popular Sunday workshop option, and are well attended. The different variations of the *Empowering Families* program served more than 750 individuals in 2012.

The program screens individuals as they sign up for the program to determine which workshop would be best for them, asking about such things as relationship status, relationship length, and experience with domestic violence. If there is an indication of domestic violence, then a domestic violence counselor is consulted. If the individual or couple attends the workshop, often a domestic violence counselor will attend to observe the couple and provide the educators with an assessment and guidance. Forty percent of their high-risk participants disclose some kind and level of relationship violence. Some are also homeless.

Engaged couples receive the Family Wellness curriculum (*MAP for Marriage*, either in Spanish or English). If couples have been cohabiting for a long time, then they are funneled into a program that uses the PREP-based

Within Our Reach program. The *MAP for Marriage* curriculum has six core sessions that include content on such things as communications skills, problem solving, teamwork, and sexual intimacy. It also stresses knowing personal values and goals as well as couple goals. In addition, the curriculum includes lessons about money management, specific stepfamily challenges, parent and in-law issues, coparenting, and the transition to parenthood. Unlike MPE programs for more advantaged couples, premarital does not necessarily mean preparental. That is, a significant proportion of lower income engaged couples already have children together or are creating a stepfamily. About 40% of the couples in the *Empowering Families* program taking the *MAP for Marriage* curriculum are parents. (Some married couples also get interested in the program and attend along with engaged couples. And some just-dating couples also attend. Even some single individuals participate.) Couples are encouraged to participate in periodic booster class sessions to promote continued commitment to marriage enrichment, but participation in the booster sessions is very low.

I had the opportunity to sit in on one of the Saturday 8-hour *MAP for Marriage* workshops in Fort Worth. The first thing I noticed was how diverse the group was. Nearly half were African American; a significant number of Hispanic individuals were there. There were many engaged couples, most getting married in a few weeks. A few participants were married but attending alone. A good number of single individuals were there too. One was currently homeless. Most were already parents. Some had been married before. It was not a group that looked like they had spent a lot of time in a college classroom, where this workshop was held. But the participants stayed engaged for most of the day and most interacted freely. The instructors were an African American middle-aged woman and a White male who was a counselor and pastor. They were down-to-earth, real, open, and entertaining. The emphasis was on active learning, although there was some lecturing. I could sit back and critique some elements of the class and curriculum. I wonder about information overload that comes with 8 hours of instruction in one setting, but given the population they were serving, getting participants to a series of weekly classes would be logistically challenging and expensive. Overall, I was impressed. The day before this workshop I met a gregarious, working-class couple that had taken the class recently and really enjoyed it. They married and then soon enrolled in a monthly marriage enrichment group sponsored by the Parenting Center because they wanted the help to keep working on their relationship. Each had been married three times before and swore it wouldn't happen again. They also were taking advantage of an 11-week parenting education class offered by the Parenting Center. And they were actively recruiting friends and coworkers to attend these classes.

The program has not yet been rigorously evaluated, although program administrators are collecting feedback data in the field and more than 70% of participants report a positive experience and say that their relationship skills improved as a result of taking the class. There have been a handful of field evaluations of programs making use of the *Family Wellness* curricula employed by the Fort Worth Parenting Center, although these have not been rigorous, randomized controlled studies.[52] These studies have focused on lower income and minority families. And these participants generally report at the end of the program significant growth and positive effects on couple relationships, communication skills, and parenting practices as a result of their participation in the program.

General effectiveness of MPE for engaged couples. In addition to individual studies of specific MPE programs, there are some studies that have examined whether MPE for engaged couples is, in general, effective. I mentioned earlier in this chapter my study with a former graduate student, Liz Fawcett. We identified nearly 50 studies of MPE programs for engaged couples and then synthesized the findings of those studies in a meta-analysis.[53] What we found was that MPE programs have a strong effect on increasing communication skills, which are especially apparent when researchers use more sensitive (and expensive) observational measures rather than participants' self-reports to detect these effects.[54] As for increasing relationship quality, at first it looks like MPE programs are effective, but on closer inspection, we found that there was a "publication bias" here. That is, if you only look at published studies, then MPE programs look like they increase relationship quality. But quite a few studies of MPE programs have never been published.[55] And when you include them in a review of MPE programs, the effects diminish to the point that they do not show reliable change. Of course, as mentioned earlier, the reality is that engaged couples usually already are very happy, so there isn't much room to improve.

Some researchers have studied married and unmarried individuals and then asked about their involvement in MPE in the past. A study by Stanley and his colleagues that surveyed a large number of individuals in several Midwestern states found that those who had invested in some kind of MPE had somewhat higher marital satisfaction, even when controlling for some known demographic differences between those who do and do not attend MPE.[56] They found a positive effect on divorce rates too, but this seemed to be limited to better educated couples. Also, stronger effects were associated with MPE of at least 10 hours (but much longer than that did not yield even stronger benefits). But many who reported participation in MPE said their class was only a couple of hours.

In addition, Steve Nock and his colleagues followed a group of marrying couples in Louisiana for several years and found that those who took a formal MPE class were less likely to divorce in the early years of marriage than those who did not (even when controlling for religious and other differences between these two groups).[57] Moreover, these researchers found that those couples at greater risk for divorce (i.e., less educated, less religious) gained the most from MPE, which is different than what Stanley and his colleagues found in the study just described.

But there are two caveats about this synthesis of research on the general effectiveness of MPE programs. First, only a few studies have followed these couples for more than 6 months after the program, so we can't be confident that these effects last. But one classic study by Howard Markman and his colleagues has provided some direct evidence of long-term effects.[58] In that study, researchers followed couples, randomly assigned to participate in a formal MPE program or to a control group, over 5 years. They found that these couples had higher levels of positive communication and lower levels of negative communication patterns compared to control-group couples who did not participate in a formal MPE program. But not all studies have found a positive effect. Another group of researchers followed a large group of newlywed couples for 4 years and found that their reports of attending some kind of MPE were not associated with relationship satisfaction or stability.[59] It's likely that these couples did not experience at high rates the high-quality MPE that the couples in Markman's study did.

Another concern with this body of research is that they studied mostly well-educated, White couples. These are not the couples at most risk for marital problems and divorce. However, in some research I did recently with a graduate student, Kaylene Fellows, we looked at some basic field outcome data (comparing pre-test and post-test program outcomes, no control group) of government-supported programs that served more than 5,000 mostly lower income and less educated individuals.[60] Looking at just the handful of MPE programs that targeted engaged couples in this analysis, we found a small but significant, positive effect of the programs on participants. Admittedly, we need more rigorous studies of MPE with low-income couples that follow them for several years to gain more confidence in the potential of these programs for those who need them most.

Relationship Development Education for Cohabiting-Parent Couples

As I mentioned earlier in this chapter, many couples are living together with aspirations for marriage, and often with children, but are not formally committed to the future together. Many couples, especially lower income and less educated couples, are living together because they have produced a baby and they want to try to give their child a stable family in which to grow up.[61] Most of these parents, both men and women, express hopes for marrying some day (especially men), but it is more of an aspiration than a plan. Thus cohabitation for them is a way of trying to provide a young child with a two-parent family while the parents figure out the future of their relationship.[62] Figuring out that future involves a complex set of variables and answering a challenging set of questions: Can the father provide adequately for my child and me or will he struggle to hold a job? Is my partner responsible and mature? Will he be a good father? Is he sufficiently disconnected from the street life, from drugs and alcohol? Will she respect me as a man? Is she mentally stable? Will he treat me right and not abuse me? Is my partner going to be sexually faithful to me? Can I really trust him or her? Will his obligations to children from previous relationships undermine his responsibility to our children? Will we lose some public assistance benefits if we marry? Are we financially stable and able to afford a respectable wedding? These are the kinds of questions that many cohabiting couples are trying to figure out.

Clearly, these are not simple questions with straightforward answers. These couples are trying to figure out whether they can make a future work; they have not committed to a future like most couples who are formally engaged. They are in a relationship. But what holds the relationship together varies. For some, there is clear affection and optimism about marriage when the time is right, despite some challenges. For others, the relationship is held together more by the baby they made and a hope to provide a stable home for that child than any deep love and history they share. Either way, they are hoping the relationship can prove itself worthy of the long-term commitment of marriage.

Nevertheless, the odds are against them. Researchers have found that fewer than half of these couples are still together after 5 years (compared to 75% of married couples),[63] which is why researchers have referred to these couples as "fragile families."[64] Many have moved on, had children with another partner, and are going through the same relationship calculus as before. This is the relationship churning that Cherlin identified and I summarized in Chapter 1. Nevertheless, the research also shows that a large majority of these couples wants to make a relationship work and aspires to marriage, especially around the time that their child is born. While there may be no "magic moment" to intervene, this early period around the birth of their child is certainly a potential window to respond to their hopes and dreams for the future of their family. These couples are struggling to get onto the highway on-ramp that will take them to their desired destination of a healthy marriage and a stable family.

In many respects, these cohabiting-parent couples would benefit from the standard fare of MPE that formally engaged couples receive. They would benefit from a more thorough introspection of their personal readiness and preparation for marriage[65] and a careful analysis of the quality of the match. Improved relationship skills might be just what they need to gain confidence in the future prospects of the relationship. And a better understanding of the institution of marriage will be helpful, especially if they have had little exposure to examples of good marriages.[66] But because there is not a full commitment to the future, a curriculum for informally engaged couples must be oriented in a different way. The curriculum needs to be tailored and adjusted to accommodate the important relationship reality that an aspiration is different from a commitment. Also, the core importance of commitment for healthy, stable relationships shouldn't be overlooked for formally engaged couples, but this topic probably needs even more time and energy in MPE for informally engaged couples.

Clearly there are some significant differences in premarital education for cohabiting-parent couples. Frankly, I wonder even if *marriage preparation education* is the best term to employ here. Yes, there is overlap between programs for formally engaged couples who have committed both privately and publicly to a future together and programs for couples aspiring to marriage but unsure and uncommitted to that course. But the differences are important conceptually and practically. I wonder if even calling this kind of program for informally engaged couples "marriage preparation education" would be a turn-off for those couples. They might assume that the program isn't quite for them because they aren't sure about their future together. I think we need a different name for MPE targeted to cohabiting-parent couples. One possibility is relationship prognosis education. But that seems unappealing even if descriptive. Instead, I recommend calling this kind of educational program *relationship development education* (RDE) to emphasize the positive need for relationship growth.

There are some important issues that need more attention in RDE. First, this group of couples is much more likely to be economically disadvantaged and stressed. Some scholars have argued—and I agree—that this high level of stress faced by lower income couples makes forming and sustaining healthy relationships more difficult.[67] As a result, a basic skill to teach in RDE for this group of couples is stress management, learning to separate life stress from relationship stress, and basic mental health hygiene. Basic financial management skills likely would add value to RDE for this group. Moreover, MPE programs that are integrated with or linked to other human services (e.g., employment, childcare, family planning, mental and physical health, substance abuse) make sense for this population. A holistic approach to the stressful lives these couples face suggests that couple relationships will improve when other stresses are diminished and that improvements in relationship quality will lessen the need for other services.

In addition, one of the most common and biggest stresses in these couples' lives is children, resident and nonresident. Included in the complex lives of many of these couples are children from previous romantic unions. Some of these children are in the current household (often the woman's children) and some are in other households (often the man's children) but nonetheless have claim on nonresidential parental resources (e.g., child support, childcare, spending time together). Moreover, connections to past children mean ongoing connections with past partners, potentially bringing up issues of conflict, trust, and fidelity.[68] Thus, there is a need to supplement the RDE curriculum with a number of topics, such as dealing with past partners, establishing basic trust, infant care, parenting skills, and stepparenting challenges.

Relationship aggression and violence is found up and down the socioeconomic spectrum, but unfortunately, it is especially prevalent among lower income cohabiting parents.[69] So RDE needs to place even greater emphasis on resolving problems without violence, managing anger, de-escalating conflict, and preserving safety.

Relationship break-ups as a result of RDE likely will be higher for cohabiting parents than it is for formally engaged couples. But again, if these break-ups end unhealthy relationships with doubtful long-term prospects and increase the odds that future relationships will be built on more solid ground, then I think we have to view these break-ups as a sign of program success. It's hard for me to assert that because I don't want to subject children in these unions to further family instability. But stability can't be viewed as the only outcome that matters. A poor-quality couple relationship is detrimental to children's well-being, too. So we need curricula that sensitively and skillfully address healthy break-ups.

Illustrating RDE for cohabiting-parent couples: The Oklahoma City Family Expectations program. Over the last decade, there has been a large increase in the number of programs targeted to lower income, less educated, cohabiting parents. This activity was spurred by federal policy makers' support of these kinds of programs with the hope of helping to strengthen these fragile-family couples in order to improve children's well-being. So there is no shortage of programs that I could use to illustrate this kind of work. But I think one stands out as one of the most comprehensive and the most rigorously evaluated effort: the *Family Expectations* (FE) program in Oklahoma City. So I'll focus a good deal of my attention on that program. In addition, FE was just one of eight sites across the United States providing RDE to fragile-family couples who were involved in a large, multisite, rigorous evaluation study funded by the federal government. Because the results for the Oklahoma City site were more positive than for the other sites, I need to highlight the differences between the Oklahoma City FE program and the programs at other sites to try to account for the differences.

Family Expectations is a RDE program developed specifically for lower income, unmarried couples having a baby together. In the first few years of the program, FE was one of eight sites across the United States to be involved in a large, rigorous study funded by the Administration for Children and Families (ACF, U.S. Department of Health and Human Services) examining the potential effectiveness of these kinds of programs for fragile-family couples and their children. About 1,000 couples volunteered to participate in the FE program in Oklahoma City. About 500 couples were randomly assigned to receive the FE program intervention; the remaining 500 or so did not get the program but participated in the study as the comparison or control group. Although the ACF-funded rigorous evaluation study of FE ended several years ago, the program continues and it serves about 1,000 couples a year.

There are three main components to the FE program model. The first, obvious component is a relatively intensive education curriculum. Couples meet for about 3 hours once a week for 11 weeks for a total of 33 hours of face-time instruction and training. Some couples only attended one or two sessions and a few couples signed up for the program yet never attended a session, but on average, couples received about 20 hours of instruction. For couples who attended at least one session, they averaged about 26 hours of instruction. Considering that most MRE programs for more advantaged individuals are only about 12 hours, FE couples were getting about twice the dosage that couples in typical MRE programs get. And given the stressful, busy, and sometimes chaotic daily lives they lead, these couples' commitment to the program was impressive. In recent years, the FE program has improved their retention efforts so that about 75% of couples that enroll in the program receive a full dosage of 33 hours. This may be an unprecedented high mark of retention in programs serving lower income individuals.

I attended one of these classes a few years ago. Classes were located in a building that has been intentionally designed to be appealing to men, something unusual for human service delivery facilities. (For instance, there were pictures on the walls of famous male sports figures.) Before the formal instruction time begins, couples arrive an hour early to eat a modest a-la-carte dinner together provided by the program and to relax and chat with other couples in the program. Free childcare is provided in an adjoining room. The brightly colored instructional room is filled with reclining love seats for each couple, arranged in semi-circles open to the front of the room, where a male–female team of trained instructors presents ideas, leads discussions, and supervises couple practice of learned skills. When 11 curriculum sessions end, it's not the end of the program. FE holds periodic reunions or booster sessions over the next year to reinforce what participants have learned (although these are not well-attended). The program is offered to couples at no cost. (Substantial government funding underwrites the costs.) FE is managed by Public Strategies, Inc., a public relations firm in the area that also manages the wider Oklahoma Marriage Initiative that I described in Chapter 2.

The FE curriculum is an adapted version of the *Becoming Parents* program developed by Pam Jordan at the University of Washington.[70] She in turn drew heavily from the PREP curriculum developed by Howard Markman and his colleagues at the University of Denver. The PREP curriculum focuses on effective communication and problem-solving skills, but also emphasizes relationship-maintenance issues such as friendship and fun. It also places a strong emphasis on commitment as a fundamental pillar of healthy, stable relationships. In addition to these basics, the FE program also includes modules on such topics as trust, fidelity, safety (managing anger, avoiding violence), forgiveness, and finances. Also, several sessions touch on infant care and parenting basics. There is attention to self-care, as well, such as building a social support network and living a healthy lifestyle to prevent depression, which is a large risk for new mothers. Moreover, the curriculum includes some important topics such as coparenting with former sexual partners and meeting responsibilities to previous children. There is explicit attention to the issue of marriage, its potential benefits, and whether it is the right thing and right time for the couple. Each of these topics provides ample opportunity to practice communication and problem-solving skills learned during the course of the program.

A valuable second component of the FE program model is that each couple receiving the program is assigned a family support coordinator whose job it is to meet regularly with couples (often before instructional sessions), reinforce program principles, and help solve logistical problems that might prevent their full involvement in the program (e.g., transportation, childcare, rescheduling missed sessions). In addition, they try to assess other problems that may be adding stress to the couples' lives, such as employment or housing difficulties, and then connect them to human service agencies and organizations that can assist them with these challenges. This is the third component of the FE program model, and over the years these coordinators have become more involved in helping these couples. They have also been well trained. For instance, all these coordinators recently were trained and certified as family mediators. Of course, they add a significant expense to the program too.

As you can see, FE is a comprehensive, well-designed program. It covers all the important areas of MPE I addressed earlier in the chapter, and then some. Of course, it was expensive to develop and run—about $11,000 per couple—but costs are coming down substantially as the program recoups some early development costs and finds efficient ways to administer the program. And if we can save $100,000 for every family break-up prevented, as the research I cited back in Chapter 2 suggests,[71] then we are getting a substantial return on our investment. Although the federally funded study of the FE program has ended, FE continues to receive state and federal support and to operate today.

But how effective has the FE program been? Historically, these kinds of social service programs for lower income individuals have struggled early on to show that they make a significant difference. For instance, a large amount of government funding has been allocated over many years to reduce problems such as teen pregnancy, drug abuse, and unemployment. Typically they have struggled to document significant impacts.[72] How has FE fared in early evaluations? When the effectiveness of the program was assessed at about a year after the end of the program, the results showed a consistent pattern of small but statistically significant differences between couples who participated in the Oklahoma City FE program and those control-group couples who did not.[73] More specifically, FE couples were more likely to still be together and romantically involved than control-group couples (82% vs. 76%), although there were no differences in rates of couples who married over this time. FE couples also reported slightly more positive attitudes about marriage than control-group couples and had slightly higher scores on relationship happiness and support. They also reported more use of constructive conflict behavior and more avoidance of destructive conflict behavior than control-group couples. FE couples also were less likely to report experiencing infidelity. There were no group differences on reports of intimate partner violence (both were low). There were some small but noteworthy effects on parenting outcomes. FE fathers were more likely to be living with their children (71% vs. 66%) and more likely to be providing financial support (80% vs. 72%) than control-group fathers. FE parents reported slightly higher scores on a measure of cooperative coparenting than control-group parents. There were no differences found between the FE group and control group on mothers' and fathers' self-reports of parenting behavior. One of the largest (but still modest) effects of the program was on mothers' reports of depression; FE mothers scored significantly lower on a measure of depression than control-group mothers. Also, FE couples reported less use of public assistance programs, such as TANF or SNAP (food stamps), compared to control-group couples (49% vs. 54%), even though the two groups were roughly equivalent in terms of family income.

One of the most interesting findings was that these positive effects generally were even stronger for African American couples who participated in FE compared to African American control-group couples, although it is not clear why this was so. For instance, compared to African American control-group couples, higher proportions of African American FE couples were married (16% vs. 11%) or still living together (51% vs. 36%). Similarly, there was evidence that the least-educated couples benefited more from the FE program than couples with more education. Given that African American and less educated couples are less likely to marry and more likely to divorce if they do marry, this pattern of stronger effects for at-risk groups is encouraging.

But the rigorous study of the FE program did not stop there. It followed them for 2 more years to see if positive effects were maintained. This second follow-up assessment proved somewhat disappointing. The general pattern of small but positive differences between FE and control-group couples disappeared at this 3-year follow-up.[74] But there was one very important exception: FE couples were more likely still to be together compared to control-group couples. That is, even though there were no significant differences in couple relationship quality and other outcomes between the groups, 49% of FE couples were still together compared to 41% of control-group couples. While that eight-percentage-point difference may not seem like much, it means that about 20% more FE couples (or about 80 couples during the study) were together than control-group couples, and this could mean significant savings to taxpayers given that family dissolution often results in higher levels of poverty and greater use of public assistance programs. Another way to look at this finding is that for every 12.5 couples served in the FE program, one is continuously together for the first 3 years of the child's life that would not have been without the program. (The typical class size is 12–14 couples, so for every class, there is one couple together 3 years later that otherwise would not be.) So FE couples stay together at higher rates even though they don't report any greater relationship happiness or better communication skills. Perhaps they have taken to heart the importance of commitment and sticking together through difficult times for the sake of their family. Commitment messages are strong in the FE curriculum. (Note that FE couples report equally low rates of intimate partner violence compared to control-group couples.)

So is the glass half empty or half full with this study of FE? On the half-empty side, it is disappointing to see that a well-developed program that was well attended was not able to maintain many of the positive effects over time. But on the half-full side, recall that African American couples, the least educated couples, and those with lower relationship quality at the beginning of the program seemed to benefit the most from FE, at least at first. These are the couples at most risk for family break-ups. If FE can improve to be able to maintain these effects, this will be a substantial benefit. Also remember that the one difference that remained—FE couples were more likely to still be together at about 3 years—may be the most significant one for policy considerations. Remember too that FE is a first-wave program. This was a pilot test. FE program developers are learning and improving the program, so it may produce better results over time.

Another technical but important thing to keep in mind is that the effectiveness of the program was evaluated with the most rigorous design (randomized controlled trial, or RCT, in which couples who volunteered for the program were randomly assigned to intervention or control groups) and with the toughest analytical approach: intent-to-treat, or ITT, analyses. ITT analyses compare all couples assigned to the intervention group—regardless of whether they ever participated in the program or how much they participated—to all couples assigned to the control group, whether they received some kind of MRE on their own or not (only a few control-group couples sought out RDE on their own).[75]

So I'm not discouraged by these results. I think the results show some important potential for FE. With further improvements, the program may show improved longer term results. But policy makers shouldn't sneeze at the finding of more couples staying together. There are real potential savings from that difference.

My discussion of the FE program and evaluation study has already been lengthy, but I need to put these findings in context. Remember that the FE program in Oklahoma City was just one of eight sites that was running an

RDE program for fragile-family couples.[76] Researchers found no pattern of significant, positive differences between intervention-group couples and control-group couples in the other seven sites at either follow-up assessment.[77] All together, the eight sites constituted what is called the Building Strong Families (BSF) study. The no-differences finding in these other seven sites is disappointing; the glass looks more than half empty now. But there may be some glass-half-full issues to take into account. For one thing, some (yet-to-be-published) follow-up analyses by Paul Amato at Penn State found a general pattern of positive benefits at 1 year after the program for the most disadvantaged participants, including less destructive conflict and less couple violence.[78] And he found this positive pattern for all BSF sites except Baltimore.[79] Also, recall that researchers found a pattern of positive results for African American couples that was seen in the Oklahoma City program, at least at first. The program increased constructive conflict management and decreased destructive conflict behaviors. African American couples in the BSF study were more likely to be faithful to each other and less likely to experience abuse. These couples also were more cooperative coparents. Unfortunately, these effects for African American families did not hold up. At the 3-year follow-up assessment, the effects had faded and there were no significant racial differences in the effects of the BSF curricula.[80] But in light of other research findings that African Americans seem to benefit more than others from MRE,[81] I think these BSF findings are noteworthy.

Also, a valuable finding at the 3-year follow-up assessment was that children of parents in the BSF intervention groups had slightly higher scores on measures of social and emotional development. This is likely due to the positive parenting education and childcare instruction that parents in the BSF intervention groups received. Because so few studies actually assess the effects of MRE programs on children's well-being, which is the ultimate endpoint of these interventions from a policy perspective, this is an important finding. In addition, there were a few differences at the 3-year follow-up assessment of all the BSF sites that showed some small, counterintuitive differences. For instance, in a couple of the program sites, BSF couples were actually a little less likely to still be together and fathers were a little less likely to be engaged with and supporting their children. At first, this seems to support the glass-half-empty perspective. But I think this difference most likely can be attributed to decisions by BSF intervention-group participants to end a relationship because they could see that it did not measure up to the relationship standards they learned in the program. In other words, participating in the BSF program taught mothers and fathers about healthy relationships and over time, if their relationship didn't live up to that, they were more likely to break up. We could debate whether this is a positive or negative outcome of the program, but I think it may be positive. Unhealthy relationships that don't change over time are not good for children or parents. These kinds of intervention programs hope to increase family stability, but not at the expense of individual well-being. So I think this finding is encouraging. It suggests that the BSF programs can promote the wise break-up of unhealthy relationships while also attempting to strengthen couple relationships.

Finally, when we examine some of the differences between the FE program in Oklahoma City and the other BSF programs at the other study sites, the glass doesn't seem quite so empty. One important difference was that the FE program was much better at retaining couples for a nearly full dose of the program compared to most of the other sites. While nearly 50% of FE couples received a strong dosage of the program, at the other seven sites, the average was closer to 10% of couples receiving a strong dosage of their program. At some sites, many couples randomly assigned to the intervention group never even came to an instructional session. A certain dosage of the medicine is probably necessary to produce some positive effects. And the Oklahoma City site was very skilled and dedicated at facilitating participation and retaining couples in the program. This included constant monitoring of FE couples and eliminating barriers to attendance. Also, the FE classes were offered several times a week, so if a couple missed a class, they could make it up. The program also was about 10 hours shorter than most of the other programs, so maybe less is more in this instance. Another noteworthy difference is that the FE program actually included both unmarried, romantically involved parents as well as lower income married parents in the same sessions. (The married parents were participating in a distinct, different study that I will describe in detail in Chapter 6. But they received the same curriculum.) This was not the case with the other program sites. One possibility is that, regardless of the curriculum, the unmarried couples may have benefited from seeing, listening to, and interacting with married couples who had achieved what most of the unmarried couples were hoping to attain: marriage. Some of these unmarried couples don't know many married couples and don't have many role models or social support. Maybe these unmarried FE couples could see more hope by learning in the same program with couples who were much like them not so long ago and now were married.

Of course, there were differences in the content of these programs that might account for some differences in the program effects. While there was a great deal of similarity, the FE program gave more emphasis, I think, to the issue of commitment and somewhat less to specific communication skills. I think the FE program also put more emphasis on building and maintaining friendship than the other programs. Unfortunately, the design of the study can't parse out these curriculum differences to see if they account for the positive effects of the FE program compared to the other programs. But it is possible that curriculum differences contributed to program effectiveness.

So again, I think the FE program and larger BSF evaluation study of RDE for cohabiting-parent couples provide at least some optimism about continued policy efforts. Admittedly, the results are mixed at this point. But given that this is the first wave of work in this area, I'm encouraged that we have some positive findings this early in our policy efforts. I think we can get better at what we do and how we do it so that more positive results are possible in the future.

Effectiveness of other RDE programs for cohabiting-parent couples. Moreover, FE and BSF are not the only programs working to help informally engaged couples, nor are they the only evaluation studies that have been conducted, although these other studies are not as rigorous as the FE and BSF studies. For instance, one group of scholars recently tested a 16-hour PREP curriculum on a group of lower income African American and Latino unmarried couples expecting a child together.[82] These researchers found short-term, significant, positive change in both men and women on measures of relationship satisfaction, positive communication skills, negative communication, friendship, commitment, and confidence in their ability to manage relationship challenges in the future.

Similarly, Ron Cox and Karen Shirer reported a pilot study evaluation of the 12-hour *Caring for My Family* (CFMF) curriculum designed for low-income unmarried parents to assess their readiness for marriage and improve relationship skills.[83] (This program is used by a handful of organizations receiving government support.) The program does not require that couples participate together; they can take it as individuals. (This was the case in one class I observed in Tuscaloosa, Alabama, that used the CFMF curriculum.) And it is not as comprehensive or intensive as the FE program. Still, results suggest that CFMF couples became more intentional about becoming a stable family and improved their decision making about this compared to control-group couples. Also, they reported healthier coparenting attitudes after the program. More studies are coming.

A program in the Minnesota Twin Cities provided almost 18 hours, on average, of an RDE program (and other life skills, such as budgeting) to unmarried, diverse, lower income couples.[84] The curriculum was delivered in-home by trained home visitors and tailored to each couple. In a quasi-experimental design study, one year after completing the home visiting program, there were no statistically significant differences in relationship stability between treatment-group couples and a comparison group of matched couples from a study of fragile-family couples in nearby Milwaukee. However, treatment-group couples were three times more likely than the comparison group to marry by one year after the program (20.8% vs. 6.3%), which has positive implications for longer term relationship stability. The researchers speculated that the personalized, in-home instruction may have provided some couples with the confidence to make a transition to marriage.

Parenthetically, a couple of other studies that I will report on in more detail in Chapter 6 tested relationship education program effects on groups with both married and unmarried parents together (and with large proportions of Latino couples) and found positive program effects regardless of marital status.[85] So I think the overall picture based on research to date suggests that RDE programs for cohabiting-parent couples show potential. Of course, more work is needed for a definitive answer to the question of whether these programs are effective.

How Do We Deliver MPE and RDE to Couples?

How can we feasibly deliver MPE and RDE to the many couples who marry each year and to the millions of cohabiting couples and parents who aspire to marriage? The primary institution we can call on to provide MPE are the churches and faith-based organizations, especially for formally engaged couples. Most marriages still take place under religious auspices. For virtually all faiths, marriage is a sacred relationship, a sacrament, a covenant with deity as well as between spouses. Faith and family are intricately intertwined.

Marriages are important religiously (and practically) to churches and other faith-based organizations and they want to see them succeed. This deep interest in the success of a marriage together with providing the venue for the wedding makes the church an ideal infrastructure for delivering MPE to engaged couples. Of course, many churches already are doing this; some research suggests that about 90% of couples who get marriage preparation education receive it from a religious source.[86] And often these sources provide the educational service for free or at low cost. So they will not need government funds to support their efforts (and wouldn't want the restrictions on their religious mission that would come with government support of their efforts).

Will religious organizations focus primarily on religious preparation or will they include the kind of secular material that I suggested earlier? My observations and investigations of this question suggest that most churches and faith-based organizations blend the secular and sacred into a solid curriculum. I think many religious organizations do a pretty good job of covering the kinds of topics that good MPE should cover. Some use formal versions of secular programs adapted to include some religious material. Some imbue what might be seen as secular topics, such as effective communication, with supportive doctrine and principles that I suspect strengthen the presentation of secular material. I'm a social scientist, but I'm also a person of faith, and I'm not worried about the content of religiously based MPE for engaged couples. At least one study documents that relationship education provided in religious settings by religious leaders is as effective as similar relationship education provided by professionally trained clinicians in university settings.[87] I'm sure there is room for improvement in what churches do for MPE,[88] but overall, I think their work is commendable, and the more engaged couples participate in these programs the better off we will be. Moreover, we shouldn't underestimate the potential value of faith-based delivery of services. In many parts of the country, the church is a prominent, respected, and trusted institution in the community across demographic lines. Many people look first to the church for services because it matches well with their own values.

But we shouldn't rely exclusively on faith-based organizations to deliver MPE. Some evidence suggests that young couples are less likely to affiliate with a religion than in the past.[89] Many couples will not desire a wedding under religious auspices and may not want to go through MPE programs with religious content included. I think there are some good and feasible secular alternatives for these couples that could be developed further with some minor financial support. One underused educational network is the Cooperative Extension system. In every state and virtually every county, the state's land-grant university has a group of faculty whose job is to translate research into educational programs and materials and deliver that valuable information and programming to the citizens of the state who could benefit from it. Most Cooperative Extension offices include educators who specialize in family and consumer sciences. These educators are well trained and capable of delivering research-based MPE curricula to engaged couples. Because Cooperative Extension offices are in local communities, they also may be able to make minor adjustments to curricula to fit better the experiences and values of the local community. In addition, because the Cooperative Extension system has a long history of serving rural communities, this may be a good option for states with significant rural populations. Cooperative Extension services are provided at very low cost as a public service, an outreach of the state's land-grant university funded by tax dollars.

Community colleges and universities could be doing more, I think, to provide MPE to young adult couples. I mentioned in Chapter 4 that higher education, especially the system of local community colleges, is a good source for delivering relationship literacy education (RLE) to young adults. I think we have a picture of college students as interested only in hooking up and hanging out, so MPE is irrelevant to their lives. But many college students become very serious and committed to a partner, and a substantial minority choose to marry during their college careers. I think colleges could do more to offer educational options geared toward seriously dating or engaged couples. These classes would not require couples to attend together; they could be structured to allow for a single partner to participate, as well. But they would need to be more than a sociological review of romantic relationships and marriage. They would need to be focused on helping a particular couple or individual assess a relationship and prepare effectively for marriage.

Some colleges and universities are doing this. The program I know the best is the one at my own institution, Brigham Young University. Each semester, hundreds of individuals and couples receive an in-depth curriculum focused on preparation for marriage led by a talented scholar–teacher in this area, Jason Carroll. The class is both rigorous and practical and provides a tremendous service to these students. I'm sure there are other talented teachers at many colleges and universities who are or could be providing a similar service.

Individuals in the military are more likely to be married at younger ages than those in the civilian populations.[90] Hence, the military could be a good source of MPE for those couples. The Army in particular has devoted significant resources, primarily through the chaplaincy, to making MRE resources available to military personnel. My sense is that the bulk of these resources are targeted to helping married military couples sustain healthy relationships through the significant stresses of military life. A modest extension of this kind of effort to engaged couples should be straightforward.

Many of these delivery infrastructures can help provide RDE for cohabiting-parent couples with aspirations to marriage. But I think human service agencies may be a prime candidate for delivering these services.[91] Many of these couples already are receiving assistance from such organizations as TANF offices, food insecurity programs such as SNAP, employment services, parenting resource centers, early childhood education programs, healthcare providers, and others. Several states have a loose network of parenting/family resource centers across the state that provide a variety of services by well-trained and caring professionals to assist parents. I've personally observed classes sponsored by these centers that attract unmarried parents (mostly but not exclusively mothers) and the participants really engage in the curricula. Many of these kinds of organizations, with funding and support from the federal Administration for Children and Families, have been experimenting with expanding their services to include RDE. Alternatively, some of these organizations have built strong collaborations with churches or other organizations that already offer RDE services. This may allow an organization to avoid mission creep and stay focused on a specific need and service while still recognizing the value that RLE could add to their clientele. Cohabiting-parent couples may not be aware that RDE services are available for their relationship needs. So it makes sense to use organizations and agencies from which they are already receiving valued services to provide RDE or to refer them to other organizations that can do so. Indeed, cross-service referral is the primary way that these organizations recruit interested participants.

A combination of religious and secular organizations can provide solid MPE and RDE programs to millions of couples each year and do so at no or low cost. The infrastructures are already in place, with talented and caring family life educators. I think our capacity may be underused right now. But if we double or triple the number of couples seeking MPE and RDE, we may need to do more to build up the supply. I don't think that will be difficult. Churches can train more lay educators. There are likely more married couples with a passion for helping couples form a strong foundation for their marriage than we are currently tapping. They can be trained to be effective educators. Likewise, my academic colleagues could ramp up and do more to prepare enthusiastic students in family studies, social work, or other behavioral science degree programs to offer MPE/RDE. If the emphasis were placed more on making these educational opportunities available to more disadvantaged, lower income, diverse couples, I think academicians would be even more likely to devote their efforts to preparing their students to be educators. Human and social service organizations are thinking more and more about integrated services to provide holistic assistance. I think they will be increasingly interested in including RDE in their portfolio of services, especially if we can show them how this add-on improves the lives of the clients they serve and their children. When we build more on-ramps to a healthy marriage, more people can get to their desired destinations.

Final Thoughts: Putting More People on the Road

Surveys report that most people think it is a good idea for couples to invest in formal marriage preparation education before getting married. About half even say they think it should be required.[92] I have heard many couples say this as they finish their own program. The more couples who invest in good MPE programs, the less likely we are to see the problems that can lead to divorce. Divorce has a large cost to taxpayers as well as taking a huge personal toll on parents and children.

Should states then require that couples take MPE as a way to strengthen families and save tax dollars? As a strong advocate of MPE, it's tempting to say yes. After all, the law often requires specific training to operate a car, own a firearm, and other common, personal actions. But I don't think this is the best way to go. First, there are practical problems. If it is mandated, does the community have the capacity to meet the demand? Some may object to the state accepting religiously based MPE programs as a violation of the Constitution's required separation of church and state. But without the religious sector, the demand could not be met. Without the low-cost services of faith-based orga-nizations, would we need to allocate substantial government funds to support MPE, and is that even feasible? Also, there could be liability issues associated with mandated MPE that would lead to a requirement for MPE providers to be insured, raising the costs. Who would approve the curriculum or specify the content? And how would couples react to this kind of government inter-vention? These and other practical matters make a mandate unwise, I think.

Instead, I support a different approach. Nine states have passed legisla-tion that provides incentives—a reduction or waiver of the marriage license fee—for couples to invest in MPE.[93] The states generally provide a small set of topics to cover in an MPE program but leave it up to the couple to choose the program they want. No big bureaucracy has been born to administer this legislation. Usually a simple letter from a provider or an official form signed by the educator suffices as proof of meeting the legislative require-ments. I think an incentive avoids the practical concerns raised above. These incentives are minimal, anywhere from a $5–$60 reduction in the license fee. Given how much couples spend on weddings these days, the incentive is more psychological than financial. With the incentive, the state signals that it values its citizens preparing more effectively for marriage because this pre-serves families and reduces the need for government services for nonintact families. And by taking advantage of the incentive, couples signal their com-mitment to approaching marriage with the seriousness it deserves.

In talking with a handful of practitioners in Texas, which passed incen-tive legislation in 2007, it is clear that an incentive motivates many couples, especially lower income couples, to participate in MPE. Some couples learn about the license fee reduction when they are getting their marriage license and want to take advantage of it, so they quickly find a class that meets as an 8-hour workshop and then get married, sometimes the next day. While participating in MPE the day before the wedding is better than nothing, I think it loses some of its potential value because part of what MPE does is provide a mechanism to evaluate the relationship and its future potential for success. I worry that a "quickie" class the day before the wedding cannot adequately give couples the temporal and psychological space to evaluate the relationship and its prognosis. And the learning goals of the class easily could be subverted by the looming emotion and hectic preparations for the wedding. I'm told that sometimes these last-second participants will come back after they are married and take the program again, which would be a good thing. Ideally, legislation to promote MPE would encourage participation at least 30 days before the wedding date. I think this is what the state wants to encourage and will best serve the purpose of the legislation. Perhaps a partial discount could be offered for those who take it within 30 days of their wedding, with a full discount reserved for those who participate more than a month before. Regardless, we need to do a good job of publicizing the discount so that couples can plan better.

States may lose a small amount of revenue in the short run with these "rebates," but I did some calculations a few years ago, and even using conservative assumptions, these costs are recouped quickly even if only 1%–2% of divorces are prevented by couples investing in MPE.[94]

No research has documented yet whether incentives actually increase the number of couples who invest in MPE. But as I mentioned earlier, I know several educators in Texas who have no doubts that it does. And my colleague Bill Doherty at the University of Minnesota, who was instrumental in passing the Minnesota legislation, reports anecdotally an increase in MPE in Minnesota of about 20% in the first few years after passage in 2001. Staff at the Oklahoma Marriage Initiative report that Oklahoma appears to have seen a substantial increase in MPE since passage of their incentive legislation. So I think states should seriously consider enacting MPE incentive legislation. Behavioral economists have learned that people are motivated more not to lose something than to gain something new.[95] I think this kind of legislation would be even more effective if states substantially reduced the cost of a marriage license but then added a substantial "penalty" if couples do not invest in formal MPE.

But I would like to see one thing mandated by the state. Earlier in the chapter I mentioned the "covenant marriage" statutes available in three states that couples can choose. To get a covenant marriage, among other things, couples need to swear an oath before the county clerk who issues the marriage license that they have disclosed to each other anything that could reasonably affect the decision to marry. I think state legislators should seriously consider adding to their statutes a requirement for this kind of oath and also publicize it so that couples anticipate more than just signing a piece of paper when they go to get their marriage license. Full disclosure is a valid expectation of the state when couples seek a marriage license.

But government policy can only go so far. I want to recommend a private-sector action that likely would be more effective at getting couples to participate in MPE than marriage license fee reductions. I think the wedding industry should do more to adopt and promote the cause of marriage preparation education. Jewelers often are a first contact point with formally engaged couples. Jewelers should collaborate with MPE practitioners to encourage more couples to consider MPE. And the earlier they participate, the more effective MPE can be, because it does not bump up against the deadline of a wedding date. Jewelers could easily do more to publicize MPE classes and advertise the benefits. I think many profitable jewelers also could give free or deeply discounted vouchers to private MPE programs, if these are needed. But given that many MPE programs are free, it may be more effective for jewelers to offer a 5% discount or rebate on wedding rings for couples who enroll and finish a good MPE program. And jewelers shouldn't be the only part of the wedding industry that gets on board this train. Dressmakers, caterers, wedding planners, and other retailers who profit financially from marriages should also enlist in this cause. Imagine if all these points of contact in the wedding planning process were encouraging MPE with advertising and discounts. Not only would this actually help save couples money in what is an expensive proposition, but it would send a strong signal about what we think is valuable in our society.

And while I'm on the topic of expenses, I want to recommend one other incentive. Researchers have found that many couples who plan to marry delay it because they want a "nice wedding"; they don't want to "disrespect" marriage by settling for a "cheap wedding."[96] I'm not going to get up on my personal soapbox about the distracting commercialization of weddings these days. But we need to offer lower income couples who want to marry an affordable and respectful way to do so. I applaud the *Family Expectations* program directors in Oklahoma City (mentioned earlier in this chapter) for a generous and innovative wedding service they offer. For couples who participate in their FE program, they offer their instructional venue one day a month for free to hold a wedding ceremony. They spruce up the space with nice decorations and hire a caterer to provide a cake and refreshments. It's not a top-of-the-line destination wedding, but it is respectful and very affordable. I think MPE practitioners can work with other commercial and nonprofit partners to provide this kind of service for couples who need it.

With solid infrastructures to deliver good MPE and some government incentives and private investments, many more couples would do what almost all say they think is wise: take a formal marriage preparation education class. And the research suggests that the more couples who do this, the more likely they are to have a happy and safe marital journey and the less likely they are to experience a breakdown on the road that threatens their dreams and aspirations of a healthy, life-long marriage.

Chapter 6

Marriage Maintenance Education: Supporting the Journey to Forever

Proposal 3: Provide more support for marriage maintenance education to help couples deal with the inevitable challenges and transitions that can rattle couples in the early years of marriage (and beyond).

With solid doses of relationship literacy education in youth and young adulthood and investment in a well-designed marriage preparation program, couples would be off to a good start in their marital journey to forever. But forever is a long time and we can't assume happily ever after. Couples will need to continue to invest in their marriage and improve relationship skills to handle the twists and turns, absorb the bumps and bruises, and manage the chills that inevitably accompany the cherished thrills of married life. So we need continuing dosages of marriage and relationship education (MRE) to keep marital relationships strong, the same way we need to replenish fuel and provide regular maintenance for our cars if we want them to last. I believe public policy can and should promote this possibility.

The Problem of Relationship Entropy

Country music superstar Brad Paisley reminded us in a recent hit song, "It's easy to take forever for granted with tin cans tied to your car." His advice to the new groom to "love her like she's leaving" may be a folksy way to say that good marriages are maintained over a lifetime, not made on our wedding day. Scientists tell us that the natural state of the universe is entropy; things naturally fall apart and disintegrate toward chaos. It takes regular doses of energy to keep a complex system ordered. This is as true for social systems as it is for physical systems. Call it the Second Law of Marital Thermodynamics: without regular inputs of energy—attention, time, effective communication and problem-solving—to counteract forces of entropy, marriages become disordered and fall apart. Marital decay is the natural course; keeping things headed in the right direction takes energy. This is the challenge facing married couples from their wedding day to forever. The higher expectations for marriage and the demands it places on individuals these days, not to mention the everyday, external stresses and strains in our lives, make it even harder to maintain a satisfying relationship. It's common to hear that you have to work on a marriage to keep it strong, but in this instance, the common wisdom is correct. But if it's harder to maintain a marriage these days, I think the evidence is thin that we are really working harder. For instance, one way to keep a system ordered is to give it time, but research shows that we are spending less time together as couples. And, as Paul Amato and his colleagues argue, there has been a decline in the social capital of married couples over the past few decades, as well as an erosion of community support for marriages that together have had pervasive, negative effects on marital quality.[1]

When a marriage falls apart, divorce is usually the outcome. Today between 40%–50% of first marriages and about 60% of second marriages end in divorce.[2] About one third of all marriages end within 10 years.[3] Although the divorce rate has actually declined over the last 30 years for a variety of reasons, things haven't changed in the same way for all groups. Divorce rates have declined substantially since 1980 for more educated Americans, but they have actually increased for less educated Americans during the last few decades; they now face divorce rates north of 50%.[4] Thus divorce is increasingly an issue that affects the less advantaged sector of our society. Couples with a university education, a decent income, a shared faith, and who start out married life without children face odds of divorce that approach single digits.[5]

But a lot of people probably don't know that. And the fear of divorce seems to be at an all-time high; it seeps down deep into the culture.[6] This hit home to me many years ago when my daughter came home from school one day complaining that all her friends' parents were divorced or getting divorced. I did a quick review in my head and calmly refuted her assertion. But my rational response to her miscalculation wasn't what was needed. She had learned from a friend that her parents were getting a divorce and her best friends' parents were already divorced. So the specter of divorce was there. Like a strong spice, a little goes a long way. The specter of divorce is a potent, entropic force working against long, happy marriages. Young adults whose parents have divorced face double the risk of going through their own divorce.[7] Just having friends who are divorced increases the risk of your own divorce, a kind of social contagion effect.[8] And fear of divorce is a big reason why many young people are hesitant to marry.

About 10% of marriages at any point in time appear to be chronically unhappy. But on the flip side of this statistic, 90% are happy. But if 90% of marriages are happy, then where do divorces come from? It probably isn't surprising to learn that marital happiness isn't set in cement. After an initial decline in happiness during the first few years of marriage—a post-honeymoon dip—marital quality generally levels out. But that's an average; there's a lot of variation in this central tendency. And it doesn't mean that all marriages are stable over time. Divorces come from marriages that were generally happy a few years ago as well as from chronically troubled marriages. Research suggests that perhaps about half of divorces come from marriages that were generally happy a few years ago and are hard to distinguish from marriages that do not end in divorce.[9] Hence the need for continuing efforts to maintain a happy marriage.

But research also finds that the seeds of marital decline are often evident even in the first few months of marriage. That is, most married couples stay happy and satisfied over the first years of marriage. But a subset of couples starts at lower levels of satisfaction and becomes substantially less satisfied over time due to initial problems in the relationship.[10] (Maybe they needed to invest more in marriage preparation education.) So some couples may need to work to repair and improve problems that affected the relationship from the start, rather than fight entropy to maintain a strong relationship.

Several studies have asked divorced individuals to report the main reasons for their divorce, and the answers are quite consistent.[11] At or near the top of the list of reasons given for divorce is infidelity. Infidelity dramatically increases the odds of experiencing a divorce.[12] Unfortunately, infidelity rates appear to have increased in recent years.[13] And whereas infidelity used to be more common among men, rates among younger cohorts of women and men are getting to be quite similar.[14] Yet the anything-and-everything sexual revolution ends at the marriage altar; the norm of fidelity remains strong and the violation of this norm shatters the sense of trust and oneness that undergirds a marriage. Most infidelity does not seem to follow in the wake of prolonged dissatisfaction but rather is a consequence of opportunity and human frailty.[15] Vigilance is fortified by regular, intentional efforts to maintain a strong marriage.

Domestic violence is not one of the most common reasons given for a divorce, although still a nontrivial 30% of divorced individuals say this played a significant role. But again, this average hides a great deal of variation. Low-income couples experience much greater rates of domestic violence that likely contribute to higher break-up rates.[16] But domestic violence is an extreme manifestation of one of the most common reasons for divorce that people report: too much arguing. The inability to handle and resolve disagreements effectively can corrode a marriage over time. Effective communication and conflict resolution are learned skills.

One of the biggest sources of conflict is parenting. Becoming an effective coparenting team is a challenge. Problems with dividing up domestic duties is another reason listed as one of the more common problems that can contribute to divorce. And parenting these days seems to require even more energy than in the past, energy that can guzzle fuel needed for maintaining the marital relationship. There is some evidence that making the transition from partners to parents hits contemporary couples harder than it did their grandparents.[17] Of course, the parenting–marriage connection goes both ways. A large body of research documents how marital conflict decreases the quality of parenting children receive.[18]

It's harder to maintain a remarriage than it is a first marriage; that is reflected in the higher divorce rate for remarriages. About a third of marriages today involve one or both spouses having been married before.[19] Trying to parent nonbiological children, ex-spouse headaches, financial strains of supporting multiple households and families, and many other challenges associated with blending families are added to garden-variety marital stresses to place more demands on remarried couples.

Finally, many scholars believe that marital bonds are weaker now than in the past; the glue that holds a marriage together is more like what is used on sticky notes than wood glue. We enjoy the freedoms that come with contemporary life and the deep psychological satisfactions that modern marriage can yield. But psychology isn't as long-lasting an adhesive as social norms. The popular social historian Stephanie Coontz argues that romantic love became an increasingly important component of marriage a few centuries ago and deepened the psychological salience of marriage. But she argues that romantic love was also a potential corrosive, capable of eating away at the old social norms that served to keep marriages together—even unsatisfying marriages—for the sake of family and social stability.[20] Combine a hegemonic importance of romance with the emergence of a strong ethic of individualism over the past two centuries[21] and you have a breeding ground for deep dissatisfaction. While I suspect that Coontz's historical narrative is oversimplified, I think she and other scholars have an important point to make about modern marriage: it is intrinsically less sticky than in the past, when strong, external social norms fortified the glue of marriage. Less constraint also may mean less cohesion. To replace those external norms, couples now must substitute an increased measure of their own internal dedication to making a marriage work. When there are strong walls built around marriages, it's easier to keep them together. When those walls become largely self-constructed and psychological, then our marriages take more personal work. I think it is unlikely that people have poorer marriage skills these days than in the past. But I also think that it is harder for us to maintain a satisfying marriage now than it was for our grandparents because of how the institution of marriage has changed, how it has been de-institutionalized, as I discussed back in Chapter 1. And I don't see much likelihood that we will see a strong re-institutionalization of marriage for the twenty-first century. In fact, it looks to me like we haven't yet seen the end of this long and winding road of de-institutionalization.

The point of this section describing the problems facing contemporary marriage is that we have to work harder to sustain a happy marriage. A lifelong, satisfying marriage needs ongoing, anti-entropic enrichment efforts. Marriage enrichment education, as it is generally called in the field, is a tool for that important work. But I prefer a more descriptive term: marriage *maintenance* education. *Enrichment* implies that something is fine but needs to be enriched from time to time. By using the term *maintenance,* I am sticking with the entropy idea: the world falls apart naturally without regular work to maintain it. So I'll use the term marriage maintenance education (MME) in this chapter to describe this part of the policy agenda I am advocating. Marriage maintenance refers to efforts to keep a relationship engine in satisfactory operating condition and includes a wide range of efforts, such as thinking, planning, learning, talking, sacrificing, and spending time together in service to the relationship.[22] (And, yes, research generally confirms the stereotype that wives are more attuned to and engage in more relationship maintenance efforts than husbands.[23] So men may need extra help to invest in maintenance efforts.) Marriage maintenance education might not be the best term to use in marketing these kinds of educational opportunities to the public. Maybe MME sounds too much like learning how to change the oil in your car. A term like marriage enrichment education may be more attractive for marketing purposes, but here I will stick with marriage maintenance education. The next section, then, provides more detail about what MME for married couples is conceptually and in practice. I also review the research on how effective it is. Finally, I discuss how we can efficiently deliver MME to large numbers of married couples.

What is Marriage Maintenance Education?

In terms of the scope or content of MME, I think it is broader than the other forms of MRE that I have discussed so far in the book, which are focused on the formation of healthy marriages and relationships.[24] This is because marriage maintenance is temporally and psychologically a longer and bigger task than relationship formation and because what couples need to maintain a healthy, stable marriage is different from couple to couple and from circumstance to circumstance over a long period of time. Still, a strong focus on communication and problem-solving skills is one of the biggest and most important components of most MME programs.[25] Of all the things that predict the satisfaction of a couple relationship over time, the quality of couple interaction and communication is clearly one of the strongest,[26] although we have less research about this for disadvantaged couples.[27] Most programs attempt to decrease negative communication behaviors (e.g., criticism, contempt, escalation) and increase positive communication behaviors (e.g., careful listening, appropriate humor, empathic response), both of which are important to long-term marital health.[28] Research indicates that MME programs overall are successful at improving communication skills.[29] Some programs have an exclusive focus on communication skills, with some even focusing on a specific skill within that domain, such as expressions of deep empathy.[30]

But even with a strong behavioral focus on communication skills and effective interaction, many programs also dive into the crucial motivations that are a foundation for our behaviors. Increasingly, MME programs put emphasis on what Frank Fincham at Florida State University and his colleagues call transformative processes.[31] Transformative processes such as forgiveness, sacrifice, commitment, and loyalty deal with deep motivations in the relationship and have powerful effects on the maintenance of healthy relationships. These programs then attempt to strengthen couples' abilities to maintain healthy relationships through greater understanding of forgiveness, sacrifice, commitment, and loyalty in marriage and ways to implement these virtues in day-to-day life.[32]

In addition, most MME programs also venture into presentation and discussion of a wide range of other topics that affect married couples. Common topics might include in-law relationships, carving out couple and family time, managing family finances, ex-spouse and stepchildren issues, sharing housework and childcare, coparenting issues, couple sexual relations, preserving fidelity, and many others.

What I have described so far might be termed the traditional concept of MME: a set, programmatic curriculum with a strong focus on communication skills, typically about 12 hours long, delivered in an interactive classroom setting to a small group of married couples. In the next chapter—an important companion to this one—I'll discuss some less traditional directions I think the field needs to take to improve on what we do to help married couples maintain and strengthen their marriages. But in this chapter I'll stay focused on this more traditional concept of programmatic MME and the potential it has to help married couples maintain a strong relationship.

Illustrating MME Programs

It's always easier to see something from a concrete example than a broad abstraction. So in this next section I'll illustrate MME with a couple of noteworthy programs, each of which have received significant government support to be able to reach substantial numbers of lower income couples who are at greater risk for divorce.

University of Central Florida's (Orlando) Project TOGETHER. The University of Central Florida claims to be the second largest university in the United States, serving nearly 60,000 students. But nestled in a corner of the campus is a building that has been remodeled to look like a home. Inside it has a comfortable and homey feel to it. This building serves as the site for the Project TOGETHER's *For Our Future, For Our Family* (FOF) program to help strengthen married couples' relationships. Since 2006, Project TOGETHER has received substantial federal funding to enable it to serve diverse, lower income couples in the Orlando area. The program director is Andrew Daire. This program also was one of eight sites chosen to participate in the largest and most rigorous evaluation study of MME for lower income couples, the *Supporting Healthy Marriage* project funded by the Administration for Children and Families.

Like all eight sites in the Supporting Healthy Marriage (SHM) project, Project TOGETHER has three main components to its MME services. First, it offers marriage education classes. Specifically, it employs the FOF curriculum that is adapted from a well-known program called *Practical Application of Intimate Relationship Skills*[33] (PAIRS) to fit the circumstances of diverse, lower income couples. All SHM program sites teach communication and problem-solving skills to decrease negative couple interactions, increase positive interactions (e.g., supportive behaviors, shared goal setting, couple time), help couples understand married life better (e.g., all couples have problems, self-effort can create positive change, the value of having support networks), and provide tools for managing stressful circumstances commonly faced by lower income couples. The FOF curriculum that is used at this Orlando site puts a special emphasis on developing emotional and physical closeness through healthy expression of emotions and overcoming past experiences that interfere with intimacy. The program has up to 30 hours of face-to-face instruction in small groups of about eight couples over about 4 months. On average, couples participating in FOF receive about 17 hours of the curriculum (due to missing some sessions). Their participation is encouraged by providing on-site childcare. Some couples also receive cash assistance for travel expenses. And there are cash incentives for couples who regularly attend the sessions.

A second component of the SHM model is supplemental organized educational and social activities for about 6 months after the main curriculum ends. Brief educational seminars teach supplementary topics such as family financial planning and effective parenting (while also reinforcing the main themes of the FOF curriculum). In addition, they sponsor formal date nights with dinners, dances, and other activities, reinforcing the FOF principle of fun couple time. On average, couples participate in about 6 hours of these supplemental activities.

The third component of the FOF model is that each couple is assigned a family support coordinator who facilitates the couple's participation in the program and events and helps meet family needs by connecting them to other community services (e.g., employment services). These coordinators can provide make-up instruction when couples can't make it to an instructional session. Many of these part-time coordinators are graduate students in clinical training programs at UCF.

As you can imagine, all this did not come cheap. The average cost per couple for involvement in this program was about $9,000. This cost isn't out of line with other kinds of social and economic intervention programs for low-income individuals, especially in a start-up, demonstration-and-evaluation phase. But it is probably still too high to make the program feasible for long-term support, so I suspect major changes in the program cost structure will be needed.

Couples who participated in the SHM evaluation study of the FOF program in Orlando enrolled in the program in 2008–2009. About 350 couples received the FOF program and accompanying services. (Another 350 couples served as the control group that did not receive services but did receive compensation for participation in the study.) Most participants were recruited in waiting rooms of local Women, Infants, and Children (WIC) program offices or in public health clinics. As a result, about 30% of couples were below the federal poverty line and another 60% were between 100%–200% of the poverty line, which is still an economically vulnerable position. Forty percent of these couples were Hispanic, 18% were White, 14% were Black, and 28% were multiracial couples or other ethnicities. About a quarter were in stepfamilies. More than half of the couples said that their marriage had been in trouble during the past year, which may be a reason why they sought out participation in the program.

One reason I chose to highlight the UCF Project TOGETHER program is that it was rigorously evaluated along with seven other sites across the United States as part of the SHM project. Like the Building Strong Families (BSF) evaluation study I discussed in Chapter 5, SHM was a rigorous, large-scale, multisite evaluation study of MME programs targeted to lower income married couples. More than 6,000 couples were randomly assigned to no-treatment control groups or to treatment groups with the kind of educational opportunities and services described above. The results I summarize below are for all eight sites combined, not just the Orlando site, but the pattern of results for the Orlando site was similar to the overall pattern.[34]

Classes and services were completed by 12 months from the time that couples enrolled in the SHM study. At that time, the SHM program showed a consistent pattern of small but statistically significant positive effects on various aspects of couple relationships. For instance, spouses who received the SHM program reported slightly higher (but statistically significant) marital happiness scores. They also were 5% less likely than control-group couples to say their marriage was in trouble, an important indicator of marital stability. Also, couples reported (and researchers observed) slightly higher scores on positive communication skills and less anger and hostility in intervention-group couples compared to control-group couples. Intervention-group couples reported less psychological abuse. Husbands also reported less physical abuse (e.g., pushing, slapping) from their wives, but there were no differences for wives' reports. However, at this 12-month assessment, SHM couples were no more likely to still be married than control-group couples. Perhaps this is to be expected, because a year is still a pretty short time to see effects for marital stability. Intervention-group individuals also reported slightly less psychological distress. There were no group differences on the level of cooperative coparenting behavior. These effects were generally consistent across the eight sites of the study, including the Orlando site. Subgroup analyses found some evidence that effects were somewhat larger and more consistent for Hispanic couples and couples who entered the program experiencing higher levels of distress.

Although the early effects of the SHM program were small, they were fairly consistent, giving greater credence to the results. I'm especially encouraged that fewer SHM couples felt their marriage was in trouble 1 year after starting the program compared to control-group couples. Many of the participants were in distressed marriages, and the program appeared to improve their relationships by 1 year after starting the program, despite the stressful circumstances of their lives.[35]

The Smart Steps program in Utah. Between 2006–2012, nearly 3,000 Utah adults in stepfamilies have received an 8-hour dosage of a curriculum called *Smart Steps*.[36] The need for this service is great. There have been more than 35,000 remarriages in Utah between 2006–2010 (about 30% of all marriages).[37] While these *Smart Steps* classes are considered a part of the Utah Healthy

Marriage Initiative that I described back in Chapter 2, the classes have been funded directly by three different federal grants from the federal Administration for Children and Families[38] rather than by Utah HMI funds. The classes are free to the public. Not all who attend are married; about a third are cohabiting couples, many of whom are thinking seriously about marriage. But I think the *Smart Steps* program is best thought of as a marriage maintenance program even though for some it may operate more like a marriage preparation or relationship development program. About two thirds of program participants are White and about 30% are Latino.

The force behind this significant effort to help remarried couples strengthen their marriages and relationships in Utah is Brian Higginbotham, a Cooperative Extension System family life specialist at Utah State University (USU). Linda Skogrand and Kay Bradford (a former graduate student of mine) at USU also have been heavily involved in the project. Classes are offered through various community family support organizations throughout Utah, including some Head Start programs and parenting resource centers. Couples attend with children, but for most of the time couples meet with other couples without their children for instruction, then have a 30-minute family activity with the children at the end of the class. (Childcare is provided for young children; older children receive some instruction to help them adjust to stepfamily life and likely benefit from the classes, as well.[39]) Classes are taught by a variety of family life educators in the state after being trained by Higginbotham and his colleagues, including receiving training in recognizing and dealing with domestic violence.[40] Classes are offered in both English and Spanish.

The *Smart Steps* curriculum has a positive focus on building couple and family strengths more than a deficit perspective of fixing common "problems" faced by remarried couples. This was evident to me when I sat in on a class while writing this chapter. The class was held in a modest Head Start facility. While the curriculum teaches some effective communication skills, it has a strong topical focus on the distinctive issues and challenges that arise in most stepfamilies. It covers many different topics, including stepfamily myths, realistic expectations, stages of stepfamily development, roles and rules, family finances, stepparent–stepchild relationships, and communicating with the other parent. But as I observed this class, I saw that classroom dynamics might be as important as the actual *Smart Steps* curriculum. Participants frequently asked, "So, how do you handle such-and-such a problem?" Facilitators encouraged class participants to respond, calling them the "experts." I sensed the class offered an appreciated support system of couples in similar situations. And facilitators consistently tried to empower participants by reinforcing their instinctive abilities to deal with their challenges.

I chose to highlight the Utah *Smart Steps* program for several reasons. It's a program that I know pretty well because of my work with the Utah Healthy Marriage Initiative, and Higginbotham is a close working colleague. Plus, I think it's important to put the spotlight on programs that are targeted specifically to remarried couples who face a higher risk of divorce. But another reason I want to highlight this program is because it has been one of the most evaluated remarriage MME efforts in the country.[41] While the federal grants funding this program did not require such extensive evaluation, Higginbotham's position as a family life education scholar–practitioner at a research-oriented university and his graduate school training, including research on stepfamilies, motivated him to devote resources to evaluating the program. Higginbotham has not had sufficient resources to conduct a rigorous, randomized controlled trial of the *Smart Steps* program in Utah, but he has put a lot of effort into collecting and analyzing field data from program participants before and after they take the program.

In general, Higginbotham and his colleagues have found a pattern of positive change for couples who participated in the program (both for married and unmarried participants). An early evaluation study of participants before and 1 month after they took the *Smart Steps* program found reports of increased commitment to the marriage, an important element of marital success. This study also found increased agreement on finances, issues with ex-partners, and coparenting issues.[42] Another study followed up with 20 participants 1 year after completing the *Smart Steps* program and interviewed them in depth about their family relationships and how they perceived the program had affected those relationships.[43] Almost unanimously, individuals reported that the program helped them to improve their couple relationship, including improved communication, stronger unity, greater commitment, and better coparenting. Those with ex-partner relationships to manage also reported better attitudes and relationships with their ex-partners. Participants also talked about perceived positive effects in their relationships with their children and greater family unity. The researchers were not able to test these positive changes against a no-treatment control group of stepfamilies, so the positive results of the *Smart Steps* program in Utah are not definitive. But I think Higginbotham and his team are to be commended for building up an infrastructure to provide a valuable service to an at-risk population of couples in remarriages that appears to give them a boost in their desire to build and maintain a strong marriage for themselves and the children in their lives.

Other Evidence of the Effectiveness of MME

I have highlighted the Orlando and Utah programs and summarized the evaluation research on them. But there is much more research on MME effectiveness. I'll try not to overwhelm you with that research in this next section, but I think it would be helpful to summarize some key studies, giving special emphasis to studies with lower income, higher risk couples.

OFA HMRI grantee meta-analysis. I'll start with a brief summary of a study I did with a graduate student, Kaylene Fellows.[44] I've described other results from this study in previous chapters. This was a meta-analysis, or a synthesis of other studies. We reviewed and quantitatively synthesized the results from 50 field studies of MRE programs that were supported by the federal Office of Family Assistance (OFA, ACF). (These programs were part of the federal Healthy Marriages and Relationships Initiative I described in Chapter 2.) These grants were used to recruit primarily lower income couples and individuals into MRE programs. The 50 programs in this study had collected basic field data before and after the program (with no control group). Here I focus on the 13 programs that specifically targeted married couples with a variety of MME curricula. There were more than 11,000 individuals who participated in and provided data to these programs. The immediate pre-post effect size for these 13 programs was statistically significant ($d = .50$) on an aggregate outcome measure that included relationship quality, communication skills, relationship confidence, relationship aggression, and coparenting. This effect size is a moderate, pretty typical effect for these kinds of programs, indicating positive change for these lower income couples.

Supporting Father Involvement program in California. An important study conducted by Phil and Carolyn Cowan at the University of California at Berkeley followed a moderately sized sample (371 couples) of low-income, mostly Hispanic couples in California for 2 years who participated in a MME program.[45] The program and evaluation study were funded by the State of California's Office of Child Abuse Prevention as a way to improve couple relationships and father involvement in order to reduce child abuse. The study examined the effects of a group-discussion–oriented educational program designed to promote fathers' engagement with their children and strengthen couples' relationships. The program was called *Supporting Father Involvement* (SFI). Note that this program explicitly blended issues around couple relationships and parenting issues, specifically, positive father involvement.

Those participants who agreed to be in the study were randomly assigned either to a fathers-only educational intervention group (with 32 hours of group interaction and discussion), a couples group (mothers and fathers attended the program together, with almost the same program content as the fathers-only group), or a comparison group (one brief meeting that emphasized fathers' importance to their children's development). The random assignment of participants to groups makes a more rigorous and reliable test of the effectiveness of the program. Like the *Smart Steps* program in Utah described above, both married and unmarried couples participated in the SFI program, but about 75% were married, so I think this program is best categorized as MME. Compared to the control group, the researchers found that both intervention groups showed small-to-modest, positive changes in couple relationship quality, father engagement, and of note, children's problem behaviors. But the couple group seemed to work better than the fathers-only group. Participants in the couples group also showed reductions in parent stress and increased marital stability as well as increased relationship quality. And the couples group showed more consistent, longer term, positive outcomes than those in the fathers-only group. This first study of the SFI program has now been replicated with two other studies of low-income families and found generally similar positive results, including a reduction in violent problem solving.[46]

A few more interesting studies. A handful of other studies evaluating MME programs provide intriguing answers to some interesting questions. For instance, one program explicitly targeted lower income couples who were experiencing a lot of conflict. Most MME programs screen for any relationship violence and refer those couples to other services rather than include them in their programs. But this educational program was designed specifically to help these kinds of couples, who were experiencing conflict but wanted to work on their relationships. (They were not mandated by a court to participate.) These high-conflict couples were experiencing what researchers call situational couple violence that involves things like pushing and kicking and is usually reciprocal. (They were not experiencing intimate partner terrorism that is men's domination and control of their female partner through use of severe physical and emotional violence.[47]) The program, *Creating Healthy Relationships* (CHR), is based on prominent marriage researcher John Gottman's sound marital house theory and emphasizes skills training to help manage conflict and deal with negative emotions. It also emphasizes building friendship, emotional intimacy, and shared goals to create a stronger sense of "we-ness" in the relationship. The program is intensive for an MME program, lasting 22 weeks with 44 hours of planned group instruction and discussion. Group instructors were trained therapists.

The evaluation study of this program randomly assigned 115 couples with incomes below the area median to participate in CHR or to a comparison group that received a referral to other services available in the community, such as a domestic violence prevention program.[48] Again, some of the couples were unmarried, but a large majority was married, and all couples had to have been in a relationship for more than a year. All couples had at least one young child. Unfortunately, more than a third of the couples did not complete the program or the study, including 19 couples who broke up during the study. So the results of this study need to be interpreted carefully and are not as strong due to this sample attrition. Couples were assessed 6–12 months after completing the program. Researchers found that both women and men in the CHR group reported increased relationship satisfaction, greater use of effective communication skills, and reduced conflict compared to the comparison-group couples. Given the at-risk nature of this sample, these are encouraging results, but more rigorous research like this is needed to see if educational programs are appropriate for and can help high-conflict couples.

The studies I've reviewed suggest that MME programs can improve relationship quality. But can they actually prevent divorce? It's harder to study divorce because you have to follow couples for a longer period of time to allow for divorce to occur. But in another rigorous study, there is some early, intriguing evidence that MME for lower income and less educated couples may decrease divorce rates. In the first study to use a randomized controlled trial to assess effects on divorce, Scott Stanley and his colleagues at the University of Denver recruited a moderately sized sample (476 couples) of couples with one spouse in the Army and followed them for a year after completing the *Prevention and Relationship Enhancement Program (PREP) for Strong Bonds* program.[49] This was a relatively low-income sample, although the military service benefits add to the economic resources of these couples. This program consisted of 14 hours of the PREP program adapted for and by the Army, with a one-day seminar occurring on a weekday on-post, followed by a weekend retreat at a hotel off-post. One year after completing the program, the researchers found that couples randomly assigned to take the *Strong Bonds* program had a divorce rate that was one third that of control-group couples (2% vs. 6%). And at 2 years, there was still a significant difference between *Strong Bonds* couples and control-group couples (8% vs. 15% divorced).[50] While statistically this seems like a moderate difference, in real-life terms this indicates a potentially large and meaningful difference at the population level. And the difference actually was bigger than this for minority couples. For instance, 5% of African American couples who participated in *Strong Bonds* were divorced after two years versus 18% of African American couples who did not participate in the program. (Among White couples, those figures were 11% versus 13%.) Interestingly, there didn't seem to be big differences in treatment and control couples on marital quality. So it appears that MME programs can increase marital stability, that is, reduce the likelihood of divorce, even if they do not significantly improve marital quality, perhaps by strengthening commitment to the marriage.

How long can positive effects of MME programs last? Some studies have found that positive effects of MME programs are not just short term (more than a couple of years), although these studies have been done with more advantaged couples. One unique study done in Germany followed a group of newly married couples who took an MME program focused on improving communication skills. The researchers found early positive effects of the program, and those effects could still be seen more than a decade later.[51] Moreover, program participants had a much lower incidence of divorce than an equivalent comparison group of couples. However, this study was with a group of more educated and well-off German couples, so we have to be careful generalizing the results to more disadvantaged couples in the United States. Another study with mostly well-educated California new parents found positive effects of a MME program on couple relationships and children's well-being 10 years after the program.[52]

I have tried to illustrate some noteworthy MME programs and provide evidence on how effective they are. I'm encouraged by the evidence so far. MME programs appear to help married couples work on and improve their relationship to keep it strong over time and prevent divorce. So how do we increase the availability of this service to married couples? That is the topic of the final section of this chapter.

How Do We Deliver MME to Married Couples?

To deliver more MME opportunities to married couples, I think we need to make use of many potential educational infrastructures. I think there are a wide variety of educational tracks or roads that are already laid down but could be improved with just small amounts of government funds. The wide variety is needed to match the large array of different needs and circumstances of married couples during the early, high-risk years of marriage and beyond.

Actually, the first educational infrastructure to consider generally doesn't seek government funds for support: the church. As I wrote in Chapter 5, the church is a primary delivery mechanism for marriage preparation education (MPE). As a result, it may also be an important means for supporting married couples in the early years of their long journey to forever. Especially if they have had a good experience with MPE with a particular church and have continued their involvement in that congregation, couples may be more receptive to invitations to continue to invest in strengthening their marriage. In fact, come to think of it, maybe I should add one more element to good MPE: it should teach engaged couples that ongoing work to keep a marriage strong is needed and formal MME can help with that task after they are married. For religious couples, the ability to clothe good principles of healthy, strong marriages in spiritual terms of faithfulness, charity, forgiveness, personal responsibility, connection to God, and other strong religious themes may be a real asset to MME. Also, often these couples will participate with other couples in the congregation they know who can be an effective support system. I've mentioned previously the research that shows that MME providers in religious organizations appear to do as good a job or better than professionally trained educators in university-based venues.[53]

But I think there are good secular tracks for delivering MME, too, that we will need to use; these can be enhanced with wise investments of small amounts of public funds. For instance, there are a number of community human service agencies, such as parenting/family resource centers, that have a long track record working with lower income families that can expand their services to include MME. The actual proportion of married couples with incomes below the poverty line is quite small. But a good number of married couples are not so far above the line that they wouldn't be in contact with these kinds of community organizations currently or in the past. One promising possibility is community organizations hosting and running Head Start programs for lower income children and their parents. Many of these organizations already provide parenting education classes or responsible fatherhood programs. I think a friendly merger of couple education and parenting education in these settings has a lot of promise. (I'll talk more about the value of this merger in the next chapter.) ACF recognized as much when it allocated about 25 five-year grants to Head Start community organizations to do this in 2007. It will be interesting to see if these MME programs have been able to set down roots and become an integral part of what Head Start programs offer their client families.[54]

I think the healthcare sector can do more to support MME for lower income couples.[55] Community health clinics, maternity and newborn care facilities, family practice offices, and various public health agencies come in contact with lower income married mothers and their children and often provide free educational services as a public health service, including prenatal care, childbirth preparation, infancy care, community health nurse home visits, nutrition education, general parenting education, and more. So serving families in behalf of providing children a better start in life is a normative part of many healthcare organizations, even if they haven't typically thought much about strengthening couple relationships. Yet given the strong research evidence on the physical and emotional health benefits to families of a healthy, stable marriage,[56] there is good reason for healthcare systems to give this more attention. Some well-placed public funds could help to spur this innovation in public health services.

Earlier in the chapter I cited research on the Army's *Strong Bonds* program. This is a research-based MME curriculum designed for military couples who face a lot of work-related stress and challenges (in addition to the regular stresses) to keeping their marriages strong and intact. The Army has invested a lot of its own resources into developing and providing MME to military personnel. And there is evidence that these programs are having some positive effects.[57] Base chaplains are trained to be the instructors for these programs. My own investigations suggest that the other branches of the military have not invested as much effort in MME, so they could stand to improve. The military can be an important and effective provider of MME services for a special category of married couples who face some distinctive challenges.

In Chapter 5, I mentioned that the Cooperative Extension Service associated with the U.S. land-grant universities could be a valuable educational infrastructure to deliver marriage preparation education, and I think they could also help make MME more available in communities. Again, the Cooperative Extension Service, with its roots in serving agricultural communities, may be particularly well-suited to reaching out in small and rural communities, many of which have high divorce rates. And services are low or no cost in the Extension Service, so that fits well with meeting the needs of a lower income group. The Extension Service already is funded by the federal government, so it's a matter of reallocating limited resources to this task. As I described in Chapter 2, the Utah Healthy Marriage Initiative funnels funding (from TANF) to the Cooperative Extension Service to make it easier for them to provide MME classes.

There are a number of different community organizations, secular and religious, that can increase the availability of MME. But some couples will prefer more private or more flexible options. So I want to conclude this section with a plug for self-guided educational options as an alternative or a supplement to more traditional face-to-face programs. I discussed the idea and potential value of self-guided programs or curricula back in Chapter 4, and I'll say more about it in Chapter 7. But there is research now that self-guided program too can strengthen couple relationships.[58] Online MME alternatives may be a valuable and increasing option, as well.

To summarize, in this chapter I have reviewed the need for and value of marriage maintenance education to help couples do the regular work to fight relationship entropy and keep a marriage strong. I illustrated some noteworthy programs that have received public support and target disadvantaged couples. I reviewed the evaluation research that shows promise for MME efforts for these kinds of programs. Nevertheless, I think we can and need to do a lot better and I have a lot to say about this subject. So instead of a "Final Thoughts" section for this chapter, I'll develop those thoughts in the next chapter. In that chapter, I pause to provide the reader with my thoughts about how we can improve MME specifically and MRE generally. Then in Chapter 8 I return to an elaboration of my integrated, strategic public policy agenda to strengthen marriage, there with a focus on preventing preventable divorces.

Chapter 7

Improving Marriage and Relationship Education: Building a Better Car for the Journey to Forever

My proposed public policy agenda to help individuals and couples form and sustain healthy marriages and relationships lives and dies with the effectiveness of marriage and relationship education (MRE). MRE is the vehicle I'm proposing to help get the job done, whether it be for youth or young adults to help them make wise choices about romantic relationships and keep them on a positive trajectory toward forming a healthy marriage, or for cohabiting parents who need tools to assess the prospects and improve the quality of their relationship, or for engaged couples to help them build a stronger foundation for a healthy, stable marriage, or for married couples who need to work to maintain a strong relationship. I've highlighted evaluation research in previous chapters that suggests that MRE can make a positive difference. But as I said back in Chapter 2, I think it needs to be better and I'm also confident that it will get better.

This chapter explores some ideas I have for improving the practice of MRE. I put a strong focus on improving marriage maintenance education (MME), so it is a close companion to Chapter 6. Some of the ideas in this chapter are relevant for improving the broader practice of MRE for those in the relationship literacy and formation stages. But I'll refer mostly to MME unless I am specifically making a broader point.

I'd like to see the kinds of improvement in MRE over the next 30 years that we've seen in cars since 1970 when I first learned to drive. We are a lot safer now than we were back in 1970, with mandatory seat and shoulder belts, child safety seats, air bags, anti-lock brakes, crumple zones, and many other improvements. Cars are much more efficient, too, getting better gas mileage and producing less pollution per mile than in the past. And they are more reliable. Cars didn't use to make the 100,000-mile mark very often; now many are just hitting their stride at 100,000 miles. They are more comfortable and look nicer. MME could stand a long-term extreme makeover to help couples better sustain healthy marriages.

I have ideas for improving the content and the process, the what and the how of MME, as well as the overall approach. I elaborate on those ideas in this chapter. I don't claim that they are my ideas alone. Neither are they brand new. In fact, we are beginning to explore possibilities in each of the ideas. So, much of what I will do in this chapter is highlight important emerging trends and encourage more efforts to improve the practice of MME.

A general theme of most of these ideas for improvement is that we need to give less attention to the traditional, programmatic, one-and-done curricula approach to MME and more attention to regular, briefer, focused, and naturalistic interventions. In Chapters 4, 5, and 6, I focused on this traditional approach to MRE. Traditional MRE involves a set curriculum that usually covers a wide variety of topics known to be important to forming and sustaining healthy marriages and relationships. In terms of content, the traditional approach generally casts a wide net to cover as much ground as possible. These curricula are typically delivered in a classroom setting. Couples and individuals attend 2-hour classes, spread over several weeks, or sometimes 1-day workshops. Eight to 12 hours is a common dosage. All pretty traditional stuff. Most of these traditional MRE curricula were developed by marriage therapist–scholars who were intent on preventing couples from needing to come to their offices for therapy. So they developed curricula designed to give individuals and couples the skills and knowledge that would prevent major marital problems. This was an important development in the field. But it can't be the last development in the field, and it isn't.

Please understand that I'm not being pejorative here. I think there is an important role for traditional MRE to help individuals and couples. I have listened to many MRE educators describe how the group dynamics during a class are key to learning for some. They describe times when participants' comments and shared experiences in the class taught a lesson better and with more authority than an instructor could do. They describe real bonding between participants who were strangers at the beginning of the program; the classes serve a support function, helping individuals and couples to feel less isolated, more supported.[1] And these educators even describe times when class participants become minor stakeholders in each others' marriages and relationships. They say that a common dynamic they observe in their classes is that couples come in thinking that they have deep problems in their relationships and leave with new confidence thinking, "Hey, we're not so bad; others have problems like ours. We just need to tweak a few things." Traditional, programmatic MRE will continue to be a mainstay of relationship literacy education (RLE) for youth and young adults. I think it will also play a key role in relationship development education (RDE) for cohabiting parents and marriage preparation education (MPE) for engaged couples. But when we get to married couples or long-term cohabiting parents, if we want to reach a larger proportion, I think we need to get more creative to fit continuing education into the normal spaces of busy people's lives. The ongoing, regular inputs of energy needed to maintain a marriage call for briefer interventions with more narrow curricula that fit naturally into the temporal rhythms of peoples' lives.

Regular Marital Checkups and Self-Directed Interventions

The day I began writing this chapter started with a dentist appointment, what we often call a checkup. If you want good dental health, you go once or twice a year to the dentist for a checkup and a routine cleaning. I have also been a good brusher and inherited a good set of teeth, so cavities have not been a big problem for me. But during this last checkup, the dental assistant checked me for gum-recession problems. This has been a problem for me lately. A few years ago, the hygienist noticed an emerging problem and told me I needed to do a better job of flossing and rinsing to prevent more gum recession that would lead to all sorts of unpleasant consequences. She showed me specifically what to do. And having had oral surgery in the past, I was highly motivated to short-circuit the need for more radical interventions. So I started flossing and rinsing twice a day and brushing my teeth directly after each meal. The result, 2 years later, is healthy gums and no looming specter of oral surgery. It took just a little better attention to a daily regimen of dental hygiene, something I thought I did pretty well because I brushed regularly. But there is more to dental health than brushing.

Similarly, we would do well to give ourselves regular marital checkups. This wouldn't be signing up for a 12-hour educational program. For some who really enjoy that kind of thing and have the time for it, taking an intensive booster program every year would be fine. But most of us would struggle to fit that into our schedules and some don't even like to do that kind of thing. (I'll discuss that issue a little later in this section.) Instead, a marital checkup is more like a once-a-year, brief process of assessing the health of the marriage and making sure we are doing basic relationship hygiene tasks, such as taking time to reconnect each day, spending some fun time and couple time together, employing positive communication techniques, giving each other the benefit of the doubt, maintaining boundaries around the relationship to reinforce a commitment to fidelity, and so on. Also, a marital checkup surfaces relational anomalies that could grow into bigger problems if not taken care of in a timely way. Maybe there is an issue that has caused some friction in the past but has now gone underground and you don't deal with it directly, but the subterranean conflict seeps out in other interactions. Early intervention to resolve the issue can keep the specific problem from damaging other parts of your relationship and prevent a bigger eruption later on. Some couples may be struggling to balance work and family time; explicit attention to this challenge may increase understanding and suggest some solutions. Maybe a parenting disagreement over a difficult child is starting to feel like a fundamental dividing line rather than an isolated point of difference. Whatever the anomaly, it's easier to address it early on rather than wait until it grows into something bigger.

Maybe a marital checkup is not quite like a yearly flu shot. For flu shots we drop by an office each autumn, sign a release form, and someone sticks a needle in us that deposits an inert substance that preps our bodies to defend themselves better against anticipated influenza bugs for the coming winter. That only takes a few minutes and is a very passive process. A marital checkup takes a little longer, we learn some things, and we anticipate needing to make some minor changes as a result. It's a more active process, albeit briefer and less intensive than traditional, programmatic MME. With checkups, we probably find that we are doing well in many areas, which is reassuring, but we could stand to do better in a few other areas, and we make some minor adjustments that are within our behavioral repertoire.

One thing a checkup does is provide a known time and space to assess and recalibrate. What this means is that small issues can remain small because we know there is a time when it is straightforward to surface the issue and address it. We don't have to litter our daily lives with the constant need to solve every problem right now. In addition, a regular marital checkup reinforces a mindset that you need to work on a relationship to keep it strong. Also, a checkup can be a formal time to recognize, appreciate, and even celebrate our marital strengths: we're firmly committed to each other, our marriage, and our children; we respect each other; we're good friends; we're generally compassionate toward each other; we feel like an us rather than an interconnected set of me's. Finally, a checkup is a private way to work on our marriage. We don't have to go to a public space and participate in a public discussion about our relationship. For some, the lack of privacy is a real deterrent to participating in MRE.[2]

Tools for regular marital checkups are emerging to make this easier. For instance, James Córdova and his colleagues at Clark University have developed a brief intervention for couples called, appropriately, *The Marriage Checkup*. Córdova refers to this intervention as the "marital health equivalent of annual physical or dental health checkups."[3] The *Checkup* is used by couples across the spectrum from highly distressed to highly functional and happy. Córdova argues that couples who eventually become highly distressed pass through earlier stages of minor problems that could be addressed but often are not because individuals—especially men—are averse to seeking help for their relationships.[4] The *Checkup* is intended to attract couples to assess the health of their relationship and identify some areas of improvement. It is advertised explicitly as not therapy. It is brief and private. Couples who take the *Checkup* come in and take a questionnaire that assesses such areas of martial health as intimacy, sex, communication, finances, and coparenting. Then, in a brief session with a trained counselor, the couple identifies what they believe are their greatest strengths—to set a positive atmosphere for the session—and their most pressing, current concerns. The counselor works briefly with the couple on their concerns. (At this point, the intervention appears to cross the line from an educational intervention to a therapeutic session, but Córdova believes that the *Checkup* is much closer to education than therapy, even though a trained therapist conducts the session.) Finally, the *Checkup* intervention involves a second session 2 weeks after the assessment session. The information from the initial assessment session is brought together in a feedback report that highlights the couple's relationship strengths, lists specific scores on questionnaire items, and points out areas of potential concern if unaddressed. The counselor asks the couples to assess whether they think the feedback is accurate. In addition, the counselor presents some options for what they could do to work on some of their concerns. Then the couple and counselor work together to develop an action plan for going forward. The goal of this feedback session is to provide the couple with accurate information and motivate them to take specific actions to preserve a healthy relationship. Some early research on the effectiveness of the *Marriage Checkup* with couples who were experiencing some distress but not motivated enough to seek therapy suggests that the brief intervention can improve relationship satisfaction, improve communication, deepen intimacy, and increase motivation to work on maintaining the health of the marriage.[5]

There are other marital checkup interventions that are even less intrusive than Córdova's *Marriage Checkup*. For example, David Olson and Peter Larson have developed an online *Couple Checkup*[6] based on the PREPARE/ENRICH questionnaire, perhaps the most used relationship inventory in the world. An online questionnaire has hundreds of questions that assess the health of the marriage. Before filling out the instrument, individuals answer questions about their relationship stage and family structure and circumstances, and then the instrument is automatically customized for that couple's situation (e.g., a middle-aged remarried couple married just a few years). Upon completing the questionnaire, the couple almost immediately receives a private, 20-page report assessing their relationship strengths and possible weaknesses and an extensive discussion guide designed to help the couple explore the results, learn new relationship skills that could help them deal with concerns raised in the assessment, and motivate them to work on the relationship. Similarly, a number of my colleagues here at BYU have developed the RELATE questionnaire. I discussed this back in Chapter 5 as a premarital relationship inventory. But it also is used as a checkup to assess the health of a marriage.

Most marital checkup options have a price tag. For instance, the *Couple Checkup* costs about $30. While this is a nominal cost for a valuable service for some couples, the ones who might stand to gain the most from it may see even a $30 price tag as a luxury. Greater government support for this kind of brief educational intervention could help defray costs and promote use by lower income married couples. The private sector could help out, too. More and more, insurance companies are paying for preventative checkups. Paying for an annual marital checkup makes sense, given the strong link between marital quality and physical and mental health.[7]

I think greater emphasis in the field on regular marital checkups is needed to help couples work on little problems before they become bigger problems. This will significantly improve educational efforts to help couples keep their marriages in good working order or fix some problems that could cause a later breakdown. And I think it will reach more couples than traditional, programmatic, classroom approaches. I think the field is making progress on this but we need to do more to promote it. Greater government support would help. I understand that the federal government recently relaxed its requirement that all MRE programs receiving government funds provide at least 8 hours of instruction. This is a positive change that will facilitate more support for relationship checkups.

A close cousin to the idea of regular marital checkups is self-directed MME. Self-directed MME is what it sounds like: an educational program to strengthen the marriage or relationship that is done mostly in private rather than in a group setting and often allows the couple to tailor the curriculum to their specific interests and needs. Privacy and timing can be significant barriers to participation in traditional MME. Some would be more interested in working on their relationship if they didn't have to display it in public. For others, life is just busy and unpredictable and they lack the flexibility to participate in traditional programs.[8] Accessibility can be an issue, too, for rural couples or those with unreliable transportation. And for the younger, tech-savvy generation that has grown up with the entire world of information constantly at its fingertips, web-based programs may be more appealing than sitting in a classroom. Self-directed MME is an attempt, then, to overcome barriers to participation such as these.

In a meta-analytic study conducted by a graduate student of mine, Shelece McAllister, we looked at all self-directed MRE programs that have been evaluated and found overall evidence that self-directed programs can work, although their effects so far appear to be fairly small.[9] (She also found that traditional programs that supplement their classroom education with significant self-directed curricula produce stronger effects.) But I think we are getting better at self-directed MME.

Some recent, specific studies suggest that online, self-directed MME can produce significant change. For instance, researchers recently evaluated a creative, web-based, self-paced MME program called *Power of Two,* with a strong emphasis on communication skills.[10] Couples who participated in the program had improved conflict resolution and marital satisfaction scores two months after the program compared to couples who were randomly assigned to a control group. In another study, my BYU colleague, Steve Duncan, compared an online version of an MME curriculum based on Gottman's Sound Marital House theory with a traditional, face-to-face, classroom version of the curriculum and a no-treatment control group.[11] There was roughly equivalent, positive change in both intervention groups compared to the no-treatment control group. Also, a recent study of a brief, PREP-based, online program for foster and adoptive parents provided evidence that those parents taking this online course on their own reported greater knowledge and use of effective communication skills compared to a control group.[12] Parenthetically, a meta-analytic study of more than 50 evaluations of online vs. face-to-face instruction with primary and secondary education students found that online instruction modestly out-performed face-to-face instruction.[13]

Also, Kim Halford at the University of Queensland (Australia) and his colleagues have developed a home-based, self-directed MME program called *Couple C.A.R.E.* (Commitment and Relationship Enhancement).[14] The curriculum has the typical dimensions of improving communication skills and intimacy. But it also has a less common and intriguing focus on what Halford calls "relationship self-regulation," which is learning to evaluate one's own behavior in the relationship across a wide range of domains, setting goals for personal change to strengthen the relationship, and implementing and evaluating the effects of those changes. *Couple C.A.R.E.* involves six lessons on DVD and an accompanying workbook with personal and couple exercises to reinforce and practice course material. In addition, a trained facilitator calls couples going through the program about once a week to encourage involvement, answer questions, briefly review lessons, and help participants implement self-change plans. In a series of studies, Halford has shown that participation in this self-directed program can improve couple communication, relationship self-regulation, and marital satisfaction, and that the effects seem to last for several years (although they diminish somewhat over time).[15] In a version of the program targeted to new parents, *Couple C.A.R.E. for Parents,* Halford's team has shown positive outcomes compared to a regular, phone-based, new-parent program for mothers, but those positive outcomes are primarily found in high-risk couples.[16]

Finally, as I was writing this chapter I became aware of two new, innovative attempts to maintain and strengthen marriages using self-guided, web-based educational programs. The first program was developed for military personnel, especially those separated from their spouses for long periods of time by deployment. It was developed by John Gottman. He developed a four-module, web-based, self-directed intervention for soldiers to learn relationship skills based on his book, *The Seven Principles for Making Marriage Work.*[17] This curriculum is embedded into the U.S. military's *Comprehensive Soldier Fitness* program. The new curriculum has not been rigorously evaluated yet, but it is another example of how program developers are making use of the Internet as a useful delivery vehicle for MME.

A second program was developed by Jacques Bazinet, a creative entrepreneur who worked with Steven Covey as a corporate trainer and is a former member of the Utah Commission on Marriage. He has launched a program called *Guarantee Your Marriage* (GYM).[18] Bazinet's team produced a series of 30-minute, web-based modules for married couples based on the PREP program. Couples who sign up for the program pay a monthly fee to engage in these marriage-maintenance modules and accompanying activities. In return, couples who actively participate in GYM and reach 20 years of marriage receive a $25,000 reward (paid out over 5 years). Moreover, if couples participate actively in GYM for at least 4 years but still divorce, they receive $10,000 payment (paid out over 5 years) to help defray the expenses of divorce. But the cost of this for-profit program would make it difficult for lower income couples to participate without some help. Still, it's an intriguing model that should be monitored. If it turns out to be cost effective, government funds could be used to underwrite participation of lower income couples; the cost would actually be less than the initial costs of the Supporting Healthy Marriage program that provided an intensive traditional program for lower income married couples.

Based on this emerging body of evaluation research of different curricula delivered in different ways, I think that self-directed and web-based MME programs can and should have a prominent place as a way to promote more access to and involvement in MME, especially for couples who would not otherwise have ready access to or interest in traditional, face-to-face programs.

Narrowcast Interventions

I've thought a lot about writing this section of my book because of a nagging sense over several years that we have overinvested in an open-mouth-insert-fire-hose pedagogy for MME. It's not hard to understand why there is this approach. There's a lot that goes into making a marriage work day-to-day, year-to-year, and decade-to-decade on the way to forever. There's a lot that can go wrong. Scholars know a lot about what makes for a healthy, stable marriage, and we're learning more every year about how to help people get there. And people's circumstances are so varied these days. With all this good information and all the needs and different circumstances, we can't resist the urge once a couple walks through our classroom door to stick fire hoses in their mouths and crank open the fire hydrant of good information. But is this really the best way for people to learn in ways that will help them tailor change to strengthen their marriage today and tomorrow? And is this the best way to attract people to our programs? I have wondered about this while observing some all-day workshops and personally experiencing information overload even though I was familiar with the curriculum. Maybe there is a useful comparison to broadcast television here. Broadcast television develops a wide range of programs and then sends them out over the airwaves or cable channels knowing that only some of what is offered will be of interest to viewers, but hoping there is something of interest for all viewers. Similarly, a participant in a MRE program can only be attuned to so much. A broadcast approach to MRE can be inefficient, especially for couples who may be experiencing a particular challenge and would like to work specifically on that challenge and not have to deal with other things right now.

So another way I think we can improve the effectiveness and value of marriage maintenance education is to put more emphasis on narrowcasting our educational offerings to focus on more specific issues and targets. Trying to be all things to all people and their wide range of issues and circumstances at all times may not be the best approach.[19] The traditional approach to MME generally puts a dominant focus on communication skills, based on the idea that if we can provide couples with strong communication and problem-solving skills, then they can apply these general skills to their own set of challenges. There is some merit to this general approach, although there is debate in the field about how well couples do at applying these general skills in their real lives.[20] But I think there also is merit to the idea that a general skill is best learned in a context that is tailored to a specific, personal challenge. Moreover, narrowcasting to a specific issue and specific demographic group probably improves our ability to market MME and attract more eager participants. A general appeal to come work on your relationship is harder to market than a specific appeal to address the particular issue that you are struggling with right now. More often than not, MME practitioners market their program as able to help everyone regardless of their relationship situation or circumstances. I think they do so thinking it expands the pool of potential participants and thus increases the number who will sign up for the program. I wonder if the opposite isn't true; a smaller target may actually yield bigger interest. Narrowcast MME could include education for a specific group, such as couples transitioning to parenthood, or education for a specific topic, such as dealing with financial disagreements that appear to be particularly potent for marital dissatisfaction and divorce.[21] The field is already starting to do more of this narrowcasting. I want to call attention to it and urge more effort.

For instance, a major transition for many couples is becoming parents. This changes the nature of the family and family roles and responsibilities, time together, sleep patterns, and a host of other things that can impact marital relationships.[22] And research documents that some couples experience a significant dip in their marital satisfaction during this time.[23] So the transition to parenthood is a prime time for doing some preventative work that can keep minor issues from mushrooming into major problems. And this is one narrowcast area that has received a good deal of attention, although many of the programs that focus on helping couples through the transition to parenthood are too long and intensive, I think, to attract many participants, especially at such a busy time in their lives. So I think we need to dial these programs down somewhat. This goes against some evidence that the more intensive transition-to-parenthood programs seem to produce somewhat stronger results.[24] But the more intensive the program, the fewer couples will participate. So I think we may need to live with this trade-off, sacrificing a little stronger impact for a much greater reach. Overall, there is a body of good research showing that these programs can be helpful,[25] including some studies that follow new-parent couples for several years.[26] But we need more program evaluation research with samples of lower income couples going through the transition to parenthood. Some of these programs also address parenting behavior, achieving modest success.[27]

A challenge faced by couples early in marriage, during the transition to parenthood, and beyond is sharing domestic labor. When couples are squabbling about how to divide housework and childcare it can wear down a marriage. This could be a fruitful area for more narrowcast MME. Earlier in my career I created a program called *Sharing the Second Shift* and in a field evaluation study (without a control-group comparison) found some positive effects on couple satisfaction with the division of domestic labor and improved relationship satisfaction.[28] But I haven't seen a lot more work in this area over the last 20 years and I think it is ripe for picking. The program I designed was too long (again, about 12 hours of face-to-face instruction). We need to shrink programs like this down to an economy size so that they will attract more interest from busy dual-earner couples.

Back in Chapter 6 I discussed the value of targeting remarried couples for specific curricula to deal with the distinctive challenges of stepfamilies. So I won't revisit that here, but I think it fits the general idea of narrowcast MME that I'm promoting. There are some other possibilities like this that I can think of, such as targeting parents who are adopting children to help them deal with their challenges. There is some evidence that adoptive parents would like help with their couple relationship as well as with their parenting.[29] The Oklahoma Marriage Initiative has an ongoing program like this for adoptive parents. Foster parenting can be hard on a marriage, too, so perhaps state agencies that oversee the foster care system could add a brief MME service to their support of parents who are providing this important service to children and their communities. At least one study has shown early positive results for MME programs targeted to these at-risk groups.[30]

There are specific problems that some married couples face that they may be reluctant to get intensive help with, but might respond to a brief, educational intervention. Alcohol abuse would be one example. Sometimes reporters and students ask me what I think is the most important thing we could do to strengthen marriages. Sometimes I reply that if a genie granted me one wish, I think I would magically do away with alcohol. While most handle alcohol well, far too many do not. I suspect alcohol abuse has done more to destroy families across time and space than any other single thing. Preventing an emerging alcohol problem from becoming an entrenched, chronic, and even relationship-dissolving problem seems like a good idea, but I only know of one empirically tested attempt to merge MME and alcohol-abuse prevention education.[31]

Another valuable narrowcast topic for MME is building a support system for the marriage. Marriages tend to be more isolated than they have been in the past.[32] And lower income married couples may feel especially isolated. Having some positive social support is a real asset to a marriage. Close family members and good friends, especially ones that are cheerleaders for the marriage, can lend a constructive, listening ear when needed and are a general resource to provide a more supportive context for our marriages. Some scholars have criticized educational efforts to help lower income couples for not addressing important factors outside the relationship that make it difficult to sustain a healthy relationship.[33] One of these external factors is the social support system. (Another is external stressors, which I address next.) But there may be some active steps couples can take to strengthen their social support systems that in turn can strengthen their marriage. The PREP program that I've highlighted several times in this book explicitly includes instruction on building positive social support networks. An interesting recent study evaluated the effectiveness of the PREP program with a group of lower income African American couples. Historically, social support networks have been especially important for African American families struggling against social injustice and discrimination. In this study, the researchers found large, positive gains for couples as a result of the program. But interestingly, they found even larger, positive changes for men when their partners reported increased feelings of social support from family and friends.[34] (They did not find an effect for women with men's social support.) This suggests to me the potential for developing a narrowcast curriculum focused on how to build better social support systems and make them be a resource for a strong marriage.

Similarly, dealing with external stresses—job loss, financial pressures, chronic or acute health problems—can take their toll on relationships.[35] And lower income couples have a disproportionate share of these kinds of external stressors. As I said in Chapter 3, I'm in favor of other effective social policies that help lower income individuals with external stresses, which in turn can reduce negative pressures on a relationship. But in addition, there may be some skills we can give couples that will help them isolate those external stresses from their effects on the relationship. This would be another fruitful area for a narrowcast educational offering to strengthen marriages.

One program that gives this issue a lot of attention is the *Fatherhood, Relationship, and Marriage Education* (FRAME) program.[36] This is an educational program specifically aimed at helping couples cope with stress to improve couple relationships and parenting behaviors. It was developed by Martha Wadsworth and her colleagues at the University of Denver, adapted from the PREP curriculum. The curriculum is broader (general relationship skills and parenting skills in addition to a primary focus on coping with stress) and more intensive (14 contact hours) than the narrowcast idea I'm promoting here. But I bring it up to examine empirically the potential of a program with a strong focus on coping with stress. In a study of the effectiveness of the FRAME program with a sample of ethnically diverse lower income couples (mostly married), Wadsworth and her colleagues found that couples who received the intervention reported reduced stress in some areas and more effective communication and problem solving around external stress issues compared to a control group, and these changes were associated with reductions in symptoms of depression. The study wasn't designed in such a way to be able to isolate the coping curriculum as the primary active ingredient implicated in the change (as opposed to other curriculum or program elements).

An earlier study by Guy Bodenmann and his colleagues in Switzerland evaluated a program that is predominantly focused on teaching couples skills for coping with stress, although this study was not with a lower income sample. But a study of the effectiveness of Bodenmann's *Couples Coping Enhancement Training* (CCET) program found positive changes in couple coping skills and increases in marital quality for CCET couples compared to control-group couples, although the effects diminished somewhat over the 2-year period of the study.[37] The field needs to develop and evaluate brief, narrowcast programs that focus on helping couples cope more effectively with external stress. When we do, I think we will find some encouraging results that will make the case for this focus in MME and appeal to larger numbers of couples.

Naturalistic Microinterventions

In some ways, I think the practice of marriage and relationship education is still trapped in the interventionist equivalent of the DOS era in computing. Younger readers may not even recognize this comparison. Older readers will remember that in the early years of personal computing, users had to learn a special language—a syntax of exact commands—to get the computer to do what they wanted it to do. It took significant training and experience to operate a computer (and it was slow). Then Steve Jobs and Apple Computer came along and blew this approach out of the water. Instead, Jobs created an operating system for the personal computer in which users were presented a menu of functions and all they had to do was point and click with a little device called a mouse. All the complex programming was hidden behind a set of menu requests. User interface was simple, intuitive, reliable, and didn't require a big investment up front to be able to work a computer. It made personal computing a tool for the masses. Even our technophobic parents and grandparents could learn how to point and click to avail themselves of the power of personal computing.

Similarly, I fear that the MRE—and more specifically, the MME—field is still comfortable with a kind of DOS approach to its work. "You have a complex but highly valuable machine called a marriage," the professional educator says to the masses of the undertrained marriage-machine operators out there. "You need significant training and some specialized skills to be able to operate that machine optimally. Come take my class. Give me 12 hours over the next few months and I'll teach you some new skills so that you can make better use of that machine and end much of the frustration you've had trying to operate it."

These marriage machines are complex, I admit. The knowledge and skills to make them work are not encoded in our genes and do not come as naturally as breathing and smiling. But can we make the operation of the machine simpler? Can we access the complexity of the machine through a set of straightforward behaviors that virtually all can do? I think this is the big challenge for the next generation of marriage and relationship scholars and educators. How can we simplify the complexity of marital health and make the hard work of marriage maintenance easier for all couples? I see some work going on in the field already that may open up our thinking about some ways to do this. These approaches make use of naturally occurring behaviors and add simple features to them that may help keep marriages healthy and growing. The upfront learning time is minimal and the learned behavior is practiced regularly as a part of prosaic pattern of daily life.

Relationship-Focused Prayer

For instance, I have been fascinated with some work by prominent psychological researcher Frank Fincham at Florida State University. With a group of talented students and colleagues, Fincham has been giving serious scholarly attention to the potential of daily prayer as a mechanism to strengthen romantic relationships. Prayer couldn't be a tool to help everyone, of course. But 80% of Americans say they are sure there is a God and nearly 60% of American adults say that they pray regularly.[38] Married people tend to be more religious than others, so I suspect that this latter figure is even higher for them, probably a solid two thirds. Fincham and his colleagues have wondered whether the regular behavior of prayer could be harnessed as a relationship-strengthening tool. Prayer is something that many married people do everyday together and by themselves. And prayer is supposed to call out our better natures. We pray for our loved ones and we pray that we can be better people. Undoubtedly people pray often about their marriages and for their spouses. Could this behavior, which occurs during the natural course of religious people's daily lives, be harnessed and enhanced in a formal way to overcome problems and strengthen marriages? Perhaps some may think that it's a bit presumptuous for social scientists to take a sacred and personal religious ordinance and tinker with it for their purposes. I'll let readers ponder the theological implications of this matter on their own. Like Fincham and his colleagues, I'm approaching this issue now from an empirical perspective. Can a naturally, regularly occurring behavior of perhaps two-out-of-three married Americans be borrowed and enhanced to become an effective microintervention to strengthen a marriage? A fascinating set of experiments suggests an intriguing potential.

In a set of experimental studies employing volunteer undergraduate students (mostly women) who were in a romantic relationship and who prayed at least occasionally, Fincham and his colleagues explored the effects of prayer on romantic relationships. The studies were with unmarried young adults, but I think the application to married relationships is relevant. For instance, in one study, students were randomly assigned to four different groups.[39] In the first group, students were assigned to set aside time each day for 4 weeks to pray for the well-being of their partners. In the second group, they were assigned to set aside time each day for 4 weeks to pray, but were not directed to pray specifically for their partners. In the third group, students were assigned to set aside time each day for 4 weeks to think positive thoughts about their partners. And in the final group, students were assigned to set aside time each day for 4 weeks to think about what they had done that day. After 4 weeks, the researchers found that students who had been assigned to the two prayer-focused intervention groups reported significantly higher scores on a measure of gratitude (for the relationship and for life generally).

Similarly, in a subsequent study, about 50 undergraduate students were randomly assigned to two conditions.[40] The first group was taken to a private room and asked to pray for their partners. The second group also was taken to a private room and asked to describe their partners' physical characteristics (recorded privately on a tape recorder). After the assigned activity, students filled out a questionnaire; those who had prayed for their partner had higher scores on a measure of forgiveness than the other group.

In another study, about 80 undergraduate students were randomly assigned to one of three groups.[41] The first group was assigned to set aside time each day for 4 weeks to pray for their partners, and were given an example of what that kind of prayer would be like. A second group was assigned to engage in undirected prayer. And the control group was assigned to think about their day. After 4 weeks, students in the partner-focused prayer group reported lower infidelity to their partner (in thoughts and deeds) than did the undirected-prayer group and the control group. Furthermore, the researchers determined that it was a sense of the relationship as sacred, which apparently came from the prayers, that was responsible for these group differences. In a follow-up study to this experiment, objective observers who didn't know to which group the students had been assigned observed the individuals participating in the study as they talked about their relationships and rated those in the partner-focused prayer group as having higher commitment to their relationships than those in the other groups.

Finally, in a similar study, about 120 undergraduate volunteers were randomly assigned to one of four groups.[42] The first group was assigned to pray for their partners each day for 4 weeks and were given a set of various relationship themes to focus their prayers, with the themes changed every 3–4 days. The second group was assigned to engage in undirected prayer each day for 4 weeks. A third group was assigned to think and write about their relationship and was given the same set of relationship themes as the first group. A final group was assigned just to take time each day to write about their daily activities. After 4 weeks, students were asked to report on their partners' alcohol consumption during this time. The researchers found that students in the two prayer groups reported that their partners drank about half as much alcohol as the partners in the two non-prayer groups.

These were a set of experimental manipulations with unmarried undergraduate students. But I can imagine some brief, formal interventions, perhaps in a religious setting, instructing married couples to pray for each other every day in specific ways to strengthen the relationship. Or maybe couples who regularly read scriptures together could enhance this time with a relationship focus: apply something learned from that day's scripture reading to help strengthen their relationship. This kind of approach piggy-backs a relationship-strengthening microintervention onto a regularly occurring behavior. It doesn't require special training as an instructor and it doesn't involve a large investment of time by couples to learn a set of new and perhaps foreign behavioral skills. Embedded within this enhanced, natural behavior of praying for a partner may be a set of relationship processes that are activated by partner-focused prayer, such as increased willingness to forgive, greater commitment, treating the relationship as special and sacred, and holding oneself to a higher standard. Each of these processes is linked to stronger relationships and stable marriages.[43] I can also imagine a similar microintervention for nonreligious couples that might teach them a basic skill of focused meditation on the relationship.

Enhanced Date Nights

Another regular and natural behavior ripe for enhancement is the typical couple date night. Of course, regular and natural might be overstating it for many; some married couples are better at this date night thing than others. Indeed, many couples struggle to carve regular time out of busy work schedules, childcare responsibilities, and personal recreation, even though they know that regular couple time is important to the health of their relationship.

I admit that my wife and I have had better and worse times for regular date nights. But I think that most married couples know this is important and want to do it. Even those who regularly carve out the time perhaps could use some help in structuring the date to be more effective at enhancing the relationship (rather than a time to gripe about the boss, talk about the kids' behavior, worry about parents, or complain about some relationship problem that continues to nag).

There hasn't been much research on the potential benefits of date nights for married couples. Nevertheless, Brad Wilcox at the University of Virginia and the National Marriage Project and Jeff Dew at Utah State University (a former student of mine) mined some large national data sets with data on couple time together to take an indirect look at how couple time was associated with marital quality.[44] They found that individuals who reported having couple time at least once a week were three times as likely to say they were very happy in their marriage compared to those who reported couple time less frequently (controlling statistically for a host of other potential demographic differences). In addition, they found that these differences in marital happiness could be explained by greater satisfaction with communication and sex, as well as higher levels of commitment among couples who invest in regular couple time. Also noteworthy, couples who reported more couple time together at one point in time were about half as likely to experience a divorce over the next 5 years. Moreover, they found that new parents who were able to maintain their couple time together after their baby was born were half as likely to experience the common decline in marital satisfaction during the transition to parenthood. Interestingly, they also found that wives who attended religious services infrequently, as well as wives with relatively low relationship-commitment scores, benefited much more from regular couple time compared to religious and high-commitment wives.

Another study randomly assigned married couples to three conditions.[45] One group engaged in a date night with a mutually-agreed-on fun and expanding activity (e.g., going to a play, hiking, skiing, dancing) for 10 weeks. A second group engaged in mutually pleasant but more commonplace activities (e.g., movie, dinner out) for 10 weeks. The third group was a no-date-night control group. After 10 weeks the special date night group reported significantly improved marital quality compared to the other two groups. So perhaps date nights are best when they involve some expanding activity that both enjoy. These findings correspond with a recent study by some colleagues of mine at the Utah State University. They conducted a formative evaluation study of a date night microintervention that they have been offering in a number of Utah locations as part of the Utah Healthy Marriage Initiative. Date nights were a 2-hour fun activity, such as a cooking class, couple massage, or rock climbing (as opposed to a movie or a dinner out). At the beginning of the event, a facilitator led a 10–15 minute presentation and discussion about some relationship concept or skill that was related to the evening's activity. For example, the couple rock-climbing exercise was preceded by a discussion of the importance of teamwork, trust, and communication. And during the rock climbing, couples were encouraged to integrate what they learned into the experience. The facilitator concludes the evening by giving couples take-home materials to reinforce the learned concept, such as a how-to book. In their simple field study of these date night microinterventions with about 150 couples, my colleagues found that both wives and husbands reported a significant increase in specific relationship knowledge as a result of the intervention. In brief qualitative comments on the evaluation form, individuals also reported specific benefits from the events, including increased communication, teamwork, time together, and fun time.[46]

I think there is real potential in this kind of microintervention for married couples. It lends itself to easy marketing with fun, brief activities. I suspect a commitment to do something fun together once a week, like going to a local rock concert together and then discussing the relationship messages in the lyrics about romantic relationships, will attract a lot more couples than a 12–20-hour, 6–10-week program of intense instruction. The initial instruction for a date night is very brief, but then a learned principle is reinforced with fun, hands-on activities. If couples can participate regularly in these events, then they could learn a pattern for improving the quality of their regular, ongoing date nights that could help them maintain a satisfying marriage.

Daily Rituals

My colleague at the University of Minnesota, Bill Doherty, talks about the potential value of couple and family rituals to fight against the relationship entropy I discussed in Chapter 6.[47] For instance, Doherty tells about a ritual that he and his wife, Leah, used for many years that helped them keep their relationship a priority.[48] When their children were young and their careers were busy, the demands on their time were great. But they made a decision to set aside a little time each day to reconnect. They made a strong commitment to have a family meal together every night, which is laudable. But after the meal was done and the dishes rinsed and put in the dishwasher, the children were told to go play on their own while Mom and Dad had some time together. They were told not to interrupt unless someone was bleeding. (I can imagine that it took some time for them to drill this into their children.) Bill and Leah put on a pot of coffee and while it brewed, they sat down and began talking with each other about their day and how they were feeling. Over coffee they reconnected. At first they found that they would use this time to address some relationship concerns, but they didn't find that very conducive to simple reconnecting and prioritizing the relationship. So they made a rule that they couldn't talk about relationship problems during this time; those were relegated to other times. Instead, they just focused on their days, getting to know each other better, reconnecting, and relaxing together. This little daily routine took about 20–30 minutes but became a ritual that they deeply valued and credit with an ability to fight the forces of marital entropy. After their last child left home and they were having dinner together alone, they got out of the habit of their post-dinner coffee time together. But they realized eventually that even though they had more time together to talk during dinner, the ritual had come to serve a distinct purpose of symbolizing the priority they put on their relationship. So they decided to keep it going.

At a conference I attended where Doherty was speaking on this topic, he took a microphone and roved the audience inviting individuals there to share their own couple rituals. I'll never forget the story told by one middle-aged woman who stood and spoke about a ritual her husband (and children) had begun several years previously. It came at a time when life was particularly busy and stressful and she was feeling its toll on her marriage. One evening as she walked through the door she noticed that her husband (and children) who were home hardly acknowledged her return from work. In contrast, the family dog came running up, jumping on her and licking her face and whipping the air with hurricane-force tail-wagging. Later that evening she shared this contrasting experience with her husband, saying that she was worried that they were drifting apart. Her husband remarked that he too had been worrying about how distant they were becoming during this time of stress. They decided to try and do something about it. Her husband came up with a particularly creative suggestion in the form of a daily reconnection ritual. He suggested that when one came home and the other was already there, they had to beat the dog to the entryway and out-do the dog in greeting enthusiasm. At first the children were utterly bemused by dad running to the door to greet mom by jumping up and down and wagging his behind and slopping kisses all over their mother! But eventually they joined in. The woman who told this story at this conference did so with a good deal of emotion and said that this daily ritual became the reminder that they needed to help them prioritize their relationship and prevent a slow deterioration that could have jeopardized their marriage and family.

I think creative interventionists could harness the power of daily or regular ritual in marriage-maintenance microinterventions. A brief, one-session class (a date night?) could teach couples about the power of daily rituals to fight relationship entropy and encourage couples to create their own rituals. Instructors could provide some guidelines for ways to do this effectively. (Doherty gives several useful guidelines in his book, *The Intentional Family*.[49]) Perhaps a follow-up booster class a few months later could then allow couples to share their experiences, learn from each other, and refine their own efforts. Or instructors could set up a social networking site for couples to share their ongoing experiences.

I suspect there are endless possibilities for different kinds of microinterventions to help married couples work on their marriages: a daily midday check-in call to chat about your day and saying you look forward to doing something together tonight; posting a daily love message to your spouse's Facebook page; a couple dishwashing chore that includes some strategic, fun touching; a bedtime foot massage ritual that includes some relaxed talk. Those were a few ideas I came up with off the top of my head as I wrote this paragraph. Some might be silly or ineffective, but there are endless possibilities to explore. The point is that it is probably more important that couples do *something* rather than something *specific*. That is, when it comes to countering relationship entropy, I'm not convinced that the specific approach and content of MRE is nearly as important as the general effort to attend to the relationship and to put some energy into the marital system at regular intervals.

Enterprising, technology-savvy entrepreneurs already are at work at developing relationship-maintenance apps for our smart phones. I'll bet there is great potential for technology-assisted regular maintenance behaviors. The point is to find natural, simple behaviors that occur on a regular basis and enhance them with a small relationship-focused element that allows couples to reconnect, experience a bit of romance, communicate in positive ways, and get in touch with the core feelings of love and friendship that easily get buried under a pile of daily cares and stresses. Creative practitioners can suggest numerous different strategies and monitor which ones work well and why. They will need to be attuned to those strategies that work best for lower income couples, as well, whose marriages face the most stress and who have more difficulty finding time together.

A possible barrier to these marriage-maintenance microinterventions is whether government administrators will accept them as legitimate and support them with funding. The programs involved in major evaluation studies by the federal government for lower income couples (i.e., Building Strong Families; Supporting Healthy Marriage) were much more intensive than the typical programs. While more intensive interventions are one approach that deserves study, I think we should be experimenting with microinterventions, too. If they can produce positive, lasting changes, they would be much more cost effective than the more traditional programs, which is always an asset in public policy. Sometimes less is more and small is often beautiful. I think the federal government should fund some rigorous projects designed to test the effectiveness of these kinds of microinterventions to help couples.

One final thought in this section advocating naturalistic, microinterventions. I've given more attention to the micro dimension than to the natural dimension. But even with more traditional, programmatic, face-to-face MRE, I think they will be more effective in more natural settings and with more familiar instructors. I suspect that asking individuals and couples to come to a strange place to learn from a strange instructor will diminish the potential effectiveness of MRE for many. What is more likely to be effective in recruiting, retaining, and positively impacting individuals and couples are settings that the participants are familiar and comfortable with and instructors who have an on-going, positive relationship with the couple.[50] One recent study found that a positive relationship or strong alliance with the instructor is associated with stronger outcomes in MRE for participants.[51]

So, for example, interventions in high schools with known teachers,[52] in faith-based settings with trusted religious leaders,[53] and on military bases with chaplains who are respected (and who get deployed alongside their participants)[54] will likely be more effective. I have heard MRE educators in small, rural towns talk about how they regularly cross paths with former participants in their classes and how natural it is to ask about how the relationship is doing. Other possibilities exist, as well.

Media Campaigns

Again, I want to reiterate that I think there is still an important role for traditional approaches to MRE, even as we experiment with other, creative approaches. One of the most significant barriers to the potential of traditional marriage and relationship education is a simple lack of awareness of what it is and how to access it. Perhaps the most important improvement to make to MRE is to get more people to use it. Accordingly, I believe we need to invest in media campaigns to counter this lack of awareness and to spur greater participation.

But there is an additional, direct benefit of MRE media campaigns. Helping people to understand its value and get access to its services may help those who then seek it out. But most media campaigns also carry with them a substantive message that can motivate a slight behavioral course change. Could media campaigns be used directly as an intervention to help couples form and sustain healthy marriages and relationships, even if they do not seek out a formal MRE experience? Are relationship attitudes and behaviors amenable to small but meaningful shifts as a result of media campaign messages? A generation of research on a wide array of media campaigns suggests that complex human behaviors can be tweaked by these messages.

I'm getting into the realm of public health now. We've all seen the extensive media campaigns aimed at reducing expensive and debilitating unhealthy behaviors: antismoking campaigns, antidrug abuse campaigns, buckle-up seat belt campaigns, prenatal care campaigns, child abuse prevention campaigns, and so forth. These campaigns use mass media to send a message and provide a resource for more information with the intent of reducing poor health behaviors. They don't eliminate the problems they address, obviously, but a generation of research now is providing evidence that these campaigns—especially sustained campaigns—can change behaviors for some and reduce the problems.[55] Even small changes multiplied across the community or nation add up to noticeable health improvement and significant savings of public funds spent on the problems.

For instance, the sustained (and well funded) American Legacy Foundation's "truth" anti-smoking campaign has shown significant population-level effects. This counter-marketing campaign cleverly counters a "smoking is hip and cool" commercial marketing message with an alternative behavioral strategy for youth to rebel against smoking-industry manipulation and assert their independence. A study documented a decline in youth smoking from 25% to 18% in a short span of time, with the "truth" media campaign accounting for about one quarter of that decline.[56] Successful campaigns have also helped to reduce unhealthy eating behaviors in children.[57] Similarly, the Parents Speak Up National Media Campaign was designed to help parents talk early and often to their teens about delaying the onset of sex. An evaluation study showed encouraging results. Parents who viewed and heard campaign messages talked more with their teens about sex and sexual responsibility than parents who did not view and hear the messages.[58]

These are just a few examples of how well-designed public health media campaigns were able to get potent messages to change behavior for some people. Smart, creative social marketers should be able to do this in ways to help couples form and sustain healthy marriages and relationships. In fact, they are already doing so. For instance, the Utah Healthy Marriage Initiative has employed one of the leading marketing firms in Utah to help get their message out, especially to the 18–29-year-old demographic. They did some research to guide the messaging. They found that while young adults in Utah had a positive view of marriage, one significant concern they had was the personal challenge of going from independent life as a single person to an interdependent life as a married couple. The marketing firm used this nagging unease to craft a series of creative cartoon TV and print ads. The ads showed, for instance, a couple humorously working alone and then together to turn the "M" in "Me" upside down to change it to "We."[59] The tag line is: "If you want a stronger marriage, work on it together." Then the ad points the viewer to the Utah Healthy Marriage Initiative web site for a list of MRE classes and other resources. So the ad accomplishes several things. First, it plants a message about the need for relationships to move beyond "me" to "we"—the value of being an "us." Second, it sends the message that people can get some educational help learning how to do this. Last, it points them to a web site that directs them to specific classes and other resources. As I mentioned in Chapter 2, in the first 3 years of this campaign, these kinds of ads were seen more than 33 million times in the target demographic of young adults. And we have anecdotal data suggesting that these efforts led more people to the classes offered in the state.

First Things First, a community-based healthy marriage and relationship initiative in Chattanooga, Tennessee, is perhaps the premier example of a community-based HMRI. With government funding, it developed a series of generic billboard, TV, radio, and print ads. (These are available for use by other initiatives because their development was underwritten by government funds.) I especially like their "commitment" series.[60] For instance, one ad shows a woman running and running, and a female voiceover talks about how commitment is needed to overcome hard days and achieve desired goals. At the end of the 30-second ad she says, "So, yeah, I'm absolutely committed . . . to my marriage." Then the ad refers viewers to the First Things First web site to find educational resources to help strengthen marriages and relationships. Again, a message is sent about the importance of commitment to marriage, and then viewers are encouraged to avail themselves of resources to work on their marriage. This same ad can be used as a radio ad and condensed to a billboard.

These are a few illustrations of the kinds of media campaigns that are being developed. I think we need to do more. The most significant barrier is funding, because good campaigns take skilled planning and sustained efforts. I'll talk a little more about how to meet this challenge in Chapter 9. But media campaigns can increase the numbers of couples investing in formal MRE and can infuse positive messages into the culture and people's lives to strengthen their marriages and relationships.

Integrating Marriage and Relationship Education and Parenting Education

My final suggestion for improving the effectiveness of MRE is to provide more educational opportunities that integrate MRE with parenting, coparenting, and responsible fatherhood education. I saved this for my last recommendation because in many ways this suggestion goes against the grain of what I have urged in this chapter. While the chapter thus far has built a case for the need for briefer, regular, focused, and naturalistic interventions, this last recommendation calls for more programmatic MRE—but with a curricular twist.

On a conceptual level, a large body of research suggests that an improved couple relationship and a stable marriage improve the quality of parenting and child outcomes.[61] And interventions focused on strengthening couple relationships have shown the spillover ability to improve parenting and child outcomes.[62] In fact, some human development scholars now say that couple relationship quality should be considered a dimension of parenting behavior.[63] The noted couple therapist and scholar Sue Johnson summarizes this body of research this way: "Better relationships between love partners are not just a personal preference, they are a social good. Better love relationships mean better families. And better, more loving families mean better, more responsive communities."[64]

On a practical level, there are reasons for marrying couple education with parenting education. The earliest MRE programs focused on engaged couples and newlywed couples; programs assumed there weren't children in the family. But times have changed dramatically and now premarital and early marital couples, especially lower income couples and remarried couples, are likely to have children. So parenting is a big challenge even for many couples who have not been together long. Moreover, arguing with each other over parenting practices and responsibilities is one of the most common areas of disagreement for couples. Dealing directly with the substance of those conflicts—differing parenting philosophies, attitudes, and practices—can help alleviate those conflicts.[65] One educator in Alabama related a story to me of a couple that had been together for several years and had several children together but had not married. Their biggest roadblock was serious disagreements about parenting. They attended a MRE workshop that included a parenting curriculum. The class ended at 9:00 p.m. but they ended up talking at home until 2:00 a.m. They talked about and resolved a number of differences in their parenting philosophies and practices. As a result, they said their parenting improved, there were fewer arguments, and they finally decided to get married.

For some there is more appeal to learning how to be a better parent than focusing on the marriage. It's hard for some to admit that they are attending a program to improve their marriage. But that same stigma would be significantly less if they were attending a program to learn how to improve their parenting skills while also addressing the importance of strong couple relationships for the benefit of their children. After all, we all need help with the challenging and often frustrating aspects of parenting, so there is less stigma attached to parenting education. Merging couple and parenting education might help recruit more couples to invest the time to focus on their family. There is some evidence that it is easier to recruit Hispanic couples for MME if programs are advertised as parenting education to strengthen family relationships, because in many Hispanic cultures, once children come into the family parenthood is prioritized over the couple relationship.[66]

So for both theoretical and practical reasons, more and more contemporary programs are seeing the value of integrating marriage and relationship education with parenting, coparenting, and responsible fatherhood education.[67] I want to draw attention to this trend and encourage more of it,[68] even though this likely means longer, more intensive interventions.

I've mentioned a number of MME programs in this and previous chapters that include a substantial parenting education component. Many of them have been spurred by government funding. For instance, the *Couple C.A.R.E. for Parents* program mentioned earlier in this chapter has additional content focused on parenting.[69] In Chapter 6, I talked about the *Family Expectations* curriculum in Oklahoma City that is a part of the Supporting Healthy Marriage project supported by federal funds. The FE curriculum includes a number of modules on parenting topics, such as cooperative coparenting, the importance of father involvement to children's well-being, and parent–infant relationships. The *Supporting Father Involvement* and the *Smart Steps* curricula also mentioned in Chapter 6 have a strong parenting education component. Interestingly, one study that reviewed the limited research on programs targeted to remarried couples found that these programs generally had positive effects on parenting outcomes but not much impact on couple relationship outcomes.[70] I think the integration of MME and parenting education is an emerging best practice in the field.

An important cross-generational rationale exists for offering parenting education as a valuable element of MME. Scholarship now points to how important it is for young children to receive competent, sensitive, positive, authoritative parenting, especially early in life, in order for them to begin to develop emotional intelligence and regulation.[71] If parenting education can improve parenting behavior—and there is evidence that good programs can do so[72]—this should help children increase their emotional intelligence and regulation, which in turn should help these children as they mature into their adolescent and early adult years to form and sustain healthier romantic relationships that will keep them on positive trajectories to strong marriages. In other words, children begin learning early in life the generic relational skills that will facilitate establishing healthy romantic relationships later in life; responsive parenting bequeaths to children greater psychic resources to be able to give and receive love and affection.[73] Their primary teachers are parents, both in how they parent and in the examples they give their children of a healthy, stable relationship. While emotional or relational intelligence is not fixed early in life and immutable after that, early learning would be a tremendous asset as children grow into adolescence and young adulthood and begin forming romantic relationships. Relationship literacy education will go farther with emotionally intelligent youth and young adults already primed by positive parenting in their earlier years.

Summary and A Final Brief Thought

If the work of MME practitioners is really going to make a noticeable difference, if it is to move beyond promising to proven, if it is going to provide a worthy return on investment of public funds, then it needs to get better. In this chapter, I have provided my list of the top five improvements that we should make: invest in the potential of regular marital checkups and self-directed MME; increase the amount of narrowcast MME that is focused on specific topics, challenges, and life course stages; develop more creative microinterventions that are built on to naturally occurring, regular human processes; invest in media campaigns to promote more use of MRE and plant effective micromessages in the culture that can help couples; and integrate couple and parenting education. Each of these improvements will increase the accessibility of and interest in MME and thus grow the numbers of couples who participate, which may be the most important improvement we can make.

Of course, building a better product takes time. The auto industry needed decades to get to the quality products that cover the roads these days, and it is still hard at work improving its products. There is a great need for better educational products to help couples form and sustain healthy marriages and relationships. I think we are already headed in a positive direction, but we could go farther, faster by giving these recommendations for improvement more attention and resources. And other good ideas will emerge.

Which leads me to one final thought. Although our knowledge about the science of love has increased over the past 25 years and MRE has benefitted from that knowledge, I believe the learning curve will be much steeper over the next 25 years. And I think the emerging integration of psychology, sociology, biology, and neurology in the service of understanding romantic love will produce breakthrough insights. I think our tools for understanding love are getting more sophisticated along with the increasing need to understand it. Thus, one of the most important innovations in MRE over the coming decades will simply be to attend to a constant stream of new knowledge about how healthy relationships and enduring marriages are formed, sustained, and repaired, and learn to apply this knowledge in our MRE efforts. Similarly, I anticipate that the science of intervention to strengthen marriages and relationships will accelerate and become more sophisticated, sensitive, and effective at achieving its aims. The combination of greater basic knowledge and more refined intervention bodes well for the future of MRE.

Chapter 8

Divorce Orientation Education to Improve Decision Making about Divorce: Helping Individuals at the Crossroads of Divorce

Proposal 4: Require divorce orientation education before filing for divorce to help individuals at the crossroads of divorce think clearly about their decision and prevent some preventable divorces.

So far I have tried to make the case for greater public support for: relationship literacy education for youth and young adults; effective premarital education for engaged couples or relationship development education for cohabiting parents; and marriage maintenance education for married couples. I am confident that effective marriage and relationship education (MRE) programs can make a meaningful difference in helping more youth and young adults stay on a positive trajectory for forming and sustaining healthy relationships and enduring marriages. But I would add one more policy recommendation, one that acknowledges the reality that many married couples, even those that get off to a good start on the road to forever, can experience deep disappointments that threaten to dissolve their marriage.

I'll use the road trip and car analogies that I employed in earlier chapters one more time here. Cars break down sometimes, even good cars with plenty of miles left on them. I've owned a fair number of cars in my life. Typically I buy used cars and try to get as many miles out of them as I can. But at some point the cars appear to be breaking down and I have to make a tough call: should I invest in some costly repairs and hope to get more good miles out of the car? Or do I walk away and swallow the expense of getting another car? I'm not a car guy so I suspect my decisions have been made based mostly on gut intuition. And being a guy, I haven't asked for much help in making the decision. I suspect I could have used more help.

Marriages can break down, too; they don't come with no-failure guarantees. As I have mentioned in previous chapters, 40%–50% of first marriages in the United States and about 60% of second marriages end in divorce. Most marriages go through rough patches, even marriages that start from a strong foundation. But sometimes those patches become so discouraging that the idea of ending the relationship seems better than to keep trying to work things out.

With the specter of divorce and our cultural acceptance of it, we can't get away from thinking that divorce is the answer. Often it is. I need to clarify my own views on this. Personally and culturally, I hold marriage in deep respect. But I also believe that many divorces are necessary. There are behaviors that violate the moral boundaries of marriage. If change won't happen, divorce likely is necessary. Sometimes relationship problems become terminal and can't be cured. Maybe there were actions that could have been taken earlier that would have prevented the death of the relationship, but a threshold has been crossed and the path forward begins with divorce. I deeply value marriage and I think we should do all that we can to preserve our own and support others' marriages, especially when children are a part of the union. They have a big stake in the health and stability of the marriage. When we make our marriage vows, we really should mean what we say: this is forever. But I also understand that marriages can break down on the way to forever and divorce may be necessary. When I talk to my students about this issue, I summarize it this way: "Divorce should not be an option, even though sometimes it's a necessity." By this I mean that our moral responsibility is to commit to forever and do all that we can to overcome those challenges that threaten our marriages. We resist the cultural voices that urge us to start over when times get rough; we persevere. Anything short of this attitude places marriages at risk in our culture. But if the marriage becomes terminal, then we probably need to end it, and move on in ways that will limit the potential negative effects on our children.

But how do people know when a marriage becomes terminal? This is such a tough question, especially in a culture that is both so in love with marriage and so accepting of divorce. My colleague Bill Doherty at the University of

Minnesota worries that we too often treat marriage like another consumer good.[1] We expect that it will wear out or we will tire of it and need to toss it out and get a new one. Or, Doherty says, sometimes we approach a distressed marriage like a bruised peach. When a peach is bruised, you can't heal the bruise; it will spread gradually and ruin the rest of the peach. It's done; you have to throw it away and get another. I believe our cultural acceptance of divorce as the answer to serious marital problems diminishes our ability to work through serious problems. Rather than take our marriage into a repair shop for some bodywork and mechanical adjustments, we cash it in for scrap metal and start looking for a new one. Doherty even worries that many marriage "mechanics"—therapists that distressed couples seek out to help them repair their marriages—are much too quick to scrap their clients' marriages and aid them with a "good divorce" rather than helping them do the hard work to save their marriage.[2] His worries may have some merit. One study found that distressed couples who seek marital counseling are more likely to divorce than distressed couples who do not.[3] But other studies have estimated that about 80% of couples see improvement in their relationship after visiting a marriage counselor and, over the short term, almost half say all of their major problems were resolved.[4]

Is there evidence that some divorces are potentially shortsighted decisions? Do some couples abandon the marriage prematurely or without thinking carefully about the potential consequences? I have come to believe that some marriages end when there is still reasonable hope for repair and happiness. Perhaps I am being naïve to think that reconciliation is a possibility for more than a few couples and that public policies can help. I recognize, of course, that divorce is an incredibly personal decision. I don't purport to know what the answer is for any particular couple. But I think there is emerging evidence now that some individuals' choices to divorce are not the best option for themselves or their children. And the costs of divorce to our society are great, so there is a public interest in preventing shortsighted divorces. One national study conservatively estimated the yearly public costs of marital breakdown at $112 billion.[5] Another study of divorce in Texas conservatively estimated the public cost of divorce there at nearly $3.2 billion a year, which is more than 10% of the annual budget for the state of Texas.[6]

In this chapter, I'll begin with a review of the evidence that a portion of divorcing couples—perhaps about 10%–20%—end the marriage when they are ambivalent about doing so and there is a reasonable chance that they could reconcile and repair the relationship. Then I will propose educational policy that could help these couples think more clearly about the road they should take. In other words, I will argue for public policy that provides a sensitive, brief program designed to help couples at the crossroads of divorce think clearly and carefully about divorce and its potential consequences as they try to decide which direction to go. (And it is a policy that can help those who go in either direction at the crossroads of divorce.)

Evidence for Preventable Divorce

Does such a thing as an "unnecessary," "shortsighted," or "preventable" divorce exist? I think there is a mounting body of evidence that it does. I've written another short book on this issue,[7] but I'll try to summarize my thoughts briefly here by addressing three interrelated questions: (1) Are regret and ambivalence common in divorce? (2) Is reconciliation a realistic possibility for some? (3) Is divorce a reliable path to personal happiness? While divorce can serve to preserve the physical or psychological safety and well-being of family members, end terminal relationships, and reinforce the ethical boundaries of the institution of marriage, a body of research also indicates that some marriages headed toward divorce could be repaired and children and adults would likely be better off if the marriage were preserved.

Are Regret and Ambivalence Common in Divorce?

A handful of surveys from various states estimate that many divorced individuals wished they had worked harder to try and overcome their differences with their ex-spouse.[8] A study that followed divorced individuals over a long period of time found that, in 75% of divorced couples, at least one partner was having regrets about the decision to divorce 1 year after the breakup.[9] A recent survey of divorced individuals in Missouri found that 25% reported they had some regrets now about getting a divorce. About 12% said that looking back, they no longer were confident that they made the right decision to divorce. Seventeen percent said that if they knew how hard things would be after the divorce, they might have worked harder to try and fix the marriage.[10] Moreover, Robert Emery, a prominent divorce scholar at the University of Virginia, reports that ambivalent or mixed feelings about a divorce are common.[11] If feelings of regret and ambivalence are not rare, this suggests that the decision to divorce for some may not have been fully considered. It seems likely to me that some individuals and couples end up sliding into divorce in much the same way that some couples slide into marriage without full consideration of the impact of this transition.[12]

My research assistants and I have interviewed over the past few years a number of individuals about their experience of going through a divorce. We have been impressed in many of these interviews at the ambivalence they felt. In one interview, a woman told us that she was still deeply in love with her ex-husband despite the fact that he was unfaithful to her numerous times. She still was in contact with him almost daily. She depended on him to do a number of utilitarian tasks for her. She was dating a "great guy" but could not commit to marry him because it wouldn't be fair to be married to him and still in love with her ex-husband. In another interview with a woman who had been divorced 20 years, we were surprised to hear that she too still had feelings of ambivalence about her divorce. I knew this woman personally and had watched the evolution of her story over time. She married a man whom she had dated for quite some time and knew well. But a week after their marriage, he decided that the marriage was wrong and wanted a divorce. She fought hard for many years to try and fix the problems. He was a devoted father and good provider. But eventually he had an affair and also began physically abusing her, so they divorced. Life as a single mom was hard for her, as it is for almost everyone, but her ex-spouse remained a good and involved father and provided his ex-wife with economic support for many years. She never remarried. Twenty years after her divorce she told us in an interview that she still wonders whether she might have been better off if she had stuck with the marriage and tried to weather the storms. She said that, looking back, the problems of the marriage weren't worse than the problems of the divorce. From my personal perspective, I think she may be wrong. But the point is that divorce does not produce a clean break of a relationship and feelings of ambivalence are common even in situations where objectively a divorce appears to be the necessary decision.

Other research is documenting feelings of ambivalence as individuals approach divorce. Professor Doherty, whom I mentioned earlier in the chapter, conducted a study in Minnesota and found that about 25% of individuals and about 10% of couples—that is, both spouses—going through a mandated divorcing parents class felt that their marriage could still be saved, even at that late stage of the legal process of divorce. Similarly, 30% of individuals and 10% of couples expressed interest in a formal reconciliation service, if it were available.[13] So for some, divorce appears to be less a personal, well-considered decision than it is a predetermined outcome of entering into the legal process for untying the marital knot. Doherty conducted this research after talking to a group of divorce lawyers and family law judges in Minnesota who expressed deep skepticism about whether there were any couples who were ambivalent about their pending divorce. But one judge was curious and asked him to find out. The judge is now a convert, having seen the data. But the legal momentum of filing for divorce and the lack of services to help these ambivalent couples still result in a divorce for all but a few. (I'll discuss what Doherty is trying to do to fix this problem later in the chapter.)

Is Reconciliation a Realistic Possibility for Some?

There hasn't been a lot of research on reconciliation, unfortunately. One study estimated that about 10% of separated couples are able to reconcile successfully.[14] That corresponds with data I have from Utah finding that about 10%–15% of couples who file for divorce do not go through with it.[15] A recent study by some Ohio State University sociologists using a national data set found that separation (formal and informal) before divorce is quite common, lasting on average about 3–4 years.[16] About 80% of those who separate eventually divorce. The remaining 20% is divided between long-term separations and couples who eventually reconcile. Long-term separations are mostly among low-income couples. Reconciliation does occur, although the researchers found virtually no reconciliation after a 3-year threshold of marital separation. A study in Great Britain found that about 20% of individuals seriously considering divorce were still married two years later, although many of them were still enduring unsatisfying relationships but holding on because of a strong commitment to the marriage.[17]

Another study with a U.S. national data set suggests that a high percentage of people who say they are unhappy in their marriage, but stick it out for several years, later report that their marriage is happy again.[18] In this study of adults who gave the lowest rating on a marital satisfaction scale when first interviewed, more than 75% reported a few years later that they were happy or very happy. In a Utah study, about 30% of currently married adults said that their marriage had been in serious trouble at some point. But more than 90% of those individuals said they were glad that they had hung on and were still together.[19] Long-lasting marital unhappiness exists but is uncommon; unhappy marriages usually improve significantly over time for those who are patient and keep trying to work things out.

Perhaps this intriguing research finding can be understood better when considering the most common reasons people give for their divorce. A national study documented that the most common reason people gave for their divorce was a lack of commitment; nearly 75% said it was a major factor.[20] Other common reasons were too much arguing (56%), infidelity (55%), unrealistic expectations (45%), lack of equality in the relationship (44%), and lack of effective preparation for marriage (41%). Surveys in Oklahoma and Utah found a similar set of common reasons.[21] Many of these reasons for divorce seem amenable to patience and effort. People can learn better communication and problem-solving skills, as I have shown repeatedly in this book. They can establish more realistic expectations (a plug for marriage preparation education.) They can learn to treat each other with greater respect and act as equal partners. There are even ways to strengthen commitment to each other and to the marriage.[22] So, I think many of the most common reasons people give for their divorce are amenable to efforts to fix the problem if the parties are willing. No doubt some have tried hard to fix the problems and have not succeeded, but others could benefit from knowing that their problems may not be terminal. Infidelity is a common reason for divorce[23] and one of the most difficult marital injuries to heal, substantially increasing the risk of divorce.[24] Yet therapists devoted to helping couples recover from infidelity report significant success for couples willing to work together.[25] While most Americans (63%) say they would not forgive their spouse and would get a divorce if they discovered he or she had been unfaithful,[26] in actuality, researchers have found that about half of men and women who have been unfaithful are still married to their same spouse.[27] While the reconciliation process can be tortuous, forgiveness and social support can help couples who are motivated to try to stay together.[28]

Generally, we think that divorces come from couples experiencing high levels of conflict. But another reason why I think that more marriages can be saved at the crossroads of divorce is because most divorces seem to come from marriages that were not experiencing abuse or high levels of conflict. One set of researchers estimated that from half to two thirds of divorces come from couples who were not having a lot of serious arguments or experiencing abuse.[29] Instead these divorces seem to come from other problems, ones that may be amenable to change with patience and work. Also noteworthy from this research is the finding that the children of low-conflict marriages who experience their parents' divorce are generally the ones who have the hardest time adjusting.[30] In high-conflict marriages, the children likely are aware of the problems and divorce may be an expected and even welcome resolution. But in low-conflict marriages that end in divorce, the children likely are surprised and bewildered; a key foundation of their world has been cracked and they struggle to deal with these unwanted and, from their perspective, unwarranted changes in their family.

Is Divorce a Reliable Path to Personal Happiness?

When a marriage becomes destructive to a person's basic human dignity, then divorce is necessary. But divorce is not a straightforward path to a happier life. Certainly there is ample evidence that the process of marital breakdown, the aftermath of divorce, and struggles to rebuild a life and meet daily challenges can leave people feeling exhausted, lost, beaten down, lacking confidence, and depressed.[31] Of course, for some adults, divorce, despite its difficulties, can be the beginning of a new, energizing, and exciting path.[32] But for most, marital breakdown and divorce carry with them difficult adjustments that challenge personal resources to adapt.[33] In this body of research findings, it is difficult to separate the effects of marital breakdown from the effects of adjustment to divorce. Most likely both contribute to adjustment difficulties. That is, problems in the marriage make people unhappy and contribute to lower well-being, but problems adjusting to divorce exacerbate these problems and likely spawn additional ones.

As I wrote the previous paragraph, I thought about a former student of mine who had shared with me recently that she and her husband had been going through some very hard times and were at the crossroads of divorce, trying to decide which way to go. She did not give me any details and I did not ask. But they had just separated when I talked to her last. I was prompted to call her up while writing this paragraph and see how she was doing. Since our last conversation, she began to experience life as a single mom: her car broke down and needed a new engine; she experienced some painful and scary personal health challenges, as well as a series of invasive and expensive medical tests for her son before ruling out a serious illness for him; and she had to take on more hours at work, which was stressful. Through this, she said that she has come to realize that she can't do it all by herself right now. She decided to accept her husband's request to either sign the divorce papers or seriously invest in reconciliation and work to repair the marriage. She has chosen to keep trying to work it out. While she doesn't know the eventual outcome of her marriage, she knows that she wants the presence of a good father to help with the children and the house, as well as the financial security of another paycheck and health insurance benefits. With a less stressful life for herself and her children, she is hoping to find the energy to work on the marriage and solve their significant problems, problems that at an earlier point she thought were much worse than the challenges of being a single mom. I expressed my sympathy and support and promised her my continued prayers.

Research finds little evidence that those who divorce rather than stay together are able reliably to rebuild a greater sense of well-being and happiness. That is, those who are unhappy in their marriage and divorce do not end up having greater emotional well-being a few years down the road compared to unhappily married individuals who stayed together.[34] This was true even for those who remarried (or repartnered) after the divorce. Remember that most who keep trying to work on an unhappy marriage report being happier later on. In contrast, those who divorce generally are not on a reliable path to improved well-being.

However, I acknowledge that this is only a general statement. Certainly there are far too many instances when one's basic human dignity or safety—as well as children's well-being—are put in jeopardy by a destructive marital relationship. Spousal abuse carries with it a high risk of destructive consequences, including poor mental and physical health.[35] So also the discovery of infidelity, especially a pattern of repeated infidelity, can produce feelings of traumatic stress, anger, depression, anxiety, disorientation, and psychological paralysis.[36] When children are witnesses to ongoing high levels of marital conflict, research indicates that most would be better off if their parents divorce.[37] For some, divorce is the necessary path.

Yet because current research suggests that some divorces may not be in the best interests of children or adults and may not be fully considered, I believe we should be exploring ways to intervene at the crossroads of divorce to encourage a more informed and careful consideration of the possibility of reconciliation. If some unnecessary divorces can be prevented, this may improve the well-being of children and adults and reduce burdens on public assistance programs.

The Need for Change

Current law and policy do not make fine distinctions between necessary and unnecessary divorce. In fact, law and policy avoid making such distinctions in order to make the divorce process as quick and easy as it can be once people file for divorce. Judges want to process divorce cases as efficiently as possible. Changes from fault-based divorce to no-fault–based divorce laws (mostly in the 1970s) were designed to make it easier and less conflictual for couples to divorce. It has gotten easier and cheaper, for sure, but I'm not convinced that it has reduced the conflict. Good intentions gone awry is how Professor Allen Parkman describes these changes.[38] Yes, the courts saw less conflict. But no-fault divorce doesn't seem to facilitate less conflict between spouses before or after the divorce. And no-fault divorce does appear to have contributed to a higher divorce rate, with most studies finding an increase on the order of about 10%–20%.[39] No-fault divorce laws and current judicial practice are not attuned to the possibility that some divorces are not in the best interests of those involved.

In the past, waiting periods for divorce were seen as a reasonable means for the state to allow couples to cool down and carefully consider whether divorce was the best course of action. Now, two thirds of states no longer have a waiting period. And of those states that do, only four have waiting periods of longer than 3 months. Three states have only a 30-day waiting period.[40] Since 1970, only Louisiana has increased its waiting period, to 1 year for parents of dependent children.

Law and policy initiatives directly intended to prevent divorce among distressed couples go against a strong legal momentum that for centuries has been making divorce easier and quicker to do.[41] One minor exception, however, is in Utah, which now mandates a brief divorce orientation education class.[42] I'll discuss the Utah case in more depth a little later. The Coalition for Divorce Reform has proposed model legislation called the Parental Divorce Reduction Act that would require all couples with minor children (where there is no domestic violence involved) to undertake a 4–8-hour divorce orientation education class and then accept a waiting period of 8 additional months before they can file for divorce.[43] No states to date have adopted this reform. Still, there are a handful of reform initiatives. Promoting divorce orientation education may be the most feasible of these initiatives. So what is divorce orientation education? The next section explores this question in some depth.

What Is Divorce Orientation Education?

There are some central elements of effective divorce orientation education (DOE). Let me begin with some general perspectives and then I'll touch on some specific curricular content.

General Perspectives

Orientation. First, I confess that for some time I was uncertain what label to put on the kind of educational experience I'm talking about in this chapter. In 2007, Utah passed legislation requiring divorcing parents to take what the bill called "divorce orientation education."[44] I was uncomfortable with the term for a while. Maybe a more generic term like "divorce prevention education" would be better, emphasizing that one of its purposes is to prevent some preventable divorces. And yet, preventing divorce is central to everything I've been discussing in the previous four chapters. So that term doesn't seem to set this idea apart. Recently I've decided that divorce orientation education is the right label. I came to this decision as a result of some research Tamara Fackrell, a recent doctoral student of mine, did for her dissertation.

Several years ago, I accepted Tamara into the doctoral family studies program at BYU. She was a practicing divorce attorney and mediator. She knew about the difficulties that faced her clients during and after the divorce and usually encouraged them to be cautious about quick decisions; if there were possibilities for reconciliation, she urged them to explore that possibility. While some divorces clearly were needed, she believed that repairing and saving a marriage was often possible. She told me a few stories of clients who succeeded in repairing their marriages and years later continued to thank her for her help when they first came to her thinking that divorce was their only option.

In all this, Tamara developed a deep curiosity about how individuals and couples go about making the decision to divorce or stay together. She wanted to understand this phenomenon and improve her skills at helping her clients (and finding ways to prevent shortsighted divorces in general). That's why she submitted to the long, tortuous road of adding a Ph.D. to her already impressive legal credentials. When she began her studies, the first thing she did was search the research literature for previous studies about how individuals go about making the divorce decision. We were both surprised to find virtually no previous research directly addressing this important topic. Given what we know about the effects of divorce on children, adults, and society, shouldn't we want to understand the divorce decision-making process better? So for her dissertation, Tamara conducted a qualitative study of how individuals make the difficult decision to divorce or keep trying to work things out. She conducted in-depth interviews with a diverse set of individuals from all across the country in various circumstances who were in different stages of thinking about divorce.

What she found after analyzing her interviews fascinated me and helped me see that the term "divorce orientation education" made sense.[45] Nearly all individuals she interviewed, regardless of their particular circumstances, were wandering in a chaotic cognitive and emotional wilderness. They were confused and bewildered, trying to process their situation and what to do about it. Not surprisingly, their thinking often appeared irrational and ineffective, and they were struggling to come to clarity about what they should do. Moreover, she discovered that for many an unsatisfying relationship alone did not necessarily push them to consider divorce, because the marriage was a separate consideration from the relationship itself. That is, apart from the quality of the relationship, the stability of the marriage had its own considerations. Similar themes were found in the study in Great Britain I mentioned earlier in this chapter.[46]

A number of major factors contributed to their confusion and were more focused on the institutional nature of the marriage rather than on the relationship per se. For instance, not surprisingly, concerns about how divorce would affect their children were usually paramount and made the decision to end an unsatisfying relationship confusing. Religion and hope loomed large for most. They generally embraced the sanctity of marriage and thus a decision to divorce took on much broader and deeper meaning. A simple calculus that the relationship was flawed was not enough for most to decide to end the marriage. Beyond religious beliefs, most remained committed to the institution of marriage and did not take their vows lightly; even when the relationship was unsatisfying and sometimes downright dysfunctional, they struggled to know what to do. Finances were a major source of concern and uncertainty. Moreover, the emotional and physical health impacts on them were often overwhelming and made it difficult to focus and pursue a rational decision-making process. Some hesitated to leave their marriage because they were afraid of losing health benefits. Finally, some individuals still clung to friendship and positive memories with their spouse, which made it more difficult to think about divorce; while the romantic relationship was unsatisfying, there were still positive ties that bound them together.

The participants in Fackrell's study were not oblivious to the bewildering condition they were in. They were aware that their cognitive and emotional capacities were stretched, making it hard to think straight about perhaps the most consequential decision they would ever make. Interestingly, the participants also seemed to sense intuitively that, even though they were overwhelmed and confused, it was necessary to wander in the wilderness for a time before they could move on, as confusing and painful as that was. Those who go through the difficult process of deciding what to do about an unsatisfying and painful relationship (or who are at the mercy of a spouse who is deciding) go through a period of disorientation; they feel lost and dazed and hardly know which way is up. Some spoke of seeking counseling, either from a secular or religious source, but counseling wasn't always helpful. I am convinced that many in this situation would benefit from some educational help at this time. They need and would appreciate some basic orientation to help them understand where they are and the potential paths forward. They need to find some clarity. Thus, I think the term "divorce orientation education" is a good label.

Decision making. A second perspective I want to emphasize follows from the first: the primary objective of DOE should be to help individuals think more clearly about the decision looming before them, not to push them one way or the other. As I said earlier, many individuals are wandering, lost in a wilderness of uncertainty and confusion, struggling to find the path that leads to clarity and peace. The purpose of DOE, then, is to provide participants solid information and reliable resources to answer questions and increase clarity about the path to take (although this may not be clarity about what the final destination will be). Information should be fair, unbiased, and based on the best available research. The purpose of DOE is not to arm-twist people into staying married for the sake of preserving all marriages or to convince them that it is best just to move on. It is a blinking red light rather than a full-on stop; come to a brief stop and look both ways before proceeding in the direction you choose. The responsibility for decision making rests with individuals and DOE should acknowledge that either direction may be the best choice. The point is to provide good information and resources that will help individuals at the crossroads make the best decision and then be able to implement the decision effectively.

Portal. A third perspective is that DOE should be conceptualized as both a defined curriculum and a portal to a more thorough and careful decision-making process. As a curriculum it should cover research-based answers to the important questions many individuals face at the crossroads of divorce. Of course, the answers that research provides are necessarily general; individuals will need to work out how those general answers may apply to them. As a portal, DOE also should provide individuals with helpful resources for assessing the relationship and point to competent assistance if they decide to keep working to repair the marriage or to valuable assistance for moving on in ways that minimize the challenges for children and adults. Pointing to reconciliation resources also means that DOE is a beginning of a process but is not the specific tool for achieving that end. Obviously, a brief, one-time class can't magically resolve serious marital problems. At best, it can open a door for some couples that can lead to repairing the marriage. I'll discuss later a process being developed by Professor Doherty that I think has potential for helping couples who want to consider reconciliation.

Individuals vs. couples. A fourth general perspective is that DOE is designed for individuals rather than couples. Divorce is sometimes a couple decision but more often it is an individual decision. While most marriage maintenance education is targeted to the couple, DOE needs to assume that an individual is seeking information to make the divorce decision. Also, there should be a sensitivity in DOE to the fact that many participants do not want the divorce; they are the passive recipients of an unwanted break-up and want to try and work things out, the leavees rather than the leavers. Sometimes there are very serious and defensible reasons for the divorce, but other times the leavee-spouse honestly disagrees about the need for a divorce and wants to work to save the marriage. DOE needs to accommodate both situations.

Parents. Fifth, DOE is targeted to parents. I'm not minimizing the challenges of distressed couples without children, but the divorce decision becomes a matter for public policy action primarily because of how it impacts children. Nonparent individuals at the crossroads of divorce should be welcome in DOE and could benefit from parts of it, but the focus should remain on the problem that divorce is potentially altering parental attention and resources that children will receive.

Targeting ambivalent individuals. Sixth, I realize that DOE would go straight over the heads of many rather than through their ears. They are not ambivalent about divorce and are not interested in or open to the questions raised in DOE and the information and resources provided; it's just another hoop to jump through. This raises the question of whether DOE should be mandatory or voluntary for divorcing individuals. I'll take on this important question later in the chapter. Suffice for now to say that, given the personal and societal costs of divorce, I'm not shy about considering a mandate. Those who would not be particularly open to DOE are hardly immune to the personal costs and potential societal costs that flow from marital breakdown. And maybe one or two things in DOE will seep in and help. But let me reiterate that DOE is designed to be of most benefit to those individuals and couples who are ambivalent or confused about whether divorce is the right option for them. Recall the Doherty study I reviewed earlier that suggests that about 25% of individuals and 10% of couples (both spouses) going through a divorce say they want to save the marriage, if possible. Individuals who are confident about the direction they are going can benefit from some of the information provided, but from a public policy perspective, the greatest benefit of DOE is the potential to identify couples for whom divorce may be preventable and to help them begin a process of repairing the relationship.

Divorce orientation vs. coparenting education. Finally, I want to make a distinction between divorce orientation education, which currently is rare, and divorcing parents' education, or coparenting education, which is now quite common in the United States. Most states now require divorcing couples with dependent children to take a brief class, usually from 2–4 hours, focused on the general effects of divorce on children and what parents can do to minimize those effects.[47] For instance, they discuss the negative effects of putting children in the middle of parental conflict, bad-mouthing the ex-spouse to children, and other harmful practices. In some research I did with Tamara Fackrell, we reviewed all the evaluation studies of these kinds of programs in a meta-analytic study and found evidence that they have small but significant positive effects.[48] So I am supportive of mandates for divorcing parents' education. But we found no evidence in our survey of the curricula for these programs that they seriously raise the topic of reconciliation. The purpose of divorcing parents' education is to help parents learn how to avoid common parenting mistakes that make children's adjustment to divorce harder. It assumes divorce and tries to help parents do it better for their kids. It is different in purpose from divorce orientation education, which is to help individuals at the crossroads of divorce make an optimal decision about what direction to go. DOE does not assume that divorce will occur. There may be some overlap in content. For instance, both classes would likely review the general effects of divorce on children. But the content overlap should be small. I'll discuss later in the chapter whether it makes sense to combine these two classes into one program for divorcing parents.

The Content of DOE

With these general perspectives in mind, what should be the content of DOE?[49]

Basic information about divorce. First, I think it is valuable to provide individuals at the crossroads of divorce some basic information about divorce. There is a lot of misinformation about divorce in our culture. I think DOE should begin with information about the percentage of marriages that end in divorce and the factors generally associated with divorce. Also, I would present the most common reasons that people give for their divorce, as I mentioned earlier in the chapter. I would raise honestly the issues of abuse, infidelity, and addictions and how these are difficult to overcome. And while some couples heroically beat the odds, it is a long, hard road. But I would also present straightforwardly that many reasons for divorce can be addressed and the marriage saved. Then I would talk about how people go about making the decision to divorce. Here the research isn't very helpful yet. But I think at least acknowledging that most people go through a period of bewildered disorientation can help. And this is a good basis for encouraging people to be careful about making decisions at a time when they are not their most rational selves.

Reconciliation possibilities. Second, I would deal directly with the question of whether unhappy marriages can become happy again. Our culture seems to promote a perspective of bad marriages rather than bad patches in marriage. Both exist. Some marriages are fundamentally flawed and probably need to be ended. But other marriages are going through bad patches and what to do is not so clear. Many marriages survive bad patches and become happy again.[50] Research on reconciliation needs to be stronger than it is, but what there is should be summarized. Moreover, the research on regrets about divorce should be presented.

Reconciliation resources. In addition, the curriculum should cover resources that can help individuals deal with their marital problems and strengthen their marriage, if there is a desire to do so. This includes both educational and therapeutic options. Some don't want or can't afford to go to a therapist, so classes should not be ignored. There are plenty of anecdotal stories of couples who were on the verge of divorce who took a marriage education class and were able to analyze and fix their major problems. I have experienced a few of these in my experiences as a community marriage educator. In one instance, a couple who took a class I taught had already tried therapy and did not find it helpful. They came to my class as the "last resort" to save their marriage. When I interviewed them 6 months after the class (for a research project) they revealed this fact to me; I didn't know it at the time of the class. They were much happier and felt confident that they were on the right track. One class I'm aware of, offered by First Things First in Chattanooga, Tennessee, and supported in part with federal funding, is advertised as a course specifically for couples in distress and thinking about divorce.[51] The program tries to provide couples first-aid skills for dealing with problems and give them hope that they can find solutions to their problems and avoid divorce. According to Julie Baumgardner, the president of First Things First, more than 90% of couples who go through this program decide to keep working on their marriage rather than seeking divorce at that time.

For some, marriage counseling may be the best option, if they can afford it. Participants in DOE will benefit from guidelines that help couples choose a competent therapist who will work with them to repair their marriage, if possible. Individuals need suggestions on how to spot an ineffective counselor or one who moves too quickly to divorce counseling. Some couples will not be able to afford counseling, so they will need financial support or other options.

Research on effects of divorce. Next, I would give individuals participating in DOE the research on the effects of divorce on adults and children. The factors that help explain why some adults thrive and others struggle after divorce should be reviewed. This needs to be presented sensitively, but not whitewashed. DOE should directly address the question of whether conflict decreases or increases as a result of divorce. In addition, I think participants would be helped by knowing the research on the general effects of divorce on adult emotional and physical health, social support, religious involvement, and the prospects for future romantic relationships. Significant attention should be given to possible financial consequences of divorce for adults and children. Also, I would not leave out the reality that the private financial struggles that most experience when a marriage ends have public costs, as well.

One of the most difficult things that people worry about at the crossroads of divorce is how divorce will affect the children involved. So the research on this should be reviewed. As I mentioned earlier, this content area in DOE could overlap somewhat with divorcing parents' education classes that are mandated in many states now. To reduce that overlap, DOE curricula may want to avoid covering issues such as effective coparenting and not putting children in the middle of adult conflicts. Instead, they should stay focused on the general impact of divorce on children, including social, emotional, educational, and religious effects, and potential effects on sexual behavior in adolescence and romantic relationship formation in early adulthood. Also, the curriculum should cover why some children struggle to adjust to divorce more than others. I think the curriculum should directly address the concept of the "good divorce," as well. Good divorces are those in which parents resolve their conflicts (or keep them away from the children) and cooperate fully in the coparenting of their children. Yet it is common to overstate the evidence about the good divorce. Children whose parents cooperate in coparenting have more involved fathers and have fewer behavior problems, but it doesn't seem to make a difference with many other outcomes such as relationships with mothers, potential problems at school, substance abuse, early sexual activity, and healthy romantic relationship formation in young adulthood.[52] A good divorce is much better than a bad divorce, but parents should know that it does not guarantee that children will be spared all of the potential negative consequences of marital dissolution.

Legal process and options. A final element of DOE curricula should be an overview of the legal divorce process and options. The legal process can be a significant source of bewilderment and stress for individuals at the crossroads of divorce. It can be especially difficult for those who do not want the divorce but find the legal process indifferent to their wishes. So DOE should help participants know what to expect as they go through the legal process, if they decide to divorce or separate. In many states, the legal divorce process does not require retaining a lawyer. Online applications and divorce kiosks make it easy and cheap to get an uncontested divorce. But most people could use help understanding whether this option is wise for them in the long run. DOE should also cover the advantages of divorce mediation for settling issues and other collaborative law approaches that are designed to prevent unnecessary conflict. Some states now require that divorcing couples begin with mediation and try to come to a fair and mutually agreeable settlement before going to court.

Facilitating personal application. I have provided an overview of the content of DOE. But a crucial element of the curriculum goes beyond information to exercises to encourage individuals to think about and apply the information to personal circumstances. This invites active and personal processing of the content rather than passive absorption of general information. For instance, an exercise to help individuals think about the merits of marriage counseling for them might be helpful to many participants. In the self-guided divorce orientation education curriculum that I have developed, there are many of these kinds of exercises designed to encourage readers to think about how general information applies to their specific circumstances and to clarify their thoughts about questions raised in the curriculum.[53] Also, an important element of DOE is to provide participants with additional recommended resources—books, web sites, community organizations and services, and so forth—that can give them further reliable information and help.

Illustrating and Critiquing DOE in Utah

Divorce orientation education remains rare. There are some marriage education programs targeted specifically to couples on the brink of divorce. But these classes are more intensive and provide specific skills to repair the relationship. I'm all for more of these kinds of classes, but they are not my focus here. As I explained in the previous section, DOE can open a portal to such programs but it is not the program to address and resolve marital problems. Utah is the only state I know that has passed legislation mandating DOE for divorcing parents, but I suspect that some states have something functionally similar.[54] Many states require coparenting education for divorcing parents, as I mentioned earlier, and while their focus is on effective coparenting after divorce, I suspect that some of these educational efforts also mention some content covered in DOE curriculum. I'll describe what is done with DOE in Utah because that is what I know the most about. However, I think there are some serious implementation problems with what is being done that limit its effectiveness. So a lot of this section will be a critique of DOE implementation in Utah and how I think it could be improved. I suspect that other states that may have DOE curricula would experience similar problems. Because DOE is a relatively new policy effort, implementation problems are to be expected. I hope my critiques are constructive. I appreciate Utah's initial efforts. But we need to do better, especially if more states are going to follow Utah's lead.

The story of DOE in Utah. In 2007, a Utah legislator who is a divorce attorney proposed and was able to pass a modification to Utah's divorce laws that added a requirement for a 1-hour divorce orientation education class for divorcing parents with dependent children. More than a decade earlier, Utah mandated a 2-hour coparenting education class for parents. But DOE was an additional requirement. The legislative language specified that in this class individuals be given neutral, unbiased information about: (a) options available as alternatives to divorce; (b) resources available from courts and administrative agencies for resolving custody and support issues without filing for divorce; (c) resources available to improve or strengthen marriage; (d) a discussion of the positive and negative consequences of divorce; (e) a discussion of the process of divorce; (f) options available for proceeding with a divorce, including mediation, collaborative law approaches, and litigation; and (g) post-divorce resources. Petitioners who file for divorce (and their spouses) are notified of this required class. Information about it is available on a state web site.[55]

I learned about the passage of this legislation by reading a brief blurb about it in a column of the local newspaper covering the legislative session. I was vice-chair of the Utah Commission on Marriage at the time and I thought I was pretty well informed about bills regarding marriage and divorce. But this one caught me by surprise. When the class was implemented a few months later, I decided to visit a class to get a better idea of what went on. I was quite surprised by what I observed and heard. Before class began I casually roamed the large institutional room in the county administration building. I estimate 50 people were there. I was a bit puzzled to see a number of couples holding hands, smiling, and talking softly to each other. I suppose it's possible that people were attending with the reason for their divorce and next intended spouse rather than their soon-to-be ex-spouse. But I later called one of the instructors and asked about this observation. She said that it was fairly common for individuals to attend with their current spouse and that some of them were still visibly affectionate.

The instructor for the class came in after registering participants and began the class. He was a licensed clinical social worker. The instructor was dressed in blue jeans and a T-shirt. He spoke very quickly so it was difficult to understand him at times. The first thing he said was that he knew that the class attendees didn't want to be there and they were only there so that they could get the proper paperwork to proceed with their divorce. The paperwork was in the back of the room to be picked up when the class was over. So right away I had my concerns that the full range of well-intentioned purposes of the legislation was not going to be taken seriously in this class. Then the instructor began to talk about his own divorce, saying it was hard but everyone survived and was doing okay. If he covered the required elements specified by the legislation I must have missed it. The exception is that towards the end he turned on an educational video on the value of mediation and collaborative law approaches, then walked out of the room. When he returned 15 minutes later, the class was over. I was not impressed.

As I wrote the previous paragraph, I decided that I needed to give this class another chance. So a few days later I attended the DOE class in my community again. I tried to keep an open mind. This time, the class was held in a courtroom, summoning to mind the legal end of the process participants were engaged in (but also providing more security as all individuals had to pass through a metal detector). Looking around the room, I again saw two or three affectionate couples physically intertwined. Overall, I think the class this time did a better job of meeting some of the required content. There was worthwhile information about divorce options, mediation, collaborative law, and the legal process of getting a divorce. There was also some sporadic coverage of the effects of divorce on children and adults. But I thought there was too much use of personal anecdote and not enough coverage of solid research. More importantly, the treatment of reconciliation and potential ways to repair relationships were inadequate, in my opinion. These issues were merely mentioned two or three times but never elaborated on and virtually absent in handout materials. A list of recommended reading included only a couple of books (out of 25) that dealt with repairing marital relationships. The instructor did vaguely mention the research that many marriages go from bad to good, but there were no details or development of this important finding. For me, the overall context for the class was an assumption that divorce was a given, not an option. This was clear when the instructor said, "I'm one of you; I went through a divorce 15 years ago." Note the assumption that he was talking to people who were as good as divorced. The dominant theme of the 60-minute class was good coparenting to help children adjust. While this is an important topic, it is the domain of the required divorcing parents class that followed the DOE class after a 10-minute biology break. So again, I was disappointed that this DOE class did not adequately address the challenge of making the best decision about whether to divorce or reconcile and how to go about a serious effort to repair the relationship. In fairness, I've had a few former students who were getting a divorce say that they appreciated the class when they attended. And I have had some research assistants sit in on other DOE classes that apparently treated the issue of reconciliation a little more seriously.

Now, back to my original narrative. Soon after observing the DOE class for the first time in 2007, I contacted the legislator who was the author and primary sponsor of the divorce orientation education legislation, Lorie Fowlke. I asked if she would be willing to talk to me about my experience with DOE. She practiced law a few miles from my office and we had lunch one afternoon. I described to her my experience with the class and my concerns about implementation of the legislation. She had similar concerns and had expressed them to the Administrative Office of the Court then and several times since, but hadn't seen much progress. I volunteered at our lunch meeting to write a curriculum that would meet the requirements of the legislation and better serve its purpose. She accepted my offer, although we didn't know whether it would be accepted and approved. I volunteered not just because the class I observed didn't meet my expectations, but because I thought it would be difficult to meet the extensive requirements of the legislation effectively in a one-hour class. I thought a self-guided curriculum that people could go through at their own pace, with exercises to apply the information to their situations, would be best. I said I would give it a try.

Fortuitously, shortly thereafter Tamara Fackrell, an experienced divorce attorney and mediator and part-time instructor at the BYU law school knocked on my door and described her passion to help distressed couples avoid the pain and fallout of divorce for themselves and their children. She wanted to return to school to supplement her law degree with a Ph.D. in family studies to improve her capabilities for reforming the divorce process. She was admitted to our program and worked with me and a group of under-graduate students to develop a self-guided DOE curriculum. It took the form of a guidebook available electronically for free. We informed instruc-tors of Utah's mandated DOE class about the book; I'm aware of only one that made use of it or recommended it to participants. We asked the AOC to approve the curriculum and even developed a web-based version of it. But to date it is not approved to meet the mandate. They did post a link to the web-based program on the bottom of the state web site that describes the DOE requirement, with a note that some might find this program useful but that it does not fulfill the state requirement. (Only about three visitors a month to the our DOE web site are coming from the state web site link, out of more than 5,000 visits a month.)

I'm not complaining because I feel slighted. I just think that this well-intentioned legislation falls short of its well-meaning purposes in the way it has been implemented. In most respects, I think the required content of the course hits many of the important areas I outlined earlier in this chapter. But I think the way the mandate has been implemented is limiting its educa-tional potential.

The problems of traditional classrooms. First, I don't think DOE is best implemented as a traditional classroom program. As it is now in Utah, the class is scheduled for a specific place and time. In my county, the class is avail-able several weeks a month on a weekday evening. It's only 5 minutes from my house, but others in the county would need to travel 30 minutes to get there. This makes it less convenient for many, especially lower income indi-viduals with chronic transportation problems. And Utahns in rural counties may have to travel more than an hour to get to a scheduled class. Moreover, the classroom setting isn't private. While that may not be a big concern for many, especially those who have already filed for divorce, it might be uncomfortable for those just considering a divorce to attend a public class. Instead, I think the DOE mandate would be better served as a self-guided intervention. An online program would be easily accessible to most. (Public libraries have Internet-access public computers for those who do not have one.) An online program could be accessed at more convenient times, as well, and might be more appealing to those who have not filed for divorce (and may not have even talked openly about their thoughts).

Curricular quality. Another concern I have with the current implementation of DOE in Utah is curricular inconsistency. There is no standardized curriculum. I have looked at outlines of the various curricula being taught by more than a dozen instructors in different counties across the state. Some curricula look better to me than others. And I have personally observed two classes now that did not meet the full requirements of the legislation and left out one of the most important elements. So I think there needs to be a standardized curriculum. Again, I think a web-based program could accomplish this most effectively. And it would be considerably cheaper. The program I helped develop had no frills, because we did not have much money to develop it.[56] We pretty much transposed the guidebook on which it was based to a web platform. But it dependably provides the needed information and more. I'm sure others could develop an even better curriculum.

Inadequate dosage. In addition, I've been concerned about the length of the DOE program ever since I first learned about it. The legislation specified that DOE be *at least* one hour in length. It has been implemented at just that. Can the objectives of DOE be adequately met in just one hour? I have my doubts. There is a lot of information to absorb. And it's not just the information that's important. As I discussed earlier, for DOE to accomplish its purposes, participants need to process the information carefully, ideally with carefully designed exercises designed to encourage thought and application of course content. Effective DOE should allow for more self-paced, individualized, and active learning. Again, a web-based program could allow for a better learning experience than a traditional, brief classroom environment.

Blurred lines. I also have concerns about combining DOE with coparenting education for divorcing parents. I suspect that this was done in Utah to make the two educational requirements for divorce more convenient for participants; they can fulfill both in one long evening. But a web-based approach would be more convenient and more efficient. Furthermore, I worry that the purpose of the 1-hour DOE class is undermined somewhat by following it immediately with a 2-hour class that assumes the divorce will occur and focuses on effective coparenting for the sake of the children. This is an important intervention, obviously, but I worry that it blunts the focus on a careful decision of which road to take. And in the DOE class I observed while writing this chapter, the majority of the time was spent on topics that fit best in the coparenting education curriculum. Content of the divorcing parents class seeped over into the divorce orientation class, making it hard for participants to see the distinct purposes of the two classes. I think the integration of these two classes diminishes the potential effectiveness of DOE.

Late timing. Related to these concerns is the timing of DOE, which has been implemented in Utah as a post-filing and usually a pre-divorce-finalization activity rather than a pre-filing requirement. The class is taken after a legal petition for divorce has been filed with the court. In fact, most take the class late in the legal divorce process, perhaps as the last step before they get their divorce finalized.[57] A former graduate student of mine, Carma Needham, visited several DOE classes and invited attendees to participate in a study about their perceptions of the class. She interviewed those who volunteered to be in the study a few weeks after the class in their homes. In many instances, the individuals were already divorced by the time she interviewed them. A question about whether the class encouraged them to think more about reconciliation seemed irrelevant to them. The decision to divorce was made (by them or by their ex-spouse) long ago and the class was a formality; the momentum of the legal process was much too strong to think about reconciliation at the time they were taking the class.[58] It makes sense to me that the sooner individuals at the crossroads of divorce can get the information provided in DOE, the more likely its full purposes can be realized. If many people are wandering in a wilderness of confusion and uncertainty, it would be better to give them some direction early on rather than wait until they are about to stumble out of the wilderness. In fact, I have had several conversations with one of the class instructors (in the two largest counties in the state) and she regularly asks participants at the end of the class whether they wished they had taken the class before they filed for divorce. Perhaps it's a leading question, but she asserts that nearly every hand in the room goes up when she asks it.

Online access to DOE would allow individuals to get this information at any time and should facilitate earlier involvement. Accordingly, in 2012 I asked a legislator to sponsor an amendment to Utah's divorce orientation education statute to require DOE before filing for divorce and open up the possibility of online education. But the bill was opposed by various interests and an impassioned legislator who had recently divorced and it was voted down in 2012. But we'll keep trying, because if divorce orientation education is going to be effective, earlier participation is needed.

As a side note, while completing this manuscript, I accepted an invitation to become the regular instructor for divorce orientation education in my county. So now I have developed a classroom curriculum that meets the legislative requirements and, in my opinion, gives adequate consideration to the possibility of reconciliation. Also, the lines between divorce orientation and coparenting education are more distinct. So even though it is still a traditional classroom, I have just 1 hour, and the timing of the class is still later in the divorce decision-making process than I would like, at least now I have an opportunity to be part of the process of improving what Utah does with DOE rather than just observing and criticizing it.

Unclear path forward. A final concern with Utah's DOE is not so much related to the implementation of DOE as to what comes after it. As I mentioned earlier in the chapter, DOE is both a curriculum and a portal to more serious consideration of reconciliation for those inclined to further explore this path. While this path may be for a minority of participants, it is important that there be a good, clear path for those who decide to go in this direction. I worry about that. Do we have the ability to help couples who want to repair their marriage? It's not that Utah has a scarcity of well-trained marriage therapists. We have several excellent clinical training programs in the state focused on marriage and family therapy, maybe more training per capita than any other state. And there are several training programs in clinical psychology, counseling psychology, and clinical social work, as well. Furthermore, Utah is a highly religious state and there is no shortage of religious counseling opportunities. We have enough counseling capacity. And even though I worry a little about the quality of counseling, having read Doherty's critique of the way many go about marital therapy, I'm also aware that marital therapy has a decent success rate for those who seriously invest in it.[59] It is more the demand side that concerns me. Researchers in Utah a few years ago found that fewer than half (48%) of individuals who divorced sought out marital counseling (either from a professional therapist or a religious leader).[60] I assume that figure is even lower for lower income individuals who might struggle to pay for this service. So my concern is that many individuals may not feel comfortable with or cannot afford marriage counseling. To help more people take advantage of counseling, I think we may need an additional service, a step between DOE and counseling that helps couples assess whether they want and can benefit from counseling.

I think Professor Bill Doherty at the University of Minnesota has a good model that if widely implemented in Utah could be a bridge that helps more people at the crossroads of divorce take the path of marriage counseling. He calls his model "discernment counseling." Discernment counseling does not try to solve marital problems. Instead, it is a short-term, serious process focused on exploring whether problems potentially could be solved and whether there is sufficient motivation to do so.[61] It helps spouses decide whether they want to give their marriage another try or head towards divorce. Discernment counseling is not for those couples where one or both spouses have made a clear decision to divorce. It's also inappropriate when there is a risk of domestic violence or a protective order from the court. Obviously, if one spouse is coercing the other to participate, discernment counseling will be ineffective. The model includes an option to discernment counseling that Doherty calls Hopeful Spouse Counseling for those individuals who still want to save their marriage but whose spouse is not interested. This option focuses on helping hopeful spouses be their best selves to facilitate a potential reconciliation or a more constructive divorce.

Discernment counseling involves 1–5 sessions about 2 hours in length. The sessions are divided between conversations with spouses together and individual conversations with the counselor. Discernment counselors help each party to see his or her own contributions to the problems and potential solutions. The goal of discernment counseling is for each spouse to gain clarity and confidence in a decision about the path forward. When a decision emerges, the counselor helps the spouses either find a professional to help them with a constructive divorce or formulate a reconciliation plan to create a healthy, mutually satisfying marriage. A reconciliation plan involves a mutual commitment to 6 months of work on the marriage, usually with a counselor, and with the divorce option off the table. To support development of this model, counselor training, and outreach to couples, the Minnesota legislature added a $5 surcharge to the marriage license fee.

I think this model shows promise for helping more couples seriously consider the possibility of reconciliation or come to more clarity that divorce is necessary. Even if reconciliation is not the eventual path they take, it provides them with greater certainty about the path forward and might reduce later feelings of regret about the divorce. So along with DOE, I think Utah needs to do more to help couples who want to explore the option of reconciliation. I think we need to devote some efforts and resources to training more marriage counselors across the state in something like Doherty's discernment counseling model. And we will need to find a way to make sure lower income couples can avail themselves of this service. It would help everyone if more insurance companies would pay for marital therapy and this kind of discernment counseling. It seems that insurance companies would likely reduce their bottom-line costs by supporting this kind of mental health service, given the toll that divorce can take on physical and mental health, not to mention absenteeism and presentism (at work but distracted).[62]

I don't mean to imply with this discussion of discernment counseling that I don't support educational programs for couples at the crossroads of divorce. Such programs exist but currently they are rare in Utah and, I suspect, in most states. I mentioned earlier the First Things First educational program for couples on the brink of divorce and the initial success they seem to be having. *Retrouvaille* is the name of a similar program that is based on Catholic theology and used by the Catholic Church to help couples on the brink of divorce.[63] It involves both religious (Christian) and secular instruction (a primary focus on improving communication skills). Perhaps there is more that could be done in Utah and elsewhere to promote the availability of these kinds of programs, as well.

Unfortunately, there is not yet any evaluation research on the effectiveness of DOE in Utah. But I don't think it has been implemented well enough to merit rigorous evaluation at this point. That is, we need to make some of the changes I've recommended before we can fairly evaluate whether DOE is achieving its stated purposes. I think well-designed and implemented DOE will be worth the investment. But the data don't exist yet to buttress that hope. Still, the public expense associated with divorce means that we don't have to prevent a lot of preventable divorces to recoup the investment.[64]

How Do We Deliver Divorce Orientation Education?

I already hinted at my answer for the best way to deliver DOE, so this section will be brief. I think the best solution is a web-based program rather than a physical infrastructure to deliver face-to-face classes. It should be required of all parents with minor children before they can file for divorce. The web-based option increases accessibility and convenience for DOE. (Public libraries and other public buildings could be tasked with making computers with access to the program available to those without personal Internet access.) Also, web-based delivery best facilitates early participation before the momentum of the legal process gets too strong. It provides for greater privacy and self-paced participation that allows for more thorough and active involvement in the curriculum and personal tailoring of the program to meet perceived individual needs. (A minimum time for viewing the program or a minimum number of exercises to complete would need to be set, but individuals are free to invest as much time and effort as they want. Computer programs have diagnostic capabilities to see how long a user spends on the web site, how many pages are viewed, etc.) Costs for supporting the program can be combined with regular legal divorce fees for couples that go on to divorce. There would be no cost for those who do not go on to divorce. (Utah now charges a $20 fee for all individuals taking DOE.) Costs would be minimal because of the web-based delivery infrastructure. A high-quality active learning program could be designed that meets the purposes of DOE with instruction, video, personal application exercises, and links to valuable resources.

If a physical infrastructure for delivery of DOE is desired as a supplement to a web-based infrastructure, then most states could append DOE to the divorcing parents' education class that they already require. But for reasons explained in the previous section, I think that option is less desirable. In some states, the Cooperative Extension System or parenting/family resource centers are being tapped to deliver coparenting education and they could be used also to provide low-cost DOE.

Are There Other Laws or Policies to Consider to Promote Reconciliation?

Before concluding this chapter, I think it might be valuable to review and critique briefly a few other divorce reform efforts that have been suggested and tried in a few places to promote greater likelihood of reconciliation for couples at the crossroads of divorce. For diverse reasons, I don't think these reform options hold as much potential as well-implemented DOE. That is, when placed in the context of other reform ideas being considered, I think DOE looks like a stronger, more feasible option.

I want to clarify that I am reluctant to support a reversal of unilateral, no-fault divorce laws, for two reasons. First, my reading of the evidence suggests that unilateral, no-fault divorce laws did not have a large, long-term effect of increasing divorce rates in the United States or Western Europe.[65] They likely contributed to a short-term spike in the years immediately after passage, probably facilitating a pent-up demand, but those rates came back down relatively quickly. I think no-fault divorce has directly contributed only a small amount to higher rates of divorce. Second, some good research suggests that a positive by-product of no-fault divorce has been meaningful reductions in domestic violence, female suicide, and spousal homicides.[66] It's not clear that there is a strong causal link between changes to no-fault divorce and these outcomes, but I am willing to give the benefit of the doubt when such serious outcomes are at stake. So I think the better course is to explore reasonable reforms that can smooth off some of the rough edges of no-fault divorce laws that currently provide few options to spouses who wish to repair the relationship and save the marriage.

Longer Waiting Periods

Some divorce reformers believe the trend to shorter (or no) waiting periods for divorce has decreased the likelihood that couples will reconcile. In the past, divorce waiting periods have been imposed by the state to encourage individuals not to end a marriage in the heat of the moment. But the legal trend has been towards very brief waiting periods consistent with the no-fault divorce trend. Only Louisiana has bucked that trend and actually increased the divorce-waiting period to 1 year for parents of dependent children (with an exception for cases with domestic violence). Virginia has a two-track system that allows a court to grant a no-fault divorce to a childless couple after 6 months of separation, while couples with children must wait a year,[67] a system similar to what is used in some Scandinavian countries.[68] There is correlational evidence that states with longer waiting periods have lower divorce rates,[69] but no policy experiments have tested a cause–effect relationship.

As an intellectual matter, I think reform proposals to increase waiting periods deserve consideration. And more than 70% of American adults agree that a 1-year waiting period is a good idea.[70] But as a practical matter, I think these reforms will be very hard to pass. Any reforms that make divorce significantly harder to get will face steep uphill battles in any legislature. I live in the reddest state in the Union with a dominant Republican party that can pass any legislation that it agrees is important. There have been a number of proposed divorce reform efforts here, yet even in socially conservative Utah, they usually fail, with DOE legislation being the notable exception. And in Utah and everywhere else, domestic violence prevention groups will oppose any move to lengthen waiting periods for divorce because they believe that it will place women in danger for longer periods of time.

I think other states can learn from the Utah experience. Legislation to help individuals at the crossroads of divorce carefully to consider their choices may have a chance at passage; legislation that lengthens the waiting period for divorce probably does not. And DOE may have the effect of slowing down the decision-making process precisely for those couples for whom reconciliation is a realistic possibility while not affecting those for whom it is not.

Time-out Laws

I know of five states (Indiana, Maine, Ohio, Pennsylvania, and Utah) that have what I call "time-out" laws. These laws allow a spouse on the receiving end of a divorce petition to ask the court to suspend the legal divorce process for a brief time so that counseling to save the marriage can be pursued. I found out about Utah's time-out law in an unusual way. An individual I knew who was involved in an unwanted divorce said she had heard about this law in Utah. I asked my then–graduate student, Tamara Fackrell, a practicing divorce attorney and mediator, about it. She said she was pretty sure that such a thing did not exist but said she would do some research. Sure enough, she found the obscure provision in Utah's divorce statutes. But she doubted that more than a handful of legal practitioners knew about it and she had never heard of this provision being used before in any divorce. She said that judges would be annoyed at any attorney who asked for this "time out" because that divorce petition would then clog his or her docket. Judges want to move cases on their dockets along as quickly and smoothly as possible. I don't know if this is the case in the other states with time-out provisions, but I doubt that they are much different from Utah.

I support the concept of time-out laws. All 50 states now have no-fault divorce, which means that a spouse can choose to end a marriage at any time for any reason (or by asserting "irreconcilable differences") and there is no possible defense against this action by a spouse who does not want the divorce. Divorce is completely unilateral. The spouse who legitimately wants to save a marriage has no recourse. Time-out laws could help with this. But there are concerns with these laws. They can be used illegitimately by abusive and domineering spouses to delay a necessary divorce and hassle (or worse) a leaving spouse. So again, domestic violence prevention groups will lobby hard against these laws, probably even if they try to carve out needed exceptions with a legal scalpel. And I wonder how well used and effective time-out laws may be when judges are impatient with them. So I don't see time-out laws as a primary or feasible means of promoting the option of reconciliation.

Covenant Marriage

A final divorce reform option that has been legislated in three states (Arizona, Arkansas, and Louisiana) is covenant marriage. Covenant marriage is an alternative set of laws that couples may choose to govern their entry into and possible exit from marriage. It has three primary features: (a) couples must participate in premarital counseling or education, from either a secular or religious source; (b) they enter a legal obligation to take all reasonable steps, including marital counseling, to preserve their marriage if serious marital difficulties arise; and (c) they legally agree to limit their grounds for divorce to issues of serious fault (e.g., adultery, abuse, addiction, abandonment, imprisonment), or separate and accept a longer waiting period for divorce (e.g., 2 years in Louisiana if there are dependent children).[71]

Each of these features is relevant to the discussion about promoting reconciliation. First, premarital education scholars note that those who take premarital education are more likely to seek counseling for marital problems than those who do not.[72] Second, obviously, those who make a legal commitment to seek counseling to preserve their marriage before seeking a divorce would be more likely actually to do so and a spouse has more leverage to insist on counseling. (There is some evidence, however, that courts do not consistently enforce this provision.[73]) And a commitment to do so may get distressed couples to counseling sooner rather than later, which facilitates a greater chance of repairing the relationship. Third, the limited grounds for divorce symbolically stress that other reasons for divorce are less convincing bases for terminating the marriage, at least without a serious attempt at reconciliation. And increasing the waiting period for divorce gives more time, at least theoretically, for reconciliation to occur.

I like the idea of covenant marriage. A decade ago I promoted its passage in Utah, but the legislation lost out by a couple of votes in the state senate. I personally would choose one. (Married couples can convert to a covenant marriage.) But again, I don't think covenant marriage will be a feasible or effective solution. Only three states have adopted covenant marriage and none has done so for more than a decade now. Any policy momentum it once had—if it ever had much—has dissipated. While it has been proposed numerous times in many states, it has not been put into law anywhere since 2001 (in Arkansas, where it was signed into law by a conservative governor and Christian pastor, Mike Huckabee). Moreover, research indicates that only a small percentage of couples—about 1% in Louisiana and probably fewer in Arizona and Arkansas—are opting for covenant marriages. And those who do generally have low risk profiles for divorce.[74] They choose covenant marriage primarily as a public symbol of the value they place on the institution of marriage. Those who choose covenant marriage would have more legal support for a serious consideration of reconciliation, but few are choosing it and those who do are unlikely to divorce. Hence, I don't think it is a primary tool for promoting the reconciliation option for couples at the crossroads of divorce.

I think well-implemented divorce orientation education laws are the most feasible and well-crafted policy tool currently available to promote the reconciliation option. And DOE can provide a valuable service to individuals who go on to divorce and who would benefit from some of the other information it provides. I think it is the most feasible option, less intrusive, and less likely to garner sturdy opposition. So I'm buying stock in this option rather than the others I've just reviewed.

I conclude with a final comment on the feasibility issue. In this chapter I have argued for a policy proposal to mandate divorce orientation education for parents with dependent children. A mandate will require legislation. But juxtaposing the terms feasibility and legislation creates an oxymoron. This is the only proposal in my strategic agenda that calls for a legislated mandate. Any legislation is hard to pass and any particular legislation stands a small chance of becoming law. When it deals with something like divorce and has opposition from the ideological right and left, it is even harder, even though opinion polls consistently reveal that nearly half of U.S. adults believe it is too easy to get a divorce these days and support policy efforts to address the problem.[75] While I think mandated DOE is more feasible than the other options discussed in this section, I don't want to pretend that it is an easy road to take.

Accordingly, while we do the hard work of passing mandated DOE legislation, I think it is sensible to think about using available public funds to promote voluntary DOE. This means developing a strong, web-based DOE program and then expending resources to advertise it and promote its value. Perhaps marriage counselors, religious counselors, legal practitioners, and others could become first-responder promoters of voluntary DOE, whereas many of these professionals might be wary of mandated DOE. Judges could get behind this idea and implement local policies to encourage DOE before entering the legal system.

I'm not giving up the cause of mandated DOE. I think policy will be most effective in preventing a preventable divorce when it is universal and holds the imprimatur of the state. But I'm not naïve about the challenge of getting mandates passed by a legislature, even mandates that have a minimal price tag. While we pursue such legislation, it makes sense to me to move forward with publically supported efforts to make DOE available on a voluntary basis. And if significant progress can be made on a voluntary basis, and if research were to show that it helps prevent some preventable divorces and save the state tax dollars, then a stronger case can be made for a mandate.

Chapter 9

Facilitating Forever:
The Logistics of
Funding, Leadership, and Support

Proposal 5. Support this strategic public policy agenda with a 1% set-aside of TANF block grant funds to the state and a modest surcharge on marriage licenses. Provide state TANF-office leadership to state-directed initiatives and guide efforts with an active, expert advisory board.

Proposal 6. Provide federal support to state-directed initiatives by funding rigorous evaluation research and disseminating the knowledge gained. Also, employ federal funds for media campaigns to increase awareness of the value of MRE and participation in these services.

In Chapters 4–8, I argued for public support of marriage and relationship education (MRE) services to help youth and young adults form healthy romantic relationships and build a strong foundation for a healthy marriage, support married couples' efforts to maintain a healthy and stable marriage, and when marriages get in trouble, help individuals think carefully and rationally about their options, including doing the hard work of reconciliation and repair. I've tried to be pragmatic about this policy agenda, recommending already-existing educational infrastructures for efficiently delivering MRE to individuals and couples, especially to those at greater risk for unhealthy and unstable relationships. But I recognize that even efficient delivery will require some financial support. And good leadership will be needed to implement and direct the agenda. Funding, leadership, and support—logistics—are the topics for this chapter. How do we finance and administer a strategic public policy initiative intended to strengthen the institution of marriage? While this chapter is briefer than the preceding ones, I view implementation issues like this to be just as crucial to the potential success of the agenda as the substantive proposals covered so far.

Let me begin this implementation discussion with a review of important points from Chapter 2. Public policy efforts to help couples form and sustain healthy marriages and relationships have been driven primarily by the federal Healthy Marriages and Relationships Initiative (HMRI). Welfare reform efforts in the 1990s recognized the value of healthy marriages and stable families for reducing poverty and for children's well-being. Welfare reform legislation in 1996 encouraged states to experiment with new initiatives to strengthen two-parent families. A few states responded with some minor efforts, but these were small in scope; with one or two exceptions, not much was happening. In 2001, Wade Horn, as assistant secretary of the Administration for Children and Families (ACF)—the federal unit that administers the Temporary Assistance to Needy Families (TANF) program—began exploring ways to improve family stability by making funding available for experimental MRE programs. These initial efforts received a major boost in 2005 when congressional reauthorization of TANF specifically allocated $100 million a year for 5 years for MRE programs targeted primarily to lower income families. This funding stream was reauthorized in 2011 for 3 more years, albeit at $75 million a year. Since 2006, ACF has awarded competitive grants to community organizations throughout the United States to support the delivery of various kinds of MRE services. These were demonstration grants to experiment with what is possible. Organizations in every state except Rhode Island received some federal HMRI funding during 2006–2011. Funds were concentrated in just 32 states for the second round of funding that expires in 2014.[1]

Also, recall that a handful of states have established their own statewide HMRIs under the auspices of the state agencies directing their TANF programs. These states also benefited from some ACF grants to community organizations for MRE programs, but further efforts were funded directly by the states. But virtually all the "state" funds were set aside out of TANF block grants from the federal government to the states. Oklahoma, Texas, and Utah autonomously supported statewide HMRIs, though the Texas initiative appears to be dying right now due to budget cuts. A few other states traveled this road for a few blocks, but turned back soon after beginning. A few other states appear to be starting up state initiatives now. Oklahoma has produced the most impressive state-directed HMRI, with a substantial dose of MRE delivered to more than 315,000 individuals and counting.

So public efforts to provide MRE services targeted to lower income individuals and couples have been underwritten by federal TANF funds. Funds have been given to community organizations through ACF grants. ACF funded what it saw as the best grant applications to demonstrate possibilities in this new area of antipoverty policy. ACF funding has dramatically increased the availability of MRE services for lower income individuals and couples since 2006. And we have learned a lot over the past decade about what can be done. I believe ACF deserves credit and kudos for bringing leadership and support to this new public policy arena.

But I have two significant concerns about the future of these federally supported efforts, one strategic and the other pragmatic. First, ACF used a scattershot approach to funding MRE programs. I'm not being pejorative here. Their approach was to fund the best grant applications to demonstrate possibilities. Their initial efforts focused on demonstrating potential for different kinds of MRE, including each kind that I have discussed in the previous chapters. Beyond that, they did not have an underlying strategic plan for how to allocate these HMRI funds. So what we don't know is what is possible when a *strategic set* of early–life course MRE services are available in a community, including relationship literacy education for youth and young adults, relationship development education for cohabiting parents, marriage preparation education for engaged couples, marriage maintenance education for married couples, and divorce orientation education for couples at the crossroads of divorce. My argument is that a strategic approach directed at the state level will produce stronger results than a scattershot demonstration approach funded by the federal government. The scattershot approach will not provide comprehensive MRE services in a particular area and I think this will diminish the potential of MRE.

A second concern with the federal HMRI is more pragmatic and proximal. Given the enormous federal budget problems we are facing, these funding streams feeding community efforts to help couples form and sustain healthy marriages and relationships are at risk. I doubt that direct federal funding for HMRIs is going to survive as a priority when we are running trillion-dollar federal deficits each year and barreling at breakneck speed down a path that may take us to the same economic destination as Greece and Spain. I suspect that eventually our national leaders will come to some working compromise to avert a long-term fiscal train wreck, a compromise that will involve deep cuts (and sometimes elimination of) nearly every aspect of spending unrelated to payments on the federal deficit, healthcare, defense, and Social Security.

But there is a silver lining in these ominous fiscal clouds for HMRI efforts. The Temporary Assistance to Needy Families program that has funded these efforts is a part of our broader federal Social Security efforts, and it will survive, although it too is facing some cuts. TANF is a joint program between the federal government and the states. Most of the funds to help needy families come from the federal government in the form of an annual block grant, but states have significant flexibility in how they use the funds to meet the purposes of TANF, including strengthening two-parent families and marriage and reducing nonmarital births.[2] So states can choose to use some of the TANF funds they receive to help couples form and sustain healthy marriages and relationships in order to reduce poverty and improve children's lives. ACF may not continue to support direct grants to community HMRI programs past the current round of grants that expires in 2014. While I have no inside information on what ACF is thinking, I'm doing the budgetary and political math and this is the equation I get. But states could choose to use their TANF funds to support strategic initiatives.

So in this chapter I will detail my recommendations for how to fund and administer state-directed HMRIs. I will also note some potential advantages to state-directed HMRIs over the current federal grants approach and discuss an important supportive role that the federal government can play. But before I get to these issues, I want to address a crucial question: Why haven't more states already elected to use TANF block grant funds to support state HMRIs?

Resistance to Use of TANF Block Grants for State-Directed HMRIs

I've wondered about the above question a lot. But recently I have had the chance to ask some knowledgeable people for their perspectives on why more states have not used some of their TANF block grant funds to support state-directed HMRIs. The responses they gave converge around two related issues. First, state TANF administrators see their primary mission as helping low-income individuals get and keep gainful employment to reduce the need for public assistance. The purposes of TANF directly state that it is designed to help low-income individuals gain self-reliance through promoting family stability and work. But historically the welfare system has focused strongly on employment, for obvious reasons. And during a period of high unemployment rates like those we have been facing, their gaze will be riveted on employment struggles. Issues of family stability perhaps are not well understood, so they do not get much attention. Second and similarly, TANF administrators see their mission as making sure poor families, primarily women and children, have the basic necessities of life. They are tasked with the responsibility in a wealthy society of preventing women and children from going hungry and residing in third-world conditions. Couple relationship issues seem too soft and fuzzy to be of immediate concern, especially in difficult economic times when food and housing insecurity have risen substantially. Any public assistance pennies that can be spared should go to more basic concerns. In terms of Maslow's classic pyramid of human needs, basic security and safety come before relational needs.[3]

Thus it's not difficult to understand why most TANF administrators have barely dipped their toes in these unfamiliar waters of healthy marriage initiatives rather than jumping cannonball style into this new policy pool. Moreover, I suspect that state administrators have been content to watch from the sidelines as the federal government experiments with a new policy focus on strengthening couple relationships. Pragmatically, they probably wonder whether the new focus will gain a political beachhead and policy traction. And it's not hard to imagine that they are happy to keep their focus on the conventional tasks of helping poor families and hope that improvements in these basic issues will trickle down to improve family stability. And to some extent, they are right. As I acknowledged in Chapter 3 and elsewhere, improvements in education and employment and other areas at the macro level affect the ability of couples to form and sustain healthy marriages and relationships at the micro level. But the arrow does not just go one way; micro decisions about relationships create family instability that is a major contributor to poverty with its pressure for public assistance, poorer educational outcomes for children, reduced job skills for adults, and so forth. If there are means to create stronger and more stable couple relationships, then this road toward helping needy families should not be virtually vacant.

Also, perhaps TANF administrators doubt that the fences built at the top of the cliff are tall enough or strong enough to prevent the falls that require ambulances at the bottom of the cliff. But I have tried to show in the preceding chapters that there are promising educational interventions to diminish relationship instability. If we are serious about reducing poverty—and I am certain that TANF administrators are—then we should give attention to these potential services to help couples form and sustain healthy marriages and relationships. And we should do so not despite these families' "hard" needs for assistance with employment and food and shelter but because these "soft" services can help prevent the hard needs in the first place. We can take prevention seriously. And I see more signs that we are. I recently had a conversation with a high-level Department of Human Services administrator from a Midwestern "blue" state who told me about a meeting he attended with peers from about 20 other states and congressional leaders. He said that these state administrators were very interested in exploring the feasibility and value of healthy marriages and relationships initiatives in their states.

One organization that could do more to support this kind of prevention policy innovation among the states is the National Conference of State Legislatures (NCSL). This is a respected nonpartisan organization whose mission is to promote policy innovation and communication among state legislatures and improve the quality and effectiveness of state legislatures.[4] NCSL covers a full range of policy issues that states grapple with, including child and family welfare policy. But a perusal of their web site suggests that the organization has little to offer states right now to help them with making decisions about state-directed HMRIs.[5] I would like to see this organization become a better resource. Perhaps there is a chicken-and-egg problem here; more states need to show interest before NCSL will devote more resources to understand and improve these efforts. But I would like to see NCSL provide leadership on this issue. Other professional organizations, such as the National Organization for Human Services[6] and the American Public Human Services Association,[7] which promote the human services professions and advocates for effective social policies, could also become platforms to support state-directed HMRI efforts.

Funding State-Directed HMRIs:
1% Solutions and Marriage License Surcharges

I am sensitive to the reality that TANF funds are tight. Accordingly, I am proposing that states set aside just 1% of TANF block grant funds to support a state-directed healthy marriage initiative. If we can't afford 1% to try to prevent a major problem that contributes to poverty, then we are shortsighted with the other 99% of funds. Noted social policy analyst Isabel Sawhill made a similar point when she called for the U.S. government to set aside 1% of U.S. GDP for programs to improve the future prospects of disadvantaged children.[8] Chris Gersten, a former deputy assistant secretary to Wade Horn at ACF and one of the architects of the federal HMRI, first called for this approach, labeling it the "1% Solution."[9] I repeat that call here, urging state TANF administrators to support a state-directed initiative with a strategic set of MRE services like those I have outlined in this book.

Utah adopted a "1% Solution" in 2007. This generated about $700,000 a year for the Utah HMI. While in government budget accounting terms $700,000 is a microscopic figure, it made a significant difference to the initiative that had struggled for nearly a decade on intermittent fiscal crumbs and scraps. With recent cuts to TANF block grant funds, new administrators in Utah have decided that the Utah Healthy Marriage Initiative is a nonessential service and have terminated the work. Texas also adopted a "1% Solution" in 2007. One percent of their TANF block grant was more than 10 times the size of Utah's, about $7.5 million a year. But massive cuts there have left "Twogether in Texas" on life support for now, a reminder that prevention programs are vulnerable in difficult times and that political will can wax and wane. Oklahoma has had the steadiest funding stream for their Healthy Marriages and Relationships Initiative with $2–$3 million a year. A handful of other states have made use of TANF funds for some HMRI activities for a year or two but don't appear to have sustained those efforts.[10]

TANF dollars are not the only government funding stream that could be tapped, of course. Certainly the goals of child welfare policy to increase child well-being merge well with the aims of HMRIs to improve children's lives by increasing family stability and couple relationship quality. I understand that Florida's now-defunct state HMRI efforts in the early 2000s were supported with various child welfare policy funds. And certainly youth in the child welfare system would benefit greatly by more exposure to relationship literacy education.[11] Similarly, the Cooperative Extension System situated in land-grant universities throughout the country supports family life education efforts; these funds can be and are being used to support MRE efforts. The Cooperative Extension System draws major funding from the U.S. Department of Agriculture. The U.S. Department of Defense funds significant MRE efforts for military personnel. And healthy couple relationships and stable two-parent families contribute to better health outcomes for children and adults, so state health departments could be tapped for support, as well. Seeking funds from various government funding sources is fine. But MRE efforts and their goals of family stability, reducing unwed births, and child well-being are core to TANF; they are written into the four guiding purposes of TANF. So funds from other sources should supplement rather than substitute for TANF funds.

In addition, recognizing the fluctuations in TANF funding (that have scuttled state initiatives in Texas and Utah), I recommend that states pursue a second, stable source of funding for state strategic HMRIs. I propose that states set aside $10–$20 of the marriage license fee (or add a surcharge) and earmark the money to support state-directed HMRI efforts. This is essentially a user fee, not unlike the fee I pay for a fishing license that helps to fund state efforts to restore and reclaim fish habitat in the state. Recognizing the public value of healthy, stable marriages, the state could reasonably ask those entering the institution of marriage to make a small contribution to its upkeep. The added amount is small enough that it should not provide any disincentive to marrying, even for lower income couples. The average marriage license appears to cost about $35, with the most common fee being $25.[12] In Utah, which has about 25,000 marriages a year,[13] a $10–$20 surcharge would generate $250,000–$500,000 additional dollars each year for its initiative. California issued about 218,000 marriage licenses in 2011,[14] which would generate about $2.2–$4.4 million a year to support a state-directed initiative there.

I think a large majority of couples would willingly pay this surcharge. Data from several state surveys show that 85%–90% of adults in Oklahoma and Utah and about two thirds of adults in Florida and Kentucky think that a statewide initiative to strengthen marriages and reduce divorce is a good or very good idea. Support is even stronger among racial and ethnic minorities and among the less educated.[15] So I am not concerned about asking couples to support these public efforts to strengthen marriages when they enter into marriage themselves. There are different mechanisms for setting and adjusting marriage license fees in each state, so efforts to implement this funding stream will differ accordingly.

Leadership for State-Directed HMRIs

So far I've been discussing state-directed HMRIs in the abstract. But real people in real positions will determine the effectiveness of these efforts. So I'll try to put a little more flesh on the bones of this proposal. If the primary funding source is the state's TANF block grant, then the state department that administers TANF is the logical government entity to manage a state-directed initiative. A lean staff will be needed to run the day-to-day operations of the state initiative. Clearly, these day-to-day administrators will need strong, sustained leadership support from the organizational hierarchy above them if they are going to succeed. Top leadership needs to understand and buy into the rationale for setting aside a fraction of funds for MRE services. I have no magic formula for creating this kind of top-level support. Certainly, it will help for researchers like me to do more—even more than they have done to date—to make a hard-headed empirical case for the value of these kinds of services and the cost effectiveness of these kinds of policies.

Civil servant administrators will benefit from outside expertise to help them make strategic decisions. The Utah HMI Coordinator consults closely with an active advisory board, the Utah Commission on Marriage, to set strategic directions for the state-directed initiative. Commission members are appointed by the Executive Director of Workforce Services and volunteer their services. They attend quarterly meetings and respond to regular email inquiries from the coordinator.

The Commission is a smorgasbord of interested professionals in Utah. Academics from many of the major universities and colleges in the state are members of the Commission, including scholars with national reputations for work in the MRE field. Their involvement has been central to setting strategic directions. Because the Utah HMI uses the land-grant university's Cooperative Extension System as a primary delivery infrastructure for educational services across the state, a family life specialist with the Cooperative Extension System plays a crucial role on the Commission. Several county extension agents who oversee local MRE programs actively serve, as well. The director of the Utah State Office of Education Family and Consumer Sciences office is the Commission's resource for efforts to provide relationship literacy education to Utah youth. An individual who works with the Utah National Guard's family support programs provides a valuable connection to a large military sector in Utah. An employee from the state Office on Domestic and Sexual Violence is a long-time, active member of the Commission and advises on domestic violence prevention issues. A responsible fatherhood advocate in the state contributes to the Commission, as well. The Commission also includes practicing marriage therapists and a local media personality with a regular broadcast on marriage and family life. Representatives from Utah's two major religions are on the Commission. The director of the Family Life Office of the Catholic Diocese in Salt Lake City and an administrator with LDS Family Services (The Church of Jesus Christ of Latter-day Saints) provide regular input to the Commission. And some wedding industry entrepreneurs, for lack of a better term, also serve on the Commission.

This is not an exhaustive list of potential interested parties. But it may illustrate some important touch points that involve a wide set of interests and experiences in guiding a state-directed initiative. The Utah Commission on Marriage is not just an advisory board in name. It sets the strategic direction in close cooperation with the state Office of Work and Family Life. It also provides needed coordination of statewide efforts, including some that are not directly funded by the Utah HMI but benefit from promotion and marketing at the state level. I think the Utah Commission on Marriage can be a model for how other states, especially smaller ones, could provide expert leadership to a state-directed HMRI. (I think this even though the Commission's bureaucratic home in the Utah Department of Workforce Services is tossing us out on the street now.)

Of course, this is not the only administrative model to consider. In Oklahoma, oversight of their initiative has come from the top of the Department of Human Services, but day-to-day work is contracted out to a local, for-profit, creative, public relations firm, Public Strategies, Inc., with extensive experience now in getting educational services to large numbers of individuals and couples. This was a controversial decision at first to use an outside, for-profit entity to manage the Oklahoma Marriage Initiative (OMI). Looking back, I believe, as do many of my colleagues, that it was a strategic decision that provided the OMI with more creativity and a stronger performance mindset than is often the case in government bureaucracies. The OMI also benefits from the input of a distinguished group of marriage scholars from Oklahoma and around the nation who meet annually to review progress. The Oklahoma administrative model may be more controversial and probably is more expensive, but the results are hard to dismiss. The OMI is the premier statewide HMRI in the country, reaching the most people with the best set of services. Another model worth considering is organizing the day-to-day leadership of a state HMRI as a nonprofit organization and having the state contract with this organization to do the work. Both of these models give added flexibility because they are outside the scope of many government regulations and restrictions. For instance, for-profit and not-for-profit organizations can pursue private funding to supplement their public funding stream. A few states already have nonprofit organizations leading private, statewide HMRIs, but they receive no funding from and do not coordinate with the state. (Their funding has come directly from the federal government.) Perhaps state governments could tap these already existing organizations to provide daily leadership.

Potential Benefits of State-Directed HMRIs

I have argued for state-directed HMRIs over the current federal direction out of concern for the future viability of the federal HMI. But on the positive side, I think there are some real benefits that could accrue from a state-directed approach.

Federalism and Variation

The founders of the United States established a constitutional government that dispersed political power rather than concentrated it. We often hear about the separation of powers between the federal legislative, executive, and judicial branches of government. We hear less often about another fundamental way that the founders distributed powers. The U.S. Constitution delegated certain powers to the various states and others to the federal government. The states then have considerable autonomy in how they go about the business of government. This approach is labeled *federalism*. To some, federalism is potential legal chaos as 50 states could have 50 different sets of laws on basic matters. (As a matter of practice, there is considerable similarity among states.) But to others, this separation of powers between federal and state governments is a necessary check on centralized power that promotes greater liberty.[16] Another potential benefit of federalism is that it promotes political experimentation. States do things differently, and some ways of doing things may be more effective than others.

I have argued for the value of state-directed HMRIs and outlined how they could be feasibly funded and administered. While funding mechanisms and leadership could be relatively similar across states, I expect and welcome the variation that would emerge out of 50 different sets of people with diverse perspectives approaching the challenge of a state-directed initiative to help couples in their particular state form and sustain healthy marriages and relationships. This diversity generally is a healthy condition for effective public policy.[17] And the resulting variation is a potential goldmine of valuable information for researchers wanting to know what works well. We are not so advanced in our knowledge of how to help couples and strengthen the institution of marriage that we can prescribe a universal, one-size-fits-all approach. We will learn and benefit from divergent approaches.

Localism

Moreover, the divergence of approach will not be random. Instead, local differences will shape local initiatives. The best approach in New Jersey may not be the best approach in New Mexico. And what works well in South Carolina may not work as well in South Dakota. So a federalist HMRI approach allows local leadership to tailor efforts to better meet local needs.

Human Services Integration

In Chapter 2 I mentioned that a current emphasis in the federal HMRI is to promote the integration of MRE services into traditional human services such as employment, child welfare, and mental health. These services have a track record of helping low-income families and could be a valuable platform for providing MRE services. I support this push. Embedded in state TANF efforts, a state-directed HMRI is in an excellent organizational position to work with traditional human services and antipoverty programs to extend the reach of MRE to those who may benefit from it the most. The Oklahoma Marriage Initiative currently does a good job of using human services agencies to deliver MRE.

Strategic Direction

Finally, an important benefit of state-directed HMRIs is a greater potential for strategic direction. I stated earlier in the chapter that the federal HMRI's approach has been to use federal grants to seed promising demonstration programs in communities around the nation to see what is possible in this new policy arena. That may have been a good place to start, but it is not the best way forward now. We need more strategic planning; state leadership is more likely to provide that, I believe. As I look at the premier state-directed initiative, the Oklahoma Marriage Initiative,[18] I see much more than a scattershot approach to promoting MRE services. I see a balance of programs targeted to each segment of the life course that I have discussed in the book: youth, young adults, cohabiting parents, engaged couples, married couples, and distressed couples. I see an array of programs designed to meet particular circumstances, such as couples transitioning to parenthood, stepfamilies, adoptive families, and so forth. I see attempts to engage multiple sectors of society in supporting MRE services, including religious, human service, education, healthcare, business, military, and others. I see these services supported with effective marketing and promoted with creative media campaigns. I see web sites that are one-stop resource centers for MRE program availability around the state. And I see decisions at times to concentrate services in particular areas to achieve potentially greater impacts. In short, I see strategic planning that I think will yield stronger results over the long haul.

Role for the Federal Government

I am calling for states to assume leadership for HMRIs from the federal government. But the federal government can still provide a valuable supporting role to help state-directed initiatives flourish. Obviously, it provides a primary funding mechanism through TANF block grants. But there are other things it can do to support state efforts.

Reward Structures

Of course, the federal Administration for Children and Families could require states to set aside 1% of their TANF block grant funds for preventative efforts to help individuals and couples form and sustain healthy relationships and enduring marriages. But as much as possible, I'm trying to avoid creating top-down mandates that would be controversial and meet with heavy resistance, resistance that might show up in the quality of the programs offered. Instead, I would rather see ACF use effective carrots rather than sticks. For instance, ACF could incent a 1% set-aside with a policy that it will reimburse for a certain period of time up to 1% of a state's TANF block grant for states that devote TANF funds for supporting these policies effectively. That is, it will use various funding streams to match dollar for dollar up to 1% the funds that states invest in healthy marriage and relationship initiatives. This would reduce the start-up costs for cooperating states while minimizing the penalty for states that do not want to pursue these kinds of efforts. The cost for this would be less than the current funding approach, especially if a number of states decide not to fund their own HMRI.

Evaluation

There is still a great deal of evaluation research needed to understand what kinds of MRE programs are most effective for whom and why. Policy should be based on a body of evidence; new policy especially needs good research. Rigorous research is expensive, time-consuming, and requires training and experience. With limited funds, however, states will struggle to devote resources to the important task of evaluation. I propose that the federal government continue and expand its role in HMRI evaluation research. This would allow states to concentrate their limited funds on service delivery but still gain the general benefits of evaluation research.

Within the ACF is an Office of Planning, Research, and Evaluation (OPRE) whose mission is to conduct high-quality research to guide more effective policy to help needy families. OPRE supported the rigorous evaluation studies of the Building Strong Families program for low-income cohabiting parents and the Supporting Healthy Marriage program for low-income married parents discussed in Chapters 5 and 6. They are currently conducting rigorous research on the effectiveness of a number of other, smaller scale MRE program initiatives. This kind of original evaluation work should continue and grow. With reduced demands on ACF to support MRE programs directly with grants, ACF could re-task some of those funds to OPRE to support more evaluation research. Obviously, OPRE probably could not evaluate programs in every state running a state-directed HMRI. But it could select promising and innovative programs being tried by several states and then widely disseminate the results to help states make decisions about how to improve their services and allocate resources more effectively. It should also conduct or support policy-level evaluations with cross-state comparison studies. OPRE also could consider a grant competition for state-directed HMRIs that have a specific evaluation need that they want to address. And it could consider regularly funding the best basic research proposals from academics whose work directly advances applied knowledge in the field.

Coordination

I think the federal government could do more than fund individual research projects that lead to improvement in the practice of MRE. I think they should support an effort to coordinate this body of research by a large group of researchers to make substantial advancements in our knowledge base. While this certainly would not be similar to the scope of the Human Genome Research Project, still, we will make more progress by coordinating and integrating the efforts of researchers in the field than by simply supporting isolated teams. There remain myriad research questions to answer to improve the effectiveness of MRE, not the least of which is to understand the mechanisms of change that produce the positive changes we seek with these interventions.[19]

Dissemination

I also recommend a strong role for the federal government in disseminating research and evidence-based practice in the field. Thus, OPRE should continue its annual Welfare Research Evaluation Conference, but I think more attention needs to be given at the conference than is currently the case to promising interventions to help couples form and sustain healthy marriages and relationships. Alternatively, ACF has regularly brought together MRE grant-holder practitioners in a brief conference. Perhaps they could re-task this conference to serve both MRE practitioners and researchers as a means of disseminating research and highlighting research-based promising practices in the field.

Training

I think the federal government could provide more support for training programs at select universities to promote more training of effective MRE educator professionals and program administrators. These programs could be housed in various disciplines, including undergraduate and graduate social work programs that traditionally prepare students to work with at-risk children and young adults. Psychology, sociology, family studies, and public health disciplines could also be fertile sites for these training programs. Funds could support the addition of specific training for marriage and relationship education efforts to traditional training efforts. ACF funded a couple of training programs for a few years in the mid-2000s, but the training efforts have now dissipated, as far as I can tell.[20] Grants will need to be much longer in order for these university training programs to gain traction and become a mainstay of professional preparation.

Resource Centers

The federal government can facilitate the kind of support systems that will help state-directed HMRIs to accomplish their work. This is something that ACF has been doing and I applaud their efforts and urge continued support. For instance, ACF recently funded the National Resource Center for Healthy Marriage and Families with a mission to support state human service providers' efforts to integrate MRE skills into traditional human service delivery systems (e.g., employment, child support and welfare, domestic violence prevention, mental health) as a part of a comprehensive family-centered approach to promote self-sufficiency.[21] This organization could be a valuable resource to state-directed initiatives in their efforts to learn how to use existing human service delivery systems to provide low-income individuals and couples with MRE services. Similarly, the National Healthy Marriage Resource Center was funded by ACF from 2004–2011 to be a support system to MRE practitioners generally and HMI grantees specifically.[22] This resource center was run by Public Strategies, Inc., which is the same group that runs the Oklahoma Marriage Initiative. The web site is a repository of valuable information that can help state-directed HMIs.

Media Campaigns

Effective media campaigns help people understand the value of MRE and draw more participants into programs. But good campaigns take hard work and creative talent to develop effective marketing ideas and are expensive to put in the field for the length of time they need to make an impact. Again, with limited funds, state-directed HMRIs will be hard pressed to sustain major media campaigns. For a number of years, the Utah HMI made a major commitment to a media campaign to support its services run by a leading social marketing firm. In fact, it was nearly half the budget. But with recent large budget cuts, decision makers had to give up the campaign. I think the federal government can play a valuable support role here and I echo the calls of other scholars for federally supported media campaigns.[23] It could concentrate funding and efforts to develop a national campaign to promote the value of MRE and direct interested individuals to web sites to learn more. The federal government also could develop marketing tools that could be adopted and branded by state initiatives.

In this chapter, I have focused on implementation of my proposed policy agenda to help couples form and sustain healthy marriages and relationships. Funding, leadership, and other logistics are crucial to turning an agenda into something that makes a real difference. Of course, there are many other details that will be involved in implementing state-directed HMRIs, and those will vary in each state according to distinctive circumstances and personalities. I hope the general implementation principles that I have explained here can provide a solid launching pad for state efforts. In the final chapter, I try to summarize the policy agenda I have been describing in this book and provide some concluding observations on how to move forward.

Chapter 10

Summary and Final Thoughts

Given the length of this book, I think it would be good in this concluding chapter for me to summarize what I've tried to say in the previous pages. I'll do so in the form of a logic model (see Figure 10.1) that connects the policy agenda I have proposed both to the societal and relationship challenges that create a need for the agenda and the intended personal and societal outcomes it attempts to enhance. Then I will be very brief with some concluding thoughts.

A Logic Model Summary

To summarize, the overarching problem that my proposed strategic public policy agenda seeks to address is decreasing family stability with its negative effects on many children and its public costs. In our contemporary society, there are many challenges to forming and sustaining healthy relationships and marriages, as outlined in the "Relationship Challenges" stratum of the logic model. Of course, these are embedded within broader, contextual challenges to forming and sustaining healthy relationships, including macroeconomic challenges such as diminishing educational and employment opportunities, incarceration, high rates of substance abuse, mental health problems, and violence and abuse, as well as historical cultural forces such as increasing individualism. Positive changes in these challenges will indirectly strengthen the institution of marriage. But as a result of these contextual and relational challenges, there is a direct and increasing need for education to help individuals and couples develop stronger relationship skills and gain greater knowledge in order to form and sustain healthy relationships and enduring marriages. And this education needs to be targeted especially to

283

less educated and lower income individuals and couples who experience more external stress and are at greatest risk for relationship problems and family instability.

Specifically, I have proposed public support for a series of educational interventions across the early life course, beginning with relationship literacy education for youth and young adults (delivered primarily through high schools, community colleges, and universities), relationship development education for cohabiting parents with aspirations for marriage (delivered primarily through human service agencies), marriage preparation education for formally engaged couples (delivered primarily through religious organizations), marriage maintenance education for married couples, especially early-married couples (delivered through a variety of religious organizations, human service agencies, and self-directed Internet programs), and divorce orientation education for couples at the crossroads of divorce to help them make careful decisions about the best path forward (delivered primarily by self-directed Internet programs). These efforts can be funded by a 1% set-aside of TANF block grant funds to state-directed Healthy Marriages and Relationships Initiatives supplemented by a $10–$20 set-aside or surcharge on marriage licenses. These funds would be administered by state TANF offices guided by an active volunteer advisory board of experts.

This integrated set of educational interventions experienced over the early life course by an increasing number of at-risk individuals and couples will produce a greater incidence of proximal, positive relational outcomes, as outlined in the "Intended Personal and Relational Outcomes" stratum of the logic model. This, in turn, increases distal outcomes such as the proportion of healthy romantic relationships and stable, two-parent families, which ultimately reduces poverty and improves child well-being in our society. This model is what I have tried to explain and advocate for in this book.

Final Thoughts: Terminology, Idealism, and Integration

With this integrated set of educational interventions, some will have noticed that I have subdivided the generic field of marriage and relationship education into five specific kinds of programs to help individuals and couples form healthy relationships and strong, enduring marriages: relationship literacy education for youth and young adults; relationship development education for cohabiting parents with aspirations to marriage; marriage preparation

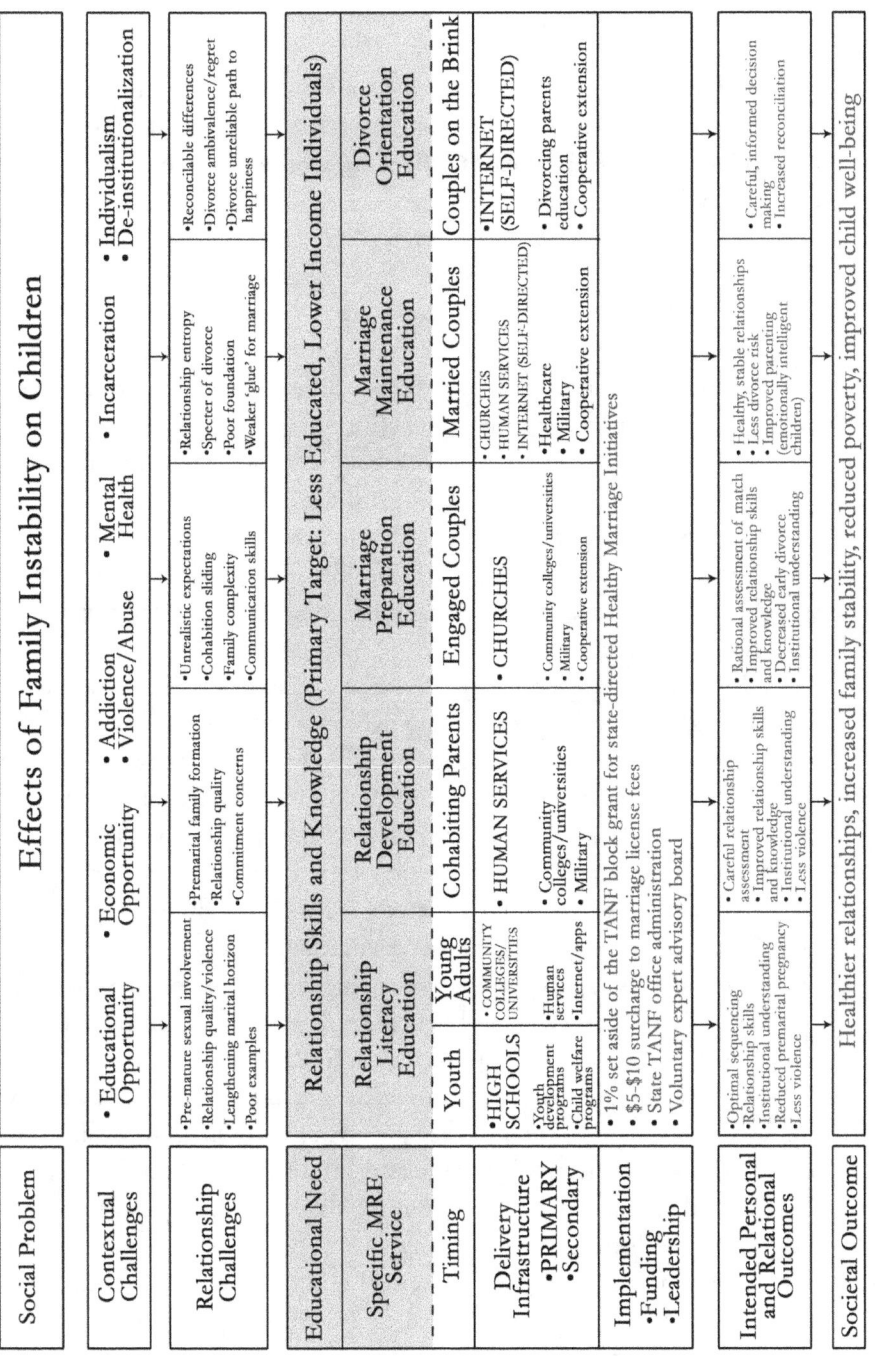

Figure 10.1. A Logic Model of a Feasible Public Policy Agenda to Promote Marriage and Relationship Education Services to Help Couples Form and Sustain Healthy Marriages and Relationships to Increase Family Stability, Decrease Poverty, and Improve Child Well-Being

education for engaged couples; marriage maintenance education for married couples; and divorce orientation education for distressed couples at the crossroads of divorce. The field is addressing diverse educational needs associated with variations in age, life course stage, and unique circumstances. As a result, I think the field's terminology needs to become more precise. I hope these terms, most of which are new recommendations to the field, will be helpful to practitioners and scholars. There has been debate and inconsistency about the umbrella label for the field. A whole set of competing terms are commonly used, including relationship education, couple education, and marriage education, along with conjunctive combinations such as marriage and relationship education (and some argument about whether marriage or relationship should come first) and couple and relationship education. There are reasons behind a preference for each term. But perhaps this diversity of generic terms for the field would be less problematic if we begin to use more specific and descriptive terms that capture the diversity of educational programs in the field.

At the same time, I recognize that these conceptually distinct kinds of marriage and relationship education (MRE) may not be so clean in the field. Participants who are seeking some relationship help are coming to any class they can get, married, unmarried, single, divorced, young, old. As I have talked to educators in the field serving lower income populations, I have been impressed with the tremendous diversity of participants that will come to a class and make an age- or family structure–focus challenging. And they may be seeking help with a wide variety of couple, family, or other relationships. So perhaps it is also appropriate to have a broad term to describe a curriculum that is delivered in a relationship nonspecific way. I recommend a generic term such as healthy relationships education (HRE).

I suspect that I am susceptible to the critique that I am idealistic in my proposed agenda and its hypothesized positive effects. On my office desk sits a small wooden statuette of Don Quixote on his trusted steed, Rocinante. The fictional account of Don Quixote spawned the word *quixotic,* which means to be idealistic, particularly in a romantic but impractical way. I admit to the idealism. And I'm happy to apply it in the service of romance. But I have tried hard to avoid the impractical in the strategic policy agenda I have proposed. Indeed, I have made feasibility a central element of my agenda. If we are going to move forward, we need an agenda that can be implemented within the serious fiscal and political constraints we are facing now and for the foreseeable future. What I have proposed requires little in the way of new funding. I have proposed using just 1% of current TANF block grants in each state to support educational initiatives, supplemented by a small marriage license fee surcharge (that likely will have strong public support). With the exception of divorce orientation education, the agenda does not require new legislation, which is a roadblock to implementation given how hard it is to pass legislation that deals with sensitive issues. I have proposed building awareness and interest in these voluntary educational services with effective media campaigns. The agenda can be implemented efficiently without a large government bureaucracy that is expensive and anathema to many. Services can be delivered best within existing civic educational infrastructures, with minor enhancements. There is emerging evidence that these kinds of services can be effective at helping couples form and sustain healthy relationships and stable marriages. And public support for the kinds of initiatives I'm proposing appears to be strong. In short, I think the policy agenda I have proposed here is doable now. The biggest barrier to implementing the agenda is vision to see how current resources could be used more effectively and how doing so would tangibly bless couples and the next generation. I hope this book has opened up that vision, especially to key policy makers in each state.

Finally, I have tried to describe (and depict in Figure 10.1) the set of proposals as an integrated strategic agenda. Early intervention is crucial, but then other educational programs need to follow at key times. The full set of interventions is more than the sum of the individual parts. My hope is that the full implementation of this agenda takes on the nature of regular support across the early life span for forming and sustaining healthy relationships and stable marriages instead of being just some educational tool that we employ once and hope to prevent or fix all problems. As I said in Chapter 1, a single dosage of MRE is unlikely to successfully inoculate individuals against relationship problems. If we are going to think of MRE as a vaccine, then we need to think of it as requiring multiple dosages across time to be most effective. A single-point intervention will struggle to make a big dent in long-term family instability rates.[1] While each individual component of the agenda is being tried in various places, there is no place yet where the full set has been strategically and effectively implemented over a significant period of time. Oklahoma comes the closest, with Utah at number two. But further progress and refinement are needed in those two states. No doubt what they accomplish will be important for other states to view as they consider adopting this policy agenda. As a few states continue to make progress and, importantly, show that it is cost effective at increasing family stability, I hope more states will see the value and commit to implementing the full strategic policy agenda.

Moreover, perhaps implementation of the full agenda could increase family stability in another way, too, by giving greater substance to a higher vision. Maybe it would tune all of us into the bigger ideas behind the various initiatives and curricula: that healthy and stable family relationships are the greatest personal and public assets we have, and that the yearnings of the human heart are deeply dependent on a demanding discipline of cognitions and behaviors that make relationships work and thrive, a discipline made more difficult by broader societal trends and stresses. Maybe a full implementation of this proposed agenda will strengthen a vision of what is good and possible. I fear too many have lost that vision. I think a strategic agenda can help us envision a modern society of healthy marriages and relationships for more than the educated elite. Vision is important too.

I admit that to get more than modest change we need to do more than provide a set of programs. We are cultural creatures; we tend to go along with the cultural current. So we need to shift the culture. But perhaps this modest policy agenda could be a catalyst for building a more powerful cultural expectation that we educate ourselves to be smarter about marriages and relationships rather than leaving things to chance. I know that it is easy to be skeptical about this. I opened this book with an important question raised by skeptics of the kinds of efforts I am proposing here: Are the forces of cultural change so overpowering and relentless and our tools to intervene so constrained and limited as to make any policy efforts merely quixotic? I think many believe we can only be fatalistic observers of where the cultural forces of change will take us. Or, some are content with observing where cultural forces are pushing contemporary romantic relationships because they believe we are just going through another historical transition and are optimistic that these currents will eventually take us to new destinations of diverse, functional family forms. I am less optimistic about where those currents are taking us. I'm certainly less patient. I don't think being a passive spectator is what is needed because there is too much evidence that people's lives are diminished by current and continuing trends and that society as a whole suffers as a result. I am advocating for an active agenda to nudge cultural forces.

Many will see my idealism exposed again in the task I have given to a set of brief educational interventions to help individuals and couples form and sustain healthy relationships and strong, stable marriages. In the face of powerful, historical, glacial forces that are pushing and reshaping the institution of marriage and constant buffetings of the contemporary winds of social and economic struggles, can these minor efforts to provide more needy couples with better relationship skills and knowledge really be anything but idealistic, maybe even misdirected do-goodism?

Well, simply, I believe in the power of education for good. That shouldn't be a surprise, as I am an educator by profession. I know that education doesn't lead everyone to make better choices all the time. But we can facilitate personal aspirations of forever. I'm encouraged by the early research and I think many individuals and couples will gain from these educational opportunities. I think the agenda of educational initiatives proposed here can make many more young people today better drivers of their romantic relationships, more competent at avoiding destructive detours, and more capable of achieving their marital aspirations and destinations. Their personal successes then become societal assets.

Furthermore, when there is important knowledge that makes people's lives better and could benefit society, I believe we have an ethical obligation to make that education available to those who need it and want it. After all, education is fundamentally a moral endeavor. When there is knowledge and wisdom that can help improve human lives and human societies, it must be available to needy learners. When reliable knowledge meets eager learners at the right time, then there is potential for meaningful personal growth. That personal growth when multiplied by significant numbers over time can create noticeable, positive, societal change, change that creates better circumstances for children. That is something we all want.

References

Abrahamson, I., Hussain, R., Khan, A., & Schofield, M. J. (2012). What helps couples rebuild their relationship after infidelity? *Journal of Family Issues, 33,* 1494–1519.

Acitelli, L. K. (2001). Maintaining and enhancing a relationship by attending to it. In J. H. Harvey & A. Wenzel (Eds.), *Close romantic relationships: Maintenance and enhancement* (pp. 153–168). Mahwah, NJ: Lawrence Erlbaum Associates.

Adler-Baeder, F., Callingas, A., Skuban, E., Keily, M., Ketring, S., & Smith, T. (2013). Linking changes in couple functioning and parenting among couple relationship education participants. *Family Relations, 62,* 284–297.

Adler-Baeder, F., Ketring, S., Smith, T., Skuban, E., McLane, J., Gregson, K., Bradford, A., Lucier, M., & Parham, R. (2011). *Overall youth: Findings for youth participants in marriage and relationship education (MRE) in years 1–5.* Auburn University: Alabama Community Healthy Marriage Initiative. Retrieved from www.alabamamarriage.org/research.php

Administration for Children and Families. (n.d.). Fact sheet: Personal Responsibility Education (PREP) evaluation. Washington, DC: Author.

Afifi, T. O., MacMillan, H., Cox, B. J., Asmundson, G. J. G., Stein, M. B., & Sareen, J. (2009). Mental health correlates of intimate partner violence in marital relationships in a nationally representative sample of males and females. *Journal of Interpersonal Violence, 24,* 1398–1417.

Allen, D. W., & Gallagher, M. (2007, July). Does divorce law affect the divorce rate? A review of empirical research, 1995–2006. *iMAPP Research Brief, 1*(1). Retrieved from http://www.marriagedebate.com/dlr.php

Allen, E. S., & Atkins, D. C. (2012). The association of divorce and extramarital sex in a representative U.S. sample. *Journal of Family Issues, 33,* 1477–1493.

Amato, P. R. (2000). The consequences of divorce for adults and children. *Journal of Marriage and the Family, 62,* 1269–1287.

Amato, P. R., & Booth, A. (1997). *A generation at risk: Growing up in an era of family upheaval.* Cambridge, MA: Harvard University.

Amato, P. R., & Hohmann-Marriott, B. (2007). A comparison of high- and low-distress marriages that end in divorce. *Journal of Marriage and Family, 69,* 621–638.

Amato, P. R., & Previti, D. (2003). People's reasons for divorcing: Gender, social class, the life course, and adjustment. *Journal of Family Issues, 24,* 602–626.

Amato, P. R., & Rogers, S. J. (1997). A longitudinal study of marital problems and subsequent divorce. *Journal of Marriage and the Family, 59,* 612–624.

Amato, P. R., Booth, A., Johnson, D. R., & Rogers, S. J. (2007). *Alone together: How marriage in America is changing.* Cambridge, MA: Harvard University.

Amato, P. R., Kane, J. B., & James, S. (2011). Reconsidering the "good divorce." *Family Relations, 60,* 511–524.

Anderson, K. L. (2010). Conflict, power, and violence in families. *Journal of Marriage and Family, 72,* 726–742.

Andrews, K. (2012). *Maybe "I do": Modern marriage & the pursuit of happiness.* Ballan, Victoria, Australia: Connor Court Publishing.

Annie E. Casey Foundation. (2012). *KIDS COUNT data book: 2012.* Baltimore, MD: Author.

Antle, B. F., Karam, E., Christensen, D. N., Barbee, A. P., & Sar, B. K. (2011). An evaluation of healthy relationship education to reduce intimate partner violence. *Journal of Family Social Work, 14,* 387–406.

Antle, B. F., Sar, B. K., Christensen, D. N., Ellers, F. S., Karam, E. A., Barbee, A. P., & van Zyl, M. A. (in press). The impact of the Within My Reach relationship training on relationship skills and outcomes for low-income individuals. *Journal of Marital and Family Therapy.*

Archer, J. (2000). Sex differences in aggression between heterosexual partners: A meta-analytic review. *Psychological Bulletin, 126,* 651–680.

Atkins, D. C., & Furrow, J. (2008, November). Infidelity is on the rise: But for whom and why? Paper presented at the annual meeting of the Association for Behavioral and Cognitive Therapies, Orlando, FL.

Barber, B. L., & Eccles, J. S. (2003). The joy of romance: Healthy adolescent relationships as an educational agenda. In P. Florsheim (Ed.), *Adolescent romantic relations and sexual behavior: Theory, research, and practical implications* (pp. 335–370). Mahwah, NJ: Lawrence Erlbaum Associates.

Beach, S. R. H., Fincham, F. D., Hurt, T. R., McNair, L. M., & Stanley, S. M. (2008). Prayer and marital intervention: A conceptual framework. *Journal of Social and Clinical Psychology, 27,* 641–669.

Berger, A., Wildsmith, E., Manlove, J., & Steward-Streng, N. (2012). Relationship violence among young adult couples. *Child Trends Research Brief,* #2012-14. Retrieved from http://www.childtrends.org/Files//Child_Trends-2012_06_01_RB_CoupleViolence.pdf

Bir, A., Lerman, R. I., Corwin, E., MacIlvain, B., Beard, A., Richburg, K., Smith, K., & Lerman, R. I. (2012). *The Community Healthy Marriage Initiative evaluation: Impacts of a community approach to strengthening families,* OPRE Report 2012-34A. Washington, DC: Office of Planning, Research, and Evaluation, Administration for Children and Families, U.S. Department of Health and Human Services.

Birch, P. J., Weed, S. E., & Olsen, J. (2004). Assessing the impact of community marriage policies on county divorce rates. *Family Relations, 53,* 495–503.

Blanchard, V. L., Hawkins, A. J., Baldwin, S. A., & Fawcett, E. B. (2009). Investigating the effects of marriage and relationship education on couples' communication skills: A meta-analytic study. *Journal of Family Psychology, 23,* 203–214.

Bodenmann, G., Pihet, S., Shantinath, S. D., Cina, A., & Widmer, K. (2006). Improving dyadic coping in couples with a stress-oriented approach: A 2-year longitudinal study. *Behavior Modification, 30,* 571–597.

Bouchet, S., Torres, L., & Hyra, A. (2012, April). *HHMI grantee implementation evaluation: Marketing, recruitment, and retention strategies.* OPRE 2012-24. Washington, DC: Office of Planning, Research, and Evaluation, Administration for Children and Families. Retrieved from http://www.acf.hhs.gov/programs/opre/resource/hhmi-grantee-implementation-evaluation-marketing-recruitment-and

Bouma, R., Halford, W. K., & Young, R. (2004). Evaluation of the Controlling Alcohol and Relationship Enhancement (CARE) program with hazardous drinkers. *Behaviour Change, 21,* 229–250.

Bowen, C. D. (1986). *Miracle at Philadelphia.* Boston: Back Bay Books.

Bradbury, T. N., & Karney, B. R. (2004). Understanding and altering the longitudinal course of marriage. *Journal of Marriage and Family, 66,* 862–879.

Bradbury, T. N., & Lavner, J. A. (2012). How can we improve preventive and educational interventions for intimate relationships? *Behavior Therapy, 43,* 113–122.

Bradford, K. P., Skogrand, L., & Higginbotham, B. J. (2011). Intimate partner violence in a statewide couple and relationship education initiative. *Journal of Couple & Relationship Therapy, 10,* 169–184.

Bradley, R. P. C., Friend, D. J., & Gottman, J. M. (2011). Supporting healthy relationships in low-income, violent couples: Reducing conflict and strengthening relationship skills and satisfaction. *Journal of Couple & Relationship Therapy, 10,* 97–116.

Bradley, R. P. C., & Gottman, J. M. (2012). Reducing situational violence in low-income couples by fostering healthy relationships. *Journal of Marital and Family Therapy, 38,* 187–198.

Braithwaite, S. R., & Fincham, F. D. (2007). ePREP: Computer-based prevention of relationship dysfunction, depression, and anxiety. *Journal of Social and Clinical Psychology, 26,* 609–622.

Braithwaite, S. R., & Fincham, F. D. (2009). A randomized clinical trial of a computer-based preventative intervention: Replication and extension of ePREP. *Journal of Family Psychology, 23,* 32–38.

Braithwaite, S. R., & Fincham, F. D. (2011). Computer-based dissemination: A randomized clinical trial of ePREP using the actor partner interdependence model. *Behaviour Research and Therapy, 49,* 126–131.

Bramlett, M. D., & Mosher, W. D. (2001). *First marriage dissolution, divorce and remarriage: United States.* (Advance data from vital and health statistics, No. 323.) Hyattsville, MD: National Center for Health Statistics.

Bray, J. H., & Jouriles, E. N. (1995). Treatment of marital conflict and prevention of divorce. *Journal of Marital & Family Therapy, 21,* 461–473.

Bridges, L. J. (2003). Trust, attachment, and relatedness. In M. C. Bornstein (Ed.), *Well-being: Positive development across the life course* (pp. 177–189). Mahwah, NJ: Lawrence Erlbaum Associates.

Brooks, D. (2010, March 30). The Sandra Bullock trade. *New York Times.* Retrieved from http://www.nytimes.com/2010/03/30/opinion/30brooks.html

Brower, N., Darrington, J., & Bradford, K. (2011). Relationship education: Encouraging participation through experiential date nights. *Journal of NEAFCS (National Extension Association for Family and Consumer Sciences), 6.* Retrieved from www.neafcs.org/assets/Journal/NEAFCS-2011-Journal.pdf

Burton, L. M., Cherlin, A., Winn, D., Estacion, A., & Holder-Taylor, C. (2009). The role of trust in low-income mothers' intimate unions. *Journal of Marriage and Family, 71,* 1107–1124.

Busby, D. M., Carroll, J. S., & Willoughby, B. J. (2010). Compatibility or restraint? The effects of sexual timing on marriage relationships. *Journal of Family Psychology, 24,* 766–774.

Busby, D. M., & Gardner, B. C. (2008). How do I analyze thee? Let me count the ways: Considering empathy in couple relationships using self and partner ratings. *Family Process, 47,* 229–242.

Busby, D. M., Holman, T. B., & Niehuis, S. (2009). The association between partner enhancement and self-enhancement and relationship quality outcomes. *Journal of Marriage and Family, 71,* 449–464.

Busby, D. M., Holman, T. B., & Taniguchi, N. (2001). RELATE: Relationship evaluation of the individual, family, cultural, and couple contexts. *Family Relations, 50,* 308–316.

Busby, D. M., Ivey, D. C., Harris, S. M., & Ates, C. (2007). Self-directed, therapist-directed, and assessment-based interventions for premarital couples. *Family Relations, 56,* 279–290.

Bush, G. W. (2002, February 26). *President announces welfare reform agenda.* Retrieved from http://georgewbush-whitehouse.archives.gov/news/releases/2002/02/20020226-11.html

Cahn, N., & Carbone, J. (2010). *Red families v. blue families: Legal polarization and the creation of culture.* New York: Oxford University Press.

Campbell, J. C. (2002). Health consequences of intimate partner violence. *Lancet, 359,* 1331–1336.

Carroll, J. S., Hymowitz, K., Wilcox, W. B., & Kaye, K. (2013). *Knot yet: The benefits and costs of delayed marriage in America.* Washington, DC: National Campaign to Prevent Teen and Unplanned Pregnancy, RELATE Institute, & National Marriage Project.

Carver, K. P., Joyner, K., & Udry, J. R. (2003). National estimates of adolescent romantic relationships. In P. Florsheim (Ed.), *Adolescent romantic relations and sexual behavior: Theory, research, and practical implications* (pp. 23–56). Mahwah, NJ: Lawrence Erlbaum Associates.

Catlett, B. S., & Artis, J. E. (2004). Critiquing the case for marriage promotion. *Violence Against Women, 10,* 1226–1244.

Cavanagh, K., & Shapiro, D. A. (2004). Computer treatment for common mental health problems. *Journal of Clinical Psychology, 60,* 239–251.

Centre for Social Justice. (2010, January). *The Centre for Social Justice Green Paper on the Family.* London: Author.

Chambers, A. L., & Kravitz, A. (2011). Understanding the disproportionately low marriage rate among African Americans: An amalgam of sociological and psychological constraints. *Family Relations, 60,* 648–660.

Cherlin, A. J. (2004). The deinstitutionalization of American marriage. *Journal of Marriage and Family, 66,* 848–861.

Cherlin, A. J. (2009). *The marriage-go-round: The state of marriage and the family in America today.* New York: Alfred A. Knopf.

Cherlin, A. J., Burton, L. M., Hurt, T. R., & Purvin, D. M. (2004). The influence of physical and sexual abuse on marriage and cohabitation. *American Sociological Review, 69,* 768–789.

Child Trends. (n.d.). *Nonmarital births: Overall trends.* Washington, DC: Author. Retrieved from http://www.childtrends.org/_docdisp_page.cfm?LID=D69BDA3A-4614-44C5-81C328964B9B7BD1

Collins, W. A. (2003). More than myth: The developmental significance of romantic relationships during adolescence. *Journal of Research on Adolescence, 13,* 1–24.

Conger, R. D., Cui, M., Bryant, C. M., & Elder, G. H., Jr. (2000). Competence in early adult romantic relationships: A developmental perspective on family influences. *Journal of Personality and Social Psychology, 79,* 224–237.

Conger, R. D., Elder, G. H., Lorenz, F. O., Conger, K. J., Simons, R. L., Whitbeck, L. B., Huck, S., & Melby, J. N. (1990). Linking economic hardship to marital quality and instability. *Journal of Marriage and the Family, 52,* 643–656.

Coontz, S. (2005a, May 1). For better, for worse. *Washington Post.* Retrieved from http://www.stephaniecoontz.com/articles/article12.htm

Coontz, S. (2005b). *Marriage, a history: How love conquered marriage.* New York: Penguin Books.

Coontz, S. (2006). The origins of modern divorce. *Family Process, 46,* 7–16.

Copen, C. E., Daniels, K., Vespa, J., & Mosher, W. D. (2012). First marriages in the United States: Data from the 2006–2010 National Survey of Family Growth. *National Health Statistics Reports: No. 49.* Hyattsville, MD: National Center for Health Statistics.

Córdova, J. V., Scott, R. L., Dorian, M., Mirgain, S., Yaeger, D., & Groot, A. (2005). The Marriage Checkup: An indicated preventive intervention for treatment-avoidant couples at risk for marital deterioration. *Behavior Therapy, 36,* 301–309.

Côté, J. E. (2000). *Arrested adulthood: The changing nature of maturity and identity.* New York University Press.

Cott, N. F. (2000). *Public vows: A history of marriage and the nation.* Cambridge, MA: Harvard University.

Cowan, C. P., & Cowan, P. A. (2000). *When partners become parents: The big life change for couples.* Mahwah, NJ: Lawrence Erlbaum Associates.

Cowan, C. P., Cowan, P. A., & Barry J. (2011). Couples' groups for parents of pre-schoolers: Ten-year outcomes of a randomized trial. *Journal of Family Psychology, 25,* 240–250.

Cowan, P. A., Cowan, C. P., Pruett, M. K., & Pruett, K. (2012, October). Supporting father involvement: A couples group approach to enhancing family well-being. Paper presented at the National Council on Family Relations Annual Conference, Phoenix, AZ.

Cowan, P. A., Cowan, C. P., Pruett, M. K., Pruett, K., & Wong, J. J. (2009). Promoting fathers' engagement with children: Preventative interventions for low-income families. *Journal of Marriage and Family, 71,* 663–679.

Cox, R. B., & Shirer, K. A.(2009). Caring for My Family: A pilot study of a relationship and marriage education program for low-income unmarried parents. *Journal of Couple & Relationship Therapy, 8,* 343–364.

Cross-Barnett, C., Cherlin, A., & Burton, L. (2011). Bound by children: Intermittent cohabitation and living together apart. *Family Relations, 60,* 633–647.

Crouch, J. D., & Beaulieu, R. (2007). No-fault divorce laws and divorce rates in the United States and Europe: Variations and correlations. In A. S. Loveless & T. B.

Holman (Eds.) *The family in the new millennium: Volume 3, Strengthening the family* (pp. 306–331). Westport, CT: Praeger.

Cui, M., Ueno, K., Gordon, M., & Fincham, F. D. (in press). The continuation of intimate partner violence from adolescence to young adulthood. *Journal of Marriage and Family*.

Cummings, E. M., Faircloth, W. B., Mitchell, P. M., Cummings, J. S., & Schermerhorn, A. C. (2008). Evaluating a brief prevention program for improving marital conflict in community families. *Journal of Family Psychology, 22*, 193–202.

Cummings, E. M., Goeke-Morey, M. C., & Graham, M. A. (2002). Interparental relations as a dimension of parenting. Monographs in parenting. In J. G. Borkowski, S. L. Ramey, & M. Bristol-Power (Eds.), *Parenting and the child's world: Influences on academic, intellectual, and social–emotional development* (pp. 251–263). Mahwah, NJ: Lawrence Erlbaum Associates.

Cummings, E. M., George, M. R. W., McCoy, K. P., & Davies, P. T. (2012). Interparental conflict in kindergarten and adolescent adjustment: Prospective investigation of emotional security as an explanatory mechanism. *Child Development, 83*, 1703–1715.

Derrington, R., Johnson, M., Menard, A., Ooms, T., & Stanley, S. (2010). *Making distinctions among different types of intimate partner violence: A preliminary guide.* Fairfax, VA: National Healthy Marriage Resource Center (and National Resource Center on Domestic Violence). Retrieved from http://www.healthy marriageinfo.org/resource-detail/index.aspx?rid=3368

Devaney, B., & Dion, R. (2010). *15-month impacts of Oklahoma's Family Expectations program.* Princeton, NJ: Mathematica Policy Research. Retrieved from http://www.mathematica-mpr.com/publications/PDFs/Family_support/BSF _15month_impacts.pdf

Dew, J., Britt, S., & Huston, S. (2012). Examining the relationship between financial issues and divorce. *Family Relations, 61*, 615–628.

Dion, M. R., Hershey, A. M., Zaveri, H. H., Avellar, S. A., Strong, D. A., Silman, T., & Moore, R. (2008). *Implementation of the Building Strong Families program.* Washington, DC: Mathematica Policy Research. Retrieved from http://www .mathematica-mpr.com/publications/PDFs/bsfimplementation.pdf

Doherty, W. J. (1995). *Soul searching: Why psychotherapy must promote moral responsibility.* New York: BasicBooks.

Doherty, W. J. (1997). *The intentional family: How to build family ties in our modern world.* Reading MA: Addison-Wesley.

Doherty, W. J (2000, August). Consumer marriage and modern covenant marriage. *Marriage and Families.* Retrieved from http://marriageandfamilies.byu.edu/ issues/2000/August/consumer.aspx

Doherty, W. J. (2001). *Take back your marriage: Sticking together in a world that pulls us apart.* New York: Guilford.

Doherty, W. J., Kouneski, E. F., & Erickson, M. F. (1998). Responsible fathering: An overview and conceptual framework. *Journal of Marriage and the Family, 60,* 277–292.

Doherty, W. J., Willoughby, B. J., & Peterson, B. (2011). Interest in marital reconciliation among divorcing parents. *Family Court Review, 49,* 313–321.

Donovan, C. A. (2011, June 7). A Marshall Plan for marriage: Rebuilding our shattered homes. *Backgrounder, No. 2567.* Washington, DC: Heritage Foundation. Retrieved from http://www.heritage.org/research/reports/2011/06/a-marshall-plan-for-marriage-rebuilding-our-shattered-homes

Doss, B. D., Rhoades, G. K., Stanley, S. M., Markman, H. J., & Johnson, C. A. (2009). Differential use of premarital education in first and second marriages. *Journal of Family Psychology, 23,* 268–273.

Duncan, S. F., Steed, A., & Needham, C. M. (2009). A comparison evaluation study of web-based and traditional marriage and relationship education. *Journal of Couple & Relationship Therapy, 8,* 162–180.

Durlak, J. A., Weissberg, R. P., Dymnicki, A. B., Taylor, R. D., & Schellinger, K. B. (2011). The impact of enhancing students' social and emotional learning: A meta-analysis of school-based universal interventions. *Child Development, 82,* 405–432.

Edin, K., & Kefalas, M. (2005). *Promises I can keep: Why poor women put motherhood before marriage.* Berkeley: University of California.

Edin, K., & Nelson, T. (2013). *Doing the best I can: Fatherhood in the inner city.* Berkeley: University of California.

Emery, R. E., & Sbarra, D. A. (2002). Addressing separation and divorce during and after couple therapy. In A. S. Gurman & N. S. Jacobson (Eds.), *Clinical handbook of couple therapy* (3rd ed., pp. 508–530). New York: Guilford.

Evans, W. D. (2008, Spring). Social marketing campaigns and children's media use. *Future of Children, 18*(1), 181–203.

Evans, W. D., Davis, K. C., & Zhang, Y. (2008). Health communication and marketing research with new media: Case study of the Parents Speak Up National Campaign evaluation. *Cases in Public Health Communication & Marketing, 2,* 140–158. Retrieved from http://www.casesjournal.org/volume2

Fackrell, T. A. (2012). *Wandering in the wilderness: A grounded theory study of the divorce or reconciliation decision-making process.* Unpublished doctoral dissertation, Brigham Young University, Provo, UT.

Fackrell, T. A., Hawkins, A. J., & Kay, N. M. (2011). How effective are court-affiliated divorcing parents education programs? A meta-analytic study. *Family Court Review, 49,* 107–119.

Farrelly, M. C., Davis, K. C., Haviland, M. L., Messeri, P., & Healton, C. G. (2005). Evidence of a dose-response relationship between "truth" antismoking ads and youth smoking prevalence. *American Journal of Public Health, 95,* 425–431.

Fawcett, E. B., Hawkins, A. J., Blanchard, V. L., & Carroll, J. S. (2010). Do premarital education programs really work? A meta-analytic study. *Family Relations, 59,* 232–239.

Fincham, F. D. (2012, October). The case for relationship education in adolescence and emerging adulthood and initial data on effectiveness. Paper presented at the National Council on Family Relations Annual Conference, Phoenix, AZ.

Fincham, F. D., Hall, J., & Beach, S. R. H. (2006). Forgiveness in marriage: Current status and future directions. *Family Relations, 55,* 415–427.

Fincham, F. D., Lambert, N. M., & Beach, S. R. H. (2010). Faith and unfaithfulness: Can praying for your partner reduce infidelity? *Journal of Personality and Social Psychology, 99,* 649–659.

Fincham, F. D., Stanley, S. M., & Beach, S. R. H. (2007). Transformative processes in marriages: An analysis of emerging trends. *Journal of Marriage and Family, 69,* 275–292.

Fleming, C. J. E., & Córdova, J. V. (2012). Predicting relationship help seeking prior to a marriage checkup. *Family Relations, 61,* 90–100.

Foroohar, R. (2012, March 12). For richer or poorer: If we want to fix marriage, we might start by fixing the economy. *Time,* 23.

Fowers, B. J. (2000). *Beyond the myth of marital happiness.* San Francisco: Jossey-Bass.

Furman, W., & Shaffer, L. (2003). The role of romantic relationships in adolescent development. In P. Florsheim (Ed.), *Adolescent romantic relations and sexual behavior: Theory, research, and practical implications* (pp. 3–22). Mahwah, NJ: Lawrence Erlbaum Associates.

Furstenberg, F. F. (2007). Should government promote marriage? *Journal of Policy Analysis and Management, 26,* 956–961.

Gallagher, M. (1996). Re-creating marriage. In D. Popenoe, J. B. Elshtain, & D. Blankenhorn (Eds.), *Promises to keep: Decline and renewal of marriage in America* (pp. 233–246). Lanham, MD: Rowman & Littlefield.

Gardner, S. P., & Boellaard, R. (2007). Does youth relationship education continue to work after a high school class? A longitudinal study. *Family Relations, 56,* 490–500.

Gates, G. J. (2011). *How many people are lesbian, gay, bisexual, and transgender?* Westwood, CA: Williams Institute at the UCLA School of Law.

Gaubert, J. M., Gubits, D., Alderson, D. P., & Knox, V. (2012, August). *The Supporting Healthy Marriage Evaluation: Final implementation findings.* OPRE Report 2012-12. Washington, DC: Office of Planning, Research, and Evaluation,

Administration for Children and Families. Retrieved from http://www.mdrc.org/publications/646/overview.html

Gersten, C. (2007, June). Getting state money: The 1% solution. Presentation at the Annual Smart Marriages Conference, Denver, CO.

Glenn, N. D. (2002). A plea for greater concern about the quality of marital matching. In A. J. Hawkins, L. D. Wardle, & D. O. Coolidge (Eds.), *Revitalizing the institution of marriage for the twenty-first century: An agenda for strengthening marriage.* Westport, CT: Praeger.

Gottman, J. M., & Declaire, J. (1997). *Raising an emotionally intelligent child.* New York: Simon & Schuster.

Gottman, J. M., & Silver, N. (1999). *The seven principles for making marriage work.* New York: Crown.

Gottman, J. M., Carrere, S., Swanson, C., & Coan, J. A. (2000). Reply to "From basic research to intervention." *Journal of Marriage and the Family, 62,* 265–273.

Gottman, J. M., Coan, J., Carrere, S., & Swanson, C. (1998). Predicting marital happiness and stability from newlywed interactions. *Journal of Marriage and the Family, 60,* 5–22.

Gottman, J. M., Gottman, J. S., & Atkins, C. L. (2011). The Comprehensive Soldier Fitness program: Family skills component. *American Psychologist, 66,* 52–57.

Graefe, D. R., & Lichter, D. T. (2008). Marriage patterns among unwed mothers: Before and after PRWORA. *Journal of Policy Analysis and Management, 27,* 479–497.

Green, M. C. (2012, July). "There but for the grace": The ethics of bystanders to divorce. *Propositions,* 1–8. Retrieved from http://www.centerforpublicconversation.org/propositions/index.php

Guzman, L., Ikramullah, E., Malove, J., Peterson, K., & Scarupa, H. J. (2009). *Telling it like it is: Teen perspectives on romantic relationships.* Child Trends Research Brief. Washington, DC: Child Trends.

Hahlweg, K., & Richter, D. (2010). Prevention and marital instability and distress: Results of an 11-year longitudinal follow-up study. *Behaviour Research & Therapy, 48,* 377–383.

Halford, W. K. (2011). *Marriage and relationship education: What works and how to provide it.* New York: Guilford.

Halford, W. K., & Wilson, K. L. (2009). Predictors of relationship satisfaction four years after completing flexible delivery couple relationship education. *Journal of Couple & Relationship Therapy, 8,* 143–161.

Halford, W. K., Chen, R., Wilson, K. L., Larson, J., Busby, D., & Holman, T. (2012). Does therapist guidance enhance assessment-based feedback as couple relationship education? *Behaviour Change, 29,* 199–212.

Halford, W. K., Moore, E., Wilson, K. L., Farrugia, C., & Dyer, C. (2004). Benefits of a flexible delivery relationship education: An evaluation of the Couple CARE program. *Family Relations, 53,* 469–476.

Halford, W. K., Petch, J., & Bate, K. (in press). Empirically based couple relationship education. In E. Lawrence & K. Sullivan (Eds.), *Relationship science and couple interventions in the 21st century.* New York: Oxford University Press.

Halford, W. K., Wilson, K. L., Watson, B., Verner, T., Larson, J., Busby, D., & Holman, T. (2010). Couple relationship education at home: Does skill training enhance relationship assessment and feedback? *Journal of Family Psychology, 24,* 188–196.

Halpern, D. (2010). *The hidden wealth of nations.* Cambridge, UK: Polity.

Halpern-Meekin, S. (2011). High school relationship and marriage education: A comparison of mandated and self-selected treatment. *Journal of Family Issues, 32,* 394–419.

Halpern-Meekin, S., Manning, W. D., Giordano, P. C., & Longmore, M. A. (2013). Relationship churning, physical violence, and verbal abuse in young adult relationships. *Journal of Marriage and Family, 75,* 2–12.

Harris, S. M., Glenn, N. D., Rappleyea, D. L., Diaz-Loving, R., Hawkins, A. J., Daire, A. P., Osborne, C., & Huston, T. L. (2008). *Twogether in Texas: Baseline report on marriage in the Lone Star State.* Austin, TX: Health and Human Services Commission. Retrieved from http://twogetherintexas.com/pdf/baselinereport.pdf

Haskins, R., & Sawhill, I. (2009). *Creating an opportunity society.* Washington, DC: Brookings Institution.

Haskins, R. Murnane, R., Sawhill, I., & Snow, C. (2012, Fall). Can academic standards boost literacy and close the achievement gap? *The Future of Children Policy Brief,* 1–8.

Haskins, R., Paxson, C., & Brooks-Gunn, J. (2009). Social science rising: A tale of evidence shaping public policy. *Future of Children Policy Brief Fall 2009.* Princeton, NJ: Princeton University.

Hawkins, A. J. (2007). Will legislation to encourage premarital education strengthen marriage and reduce divorce? *Journal of Law & Family Studies, 9*(1), 79–99.

Hawkins, A. J., & Fackrell, T. A. (2009). *Should I keep trying to work it out? A guidebook for individuals and couples at the crossroads of divorce (and before).* Salt Lake City: Utah Commission on Marriage.

Hawkins, A. J., & Fellows, K. J. (2011). *Findings from the field: A meta-analytic study of the effectiveness of healthy marriage and relationship education programs.* Washington, DC: National Healthy Marriage Resource Center. Retrieved from http://www.healthymarriageinfo.org/resource-detail/index.aspx?rid=3928

Hawkins, A. J., & Ooms, T. (2010). *What works in marriage and relationship education? A review of lessons learned with a focus on low-income couples.* Oklahoma

City: National Healthy Marriage Resource Center Research Report. Retrieved from http://www.healthymarriageinfo.org/docs/WhatWorks.pdf

Hawkins, A. J., & Ooms, T. (2012). Can marriage and relationship education be an effective policy tool to help low-income couples form and sustain healthy marriages and relationships? A review of lessons learned. *Marriage & Family Review, 48,* 524–554.

Hawkins, A. J., Amato, P. R., & Kinghorn, A. (in press). Are government-supported healthy marriage initiatives affecting family demographics? A state-level analysis. *Family Relations, 62,* 501–513.

Hawkins, A. J., Blanchard, V. L., Baldwin, S. A., & Fawcett, E. B. (2008). Does marriage and relationship education work? A meta-analytic study. *Journal of Consulting & Clinical Psychology, 76,* 723–734.

Hawkins, A. J., Gilliland, T., Christiaens, G., & Carroll, J. S. (2002). Integrating marriage education into perinatal education. *Journal of Perinatal Education, 11*(4), 1–10.

Hawkins, A. J., Lovejoy, K. R., Holmes, E. K., Blanchard, V. L., & Fawcett, E. (2008). Increasing fathers' involvement in child care with a couple-focused intervention during the transition to parenthood. *Family Relations, 57,* 49–59.

Hawkins, A. J., Roberts, T., Christiansen, S. L., & Marshall, C. M. (1994). An evaluation of a program to help dual-earner couples share the second shift. *Family Relations, 43,* 213–220.

Hawkins, A. J., Stanley, S. M., Blanchard, V. L., & Albright, M. (2012). Exploring programmatic moderators of the effectiveness of marriage and relationship education programs: A meta-analytic study. *Behavior Therapy, 43,* 77–87.

Hawkins, A. J., Stanley, S. M., Cowan, P. A., Fincham, F. D., Beach, S. R. H., Cowan, C. P., Rhoades, G. K., Markman, H. J., & Daire, A. P. (2013). A more optimistic perspective on government-supported marriage and relationship education programs for lower income couples: Response to Johnson (2012). *American Psychologist, 63,* 110–111.

Hawkins, A. J., Wardle, L. D., & Coolidge, D. O. (2002). *Revitalizing the institution of marriage for the twenty-first century: An agenda for strengthening marriage.* Westport, CT: Praeger.

Heath, M. (2012). *One marriage under God: The campaign to promote marriage in America.* New York University.

Heath, C. J., Bradford, K., Whiting, J., Brock, G., & Foster, S. (2004). *The Kentucky marriage attitudes study: 2004 baseline survey.* Lexington: Research Center for Families and Children, University of Kentucky.

Heaton, T. B. (2002). Factors contributing to increasing marital stability in the United States. *Journal of Family Issues, 23,* 392–409.

Hendrick, H. (n.d.). *Managing a statewide healthy marriage initiative: Tips from my experience as a state policymaker.* Oklahoma City: National Healthy Marriage Resource Center. Retrieved from http://www.healthymarriageinfo.org/resource -detail/index.aspx?rid=3718

Hetherington, E. M., & Kelly, J. (2002). *For better or for worse: Divorce reconsidered.* New York: W. W. Norton.

Higginbotham, B. J., & Skogrand, L. (2010). Relationship education with both married and unmarried stepcouples: An exploratory study. *Journal of Couple & Relationship Therapy, 9,* 133–148.

Higginbotham, B. J., Miller, J. J., & Niehus, S. (2009). Remarriage preparation: Usage, perceived helpfulness, and dyadic adjustment. *Family Relations, 58,* 316–329.

Hochschild, A. R. (1989). *The second shift: Working parents and the revolution at home.* New York: Viking.

Holman, T. B. (2001). *Premarital prediction of marital quality or breakup: Research, theory, and practice.* New York: Kluwer.

Holmes, E. K., Cowan, P. A., Cowan, C. P., & Hawkins, A. J. (2013). A call for greater integration of marriage, fatherhood, and parenting programming. In N. J. Cabrera & C. S. Tamis-LeMonda (Eds.) *Handbook of father involvement: Multidisciplinary perspectives* (2nd ed., pp. 438–454). New York: Routledge.

Holmes, E. K., Huston, T. L., Vangelisti, A. L., & Guinn, T. D. (2013). On becoming parents. In A. L. Vangelisti (Ed.) *The Routledge handbook of family communication* (2nd ed., pp. 80–96). New York: Routledge.

Holt-Lunstad J., Smith T. B., & Layton, J. B. (2010). Social relationships and mortality risk: A meta-analytic review. *PLoS Medicine 7*(7), 1–19.

Holzer, H. J. (2009). Workforce development as an antipoverty strategy: What do we know? What should we do? In M. Cancian & S. Danziger (Eds.), *Changing poverty, changing policies* (pp. 301–329). New York: Russell Sage Foundation.

Horn, W. F. (2002). Promoting marriage as a means for promoting fatherhood. In A. J. Hawkins, L. D. Wardle, & D. O. Coolidge (Eds.), *Revitalizing the institution of marriage for the twenty-first century: An agenda for strengthening marriage* (pp. 101–110). Westport, CT: Praeger.

Hornik, R. C. (2002a). *Public health communication: Evidence for behavior change.* Mahwah, NJ: Lawrence Erlbaum Associates.

Hornik, R. C. (2002b). Public health communication: Making sense of contradictory evidence. In R. C. Hornik (Ed.), *Public health communication: Evidence for behavior change* (pp. 1–22). Mahwah, NJ: Lawrence Erlbaum Associates.

Hsueh, J., Alderson, D. P., Lundquist, E., Michalopoulos, C., Gubits, D., Fein, D., & Knox, V. (2012). *The Supporting Healthy Marriage evaluation: Early impacts on low-income families.* OPRE Report 2012-11. Washington, DC: Office of

Planning, Research, and Evaluation, Administration for Children and Families, U.S. Department of Health and Human Services.

Huston, T. L., & Melz, H. (2004). The case for (promoting) marriage: The devil is in the details. *Journal of Marriage and Family, 66,* 943–958.

Hymowitz, K. (2006). *Marriage and caste in America: Separate and unequal families in a post-marital age.* Chicago: Ivan R. Dee.

Institute for Marriage and Public Policy. (2012, July 9). iMAPP Fact Sheet: State divorce laws. Retrieved from http://www.marriagedebate.com

Jacob, B. A., & Ludwig, J. (2009). Improving educational outcomes for poor children. In M. Cancian & S. Danziger (Eds.), *Changing poverty, changing policies* (pp. 266–300). New York: Russell Sage Foundation.

James, S. L. (2012). Variation in trajectories of marital quality across the American life course. Working manuscript, Brigham Young University, Provo, UT.

Johnson, M. D. (2012). Healthy marriage initiatives: On the need for empiricism in policy implementation. *American Psychologist, 67,* 296–308.

Johnson, M. D., & Anderson, J. R. (in press). The longitudinal association of marital confidence, time spent together, and marital satisfaction. *Family Process.*

Johnson, C. A., Stanley, S. M., Glenn, N. D., Amato, P. R., Nock, S. L., Markman, H. J., & Dion, M. R. (2002). *Marriage in Oklahoma: 2001 baseline statewide survey on marriage and divorce.* Stillwater: Oklahoma State University Bureau for Social Research.

Johnson, S. (2008). *Hold me tight: Seven conversations for a lifetime of love.* New York: Little, Brown and Company.

Jones, J. M. (2008, March 25). Most Americans not willing to forgive unfaithful spouse. Gallup Poll. Retrieved from: www.gallup.com/poll/105682/Most-Americans-Willing-Forgive-Unfaithful-Spouse.aspx

Jordan, P. L., Stanley, S. M., & Markman, H. J. (1999). *Becoming parents: How to strengthen your marriage as your family grows.* San Francisco: Jossey-Bass.

Judgment of divorce, time periods, Louisiana House Bill 1379, La. Civ. Code Ann. art 103.1 (2006).

Kalinka, C. J., Fincham, F. D., & Hirsch, A. H. (2012). A randomized clinical trial of online-biblio relationship education for expectant couples. *Journal of Family Psychology, 26,* 159–164.

Kamp Dush, C. M., & Taylor, M. G. (2012). Trajectories of marital conflict across the life course: Predictors and interactions with marital happiness trajectories. *Journal of Family Issues, 33,* 341–368.

Kamp Dush, C. M., Taylor, M. G., & Kroeger, R. A. (2008). Marital happiness and psychological well-being across the life course. *Family Relations, 57,* 211–226.

Karney, B. (2011, November). What's (not) wrong with low-income couples:

Maintaining intimacy in more and less affluent marriage. Presentation at the National Council on Family Relations Annual Conference, Orlando, FL.

Karney, B. R., Beckett, M. K., Collins, R. L., & Shaw, R. (2007). *Adolescent romantic relationships as precursors of healthy adult marriages: A review of theory, research, and programs.* Santa Monica, CA: RAND Corporation.

Karney, B. R., & Bradbury, T. N. (2005). Contextual influences on marriage: Implications for policy and intervention. *Current Directions in Psychological Science, 14,* 171–174.

Karney, B. R., Garvan, C. W., & Thomas, M. S. (2003). *Family formation in Florida: 2003 baseline survey of attitudes, beliefs, and demographics relating to marriage and family formation.* Gainesville: University of Florida Survey Research Center.

Kearney, M. S., & Levine, P. B. (2008). *Reducing unplanned pregnancies through Medicaid family planning services.* CCF Brief #39. Washington, DC: Brookings Institution, Center on Children and Families. Retrieved from http://www.brookings.edu/papers/2008/07_reducing_pregnancy_kearney.aspx

Kenrick, D. T., Griskevicius, V., Neuberg, S. L., & Schaller, M. (2010). Renovating the pyramid of needs: Contemporary extensions build upon ancient foundations. *Perspectives on Psychological Science, 5,* 292–314.

Kerpelman, J. L. (2012, October). "Relationship Smart" youth: A statewide study of relationship education for high school students. Paper presented at the National Council on Family Relations Annual Conference, Phoenix, AZ.

Kerpelman, J. L., Pittman, J. F., Adler-Baeder, F., Eryigit, S., & Paulk, A. (2009). Evaluation of a statewide youth-focused relationships education curriculum. *Journal of Adolescence, 32,* 1359–1370.

Kerpelman, J. L., Pittman, J. F., Adler-Baeder, F., Stringer, K. J., Eryigit, S., Cadely, H. S., & Harrell-Levy, M. K. (2010). What adolescents bring to and learn from relationship education classes: Does social address matter? *Journal of Couple & Relationship Therapy, 9,* 95–112.

Kneip, T., & Bauer, G. (2009). Did unilateral divorce laws raise divorce rates in Western Europe? *Journal of Marriage and Family, 71,* 592–607.

Knox, V., Cowan, P. A., Cowan, C. P., & Bildner, E. (2011). Policies that strengthen fatherhood and family relationships: What do we know and what do we need to know? *ANNALS of the American Academy of Political and Social Science, 635,* 216–239.

Krishnakumar, A., & Buehler, C. (2000). Interparental conflict and parenting behaviors: A meta-analytic review. *Family Relations, 49,* 25–44.

Lambert, N. M., Fincham, F. D., Braithwaite, S. R., Graham, S. M., & Beach, S. R. H. (2009). Can prayer increase gratitude? *Psychology of Religion and Spirituality, 1,* 139–149.

Lambert, N. M., Fincham, F. D., Marks, L. D., & Stillman, T. F. (2010). Invocations and intoxication: Does prayer decrease alcohol consumption? *Psychology of Addictive Behaviors, 24,* 209–219.

Lambert, N. M., Fincham, F. D., Stillman, T. F., Graham, S. M., & Beach, S. R. H. (2010). Motivating change in relationships: Can prayer increase forgiveness? *Psychological Science, 21,* 126–132.

Larson, J. H., Vatter, R. S., Galbraith, R. C., Holman, T. B., & Stahmann, R. F. (2007). The RELATionship Evaluation (RELATE) with therapist-assisted interpretation: Short-term effects on premarital relationships. *Journal of Marital and Family Therapy, 33,* 364–374.

Lavner, J. A., & Bradbury, T. N. (2012). Why do even satisfied newlyweds eventually go on to divorce? *Journal of Family Psychology, 26,* 1–10.

Lavner, J. A., Bradbury, T. N., & Karney, B. R. (2012). Incremental change or initial differences? Testing two models of marital deterioration. *Journal of Family Psychology, 26,* 606–616.

Lavner, J. A., Karney, B. R., & Bradbury, T. N. (2012). Do cold feet warn of trouble ahead? Premarital uncertainty and four-year marital outcomes. *Journal of Family Psychology, 26,* 1012–1017.

Lerman, R. I. (2005, March). The economic benefits of marriage and the implications for public policies to promote healthy marriages. Paper presented at the annual meeting of the Eastern Sociological Society, Washington, DC.

Lerman, R. I. (2010). Capabilities and contributions of unwed fathers. *Future of Children, 20*(2), 63–85.

Lichter, D. T., Graefe, D. R., & Brown, J. B. (2003). Is marriage a panacea? Union formation among economically disadvantaged unwed mothers. *Social Problems, 50,* 60–86.

Lipsey, M. W., & Wilson, D. B. (2001). *Practical meta-analysis.* Thousand Oaks, CA: Sage.

Loew, B., Rhoades, G., Markman, H., Stanley, S., Pacifici, C., White, L., & Delaney, R. (2012). Internet delivery of PREP-based relationship education for at-risk couples. *Journal of Couple & Relationship Therapy, 11,* 291–309.

Logan, C., Holcombe, E., Manlove, J., & Ryan, S. (2007). *The consequences of unintended childbearing: A white paper.* Washington, DC: Child Trends.

Love Thinks. (n.d.). *Love thinks program research.* Retrieved from http://www.love thinks.com/ResearchesGrants/Love_Thinks_Research

Lucier-Greer, M., & Adler-Baeder, F. (2012). Does couple and relationship education work for individuals in stepfamilies? A meta-analytic study. *Family Relations, 61,* 756–769.

Lundquist, J. H., & Smith, H. L. (2005). Family formation among women in the U.S. military: Evidence from the NLSY. *Journal of Marriage and Family, 67,* 1–13.

Mahoney, A., Pargament, K. I., Tarakeshwar, N., & Swank, A. B. (2001). Religion in the home in the 1980s and 1990s: A meta-analytic review and conceptual analysis of links between religion, marriage, and parenting. *Journal of Family Psychology, 15,* 559–596.

Manning, W. D., & Cohen, J. A. (2012). Premarital cohabitation and marital dissolution: An examination of recent marriages. *Journal of Marriage and Family, 74,* 377–387.

Manning, W. D., Trella, D., Lyons, H., & du Toit, N. (2010). Marriageable women: A focus on participants in a community healthy marriage program. *Family Relations, 59,* 87–102.

Manning, W. D., Trella, D., Lyons, H., Gulbis, A., & du Toit, N. (2008). Healthy relationships and healthy marriages: Final report. Bowling Green, Ohio: Center for Family and Demographic Research, Bowling Green State University. Retrieved from http://www.bgsu.edu/organizations/cfdr/page41881.html

Markman, H. J., Renick, M. J., Floyd, F. J., Stanley, S. M., & Clements, M. (1993). Preventing marital distress through communication and conflict management training: A four- and five-year follow-up. *Journal of Consulting & Clinical Psychology, 61,* 70–77.

Markman, H. J., & Rhoades, G. K. (2012). Relationship education research: Current status and future directions. *Journal of Marital and Family Therapy, 38,* 169–200.

Markman, H. J., Rhoades, G. K., Stanley, S. M., Ragan, E. P., & Whitton, S. W. (2010). The premarital communication roots of marital distress and divorce: The first five years of marriage. *Journal of Family Psychology, 24,* 289–298.

Markman, H. J., Stanley, S. M., & Blumberg, S. L. (2010). *Fighting for your marriage* (3rd ed.). San Francisco: Jossey-Bass.

Markman, H. J., Whitton, S. W., Kline, G. H, Stanley, S. M., Thompson, H., St. Peters, M., et al. (2004). Use of an empirically based marriage education program by religious organizations: Results of a dissemination trial. *Family Relations, 53,* 504–512.

Marquardt, E., Blankenhorn, D., Lerman, R. I., Malone-Colon, L., & Wilcox, W. B. (2012). The President's marriage agenda for the forgotten sixty percent. *The state of our unions: Marriage in America 2012.* Charlottesville, VA: National Marriage Project & Institute for American Values.

Martin, J. A., Hamilton, B. E., Sutton, P. D., Ventura, S. J., Menacker, F., Kimeyer, S., Mathews, T. J. (2009, January). Births: Final data for 2006. *National Vital Statistics Report, 57*(7), 1–102.

Martin, S. P. (2006). Trends in marital dissolution by women's education in the United States. *Demographic Research, 15,* 537–560.

Maslow, A. H. (1970). *Motivation and personality.* New York: Harper & Row.

McAllister, S., Duncan, S. F., & Hawkins, A. J. (2012). Examining the early evidence for self-directed marriage and relationship education: A meta-analytic study. *Family Relations, 61,* 742–755.

McDermott, R., Fowler, J. H., & Christakis, N. A. (2009, October 18). Breaking up is hard to do, unless everyone else is doing it too: Social network effects on divorce in a longitudinal sample followed for 32 years. *Social Science Research Network.* Retrieved from http://ssrn.com/abstract=1490708

McHale, J., Waller, M. R., & Pearson, J. (2012). Coparenting interventions for fragile families: What do we know and where do we need to go next? *Family Process, 51,* 284–306.

McLanahan, S., & Beck, A. N. (2010). Parental relationships in fragile families. *Future of Children, 20*(2), 17–37.

Means, B., Toyama, Y., Murphy, R., Bakia, M., & Jones, K. (2009). *Evaluation of evidence-based practices in online learning: A meta-analysis and review of online learning studies.* Washington, DC: Office of Planning, Evaluation, and Policy Development, Department of Education. Retrieved from http://www.breining .edu/USDEDistLearning.htm

Miller, A. J., Sassler, S., & Kusi-Appouh, D. (2011). The specter of divorce: Views from working- and middle-class cohabitors. *Family Relations, 60,* 602–616.

Montañez, M. (2011). Family wellness: Strengthening familial dynamics among underserved populations: Evidence from a quasi-experimental research design employing an intervention and control group. Unpublished report, New Mexico State University. Retrieved from http://www.familywellness.com/research.php

Montgomery, M. J. (2005). Psychosocial intimacy and identity: From early adolescence to emerging adulthood. *Journal of Adolescent Research, 20,* 346–374.

Mooradian, J. K., Hock, R. M., Jackson, R., & Timm, T. M. (2011) What couples who adopt children from child welfare want professionals to know about supporting their marriages. *Families in Society, 92,* 390–396.

Moore, K. A., Kinghorn, A., & Bandy, T. (2011). Parental relationship quality and child outcomes across subgroups. *Child Trends Research Briefs,* #2011-13. Washington, DC: Child Trends. Retrieved from http://www.childtrends.org/wp-content/uploads/2011/04/Child_Trends-2011_04_04_RB_MaritalHappiness. pdf

Morrill, M. I., Eubanks-Fleming, C. J., Harp, A. G., Sollenberger, J. W., Darling, E. V., & Córdova, J. V. (2011). The Marriage Checkup: Increasing access to marital health care. *Family Process, 50,* 471–485.

Murray, C. (2012). *Coming apart: The state of White America 1960–2010.* New York: Crown Forum.

Musick, K., & Bumpass, L. (2012). Reexamining the case for marriage: Union formation and changes in well-being. *Journal of Marriage and Family, 74,* 1–18.

National Center for Family & Marriage Research. (2009). Fatherhood in the U.S.: The decoupling of marriage and childbearing. Bowling Green, OH: Author.

National Center for Family & Marriage Research. (2010). *Trends in cohabitation: Twenty years of change, 1987–2008.* Bowling Green, OH: Author. Retrieved from http://ncfmr.bgsu.edu/page78050.html

National Fatherhood Initiative. (2005). *With this ring... a national survey of marriage in America.* Gaithersburg, MD: Author. Retrieved from http://www.fatherhood .org/page.aspx?pid=710

National Healthy Marriage Resource Center. (2010). *Administration for Children and Families Healthy Marriage Initiative, 2002–2009.* Fairfax, VA: Author. Retrieved from http://www.healthymarriageinfo.org/about/faq/download.aspx?id=337

National Healthy Marriage Resource Center. (2010). *Relationships matter: Strengthening vulnerable youth: Proceedings summary.* Fairfax, VA: Author. Retrieved from http://www.healthymarriageinfo.org/resource-detail/index.aspx?rid=3653

National Healthy Marriage Resource Center. (n.d.). *Relationship education and teen pregnancy prevention: What's the connection?* Washington, DC: Author.

National Healthy Marriage Resource Center. (n.d.). *TANF funds and healthy marriage activities.* Washington, DC: Author.

National Marriage Project & Institute for American Values. (2010). *The state of our unions: Marriage in America 2010.* Charlottesville, VA: Authors.

NCFMR Family Profiles. (n.d.). *Remarriage rate in the U.S., 2010.* Bowling Green, OH: National Center for Families and Marriage Research. Retrieved from http://ncfmr.bgsu.edu/page78050.html

Needham, C. M. (2010). At the crossroads of divorce: A formative evaluation of a self-directed intervention for participants of Utah's divorce orientation education class for divorcing parents. Unpublished master's thesis, Brigham Young University, Provo, UT.

Nielsen, A., Pinsof, W., Rampage, C., Solomon, A. H., & Goldstein, S. (2004). Marriage 101: An integrated academic and experiential undergraduate marriage education course. *Family Relations, 53,* 485–494.

Nock, S. L. (1998). *Marriage in men's lives.* New York: Oxford University Press.

Nock, S. L. (2005). Marriage as a public issue. *Future of Children, 15*(2), 13–32.

Nock, S. L., & Einolf, C. J. (2008). *The one hundred billion dollar man: The annual public costs of father absence.* Gaithersburg, MD: National Fatherhood Initiative.

Nock, S. L., Sanchez, L. A., & Wright, J. D. (2008). *Covenant marriage: The movement to reclaim tradition in America.* New Brunswick, NJ: Rutgers University Press.

Nowak, C., & Heinrichs, N. (2008). A comprehensive meta-analysis of Triple

P-Positive Parenting Program using hierarchical linear modeling: Effectiveness and moderating variables. *Clinical Child and Family Psychological Review, 11,* 114–144.

Obama, B. (2006). *The audacity of hope: Thoughts on reclaiming the American dream.* New York: Crown.

Office of Planning, Research, and Evaluation. (2010). Head Start impact study: Final report, January 2010. Washington, DC: Author.

Olmstead, S. B., Pasley, K., Meyer, A. S., Stanford, P. S., Fincham, F. D., & Delevi, R. (2011). Implementing relationship education for emerging adult college students: Insights from the field. *Journal of Couple & Relationship Therapy, 10,* 215–228.

Olson, D. H., DeFrain, J., & Skogrand, L. (2011). *Marriages and families: Intimacy, diversity, and strengths.* New York: McGraw-Hill.

Olson, D. H., Larson, P. J., Olson-Sigg, A. (2009). Couple checkup: Tuning up relationships. *Journal of Couple & Relationship Therapy, 8,* 129–142.

Ooms, T., & Wilson, P. (2004). The challenges of offering relationship and marriage education to low-income populations. *Family Relations, 53,* 440–447.

Ooms, T., Boggess, J., Menard, A., Myrick, M., Roberts, P., Tweedie, J., & Wilson, P. (2006). *Building bridges between healthy marriage, responsible fatherhood, and domestic violence programs.* Washington, DC: Center for Law and Social Policy.

Orszag, P. R. (2009, October 7). Valuing evaluation [Web log post]. Retrieved from http://www.whitehouse.gov/omb/blog/09/10/07/ValuingEvaluation/

Osborn, J. L. (2012). When TV and marriage meet: A social exchange analysis of the impact of television viewing on marital satisfaction and commitment. *Mass Communication and Society, 15,* 739–757.

Osborne, C. (2011). *Evaluation of the Parenting and Paternity Awareness curriculum: Final report 2008–2010.* Austin, TX: LBJ School of Public Affairs, University of Texas.

Owen, J., Chapman, L. K., Quirk, K., Inch, L. J., France, T., & Bergen, C. (2012). Processes of change in relationship education for lower-income African American couples. *Journal of Couple & Relationship Therapy, 11,* 51–68.

Owen, J., Quirk, K., Bergen, C., Inch, L., & France, T. (2012). The effectiveness of PREP with lower-income racial/ethnic minority couples. *Journal of Marital & Family Therapy, 38,* 296–307.

Owen, J., Rhoades, G. K., Stanley, S. M., & Markman, H. J. (in press). The role of leaders' working alliance in premarital education. *Journal of Family Psychology.*

Oyserman, D., Bybee, D., & Terry, K. (2006). Possible selves and academic outcomes: How and when possible selves impel action. *Journal of Personality and Social Psychology, 91,* 188–204.

Palm, G., & Fagan, J. (2008). Father involvement in early childhood programs:

Review of the literature. *Early Child Development & Care, 178*, 745–759.

Parkinson, P. (2011). Another inconvenient truth: Fragile families and the looming financial crisis for the welfare state. *Family Law Quarterly, 45*, 329–352.

Parkman, A. M. (2000). *Good intentions gone awry: No-fault divorce and the American family.* Lanham, MD: Rowman & Littlefield.

Parrott, L., III, & Parrott, L. (1995). *Saving your marriage before it starts.* Grand Rapids, MI: Zondervan.

Pearson, M., Stanley, S., & Rhoades, G. (2008). *Within My Reach instructor's manual.* Denver, CO: PREP.

Peipert, J. F., Madden, T., Allsworth, J. E., & Secura, G. M. (in press). Preventing unintended pregnancies by providing no-cost contraception. *Obstetrics & Gynecology.*

Petch, J. F., Halford, W. K., Creedy, D. K., & Gamble, J. (2012a). A randomized controlled trial of a couple relationship and coparenting education program (Couple CARE for Parents) for high- and low-risk new parents. *Journal of Consulting & Clinical Psychology, 80*, 662–673.

Petch, J. F., Halford, W. K., Creedy, D. K., & Gamble, J. (2012b). Couple relationship education at the transition to parenthood: A window of opportunity to reach high-risk couples. *Family Process, 51*, 498–511.

Pew Research Center. (2010a). *Religion among the millennnials.* Washington, DC: Author. Retrieved from http://www.pewforum.org/Age/Religion-Among-the-Millennials.aspx

Pew Research Center. (2010b). *The decline of marriage and rise of new families.* Washington, DC: Author. Retrieved from http://pewresearch.org/pubs/1802/decline-marriage-rise-new-families

Phillips, R. (1991). *Untying the knot: A short history of divorce.* New York: Cambridge University Press.

Pinquart, M., & Teubert, D. (2010a). A meta-analytic study of couple interventions during the transition to parenthood. *Family Relations, 59*, 221–231.

Pinquart, M., & Teubert, D. (2010b). Effects of parenting education with expectant and new parents: A meta-analysis. *Journal of Family Psychology, 24*, 316–327.

Pollet, S. L., & Lombreglia, M. (2008). A nationwide survey of mandatory parent education. *Family Court Review, 46*, 375–394.

Prinz, R. J., Sanders, M. R., Shapiro, C. J., Whitaker, D. J., & Lutzker, J. R. (2009). Population-based prevention of child maltreatment: The U.S. Triple P system population trial. *Prevention Science, 10*, 1–12.

Putnam, R. D., & Campbell, D. E. (2010). *American grace: How religion divides and unites us.* New York: Simon & Schuster.

Rackin, H., & Gibson-Davis, C. M. (2012). The role of pre- and postconception relationships for first-time parents. *Journal of Marriage and Family, 74*, 526–539.

Raley, R. K., & Bumpass, L. (2003). The topography of the divorce plateau: Levels and trends in union stability in the United States after 1980. *Demographic Research, 8,* 245–260.

Rasmussen Reports (2011, May 25). 85% of Americans view their marriages positively. Retrieved from http://www.rasmussenreports.com/public_content/lifestyle/general_lifestyle/may_2011/85_of_americans_view_their_marriages_positively

Ratcliffe, C., & McKernan, S. (2012). *Child poverty and its lasting consequence.* Washington, DC: Urban Institute.

Rector, R. (2012, September 5). *Marriage: America's greatest weapon against child poverty.* Special Report No. 117. Washington, DC: Heritage Foundation. Retrieved from http://www.heritage.org/research/reports/2012/09/marriage-americas-greatest-weapon-against-child-poverty

Reed, J. M. (2006). Not crossing the "extra line": How cohabitors with children view their unions. *Journal of Marriage and Family, 68,* 1117–1131.

Regnerus, M. (2009, August). The case for early marriage. *Christianity Today.* Retrieved from http://www.christianitytoday.com/ct/2009/august/16.22.html

Regnerus, M. (2012). How different are the adult children of parents who have same-sex relationships? Findings from the New Family Structures Study. *Social Science Research, 41,* 752–770.

Regnerus, M., & Uecker, J. (2011). *Premarital sex in America: How young Americans meet, mate, and think about marrying.* New York: Oxford University Press.

Reissman, C., Aron, A., & Bergen, M. R. (1993). Shared activities and marital satisfaction: Causal direction and self-expansion versus boredom. *Journal of Social and Personal Relationships, 10,* 243–254.

Rhoades, G. K., & Stanley, S. M. (2009). Relationship education for individuals: The benefits and challenges of intervening early. In H. Benson and S. Callan (Eds.), *What works in relationship education: Lessons from academics and service deliverers in the United States and Europe* (pp. 45–54). Doha, Qatar: Doha International Institute for Family Studies and Development.

Rhoades, G. K., & Stanley, S. M. (2011). Using individual-oriented relationship education to prevent family violence. *Journal of Couple & Relationship Therapy, 10,* 185–200.

Rhoades, G. K., Kamp Dush, C. M., Atkins, D. C., Stanley, S. M., & Markman, H. J. (2011). Breaking up is hard to do: The impact of unmarried relationship dissolution on mental health and life satisfaction. *Journal of Family Psychology, 25,* 366–374.

Rhoades, G. K., Stanley, S. M., & Markman, H. J. (2009a). The pre-engagement cohabitation effect: A replication and extension of previous findings. *Journal of Family Psychology, 23,* 107–111.

Rhoades, G. K., Stanley, S. M., & Markman, H. J. (2009b). Working with cohabitation in relationship education and therapy. *Journal of Couple & Relationship Therapy, 8,* 95–112.

Sassler, S., Addo, F. R., & Lichter, D. T. (2012). The tempo of sexual activity and later relationship quality. *Journal of Marriage and Family, 74,* 708–725.

Sawhill, I. (2012, May 27). Why Dan Quayle was right about Murphy Brown. *Washington Post,* B3.

Sawhill, I. V. (2003). *One percent for the kids.* Washington, DC: Brookings Institution.

Scafidi, B. (2008). *The taxpayer costs of divorce and unwed childbearing: First-ever estimates for the nation and all fifty states.* New York: Institute for American Values and Georgia Family Council.

Schramm, D. G., Futris, T. G., Galovan, A. M., & Allen, K. (2013). Is relationship and marriage education relevant and appropriate to child welfare? *Children and Youth Services Review, 35,* 429–438.

Schramm, D. G., Harris, S. M., Whiting, J. B., Hawkins, A. J., Brown, M., & Porter, R. (2013). Economic costs and policy implications associated with divorce: Texas as a case study. *Journal of Divorce and Remarriage, 54,* 1–24.

Schramm, D. G., Marshall, J. P., Harris, V. W., & George, A. (2003). *Marriage in Utah: 2003 baseline statewide survey on marriage and divorce.* Salt Lake City: Utah Department of Workforce Services.

Schulz, M. S., Cowan, C. P., & Cowan, P. A. (2006). Promoting healthy beginnings: A randomized controlled trial of a preventative intervention to preserve marital quality during the transition to parenthood. *Journal of Consulting & Clinical Psychology, 74,* 20–31.

Scott, M. S., DeRose, L. F., Lippman, L. H., & Cook, E. (2013). *Two, one, or no parents? Children's living arrangements and educational outcomes around the world.* Washington, DC: Child Trends. Retrieved from http://worldfamilymap. org/2013/wp-content/uploads/2013/01/WFM-2013-Final-lores-11513.pdf

Scott, M. E., Moore, K. A., Hawkins, A. J., Malm, K., & Beltz, M. (2012, December). *Putting youth relationship education on the child welfare agenda: Findings from a research and evaluation review: Executive summary.* Washington, DC: Child Trends. Retrieved from http://www.childtrends.org/_listAllPubs.cfm?LID= 4D7366E5-AEF5-4F94-8B842104664487A6

Scott, M. E., Schelar, E., Manlove, J., & Cui, C. (2009). Young adult attitudes about relationships and marriage: Time may have changed, but expectations remain high. *Child Trends Research Brief,* Publication #2009-30. Retrieved from http://www.childtrends.org/_docdisp_page.cfm?LID=248A8BBE-0415-48D2 -BDC9A5731DBDFB93

Scott, M. E., Steward-Streng, N. R., Manlove, J., Schelar, E., & Cui, C. (2011). Characteristics of young adult sexual relationships: Diverse, sometimes violent, often loving. *Child Trends Research Brief,* Publication # 2011-01. Retrieved from http://www.childtrends.org/_listAllPubs.cfm?LID=9B37B55C-75A1-4061 -8856FFA5123A43A7

Shuger, L. (2012). *Teen pregnancy and high school dropout: What communities can do to address these issues.* Washington, DC: National Campaign to Prevent Teen and Unplanned Pregnancy and America's Promise Alliance.

Shulman, S. (2003). Conflict and negotiation in adolescent romantic relationships. In P. Florsheim (Ed.), *Adolescent romantic relations and sexual behavior: Theory, research, and practical implications* (pp. 109–135). Mahwah, NJ: Lawrence Erlbaum Associates.

Skogrand, L., Barrios-Bell, A., & Higginbotham, B. (2009). Stepfamily education for Latino families: Implications for practice. *Journal of Couple & Relationship Therapy, 8,* 113–128.

Skogrand, L., Dansie, L., Higginbotham, B. J., Davis, P., & Barrios-Bell, A. (2011). Benefits of stepfamily education: One-year post-program. *Marriage & Family Review, 47,* 149–163.

Skogrand, L., Davis, P., & Higginbotham, B. J. (2011). Stepfamily education: A case study. *Contemporary Family Therapy, 33,* 61–70.

Smith C., Christoffersen, K., Davidson, H., & Herzog, P. S. (2011). *Lost in transition: The dark side of emerging adulthood.* New York: Oxford University Press.

Snyder, D. K., Baucom, D. H., & Gordon, K. C. (2007). *Getting past the affair.* New York: Guilford.

Solot, D., & Miller, D. (2002). *Let them eat wedding rings: The role of marriage promotion in welfare reform.* Albany, NY: Alternatives to Marriage Project. Retrieved from http://www.unmarried.org/let-them-eat-wedding-rings-report.html

Sparks, A. (2008, July). Implementation of "Within My Reach": Providing a relationship awareness and communication skills program to TANF recipients in Oklahoma. *National Poverty Center Working Paper Series #08-11.* Ann Arbor, MI: National Poverty Center.

Stanley, S. M. (2001). Making a case for premarital education. *Family Relations, 50,* 272–280.

Stanley, S. M. (2005). *The power of commitment: A guide to active, lifelong love.* San Francisco: Jossey-Bass.

Stanley, S. M. (2012, July). The impact of marriage education on Army couples. Presentation at the annual meeting of the National Association of Relationship and Marriage Education, Baltimore, MD.

Stanley, S. M., Allen, E. S., Markman, H. J., Rhoades, G. K., & Prentice, D. L. (2010).

Decreasing divorce in U.S. Army couples: Results from a randomized controlled trial using PREP for Strong Bonds. *Journal of Couple & Relationship Therapy, 9,* 149–160.

Stanley, S. M., Amato, P. R., Johnson, C. A., & Markman, H. J. (2006). Premarital education, marital quality, and marital stability: Findings from a large, random household survey. *Journal of Family Psychology, 20,* 117–126.

Stanley, S. M., Bradbury, T. N., & Markman, H. J. (2000). Structural flaws in the bridge from basic research on marriage to interventions for couples. *Journal of Marriage and the Family, 62,* 256–264.

Stanley, S. M., Markman, H. J., Prado, L. M., Olmos-Gallo, P. A., Tonelli, L., St. Peters, M., … & Whitton, S. W. (2001). Community-based premarital prevention: Clergy and lay leaders on the front lines. *Family Relations, 50,* 67–76.

Stanley, S. M., Rhoades, G. K., & Whitton, S. W. (2010). Commitment: Functions, formation, and the securing of romantic attachment. *Journal of Family Theory & Review, 2,* 243–257.

Stapleton, L. T., & Bradbury, T N. (2012). Marital interaction prior to parenthood predicts parent–child interaction 9 years later. *Journal of Family Psychology, 26,* 479–487.

Staton, J., & Ooms, T. (n.d.). *Marriage and relationship factors in health: Implications for improving health care quality and reducing costs.* Washington, DC: National Healthy Marriage Resource Center.

Stevenson, B., & Wolfers, J. (2006). Bargaining in the shadow of the law: Divorce laws and family distress. *Quarterly Journal of Economics, 121,* 267–288.

Stokes, C. E., & Ellison, C. G. (2010). Religion and attitudes towards divorce laws among U.S. adults. *Journal of Family Issues, 31,* 1279–1304.

Sullivan, K. T., & Bradbury, T. N. (1997). Are premarital prevention programs reaching couples at risk for marital dysfunction? *Journal of Consulting & Clinical Psychology, 65,* 24–30.

Szarzynski, A., Porter, R., Whiting, J. B., & Harris, S. M. (2012). Low-income mothers in marriage and relationship education: Program experiences and beliefs about marriage and relationships. *Journal of Couple & Relationship Therapy, 11,* 322–342.

Tach, L. M., & Halpern-Meekin, S. (2012). Marital quality and divorce decisions: How do premarital cohabitation and nonmarital childbearing matter? *Family Relations, 61,* 571–585.

Teachman, J. (2003). Premarital sex, premarital cohabitation, and the risk of subsequent marital dissolution among women. *Journal of Marriage and Family, 65,* 444–455.

Thaler, R. H., & Sunstein, C. R. (2008). *Nudge: Improving decisions about health, wealth, and happiness.* New Haven, CT: Yale University Press.

Thompson, R. A., & Meyer, S. (2007). Socialization of emotion regulation in the family. In J. J. Gross (Ed.), *Handbook of emotion regulation* (pp. 249–268). New York: Guilford.

Trail, T. E., & Karney, B. R. (2012). What's (not) wrong with low-income marriages. *Journal of Marriage and Family, 74,* 413–427.

Treas, J., & Giesen, D. (2000). Sexual infidelity among married and cohabiting Americans. *Journal of Marriage and Family, 62,* 48–60.

Tumin, D., & Qian, Z. (2012, May). Marital separation, divorce, and health consequences. Paper presented at the annual conference of the Population Association of America, San Francisco, CA.

Twenge, J. M., Campbell, W. K., & Foster, C. A. (2003). Parenthood and marital satisfaction: A meta-analytic review. *Journal of Marriage and Family, 65,* 574–583.

U.S. Department of Health and Human Services. (2009). *Emerging findings from the Office of Family Assistance Healthy Marriage and Responsible Fatherhood grant programs: A review of select grantee profiles and promising results.* Washington, DC: Author. Retrieved from www.healthymarriageinfo.org/resource-detail/index.aspx?rid=3305

U.S. Department of Health and Human Services. (2012). *School of thought: Healthy marriage and relationship education matters to our youth.* Washington, DC: Author. Retrieved from http://www.healthymarriageinfo.org/for-the-media/news/news-detail/index.aspx?nid=293

United States Government Accountability Office. (2011). *Multiple employment and training programs: Providing information on colocating services and consolidating administrative structures could promote efficiencies* (Report No. GAO-11-92). Washington, DC: Author.

Utah Department of Health. (2012, March). *Utah's vital statistics: Marriages and divorces, 2009 and 2010.* Technical Report No. 275. Salt Lake City, UT: Department of Health, Center for Health Data, Office of Vital Records and Statistics.

van Acker, E. (2008). *Governments and marriage education policy: Perspectives from the UK, Australia and the US.* New York: Palgrave MacMillian.

Van Epp, J. (2003). The P.I.C.K. a Partner educational program (Premarital Interpersonal Choices & Knowledge): Partner-selection education. Retrieved from www.lovethinks.com/researchesgrants/

Van Epp, M. C., Futris, T. G., Van Epp, J. C., & Campbell, K. (2008). The impact of the PICK a Partner relationship education progam on single Army soldiers. *Family and Consumer Sciences Research Journal, 36,* 328–349.

Vennum, A., & Fincham, F. D. (2011). Assessing decision making in young adult romantic relationships. *Psychological Assessment, 23,* 739–751.

Wadsworth, M. E., & Markman, H. J. (2012). Where's the action? Understanding what works and why in relationship education. *Behavior Therapy, 43,* 99–112.

Wadsworth, M. E., Santiago, C. D., Einhorn, L., Etter, E. M., Rienks, S., & Markman, H. (2011). Preliminary efficacy of an intervention to reduce psychosocial stress and improve coping in low-income families. *American Journal of Community Psychology, 48,* 257–271.

Waite, L. J., & Gallagher, M. (2000). *The case for marriage.* New York: Doubleday.

Waite, L. J., Browning, D., Doherty, W. J., Gallagher, M., Luo, Y., & Stanley, S. M. (2002). *Does divorce make people happy? Findings from a study of unhappy marriages.* New York: Institute for American Values.

Waite, L. J., Luo, Y, & Lewin, A. C. (2009). Marital happiness and marital stability: Consequences for psychological well-being. *Social Science Research, 38,* 201–212.

Waldfogel, J. (2009). The role of family policies in antipoverty policy. In M. Cancian & S. Danziger (Eds.), *Changing poverty, changing policies* (pp. 242–265). New York: Russell Sage Foundation.

Walker, J., McCarthy, P., Stark, C., & Laing, K. (2004). *Picking up the pieces: Marriage and divorce two years after information provision.* London: Department for Constitutional Affairs. Retrieved from http://eprint.ncl.ac.uk/pub_details2.aspx?pub_id=642

Wallerstein, J., Lewis, J., & Blakeslee, S. (2000). *The unexpected legacy of divorce: A 25-year landmark study.* New York: Hyperion.

Ward, D. B., & McCollum, E. E. (2005). Treatment effectiveness and its correlates in a marriage and family therapy training clinic. *American Journal of Family Therapy, 33,* 207–223.

Wardle, L. D. (2005). Tyranny, federalism, and the federal marriage amendment. *Yale Journal of Law and Feminism, 17,* 221–265.

Weick, K. E. (1979). *The social psychology of organizing* (2nd ed.). Reading, MA: Addison-Wesley.

Whitehead, B.D. (1993, April). Dan Quayle was right. *Atlantic.* Retrieved from http://www.theatlantic.com/magazine/archive/1993/04/dan-quayle-was-right/7015/

Whitehead, B. D. (1996). *The divorce culture: Rethinking our commitments to marriage and family.* New York: Vintage Books.

Whitehead, B. D., & Pearson, M. (2006). *Making a love connection: Teen relationships, pregnancy, and marriage.* Washington, DC: National Campaign to Prevent Teen Pregnancy.

Wilcox, W. B. (2010). When marriage disappears: The retreat from marriage in middle America. In W. B. Wilcox & E. Marquardt (Eds.), *The state of our unions: Marriage in America 2010* (pp. 13–60). Charlottesville, VA: National Marriage Project & Institute for American Values.

Wilcox, W. B., & Dew, J. (2012). *The date night opportunity: What does couple time tell us about the potential value of date nights?* Charlottesville, VA: National Marriage Project.

Wilcox, W. B., & Marquardt, E. (2011). When baby makes three: How parenthood makes life meaningful and how marriage makes parenthood bearable. In W. B. Wilcox & E. Marquardt (Eds.), *The state of our unions: Marriage in America 2011.* Charlottesville, VA: National Marriage Project & Institute for American Values.

Wilcox, W. B., Anderson, J. R., Doherty, W., Eggebeen, D., Ellison, C. G., Galston, W., ... & Wallerstein, J. (2011). *Why marriage matters, third edition: Thirty conclusions from the social sciences.* New York: Institute for American Values & National Marriage Project.

Wilde, J. L., & Doherty, W. J. (in press). Outcomes of an intensive couple relationship education program with fragile families. *Family Process.*

Wildeman, C., & Western, B. (2010). Incarceration in fragile families. *Future of Children, 20*(2), 157–177.

Wildsmith, E., Steward-Streng, N. R., & Manlove, J. (2011). Childbearing outside of marriage: Estimates and trends in the United States. *Child Trends Research Brief,* #2011-29. Washington, DC: Child Trends.

Willoughby, B. J., Olson, C. D., Carroll, J. S., Nelson, L. J., & Miller, R. B. (2012). Sooner or later? The marital horizon of parents and their emerging adult children. *Journal of Social and Personal Relationships, 29,* 967–981.

Wilmoth, J. D., & Smyser, S. (2012). A national survey of marriage preparation provided by clergy. *Journal of Couple & Relationship Therapy, 11,* 69–85.

Wilson, J. Q. (2002). *The marriage problem: How our culture has weakened families.* New York: HarperCollins.

Wilson, R. F. (2008). The harmonisation of family law in the United States. In K. Boele-Woelki & T. Sverdrup (Eds.), *European challenges in contemporary family law* (pp. 27–49). Antwerp, Belgium: Intersentia.

Wineberg, H. (1995). An examination of ever-divorced women who attempted a marital reconciliation before becoming divorced. *Journal of Divorce & Remarriage, 22*(3/4), 129–146.

Wolfers, J. (2006). Did unilateral divorce laws raise divorce rates? A reconciliation and new results. *American Economic Review, 96,* 1802–1820.

Wolfinger, N. H. (2005). *Understanding the divorce cycle: The children of divorce in their own marriages.* New York: Cambridge University Press.

Wood, R. G., McConnell, S., Moore, Q., Clarkwest, A., & Hsueh, J. (2010, May). *The Building Strong Families project: Strengthening unmarried parents' relationships: The early impacts of Building Strong Families.* Princeton, NJ: Mathematica Policy Research. Retrieved from http://www.mathematica-mpr.com/publications/

redirect_PubsDB.asp?strSite=PDFs/family_support/BSF_TOT_fnlrpt.pdf

Wood, R. G., Moore, Q., & Clarkwest, A. (2011). *The Building Strong Families project: BSF's effects on couples who attended group relationship skills sessions: A special analysis of 15-month data.* OPRE Report # 2011-17. Washington, DC: Office of Planning, Research, and Evaluation, Administration for Children and Families, U.S. Department of Health and Human Services. Retrieved from http://www.acf.hhs.gov/programs/opre/strengthen/build_fam

Wood, R. G., Moore, Q., Clarkwest, A., Killewald, A., & Monahan, S. (2012). *The long-term effects of Building Strong Families: A relationship skills education program for unmarried parents,* OPRE Report #2012-28A. Washington, DC: Office of Planning, Research, and Evaluation, Administration for Children and Families, U.S. Department of Health and Human Services. Retrieved from http://www.acf.hhs.gov/programs/opre/index.html

Endnotes

Chapter 1

1. U.S. Department of Health & Human Services, 2009, p. 18.

2. U.S. Department of Health & Human Services, 2009, p. 10.

3. There are a lot of good books designed to help couples directly with their marriages and relationships. Here are two I recommend: Gottman & Silver, 1999; Markman, Stanley, & Blumberg, 2010.

4. For instance, see: Amato & Booth, 1997; Amato, Booth, Johnson, & Rogers, 2007; Cherlin, 2009; Coontz, 2005; Edin & Kefalas, 2005; Hymowitz, 2006; Regnerus & Uecker, 2011; Wilson, 2002.

5. For instance, see: Cott, 2000; Nock, 2005.

6. Parkinson, 2011.

7. See Scafidi, 2008, for one estimate of the public costs of family fragmentation.

8. Nock & Einolf, 2008.

9. See Coontz, 2006. Also see Coontz, 2005.

10. See Wilson, 2002, p. 221.

11. Nock, 2005.

12. Murray, 2012.

13. In fact, Murray sees an inexorable, slow death of the modern welfare state and its intellectual underpinnings.

14. Heath, 2012.

15. Heath, 2012, p. 183.

16. My colleague Maggie Gallagher, with the Institute for Marriage and Public Policy, has used this phrase a number of times. See, for instance, Gallagher, 1996, p. 233.

17. Amato, Booth, Johnson, & Rogers, 2007.

18. Cherlin, 2009.

19. Cherlin, 2009, p. 194.

20. Edin & Kefalas, 2005.

21. Cahn & Carbone, 2010.

22. Cahn & Carbone, 2010, p. 168.

23. Waite & Gallagher, 2000.

24. Donovan, 2011.

25. Obama, 2006.

26. Smith et al., 2011, p. 239.

27. Smith et al., 2011, p. 243.

28. Smith et al., 2011, p. 239.

29. Smith et al., 2011, p. 240, emphasis in original.

30. For instance, see Weick, 1979.

31. Wilcox et al., 2011. Trend data for many of the statistics presented in this section can be found in Pew Research Center, 2010.

32. McLanahan & Beck, 2010.

33. Wildsmith et al., 2011.

34. Wilcox, 2010; see Figure 5, p. 23.

35. See Edin & Kefalas, 2005; Edin & Nelson, in press.

36. Wilcox et al., 2011.

37. Burton et al., 2009; Edin & Kefalas, 2005.

38. Coppen et al., 2012; Bramlett & Mosher, 2001.

39. Wilcox, 2010; see Figure 1, p. 19.

40. National Center for Family & Marriage Research, 2009.

41. Cherlin, 2009.

42. Cherlin, 2009, p. 5. Cherlin does an excellent job of documenting the exceptional amount of churning that American children experience.

43. See Cherlin, 2004, for a more detailed treatment of the concept of the deinstitutionalization of marriage.

44. Cherlin, 2004, p. 848.

45. Cherlin, 2004, 2009.

46. Cherlin, 2004, p. 848.

47. Cherlin, 2004.

48. Rector, 2012.

49. Scott et al., 2013.

50. Diane Sollee, founder of the Coalition for Marriage, Families, and Couple Education, should get credit for popularizing the term, "smart marriage." See www.smartmarriages.com.

51. Lichter, Graefe, & Brown, 2003.

52. See van Acker, 2008, and Andrews, 2012, for a treatment of policies in Australia and the United Kingdom. Australia since 2006 has supported a set of more

than two dozen Relationship Centres across the country, but operationally they have focused almost exclusively on helping divorcing couples reduce conflict and acrimony rather than on preventative education services.

53. See Marquardt et al., 2012; Haskins & Sawhill, 2009.

54. Williams, 2011.

55. Regnerus, 2012.

56. Knox et al., 2011.

57. Wilcox, 2010.

58. Many scholars have made this point about the potential effectiveness of MRE for very disadvantaged couples. For illustrations, see Wadsworth & Markman, 2012; Waldfogel, 2009.

59. Hawkins, Amato, & Kinghorn, 2013.

60. Hawkins, Wardle, & Coolidge, 2002.

61. For an excellent treatment of distinctions and overlap between MRE and couple therapy, see Markman & Rhoades, 2012.

62. Halford, 2011, p. ix.

63. Halford, 2011, provides a good overview of how MRE is distinguished from couple therapy, especially with its emphasis on prevention.

64. See Hawkins et al., 2008.

65. For meta-analytic studies of the effectiveness of MRE programs, see: Blanchard, Hawkins, Baldwin, & Fawcett, 2009; Fawcett, Hawkins, Blanchard, & Carroll, 2010; Hawkins, Blanchard, Baldwin, & Fawcett, 2008; Hawkins, Stanley, Blanchard, & Albright, 2012; McAllister, Duncan, & Hawkins, 2012.

66. For a review of the work evaluating MRE programs for more disadvantaged individuals, see Hawkins & Ooms, 2010, 2012.

Chapter 2

1. The Tenth Amendment to the U.S. Constitution is generally cited for the reservation to the states of the regulation of family relations. But this federalist approach to family law appears to be changing somewhat; see Wardle, 2005.

2. Whitehead, 1993.

3. A few (11–15) waivers were granted during this period by the Office of Child Support Enforcement (a part of ACF) to experiment with programs and initiatives that dealt with serving unmarried couples in various ways.

4. For a review of Horn's thoughts on this topic, see Horn, 2002.

5. Bush, 2002.

6. Federal agencies within the Administration for Children and Families that began early, with Horn's encouragement, to experiment with developing educational programs to help couples form and sustain healthy marriages included:

Administration for Native Americans, Children's Bureau, Office of Child Support Enforcement, Office of Community Services, and Office of Refugee Resettlement. Later the Office of Head Start also funded demonstration grants to Head Start provider organizations to make MRE services available to the parents of Head Start children.

7. For more details about the ACF Healthy Marriages and Relationships Initiative, see National Healthy Marriage Resource Center, 2010.

8. See: http://www.acf.hhs.gov/programs/ofa/resource/the-healthy-marriage -initiative-hmi

9. For more information, see Wood et al., 2010.

10. For more information, see Hsueh et al., 2012.

11. The legislation barely passed; Vice President Cheney had to cast the deciding vote. The healthy marriage initiative parts, however, did not get much attention and were not a primary source of partisan disagreements.

12. These were not new funds, however. The first iteration of TANF included a program to reward states that did the most to reduce unwed births. There was wide agreement among policy makers that this program had been ineffective, so these funds were re-tasked for the federal HMRI.

13. Religious organizations receiving funds operated under strict rules about how they could be used. For instance, religious doctrine could not be preached along side MRE. Also, MRE services had to be made available to participants without regard to religious affiliation.

14. Unfortunately, ACF has not yet compiled the data on how many individuals have received MRE services as a result of the dollars invested. I complain about this data void in several places throughout the book.

15. See http://ncfmr.bgsu.edu. I serve on the National Advisory Board for this Center.

16. These studies are being conducted by the respected social policy research organization Mathematica Policy Research, the same organization that conducted the BSF study. The studies, referred to collectively as PACT (Parents and Children Together), are rigorous randomized controlled designs with a 12-month follow-up impact study and also include implementation studies. In addition, there is a qualitative component of the study with in-depth interviews with program participants. There will be a handful of responsible fatherhood programs evaluated as well as the MRE programs.

17. Obama, 2006, p. 334.

18. PREP stands for *Prevention and Relationship Enhancement Program,* developed by researcher-practitioners at the University of Denver. For more information, go to www.prepinc.com

19. A new governor, Jon Huntsman, purged a large number of commissions and other initiatives that had accumulated in the governor's office when he took office. The Marriage Commission was included in that purge.

20. See Halford, 2011.

21. Bradford et al., 2011.

22. A program for displaced homemakers was funded by a $20 set-aside of marriage license fees, but this program sunsetted in 2012; the legislation would reallocate that $20 to support the UT HMI.

23. It also has provided some support to divorce orientation education to couples at the crossroads of divorce. I discuss this in depth in Chapter 8.

24. I have served on the OMI Research Advisory Group since 2009.

25. Markman et al., 2010.

26. Jordan et al., 1999.

27. Annie E. Casey Foundation, 2012.

28. Harris et al., 2008.

29. Osborne, 2011.

30. The one law that did pass in 2007 that mandated divorce orientation education for all divorcing parents, which I will describe in more depth in Chapter 8, I read about in the paper after the fact; I wasn't involved with it.

31. Heaton, 2002.

32. For a more detailed summary of these implementation studies, see Hawkins & Ooms, 2012. See also Bouchet, Torres, & Hyra, 2012; Gaubert, Bubits, Alderson, & Knox, 2012.

33. For a brief summary of this evaluation work on Head Start and other preschool programs, see Haskins & Sawhill, 2009, pp. 132–136. See also Office of Planning, Research and Evaluation, 2010. In short, positive effects for Head Start children exist but appear small. High-quality programs have shown that they benefit children's cognitive and social development. But most Head Start programs are not implemented very well and thus do not produce the positive effects intended.

34. I'm grateful to my team of research assistants on this project: Lacey Aukema, Jeni Awerkamp, Jessica Bartlett, Kelsey Cropper, Trevor Dahle, Sage Erickson, Abigail Fisher, Andrea Kinghorn, Faith Simonsen, and Chelsea Underwood.

35. For more details on this study, see Hawkins, Amato, & Kinghorn, 2013.

36. Wood et al., 2010.

37. Lerman, 2005.

38. See First Things First 2011 Report Card at: http://firstthings.org/page/about-us/what-is-first-things-first

39. Birch et al., 2004. I am currently conducting a replication of this study that includes more recent data.

40. For more about Community Marriage Policy communities, see: http://www.communitymarriagepolicy.org.

41. I am grateful to the National Healthy Marriage Resource Center for providing me some funding to conduct this study.

42. Hawkins & Fellows, 2011. For more details on meta-analytic studies, see Lipsey & Wilson, 2003.

Chapter 3

1. Foroohar, 2012.

2. For an illustration of this point, see: Karney, 2011; Trail & Karney, 2012.

3. For a more detailed illustration of this critique, see Huston & Melz, 2004.

4. Karney & Bradbury, 2005, p. 174.

5. This is the strong message of Kahn & Carbone, 2010.

6. See Burton et al., 2009; Cherlin et al., 2004.

7. Twenty percent of births to married women are unintended; 50% of births to cohabiting women are unintended; 65% of births to unmarried and noncohabiting women are unintended. See Wildsmith et al., 2011.

8. Wilderman & Western, 2010.

9. Edin & Kefalas, 2005.

10. For instance, the progressive Urban Institute's Ratcliffe & McKernan, 2012, analyze child poverty and call for policies that attend to the romantic relationship and to parenting, as well as to such things as employment, education, and mental health. Also, the progressive and prominent family historian Stephanie Coontz calls for both approaches: "Government should focus on strengthening economic security and developing more living-wage jobs while simultaneously providing relationship skills training," see http://www.economist.com/debate/days/view/908

11. Brooks, 2010.

12. Halpern, 2010.

13. Heaton, 2002.

14. Haskins et al., 2012; Wilcox, 2010.

15. See Haskins et al., 2012, and Jacob & Ludwig, 2009, for a reasonable set of policy actions to reduce the academic achievement gap.

16. Lerman, 2010.

17. For a summary, see McLanahan & Beck, 2010.

18. U.S. G.A.O., 2011.

19. Holzer, 2009.

20. Holzer, 2009.

21. See Cherlin et al., 2004; Burton et al., 2009.

22. Catlett & Artis, 2004.

23. See Ooms et al., 2006.

24. For instance, see Bradford et al., 2011; Bradley et al., 2011.

25. A special issue of the *Journal of Couple & Relationship Therapy*, 2011, Issue No. 2, which I co-edited, focused on this issue. For instance, see Rhoades & Stanley, 2011.

26. See Antle, et al., 2011; Bradley & Gottman, 2012; Bradley et al., 2011.

27. Graefe & Lichter, 2008.

28. For instance, the noted social policy scholar Isabel Sawhill takes this position; see Haskins & Sawhill, 2009, Chapter 10.

29. Child Trends, n.d.; Wildsmith et al., 2011.

30. Child Trends, n.d.; Wildsmith et al., 2011.

31. Peipert et al., 2012.

32. Martin et al., 2009; see especially Table 18.

33. Logan et al., 2007.

34. McLanahan & Beck, 2010.

35. See Kearney & Levine, 2008.

36. Musick & Bumpass, 2012.

37. A transcript of this NPR interview on June 12, 2012, can be read at http://www.npr.org/2012/06/12/154853988/improving-the-lives-of-single-moms-and-their-kids

38. Haskins & Sawhill, 2009.

39. Halpern, 2012.

40. See Halpern, 2012, p. 257.

41. See Furstenberg, 2007, for a critique that makes a number of the pragmatic skepticism arguments, as well as marital ecology arguments.

42. See Bradbury & Lavner, 2012; Huston & Melz, 2004.

43. See Huston & Melz, 2004.

44. See Johnson, 2012. But see Hawkins et al., in press.

45. See Catlett & Artis, 2004.

46. Bradbury & Karney, 2004; Bradbury & Lavner, 2012.

47. See Huston & Melz, 2004.

48. Wallerstein et al., 2000; Wolfinger, 2005.

49. Cummings et al., 2002; Cummings et al., 2012.

50. Doherty et al., 1998.

51. For instance, see Cowan et al., 2011; Cowan et al., 2009.

52. Adler-Baeder et al., 2013; Cummings et al., 2008.

53. McHale et al., 2012.

54. See Huston & Melz, 2004.

55. See Glenn, 2002.

56. For instance, see Cherlin, 2009; Edin & Kefalas, 2005.

57. Rhoades et al., 2009a; Rhoades et al., 2009b.

58. For a summary of research on cohabitation and marital success, see Stanley et al., 2009; Manning & Cohen, 2012.

59. See Manning & Cohen, 2012.

60. See Stanley, 2001.

61. See Johnson, 2012.

62. See Hawkins & Ooms, 2010; Hawkins, et al., 2008.

63. Ooms & Wilson, 2004.

64. Johnson, 2012.

65. See Hawkins & Fellows, 2011; Hsueh et al., 2012; Wood et al., 2010.

66. See Wood et al., 2010.

67. See Cowan et al., 2009; Hsueh et al., 2012.

68. See Halford et al., in press; Petch et al., 2012a.

69. For a review, see Hawkins & Ooms, 2010.

70. See Haskins & Sawhill, 2009, especially Chapter 8.

71. Office of Planning, Research, and Evaluation, 2010.

72. No known relationship to me.

73. Prinz et al., 2009.

74. For example, see: Devaney & Dion, 2010; Hsueh et al., 2012; Markman et al., 2004.

75. For the BSF program costs, see Dion et al., 2008. For the SHM program costs, see Hsueh et al., 2012.

76. For instance, see Haskins et al., 2009; Orzag, 2009.

77. Scafidi, 2008.

78. Nock & Einolf, 2008.

79. Schramm et al., 2012.

80. For instance, see Coontz, 2005, for an argument about how powerful social–historical changes have been in shaping family behavior.

81. See Hornik, 2002a.

82. Nudging as public policy, and the social science of behavioral economics behind it, are reviewed by Thaler & Sunstein, 2008.

83. For reviews of how marriage and family life have changed over time and "survived" dramatic changes in the social organization of life, see for instance, Coontz, 2005; Cott, 2000.

84. For an illustration of this line of argument, see Solot & Miller, 2002.

85. Coontz, 2005.

86. For an excellent review of this argument, see Nock, 2005; Whitehead, 1996.

87. Green, 2012.

Chapter 4

1. Guzman et al., 2009.

2. Rhoades & Stanley, 2009.

3. Carver et al., 2003.

4. Collins, 2003.

5. Scott et al., 2011.

6. Berger et al., 2012.

7. Heaton, 2002.

8. Furman & Shafer, 2003; Barber & Eccles, 2003.

9. Côté, 2000.

10. Wilcox, 2010; see especially Figure 14, p. 99.

11. Scott et al., 2009.

12. Fincham, 2012.

13. Rhoades & Stanley, 2009, pp. 46, 47.

14. Karney et al., 2007, pp. xiv, xvii.

15. Knox et al., 2011, p. 235.

16. Manning et al., 2010, p. 100.

17. Barber & Eccles, 2003.

18. Smith et al., 2011, p. 238.

19. Regnerus & Uecker, 2011, p. 170.

20. Whitehead & Pearson, 2006, p. 14.

21. Chambers & Kravitz, 2012, p. 656.

22. Smith et al., 2011, p. 238.

23. For more details about RLE programs, an excellent web site to browse is www.dibbleinstitute.org. Also see National Healthy Marriage Resource Center, 2010; U.S. Department of Health and Human Services, 2012. Karney et al., 2007 also provided an excellent review and critique of relationship education for youth, especially Chapter 6.

24. Gardner & Boellaard, 2007.

25. See National Healthy Marriage Resource Center, 2010.

26. U.S. Department of Health and Human Services, 2012.

27. National Healthy Marriage Resource Center, 2010.

28. For a discussion of these issues, see Barber & Eccles, 2003.

29. Whitehead & Pearson, 2006, p. 11.

30. Busby et al., 2011; Sassler et al., 2012.

31. For one perspective on this question, see National Healthy Marriage Resource Center, n.d.

32. Administration for Children and Families, n.d.

33. Furman & Shaffer, 2003.

34. Shulman, 2005.

35. See Archer, 2000; Scott et al., 2011. Also, 30% of married young adults say they have experienced relationship violence. Relationship violence appears to be more common among Black and Hispanic couples.

36. Halpern-Meekin et al., 2013.

37. Cui et al., in press.

38. Montgomery, 2005.

39. See Whitehead & Pearson, 2006.

40. Osborne, 2012.

41. Pew Research Center, 2010; see especially tables on pp. 21, 15, 36.

42. Waite & Gallagher, 2000.

43. Rhoades et al., 2009a.

44. Teachman, 2003.

45. Busby et al., 2010.

46. Stanley, 2005.

47. Burton et al., 2009; Cherlin et al., 2004.

48. See: Carroll et al., in press; Scott et al., 2011.

49. Wolfinger, 2005.

50. For instance, see Whitehead & Pearson, 2006.

51. Nock, 1998.

52. Whitehead & Pearson, 2006, p. 18.

53. See Wilcox et al., 2011.

54. Hymowitz, 2006, pp. 10–11.

55. Oyserman et al., 2006. Also see Loew et al., 2012.

56. Whitehead & Pearson, 2006.

57. Gardner & Boellaard, 2007.

58. This project has gone under a set of names that have changed over time. I will refer to it as the Alabama Healthy Marriages and Relationships Initiative. Visit the project's website at www.alabamamarriage.org.

59. See Kerpelman et al., 2010, for an overview of this pilot study.

60. See Adler-Baeder et al., 2011, for an overview of this project.

61. For a more detailed description of the RS+ curriculum, see Kerpelman et al., 2009, Table 1.

62. These are taken from Adler-Baeder et al., 2011, pp. 4–5.

63. See Kerpelman et al., 2009; Kerpelman et al., 2010.

64. Kerpelman, 2012.

65. More details than I provide here about the *p.a.p.a.* program are available in Osborne, 2011; available at: https://www.oag.state.tx.us/cs/ofi/papa/#is

66. Annie E. Casey Foundation, 2012; see especially p. 49.

67. Osborne, 2011, reports the results of this evaluation study.

68. I have not been able to get reliable data on the number of students currently taking the class, so caution is recommended with this figure.

69. Halpern-Meekin, 2011.

70. Gardner & Boellaard, 2007.

71. Hawkins & Fellows, 2011; see Table 3, p. 11.

72. U.S. Department of Health and Human Services, 2012.

73. A version of this curriculum for unmarried couples in a serious or cohabiting relationship, *Within Our Reach*, will be discussed in the next chapter. For more details about *Within My Reach*, see Rhoades & Stanley, 2009. For a copy of the curriculum manual, see Pearson et al., 2008.

74. See Markman et al., 2010.

75. Antle et al., in press.

76. Antle et al., 2011. Note, however, that there was a high rate of attrition at the 6-month follow-up, so these findings should be interpreted cautiously.

77. Sparks, 2008.

78. The theory and research behind this program is provided in Van Epp, 2003.

79. Van Epp et al., 2008. The first author is John Van Epp's daughter, who studied this curriculum during her master's degree program at Ohio State University.

80. Manning et al., 2008. See also Manning et al., 2010.

81. Vennum & Fincham, 2011.

82. Braithwaite & Fincham, 2007, 2009, 2011.

83. Braithwaite & Fincham, 2011.

84. In 1998, Florida Governor Childs signed the Marriage Preparation and Preservation Act, which made the teaching of marriage skills a required part of the high school curriculum. To the best of my knowledge, Florida is still the only state to have done this. However, according to one report, this portion of the legislation has been rescinded, but I have not been able to confirm this. The act also encourages premarital preparation by reducing the marriage license fee by 50% for those who complete a marriage preparation course. HB 1019, Fla. Stat. 98-403; see http://www.myflorida house.gov/Sections/Bills/billsdetail.aspx?BillId=20820&SessionIndex=1&Session Id=48&BillText=&BillNumber=1019&BillSponsorIndex=0&BillListIndex=0& BillStatuteText=&BillTypeIndex=0&BillReferredIndex=0&HouseChamber=H &BillSearchIndex=10

85. U.S. Department of Health and Human Services, 2012.

86. I would like to see the federal government, perhaps through ACF and the Department of Education, support with small grants more training and continuing education opportunities for teachers who want to do more of this for needy youth.

87. Halpern-Meekin, 2011.

88. Shuger, 2012.

89. Durlak et al., 2011.

90. Palm & Fagan, 2008.

91. Haskins & Sawhill, 2009; see especially p. 223.

92. Olmstead et al., 2011. See also Nielson et al., 2004.

93. See www.twoofus.org, which was developed under a U.S. federal grant to the National Healthy Marriage Resource Center, for an example of a website targeting young adults with healthy marriage and relationship information.

94. Heaton, 2002.

95. Carroll et al., in press.

96. Willoughby et al., 2012.

97. See http://marquee.blogs.cnn.com/2012/11/26/oprah-gives-marriage-advice-to-justin-bieber

98. Regnerus, 2009.

99. Carroll et al., in press; Scott et al., 2011.

100. See Regerus & Uecker, 2011, especially Chapters 4 and 5; and Smith et al., 2011, especially Chapter 4.

101. Smith et al., 2011.

102. See Edin & Kefalas, 2005; Miller et al., 2012.

103. See Martin, 2006; National Marriage Project & Institute for American Values, 2010; see pp. 73–74.

104. Rhoades et al., 2011.

Chapter 5

1. This figure comes from Clark University's Poll of Emerging Adults conducted in April 2012. It was a national poll of 1,029 young adults, 18–29 years old. See http://www.clark.edu/clarkpoll/

2. Bramlett & Mosher, 2001.

3. James, 2012; Kamp Dush & Taylor, 2011; Kamp Dush et al., 2008; Lavner & Bradbury, 2012; Lavner et al., 2012.

4. National Fatherhood Initiative, 2005.

5. I borrow this from the popular book, *Saving Your Marriage Before It Starts: Seven Questions to Ask Before and After You Marry,* by Les Parrott & Leslie Parrott, 1995.

6. Wolfinger, 2005.

7. Doss et al., 2009.

8. For this risk factor and others, see Wilcox, 2010.

9. Doss et al., 2009; Halford, 2011.

10. Stanley et al., 2006. Some other surveys in particular states have found slightly higher rates for couples marrying within the last decade. See Schramm et al., 2003; the Utah survey puts the rate for recent marriages a little above 40%, but this may include some less formal forms of marriage preparation education. Also, see Johnson et al., 2002; in Oklahoma, 43% of married couples have participated in marriage preparation education.

11. National Fatherhood Initiative, 2005.

12. Johnson et al., 2002; Schramm et al., 2003.

13. Harris et al., 2008.

14. In the movie, any concerns the father (played by Steve Martin) has about the cost of an elaborate wedding are seen as miserly and uncaring, and there is no mention at all of anything like the value of marriage preparation education. A wonderful website to check out that can help with this overemphasis on the commercial and party aspects of weddings is: www.firstdance.com

15. These MPE programs are often referred to as "Pre Cana." Cana is a New Testament town in which Jesus performed his first miracle of turning water into wine at a wedding, see John 2:1–12.

16. See Wilcox, 2010, Figure 19, p. 103.

17. See National Center for Family and Marriage Research, 2010.

18. For a good review of this research, see Rhoades et al., 2009b.

19. Rhoades et al., 2009a.

20. Stanley et al., 2010.

21. Teachman, 2003.

22. Wadsworth & Markman, 2012, provide an excellent treatment of central concepts and processes in marriage and relationship education generally rather than MPE specifically.

23. Lavner et al., 2012.

24. See www.prepare-enrich.com. PREPARE/ENRICH is probably the most frequently used relationship inventory.

25. See www.foccusinc.com

26. For more information on RELATE, go to: http://www.relate-institute.org

27. Busby et al., 2007; Halford et al., 2012; Larson et al., 2007.

28. For instance, see: Busby & Gardner, 2008; Busby et al., 2001; Busby et al., 2009.

29. For a good summary of this research, see Rhoades et al. 2009a, 2009b.

30. See Tach & Halpern-Meekin, 2012.

31. For a brief summary of marital homogamy, see Olson et al., 2011, pp. 294–295.

32. See Holman, 2001.

33. Stanley, 2001.

34. Johnson & Anderson, 2012.

35. Blanchard et al., 2009; Wadsworth & Markman, 2012. For a good how-to book on effective communication and problem-solving in marriage, I recommend Gottman & Silver, 1999.

36. Fawcett et al., 2010.

37. For an excellent treatment of forgiveness in marriage, I recommend Fincham et al., 2006.

38. For an excellent treatment of marital virtues such as forgiveness, fairness, and appreciation, I recommend Fowers, 2000.

39. Stanley, 2001. The Start Smart (see LivetheLife.org) MPE program developers also reported to me that they estimate a 10%–15% relationship-termination rate in their program.

40. NCFMR Family Profiles, n.d.. This estimate of remarriages is based on marriages in 2010 and estimated based on data from the U.S. Census Bureau's yearly American Community Survey.

41. Bramlett & Mosher, 2001.

42. Higginbotham et al., 2009.

43. Higginbotham et al., 2009.

44. Higginbotham et al., 2009.

45. Dew et al., 2012.

46. Mahoney et al., 2001.

47. Mahoney et al., 2001.

48. Stanley, 2005. A second kind of commitment is *dedication commitment*, the strong, positive desire to invest in a future for a relationship. In the long run, dedication commitment is more important. But in the short run, constraint commitment sometimes serves a useful purpose of keeping a basically good marriage together through rough times without the partners bailing out prematurely.

49. Stanley, 2005.

50. Snyder et al., 2007.

51. In 2007, Texas passed legislation that made a marriage license free for those taking an approved MPE class. Also, a few couples will sign up for the program in order to get a waiver of Texas' 3-day waiting period for a marriage license.

52. Reports of those studies are available at http://www.familywellness.com/research.php. For instance, see Montañez, 2011. But I could find no evidence that these studies have been published in peer-reviewed journals.

53. Fawcett et al., 2010.

54. Observational measures involve recording a discussion about an issue by a couple, usually for about 10 minutes; trained researchers then code those recorded conversations, looking for specific positive and negative communication behaviors.

Self-report communication measures, where an individual reports her or his perception about their communication as a couple, are not as sensitive to changes in communication behavior, apparently, because the effects are much smaller when researchers just use self-report measures.

55. Most of these unpublished studies were doctoral dissertations or master's theses.

56. Stanley et al., 2006.

57. Nock et al., 2008.

58. Markman et al., 1993.

59. Sullivan & Bradbury, 1997.

60. Hawkins & Fellows, 2011.

61. Reed, 2006.

62. A number of scholars recentlyhave shed a great deal of light on low-income, cohabiting parents and their relationship aspirations. See Burton et al., 2009; Cherlin, 2009; Cross-Barnett et al., 2011; Edin & Kefalas, 2005; McLanahan & Beck, 2010.

63. See Bramlett & Mosher, 2001; McLanahan & Beck, 2010.

64. Rackin & Gibson-Davis, 2012.

65. Szarzynski et al., 2012.

66. Szarzynski et al., 2012.

67. Johnson, 2012; Karney & Bradbury, 2005.

68. For a more in-depth understanding of the challenging issues these couples face, see Burton et al., 2009; Cherlin et al., 2004; Edin & Kefalas, 2005.

69. See Anderson, 2010.

70. See Jordan, 1999, for details about the Becoming Parents program.

71. Lerman, 2005.

72. See the United States Government Accountability Office, 2011, report on jobs programs, where the rarely documented effects tend to be small, inconclusive, or restricted to short-term impacts.

73. For details, see Devaney & Dion, 2010.

74. Wood et al., 2012.

75. Further analyses of these data evaluating the BSF program explored effects using a series of treatment-on-the-treated, or TOT, analyses as opposed to intent-to-treat, or ITT, analyses. These analyses used different methods for examining the effects of the BSF program on those who participated in the program as intended, attempting to compensate for the methodological reality that doing so risks jeopardizing the randomized nature of the study design. The TOT results generally replicated the ITT analyses; they did not suggest that higher dosages of the program would have produced significant results for the treatment-group participants. See Wood et al., 2011.

76. The other BSF sites were Florida (Orange and Broward counties); Atlanta, GA; Baton Rouge, LA; Baltimore, MD; Houston, TX; Indiana (Allen, Marion, and Lake counties); and San Angelo, TX.

77. See Wood et al., 2010.

78. Amato's measure of disadvantage included a variety of social indicators available in the data set.

79. These other sites used curricula that were different from the Oklahoma City site.

80. Amato's finding of positive effects for the most disadvantaged couples will need to be checked at the 3-year follow-up when those data are released for analyses by other scholars.

81. For review, see Hawkins et al., in press.

82. Owen et al., 2012.

83. Cox & Shirer, 2009.

84. Wild & Doherty, 2012.

85. See Cowan et al., 2009; Higginbotham & Skogrand, 2010.

86. Johnson et al., 2002; National Fatherhood Initiative, 2005; Schramm et al., 2003.

87. Stanley et al., 2001.

88. For a formal analysis of improvements in best practices, see Wilmoth & Smyser, 2012.

89. Pew Research Center, 2010; see especially p. 1.

90. Lundquist & Smith, 2005.

91. Schramm et al., 2013.

92. National Fatherhood Initiative, 2005.

93. The states are Florida, Georgia, Maryland, Minnesota, Oklahoma, South Carolina, Tennessee, Texas, and West Virginia. South Carolina's incentive is a partial rebate of the marriage license after marrying rather than a discount on the actual license.

94. Hawkins, 2007.

95. Thaler & Sustein, 2008.

96. For instance, see Edin & Kefalas, 2005; Loew et al., 2012.

Chapter 6

1. Amato et al., 2007.

2. Bramlett & Mosher, 2001.

3. Bramlett & Mosher, 2001.

4. Raley & Bumpass, 2003; Wilcox, 2010.

5. Martin, 2006; Wilcox, 2010.

6. Green, 2012.

7. Wolfinger, 2005.

8. McDermott et al., 2009.

9. Amato & Hohmann-Marriott, 2007. See also Waite et al., 2002.

10. Lavner et al., 2012.

11. Amato & Prevetti, 2003; Johnson et al., 2001; National Fatherhood Initiative, 2005; Schramm et al., 2003.

12. Allen & Atkins, 2012.

13. Atkins & Furrow, 2008.

14. Atkins & Furrow, 2008.

15. Treas & Giesen, 2000.

16. Cherlin et al., 2004.

17. Twenge et al., 2003.

18. For a summary, see Cummings et al., 2002.

19. Bramlett & Mosher, 2001.

20. Coontz, 2005.

21. Amato et al., 2007; Cherlin, 2009; Whitehead, 1996.

22. Acitelli, 2001.

23. Acitelli, 2001.

24. Wadsworth & Markman, 2012, provide an excellent treatment of central concepts and processes in marriage and relationship education generally rather than MME specifically.

25. Blanchard et al., 2009; Wadsworth & Markman, 2012.

26. Bradbury & Karney, 2004; Gottman & Silver, 1999; Halford, 2011.

27. Johnson, 2012.

28. Markman et al., 2010; Wadsworth & Markman, 2012.

29. Blanchard et al., 2009.

30. The Relationship Enhancement, or RE programs, first developed by Bernard and Louise Guerney at The Pennsylvania State University, place a strong focus on developing empathy.

31. Fincham et al., 2007.

32. Fowers, 2000.

33. See www.pairs.com for more details about the P.A.I.R.S. program.

34. Hsueh et al., 2012.

35. The SHM study included a follow-up assessment at about 30 months post-treatment. But those results were not available at press time for this book.

36. See http://www.stepfamilies.info/smart-steps.php. Participation data shared by project director Brian Higginbotham, August 23, 2012.

37. Utah Department of Health, 2010. See p. S-5.

38. Office of Family Assistance 2006–2011 & 2011–2014, and Office of Head Start, 2007–2012. See http://extension.usu.edu/stepfamily/htm/project-history

39. Higginbotham et al., 2010.

40. Bradford et al., 2011.

41. For an ongoing list of research studies and reports related to this project, see http://extension.usu.edu/stepfamily/htm/project-findings-and-reports

42. Higginbotham & Skogrand, 2010.

43. Skogrand, Dansie, Higginbotham, Davis, & Barrios-Bell, 2011. See also: Skogrand, Davis, & Higginbotham, 2011.

44. Hawkins & Fellows, 2011.

45. Cowan et al., 2009.

46. Cowan, Cowan et al., 2012.

47. For a discussion of the difference between situational couple violence and intimate partner terrorism, see Derrington et al., 2010.

48. Bradley et al., 2011.

49. Stanley et al., 2010.

50. Stanley, 2012.

51. Hahlweg & Richter, 2010. See also Halford & Wilson, 2009.

52. Cowan et al., 2011.

53. Stanley et al., 2001.

54. I'm not aware of any evaluation research specifically targeting these Head Start MRE efforts. Higginbotham's study of the *Smart Steps* program in Utah included classes offered to Head Start parents, but he has not reported a study focused exclusively on these couples.

55. Hawkins et al., 2002.

56. See Holt-Lunstad et al., 2010; Stanton & Ooms, n.d.; Waite & Gallagher, 2000.

57. Stanley et al., 2010.

58. See: Halford, 2011; McAllister et al., 2012.

Chapter 7

1. Szarzynski et al., 2012.

2. Olson et al., 2009.

3. Morrill et al., 2011, p. 472.

4. Fleming & Córdova, 2012.

5. Córdova et al., 2005.

6. See www.couplecheckup.com. Also see Olson et al., 2009.

7. See Holt-Lunstad et al., 2010; Stanton & Ooms, n.d.; Waite & Gallagher, 2000.

8. Loew et al., 2012.

9. McAllister et al., 2012.

10. Kalinka et al., 2012.

11. Duncan et al., 2009.

12. Loew et al., 2012.

13. Means et al., 2009.

14. Halford, 2011.

15. Halford et al., 2004; Halford & Wilson, 2009; Halford et al., 2010.

16. Petch et al., 2012b.

17. Gottman et al., 2011.

18. See www.guaranteeyourmarriage.com

19. Bradbury & Lavner, 2012.

20. See Gottman et al., 1998; Gottman et al., 2000; Stanley et al., 2000.

21. Dew et al., 2012.

22. Cowan & Cowan, 2000; Wilcox & Marquardt, 2011.

23. See Doss et al., 2009; Holmes et al., in press.

24. Pinquart & Teubert, 2010a.

25. Pinquart & Teubert, 2010a.

26. Schulz et al., 2006.

27. Pinquart & Tuebert, 2010b.

28. Hawkins et al., 1994. The term *second shift* was coined by Arlie Hochschild, 1989, in her book of the same title.

29. Mooradian et al., 2011.

30. Loew et al., 2012.

31. Bouma et al., 2004.

32. Amato et al., 2007.

33. Bradbury & Lavner, 2012; Trail & Karney, 2012.

34. Owen et al., 2012.

35. Conger et al., 1990.

36. Wadsworth et al., 2011.

37. Bodenmann et al., 2006.

38. Putnam & Campbell, 2010.

39. Lambert et al., 2009.

40. Lambert, Fincham, Stillman, Graham, & Beach, 2010.

41. Fincham, Lambert, & Beach, 2010.

42. Lambert, Fincham, Marks, & Stillman, 2010.

43. Beach et al., 2008.

44. Wilcox & Dew, 2012.

45. Reissman et al., 1993.

46. Brower et al., 2011.

47. Doherty, 1997; Doherty, 2003.

48. See Doherty 1997, pp. 68–69.

49. Doherty, 1997.

50. Markman & Rhoades, 2012.

51. Owen, Rhoades, Stanley, & Markman, in press.

52. Kerpelman et al., 2010.

53. Stanley et al., 2001.

54. Stanley et al., 2010.

55. For excellent reviews of the potential of public health media campaigns, or social marketing campaigns, see Evans, 2008; Hornik, 2002. Note that the entire edited volume that contains the Hornik chapter provides many interesting studies of the effectiveness of public health media campaigns.

56. Farrelly et al., 2005.

57. Evans, 2008.

58. Evans et al., 2008.

59. To see this and other ads, go to http://strongermarriage.org/htm/tv-spots. Also see http://www.youtube.com/watch?v=tiMBJMbVGKM

60. To see these ads, go to http://firstthings.org/page/media/marketing-materials

61. For example, see Bridges, 2003; Krishnakumar & Buehler, 2000; Moore et al., 2011; Stapleton & Bradbury, 2012.

62. Adler-Baeder et al., 2013; Cowan et al., 2009; Cummings et al., 2008; Hawkins et al., 2008.

63. Cummings et al., 2002.

64. Johnson, 2008, p., 261.

65. Cummings et al., 2008.

66. Skogrand et al., 2009.

67. Holmes et al., 2013; McHale et al., 2012.

68. The Center for Social Justice, 2010, in the UK makes a call for greater public support of parenting education based on a similar logic presented here.

69. Halford et al., 2012.

70. Lucier-Greer & Adler-Baeder, 2012.

71. See Gottman & DeClaire, 1998; Thompson & Meyer, 2007.

72. Nowak & Heinrichs, 2008.

73. For instance, see Conger et al., 2000.

Chapter 8

1. Doherty, 2000.

2. See Doherty, 1995.

3. Nock et al., 2008.

4. Bray & Jouriles, 1995; Ward & McCollum, 2005.

5. Scafidi, 2008.

6. Schramm et al., 2013.

7. Hawkins & Fackrell, 2009. An electronic pdf version of this book is available for free at http://divorce.usu.edu/htm/about-the-program. A web-based program based on this book is available at divorce.usu.edu

8. See Hawkins & Fackrell, 2009, Chapter 4, for a summary.

9. Hetherington & Kelly, 2002.

10. These figures come from unpublished data collected by David Schramm in 2012, University of Missouri Cooperative Extension Service.

11. Emery & Sbarra, 2002.

12. The possible lack of full consideration regarding divorce corresponds with what we know about the timing of divorce; many who divorce have been married for a relatively short period of time. Research documents that the first 5 years of a marriage are the years with the highest risk of divorce; these risks are even higher for remarriages. See Bramlett & Mosher, 2002.

13. Doherty et al., 2011.

14. Wineberg, 1995.

15. Original data analysis by Patricia Nosanchuk, data analyst with the Division of Utah Courts, August 16, 2007.

16. Tumin & Qian, 2012.

17. Walker et al., 2004; see especially Chapter 3.

18. Waite & Gallagher, 2000; Waite et al., 2002; Waite et al., 2009.

19. Schramm et al., 2003; see Table 21.

20. National Fatherhood Initiative, 2005.

21. Johnson et al., 2002; Schramm et al., 2003.

22. See Stanley, 2005.

23. Amato & Previti, 2003; Amato & Rogers, 1997.

24. Allen & Atkins, 2012.

25. Snyder et al., 2007.

26. Jones, 2008.

27. Allen & Atkins, 2012.

28. Abrahamson et al., 2012.

29. Amato & Booth, 1997; Amato & Hohmann-Marriott, 2007.

30. Amato & Booth, 1997.

31. Hetherington & Kelly, 2002; Wallerstein et al., 2000.

32. Hetherington & Kelly, 2002.

33. Amato, 2000.

34. Waite et al., 2002; Waite et al., 2009.

35. Afifi et al., 2009; Campbell, 2002.

36. Snyder et al., 2007.

37. Amato & Booth, 1997. Note that children viewing spouse abuse is considered a form of child abuse in most states now.

38. Parkman, 2000.

39. Allen & Gallagher, 2007.

40. Institute for Marriage and Public Policy, 2012.

41. Phillips, 1991.

42. There may be a handful of other states that have similar laws, but I have not found documentation on them.

43. See http://divorcereform.us

44. See http://le.utah.gov/~2007/bills/hbillenr/hb0128.htm

45. Fackrell, 2012.

46. Walker et al., 2004.

47. Pollet & Lombreglia, 2008.

48. Fackrell et al., 2011.

49. Fackrell and I have written a book for the general public that provides an example of the content of divorce orientation education, Hawkins & Fackrell, 2009. The book is free online at: http://divorce.usu.edu/htm/about-the-program

50. Waite & Gallagher, 2000.

51. See http://firstthings.org/fm/classes/detail/id/10

52. Amato et al., 2011.

53. See Hawkins & Fackrell, 2009.

54. A recent conversation with a divorcing parents educator in Texas led me to believe that most divorcing parents in Texas have something similar to Utah's divorce orientation education.

55. See http://www.utcourts.gov/specproj/dived/

56. See divorce.usu.edu

57. I now teach this class and regularly ask participants at the beginning of class how many are near the end of the divorce process. I estimate that three-fourths raise their hands. The most common written feedback I get on the class evaluation forms is that the class should be required earlier in the divorce process.

58. Needham, 2010.

59. Bray & Jouriles, 1995; Ward & McCollum, 2005.

60. See Schramm et al., 2003. Of those who got counseling, about 40% went to a professional therapist and 60% went to a religious leader, with about half of those religious leaders also being professionally trained.

61. More details are available at http://www.cehd.umn.edu/fsos/projects/mcb/couples.asp

62. See Waite & Gallagher, 2000.

63. See www.retrouvaille.org

64. Scafidi, 2008.

65. Kneip & Bauer, 2009; Wolfers, 2006.

66. Stevenson & Wolfers, 2006.

67. Judgment of divorce, 2006.

68. Wilson, 2008.

69. Crouch & Beaulieu, 2007.

70. National Fatherhood Initiative, 2005.

71. Nock et al., 2008.

72. Stanley, 2001.

73. Nock et al., 2008.

74. Nock et al., 2008.

75. For instance, see National Fatherhood Initiative, 2005; Rasmussen Reports, 2011. Also, see Stokes & Ellison, 2010 for a study predicting attitudes towards more stringent divorce laws.

Chapter 9

1. States currently not receiving federal HMI funding from ACF include: AK, CT, DE, HI, IA, ID, KS, LA, MN, MT, ND, NE, NH, NJ, NV, RI, SC, VT, and WV. See http://www.acf.hhs.gov/programs/ofa/grantees/list10-06.htm

2. See National Healthy Marriage Resource Center, n.d., for a brief on how TANF funds can be used to support healthy marriage initiative activities.

3. Maslow, 1970. A recent proposed revision of Maslow's hierarchy of needs interestingly replaces the self-actualization capstone with needs for mate acquisition, retention, and parenting; see Kenrick et al., 2010.

4. See http://www.ncsl.org

5. See http://www.ncsl.org/issues-research/human-services.aspx?tabs=858,55,56#858

6. See http://www.nationalhumanservices.org

7. See http://www.aphsa.org/Home/home_news.asp

8. Sawhill, 2003.

9. See Gersten, 2007.

10. See Hawkins & Ooms, 2010; National Healthy Marriage Resource Center, n.d.

11. Scott et al., 2012.

12. These figures were estimated based on data provided at http://www.wedalert.com/content/planning/marriage_laws.asp

13. See Utah Department of Health, 2012.

14. See http://www.cdph.ca.gov/data/statistics/Pages/OHIRMarriageData.aspx

15. For FL data, see Karney et al., 2003; for KY data, see Heath et al., 2004; for OK data, see Johnson et al., 2002; for UT data, see Schramm et al., 2003.

16. Bowen, 1986.

17. Halpern, 2010.

18. See Hendrick, n.d.

19. See Wadsworth & Markman, 2012, for an excellent discussion of this point.

20. Materials developed for one grant at Syracuse University are still available at http://www.thrivingcouplesthrivingkids.syr.edu

21. See https://healthymarriageandfamilies.org

22. See http://www.healthymarriageinfo.org/index.aspx

23. For instance, see Haskins & Sawhill, 2009.

Chapter 10

1. Knox et al., 2011.

Index

young adults *(cont.)*
  relationship literacy education for,
    14, 22
    importance of, 105–106, 107–108
    in Louisville, Kentucky, 125–127
    in Utah, 127–131
    and violence, 106, 112
youth
  barriers to successful marriage of,
    108–109, 112–113, 116
  expectations for marriage of, 112–113
  sexual freedom of, 108–109

youth relationship literacy education, 26,
    52, 63–64
  feedback about, 120–121
  format of, 110–111
  importance of, 105–106, 107–108
  parental involvement in, 117–118
  and sex education, 111–112
  skepticism concerning, 105
  and teaching mate selection, 114
  and teaching the success sequence of
    marriage, 114–115, 122

www.ingramcontent.com/pod-product-compliance
Lightning Source LLC
Chambersburg PA
CBHW070627290526
45790CB00001B/20